The Oral-Literate Connection

Perspectives on L2 Speaking, Writing, and Other Media Interactions

The Oral-Literate Connection

Perspectives on L2 Speaking, Writing, and Other Media Interactions

Edited by

Diane Belcher
Georgia State University

and

Alan Hirvela
Ohio State University

Ann Arbor
THE UNIVERSITY OF MICHIGAN PRESS

Published in the United States of America
The University of Michigan Press
Manufactured in the United States of America

∞ Printed on acid-free paper

ISBN-13: 978-0-472-03232-7

2011 2010 2009 2008 4 3 2 1

Foreword

Several years ago I wrote a foreword for a volume entitled *Linking Literacies: Perspectives on L2 Reading-Writing Connections*. Recently, I was asked by the same editors, Diane Belcher and Alan Hirvela, to write a similar small piece for this new volume—one that deals essentially with L2 speaking-writing connections. The former task was relatively straightforward because of the obvious synergies and synapses that link academic reading and writing and the many "school genres" that exploit and develop those intersections: book reports, summaries, reviews, critiques, responses to readings, as well as the "researched papers" that are often taught as the centerpieces of undergraduate composition courses.

The Oral-Literate Connection (as the title of this fine collection is called) is less self-evident, as several of the contributors themselves suggest. After all, most introductory linguistics courses around the world devote considerable time and attention to significant differences between speech and writing; indeed, it is not uncommon to find examination questions asking the students to cite as many of those differences as they can. Michael Halliday (2002) has written particularly memorably about these contrasts as they pertain to English. He notes that spoken English tends to be grammatically intricate but lexically sparse, while the converse holds for formal writing. Lucy Pickering and Patricia Byrd, in Chapter 6 in this volume, sum this up well when they note that academic speech tends to be "verb-centric," while academic writing is "noun-centric." But Halliday goes on to say that the complexity of English speech is *choreographic* as opposed to the *crystalline* complexity of prose. He concludes, "The complexity of spoken language is in its flow, the dynamic mobility whereby each figure provides a context for the next one, not only defining its point of departure but also setting the conventions by reference to which it is to be interpreted" (2002, p. 336). My own investigations of the discourses collected in the Michigan Corpus of Academic Spoken English (MICASE) reinforce this sense of the divide between spoken and written academic language because the former register turns out to be primarily conversational and consensual, while the latter is formal and not without its competitive and critical elements. Further, the linguistic characteristics of academic spoken utterances—highly fragmented yet highly phraseological—mean that they cannot be easily or simply mapped onto the subject-verb-complement patterns of written academic sentences, and thus raise questions about whether the "same grammar" of English will work equally well across the mode divide.

And yet there are affordances that mitigate these stylistic divergences. One is the reliance on "inner" or "private" speech (I am not entirely sure I always perceive the difference). Every time we are faced with a non-trivial speaking or writing task, we run through options in our minds as we prepare to either address an audience or place our fingers on the keyboard. We rehearse, and we try to imagine the effects of various possible plays, as indeed I did when I considered how much of Halliday to quote directly in the previous paragraph. (I changed my mind a couple of times.) Another is the emergence of hybrid communicative styles in electronic genres such as emails and blogs, the latter excellently discussed in the final chapter by Joel Bloch. A third affordance, which is linked to the second, concerns the growing interconnectedness of individual members of the academic world. When I first arrived at the University of Michigan more than twenty years ago, the doctoral students I met in humanities departments such as Linguistics and English functioned largely independently, often immured in their library carrels, emerging only occasionally for meetings with their advisors. Today, in my home department of Linguistics, there are formal sub-groupings of faculty and graduate students in each specialty as well as various kinds of informal collectivities for study and/or mutual support. The advantages of these arrangements are well brought out in Chapter 4 by Lisya Seloni, who concludes her careful ethnographic study with the following: "Looking at intertextual links doctoral students establish on the way of acquiring academic literacy practices does not only expand our views of academic textual worlds, but it also increases awareness of the juxtaposed and interactive nature of texts and events (i.e., spoken, written, electronic, etc.)."

These juxtapositions give rise to a fourth affordance. The fact that today we have a growing body of research that gives us insights into the structures and functions of spoken genres in the academic and research worlds—such as proposal meetings, student presentations, research group meetings and thesis defenses—means that these speech events are now seen as integral rather than peripheral to educative and communicative processes. Chapters that further explore this kind of speaking-writing connection include Christine Tardy's discussion (Chapter 10) of student-generated genre-system portfolios and that by Don Rubin and Okim Kang (Chapter 11), which, inter alia, discusses the forms of oral interaction that swirl around the scientific poster presentation. More generally, Rubin and Kang argue that models of speaking-writing interaction tend to consider the oral component as subordinate or preparatory and suggest instead that:

> A more apt model might be a double helix with a writing strand and a speaking strand intertwined. At any particular stage one strand may be the focal outcome, drawing upon the other. But as a whole, the two strands are reciprocally supportive and leading in the same direction.

In a volume with this title, it is not surprising to find a fair number of papers that discuss the various roles of group and peer discussion, both online and face-to-face, in the creation and development of written texts. Of these, I would single out the very impressive essay by Robert Weissberg (Chapter 2), which provides a critical review of the currently popular socio-cultural approaches to both first and second literacy education, typically inspired by Vygotskian perspectives of various kinds. While not unsympathetic to these approaches, Weissberg offers a number of important caveats about their simplistic adoption in second language (L2) settings. Among other concerns, he notes, "Because SCT [socio-cultural theory] invariably sees social interaction as the necessary trigger for cognition, it leaves us with a monolithic account of literacy acquisition, insensitive to differences in modality strength and cognitive style among L2 learners."

Two of the chapters I have already mentioned—those by Rubin & Kang and by Weissberg—are of considerable theoretical interest. A third is the opening chapter by Jessica Williams, particularly her exploration of "the less obvious" side of the bidirectional relationship: the move from writing into speaking. She notes that the slower and more decontextualized pace of writing offers greater opportunities for planning (perhaps via inner speech) and greater opportunities for focusing on form; as a consequence, L2 learners may be better able to recognize "holes" in their own competence. However, she also concludes that the literature on this directional connection is somewhat less robust than on the much more traveled converse.

Despite the pioneering work of a few scholars such as Don Rubin, a collection of papers by a wide range of authors on the speaking-writing connection would not have been possible a decade ago. The editors are therefore to be congratulated for putting it all together at this opportune time and bringing it to our attention. Readers will find much to reflect on here, such as the effect of new technologies (not excluding corpus linguistics), the interrupted literacy trajectories of Generation 1.5 students, the continuing influence of Vygotsky and Bakhtin, the role of "backstage" fora as a useful surrogate for L2 students, and the need for students to understand the genre repertoires with which they need to engage. Readers will also find in many of these chapters numerous useful pedagogical suggestions and ideas that can be experimented with in their own classrooms and tutorial settings. Finally, the volume raises some important questions for future research, such as when today's increasingly socialized writing classroom can operate to the disadvantage of certain types of second language learner, and how differently or how similarly speech and writing relate to second language acquisition. Finally, we might further ponder the double helix analogy for our better understanding of speaking-writing connections.

REFERENCE

Halliday, M. A. K. (2002). *On grammar.* London: Continuum.

John M. Swales
The University of Michigan
Ann Arbor

Contents

■ Introduction

DIANE BELCHER AND ALAN HIRVELA

Although many, including ourselves (Belcher & Hirvela, 2001), have complained about the limited attention given to reading-writing interactions, the speaking-writing relationship, in fact, has been far more neglected (but see such recent works as Horowitz, 2007; Weissberg, 2006). This relative neglect is no doubt partly the result of second language (L2) writing specialists' desire to legitimatize writing as a research and pedagogical area, to encourage a view of writing as more than a pale reflection and means of reinforcement of spoken discourse (for more nuanced views of the history of the field of L2 writing, see Matsuda 2001, 2003). Ken Hyland (2002) has suggested that viewing writing and speaking as though on opposite sides of a "great divide" is not only simplistic and unrealistic but may also be unhelpful to writers, as writing, like speaking, is a communicative act with interlocutors, an act for which "appropriate interactional tenor" (p. 52) does matter. We would like to argue that the current speaking-writing disconnect can be equally unproductive for speakers, not just because writing provides a means of practicing the language one is learning to speak (though it obviously does), but because the reflection that the act of writing inevitably calls for slows down cognitive processing of language, allowing for explicit attention, or noticing (see Adams & Ross-Feldman and Williams, this volume). Repeated use of explicit knowledge is likely to support, many SLA specialists now suggest (Nan Jiang, personal communication), an increase in implicit knowledge—that is, the automaticity needed for oral fluency.

The reasons just mentioned, however, are by no means the only reasons why a reconsideration of the speaking-writing relationships is needed. Since the "process" revolution in writing pedagogy, teacher-student conferencing and face-to-face peer responding have become common, if not universally accepted or widely enough researched, oral practices in writing instruction (see Ferris, 2003; F. Hyland, this volume; Hyland & Hyland, 2006). At the same time, those who teach spoken discourse, or speech communication, have long been aware of the value of writing as a means of organizing one's thoughts and mentally rehearsing what will be said. These pragmatic realizations, however, have not automatically translated into the attention from researchers, teacher trainers, curriculum and materials designers, and others that one might expect. Nevertheless, popular movements in language education have certainly been nudging practitioners toward more combined speaking and writing instruction—movements such as "whole language" at the pre-secondary level, content-based integrated-skills approaches in intensive language programs, and authentic/simulated task-based and problem-solving learning in English for academic or other specific purposes curricula. In other words, countless practitioners may already be teaching speaking and writing together in their language classes, yet they, like many others, may know far less than they would like about why, how, or whether or not this linkage actually is effective for L2 learners. Our volume attempts to bring such questions to the fore and provide a forum for those interested in both L2 speaking and writing, and in how the two modalities very probably synergistically contribute to each other and to L2 proficiency overall.

Overview of Contents

The organization of this volume proceeds from more theoretical and research-oriented issues to more classroom-based perspectives. The first of this volume's four sections looks primarily at what research and theory with various foci can tell us about the L2 speaking-writing relationship, while the next three sections contain more classroom-oriented investigations and discussions. This theory-and-research/practice demarcation, as often the case in an applied field such as ours, is only a rough dividing line, as pedagogical insights are far from absent from Section 1, and Sections 2–4 are informed by theory and often report research findings. Of the latter, more pedagogical sections, the middle two, 2 and 3, consider directional scaffolding issues: how speaking works, ideally, to scaffold writing and the less commonly recognized ways in which writing can support speaking. Technology plays a role in a number of the chapters in this volume, but the final section, 4, focuses more directly on technology as a mediational tool capable of bridging spoken and written discourse by presenting both an occasion for and means of linking the two modalities for mutual support.

Part 1: Theory and Research on Speaking-Writing Interactions

Recent research on language learning, as Jessica Williams remarks in her masterful review essay opening the section, now provides abundant evidence of the bidirectionality of L2 speaking and writing. As Williams notes, that talk aids writing, probably never much doubted, is increasingly well supported empirically. Research on student-to-peer/tutor/teacher talk about writing confirms the likelihood of draft-to-draft progress as a result of such negotiation. That writing can boost the underlying proficiency needed for L2 talk, however, has only more recently received much attention. Among the potential benefits of writing, as planned (not real-time or immediately public) production of language, it may lower the affective filter enough to make learners feel freer to try new forms of language, and hence gain a level of confidence that may eventually transfer to speech. We are likely to learn still more about speaking-writing interactions, Williams suggests, from ongoing research on genres that actually mix modes—for example, journaling and online chat.

From a more purely theoretical (or even philosophical) perspective, the increasingly popular work of Lev Vygotsky and Mikhail Bakhtin provides persuasive rationales for paying considerable attention to the speaking-writing relationship. Robert Weissberg, however, argues in Chapter 2 for a "weaker version" of Vygotskian socio-cultural theory, one that takes into consideration differences between first and second language learning, between younger and older learners, and among the varied learning styles likely in evidence in any language classroom. What Weissberg mounts a compelling case for is a "dialogue approach to L2 writing" that recognizes "not *all instructional dialogue need be external,* that we can appeal to the power of speech without always operationalizing it in the form of talk."

In her chapter on Bakhtinian theory, Ludmila Marchenkova's comments resonate with Weissberg's when she points out the too-frequent neglect of the importance of internal, rather than merely external, dialogue in Bakhtin's conceptualization of language. From the Bakhtinian perspective, Marchenkova informs us, speaking and writing share an internal orientation toward prior and anticipated utterances. What an understanding of inner dialogism offers, among other things, Marchenkova argues, is a window on how externally authoritative discourse can become internally persuasive—that is, transformed and taken ownership of in learners' own spoken and written utterances.

A multifaceted view of dialogue is integral to the model of an "academic culture of collaboration" that Lisya Seloni presents in Chapter 4. Rejecting a more traditional context-free cognitive view of literacy, Seloni proposes a model that focuses on the dynamic inter-relationships of people, texts, and events, or the textualizing of experience that results when people interact through language, jointly constructing meaning and taking action. Seloni's "intertextual analysis" of a group of multilingual doctoral students' oral and written grappling with advanced academic literacy practices, or in Bakhtinian terms, "externally authoritative discourse," not only helps concretize her model but illustrates the power of collective interaction to help newcomers own their own discourse, to "resist, challenge, and eventually creatively construct the rhetorics and texts around them."

Both Vygotsky and Bakhtin are invoked in Christine Pearson Casanave and Miguel Sosa's argument for tackling intellectually and culturally "difficult" ideas in relatively risk-free classroom environments with multiple and varied opportunities for dialogue. Casanave and Sosa's accounts of their own efforts to create and participate as learners themselves in such environments provide vivid examples of theory-put-into-practice—that is, use of writing and speaking to mutually scaffold the transformation of complex, multidimensional thoughts into lines of spoken and written words.

While writing and speaking are arguably and even demonstrably mutually supportive, Lucy Pickering and Pat Byrd remind us that there are, nevertheless, significant differences between written and spoken discourse that language educators should keep in mind. Pickering and Byrd's analysis of common four-word lexical bundles in the Academic Word List and the Michigan Corpus of Academic Spoken English (MICASE) calls attention to the fact that even the same phrases may be used for quite different communicative purposes by writers and speakers as a result of the varying resources available in the two modalities—for example, the intonational structure unique to speaking. Modal differences are not an argument for a return to discrete "skills" teaching, however. Pickering and Byrd suggest instead that "students will benefit from specific instruction on how to mediate between parallel written and spoken forms."

Part 2: How Speaking Scaffolds Writing

Literacy, especially early literacy, is "influenced and shaped by story experiences," argues Linda Blanton through her own compelling use of narrative in the opening chapter of this section. Images of loss from Hurricane Katrina, loss experienced by the author herself, serve as a poignant metaphor for lost opportunities for literacy in any language when formal education is truncated in the home language and replaced by prematurely accurate and rhetorical form-oriented instruction in a new language. For immigrant learners who have missed the crucial stage in early literacy development when oral language becomes written language, what's needed, Blanton argues, is a re-linking of oracy and literacy: "Such students need to write themselves back into the picture after an absence of long duration. Their thought [or Vygotskian "inner speech"], their expression, must have the chance to manifest itself in writing."

For those fortunate enough to reach more advanced literacy development, oracy and literacy tend to become, as Blanton (this volume) has observed, more distinct, "settling into a co-existence," yet remaining intertwined. Just how connected talk can be to the discipline-specific writing of highly literate language learners is made readily apparent in Luxin Yang's chapter (8) examining the group writing projects of Chinese commerce students in English-medium university settings. One of the few L2 investigations of group work outside the language classroom, Yang's Vygostky-inspired study found that through multiple face-to-face and email interactions, group members managed to create "a group zone of proximal development," where they learned as individuals and whole groups. Perhaps most interestingly, Yang saw this successful coconstruction resulting not just from positive reinforcement in the form of encouraging dialogue but also from "criticism, rejection, and resistance to dialogue," which forced the groups to resolve conflict and work toward understanding of each other's views and the task at hand, a process that, in the end, enhanced their performance as thinkers and writers.

Although peer interaction has become a mainstay in many writing classes, L2 specialists, Fiona Hyland reminds us in Chapter 9, have long cautioned that peer group interaction, particularly in culturally heterogeneous groups, is not necessarily supportive of the writing process. In her study, however, of two instructors with very different approaches to their culturally diverse ESL writing workshops—one creating small-group microcommunities, the other an inclusive whole-class macrocommunity—Hyland found that peer support thrived in both, as the students themselves seemed to recognize the value of such interaction. Hyland notes, though, that by not considering the interactions students engage in *outside* our classrooms, their self-selected use of resources for feedback, we may be missing an opportunity to help them learn to make the best use of the type of support networks they will likely rely on after leaving our writing classes.

Access to support networks is, in fact, a major concern of Christine Tardy, who focuses in Chapter 10 on the needs of graduate students as newcomers to discipline-specific communities of practice. Eager to equalize "resource availability" for "off-networked" students, Tardy advocates an approach to advanced academic literacy that includes use of spoken texts to build knowledge of the patterns of communication—for example, types of argumentation—essential to written texts as well. Tardy acknowledges that no classroom can replicate disciplinary settings and the complex systems of oral and written genres unique to each, but instructors can provide a supportive environment for gradual genre engagement, where learners can "explore, analyze, and critique ... to build a meta-awareness of individual genres *and* the systems that they exist within."

Part 3: How Writing Scaffolds Speaking

As Williams (this volume) has pointed out, when attention has been given to the L2 speaking-writing nexus, it has tended to be somewhat lopsided, with more focus on the role of speaking in scaffolding writing than on the reverse. Don Rubin and Okim Kang, in the opening chapter of Section 3, help us understand both the likely reasons for this imbalance—from ontogenetic, phylogenetic, and cognitive vantage points—and the reasons why it should be remedied. Rubin's own highly influential earlier conceptualization of the bidirectionality of literacy and oracy is revisited in this chapter, and a more complex double-helix configuration proposed to "capture the recurrent interplay between writing and speaking both in individuals' development as language users and in social and organizational uses of language." Rubin and Kang argue that if language educators are "serious about cultivating synergy between speaking and writing and about the primacy of social interaction," they should pay more attention to the teaching of valued oral genres, such as the briefing report and poster presentation.

Striking evidence for writing as a means of mediating speaking is presented in Gayle Nelson and Yanbin Lu's chapter (12). Mindful of the theoretical lens of legitimate peripheral participation, Nelson and Lu chart Lu's own increasingly fuller participation in her new community of practice as a doctoral student at first reluctant to engage in class discussion. Writing, in the form of posting on class discussion boards, became a virtual point of entry for later face-to-face class discussion. Through engagement in online interaction with her peers, Lu began to see learning as collaboration, to appreciate that she could learn from fellow learners and they from her. While the authors, understandably, make no claims of a direct causal relationship between posting and speaking, Lu herself is certain that her experience with online communication contributed to greater self-confidence and interest in participating in her peer community that accompanied her into the classroom.

Whether writing can contribute to greater accuracy in language production is, as Rebecca Adams and Lauren Ross-Feldman note in Chapter 14, of increasing interest to SLA researchers. One reason why writing may lead to more productive noticing, Adams and Ross-Feldman report, may be that for writers, language is necessarily both object and communication tool (see Williams, this volume). In their own research, Adams and Ross-Feldman have observed that writing before engaging in spoken interaction does appear to encourage learner attention to form, and that giving learners a chance to process content orally before writing may lead to more successful resolution of form-focused oral interactions. Thus, both writing and speaking-then-writing before engaging in spoken interaction appeared to offer distinct language learning opportunities, or ways of taking advantage of them, that educators may want to make available to learners.

Part 4: How Technology Bridges Speaking and Writing

Though many are convinced of the value of corpus linguistics not just for linguistic research but also for the language classroom, pedagogical corpus use has so far not been much examined. As both a corpus-oriented researcher and highly experienced language instructor, Lynne Flowerdew brings her knowledge of both realms to Chapter 14, where she considers how corpus activities can bridge speaking and writing in the L2 classroom. Flowerdew's goal in her own classroom, she reports, was not just to get writing students talking but to get them talking about language issues they had a vested interest in, and, as a result, learning how to critically assess electronic resources' ability to shed light on those issues. Corpus tasks, it is suggested, can serve as catalysts for talk about language that heightens awareness of lexis and grammar in ways that can improve writing. As Flowerdew eloquently observes, "The role that corpora can play in this partnership of [speaking and writing] modalities opens up many as yet relatively unexplored but tantalizing possibilities."

Computer-mediated-communication (CMC) has for several decades attracted the attention of language researchers and educators as, in Joel Bloch's words (this volume), an interesting "amalgam of both oral and written forms of discourse." Blogging, now among the most popular of all CMC forms, is especially intriguing, Bloch argues, in its ability, via easily updated web pages, to archive and inspire dialogue. Bloch reports in the capstone chapter of the volume on efforts to enlist blogging as a means of helping immigrant language learners, or "students interrupted" as Blanton (this volume) would say, in their transition from a more vernacular, speech-like literacy to a more formally academic literacy. Bloch suggests that blogging can give "the oral voice a sense of textuality" and facilitate "shuttling" between modalities. Technologies such as blogging, however, Bloch provocatively asserts, are far more than just helpmates on the road to other learning objectives; they are significant new modes of communication that merit attention in and of themselves. The implication we are left with as readers (and editors) at the end of the final chapter of this volume is that, perhaps more insistently than any other intellectual developments, new communication technologies are challenging us to rethink the value of continuing to envision speaking and writing as two entirely separate modalities.

Acknowledgments

Many people have supported us in various ways over the course of this project, and we are grateful to all of them, but there is a short-list of those without whom this project absolutely would not have been possible: all of our contributors, who care enough about the L2 speaking-writing connection to examine and write about it, and our remarkably patient and always supportive editor at the University of Michigan Press, Kelly Sippell.

REFERENCES

Belcher, D., & Hirvela, A. (2001). *Linking literacies: Perspectives on L2 reading-writing connections.* Ann Arbor: University of Michigan Press.

Ferris, D. (2003). *Response to student writing: Implications for second language students.* Mahwah, NJ: Lawrence Erlbaum.

Horowitz, R. (2007). *Talking texts: How speech and writing interact in school learning.* Mahwah, NJ: Lawrence Erlbaum.

Hyland, K. (2002). *Teaching and researching writing.* Harlow, UK: Pearson.

Hyland, K., & Hyland, F. (2006). *Feedback in second language writing.* Cambridge, UK: Cambridge University Press.

Matsuda, P. (2001). Reexamining audiolingualism: On the genesis of reading and writing in L2 studies. In D. Belcher & A. Hirvela (Eds.), *Linking literacies: Perspectives on L2 reading-writing connections* (pp. 84–105). Ann Arbor: University of Michigan Press.

Matsuda, P. (2003). Process and post-process: A discursive history. *Journal of Second Language Writing, 12,* 65–83.

Weissberg, R. (2006). *Connecting speaking & writing in second language writing instruction.* Ann Arbor: University of Michigan Press.

Part 1

Theory and Research on Speaking-Writing Interactions

1

The Speaking-Writing Connection in Second Language and Academic Literacy Development

JESSICA WILLIAMS

Abstract

The connection between L2 speaking and writing goes in both directions: A large body of research suggests that L2 speaking can facilitate the acquisition of L2 literacy, but there is also growing evidence that L2 writing may have an impact on the development of L2 proficiency. The first direction is the more expected one, with ample evidence that writers are more likely to develop and revise their writing when they have an opportunity to discuss it. This has been demonstrated in at least three contexts: student-teacher conferences, peer review groups, and writing center tutoring sessions. The second direction is perhaps less obvious. Writing may aid in L2 development at two points: first, soon after initial acquisition, as learners test out new forms, and second, later in the process, as they access acquired forms they do not yet fully control. Because written production occurs under planned conditions, with less pressure than speaking, it allows learners to draw on both their explicit and implicit knowledge of the L2.

The relationship between development of writing ability and oral proficiency is a dynamic and complex one. In the early days of second language acquisition, written language and the acquisition of literacy skills were considered secondary to the development of oral language, which was held to be the truest reflection of interlanguage (IL) competence. To read early writing on the topic was to learn that real IL was produced in spontaneous, real-time contexts in which the focus was on meaning and not form, in other words, for the most part, in conversational interaction (e.g., Krashen, 1981, 1982; Tarone, 1982). Written language potentially has few of these features although it may have some of them in certain contexts. Compared to conversational oral production, it tends to be planned, off-line, and may entail attention to the formal features of language. So what good is writing insofar as language acquisition is concerned? "Very little" might have been the response in the early days of the field. It was considered a reflection of competence, not a factor in its development (Krashen, 1984) and as such, generally took a back seat to oral proficiency in second language research and pedagogy (Harklau, 2002; White, 1987).

Our understanding of the connection between speaking and writing in a second language has come a long way, yet it is still not an area of extensive research. Harklau (2002) maintains that there remains "an implicit assumption of the primacy of spoken interaction that still underlies and shapes many studies of classroom second language acquisition," and she asks further why "applied linguists are more likely to ask *how students learn to write in a second language* than to ask *how students learn a second language through writing* (p. 332, emphasis in original).

It has long been assumed that the development of L2 proficiency is an important component of L2 writing proficiency (Cumming, 1989; Sasaki & Hirose, 1996; Schoonen et al., 2003), though connections between L2 oral proficiency specifically and writing development have not often been made. Most research on cross-skill influence has pointed to connections within modalities, either between reading and writing (e.g, Carson, 1993; Grabe, 2003) or speaking and listening (e.g., Vandergrift, 2006). Yet it is increasingly apparent that the act of writing may also promote general proficiency in ways that have not always been acknowledged. Thus, it is now possible to consider the influence of the development of L2 speaking and writing proficiency to be bidirectional as well.

Writing into Speaking

Perhaps the less obvious side of this bidirectional relationship is the influence of writing on the development of L2 oral proficiency. First a caveat: in discussing the effect of output activities, such as writing, on the development of L2 proficiency, I begin with the assumption that the forms produced during these output activities are *already* part of the mental representation of the language—that is, that at least an initial form-meaning connection has been made (VanPatten, Williams, & Rott, 2004). Therefore, it is not possible, strictly speaking, to propose any direct influence of writing on the development of the L2 competence that underlies oral proficiency. Any influence of production, either written or oral, would be indirect; that is, the act of writing would affect the learner's processing of future input. In this sense, the earlier conceptions of the role of writing were correct: written production, like all production, *is* a reflection of, not a direct causal factor in, the development of IL competence. The difference in the argument I am presenting is that this is no more true for writing than for speech. Writing, like speaking, can have an indirect role in facilitating second language acquisition.

This is not an assumption that is universally accepted, of course (cf. DeKeyser, 2003, 2007; Ellis, 2007), but even if we accept the assumption that all IL forms that are produced already have some mental representation (except in the more trivial cases of production during mechanical drills), this does not entail the assumption that the first evidence of these IL forms will emerge in oral production. In fact, there is a small but growing body of research that suggests some forms may be used in the written language before they are produced in speech (Weissberg, 2000a, 2000b). Why should this be so, and what is the evidence?

One of the most important factors in considering the role of writing is planning (De Larios, Marin, & Murphy, 2001; Ellis & Yuan, 2004; Whalen & Menard, 1995). It has also been claimed that planned language is likely to be the context in which learners try out the forms that they do not fully control. Again, this is still not an argument for a direct effect of planning on acquisition. In order to "try out" forms, there must already be some mental representation of them. A large body of research suggests that learners use more complex and varied forms in their oral production when they have time to plan and especially if they are directed to focus on formal features of their production (Ortega, 1999; Mehnert, 1998; Skehan & Foster, 2001, Yuan & Ellis, 2004). In some cases, learners are able to increase their accuracy as well (Skehan & Foster, 1997; Yuan & Ellis, 2004). Ellis & Yuan (2003; 2004) demonstrated that for both speaking and writing, the opportunity for pre-task planning was the crucial factor in allowing learners to include new and more complex forms as they formulated their message. On the other hand, more time on task—that is, unlimited time during the task itself—again in both speaking and writing, was associated with more accurate performance. Ellis and Yuan suggest this is because the extra time on task led to increased monitoring of the output.

Although most of this work, with the exception of Ellis and Yuan (2004), has been limited to planned spoken production, the same argument may be applied to writing. Most writing is done at a more leisurely pace than speaking, allowing at least some time for planning. By its very nature, writing tends to direct the learner's attention to form as well as meaning (Cumming, 1989). Another important byproduct of the slower pace of writing is that it permits learners to draw on their explicit knowledge, which may not be available to them while speaking. This effect of this process is the subject of some controversy, namely whether retrieving this knowledge facilitates its transformation into implicit knowledge. Ellis (1993) proposes a weak interface position, in which explicit knowledge is never converted directly into implicit knowledge. Rather, explicit knowledge indirectly affects the development of implicit knowledge by facilitating the processes thought to be essential to second language learning. These include noticing new forms in the input and noticing the gap between the target input and IL forms. In addition, as noted, explicit knowledge can be an important resource for monitoring output.

Trying out new forms for the first time in writing is just one of the ways in which writing may facilitate the development of L2 proficiency. Some IL form-meaning connections may not be brand new, but rather, simply weak. They may not be fully controlled, yet learners can deliberately choose to use them when they have the time and attention available to do so. Cognitive views of second language learning, particularly skill theory, suggest that repeated retrieval for both comprehension and production assists in automization (DeKeyser 2001, 2007). The implication of this position is that retrieving a form repeatedly in planned production, such as in writing, increases the likelihood that it will be produced later in a more spontaneous setting such as conversation. Indeed, DeBot (1996) argues that this repeated access for use is more likely to strengthen form-meaning connections than simply perceiving forms in the input. Thus the opportunity to use these weaker forms in a context with less time pressure may be one way of facilitating automization because it is only in such a context that this repeated access for use may be possible. Speaking, in comparison, because it is time-bound, permits little opportunity for either reflection or monitoring. Under the pressure of spontaneous production, many speakers may only be able to produce what they can access automatically.

In summary, recent research suggests that writing may aid in the development of proficiency at two possible points: first, soon after the initial point of acquisition, as learners try out new and more complex forms or familiar forms in new contexts, and second, considerably later in the process, as they access acquired forms over which they do not yet have full control, as part of their automization.

These proposals are not new. All of these functions have been suggested for output more generally. Swain (1995, 1998) has noted the potentially important role that output activities may play in helping learners to process input—specifically, to notice discrepancies between their own production and the input they hear or read, in other words, to "notice the gap." It may also help them to notice "holes" in their own competence; that is, in the act of production, learners may notice that they do not have the knowledge to say or write what they want to convey (Izumi & Bigelow, 2000; Rott, Williams & Cameron, 2002; Swain, 1998, Swain & Lapkin, 1995). It is possible that the realization of what they do not know primes them to notice relevant forms in future input (Williams & Fernández, 2007). No specific work has been done comparing the relative value of output for noticing in written versus spoken production,[1] but all of the reasons cited—time, planning opportunity, focus on form—usually also pertain for writing, perhaps more than in even planned spoken production. When learners write, they often have more opportunity to notice these gaps or holes, which can be registered only fleetingly in conversational interaction.

One area of research relevant to the speaking-writing connection addresses the effects of written reformulation and task repetition (Adams, 2003; Izumi, 2002; Izumi & Bigelow, 2000; Qi & Lapkin, 2001; Sachs & Polio, 2007; Swain and Lapkin, 2002; Thornbury, 1997). In reformulation, writers compare their original work with a new version that has been reformulated by a native speaker and, subsequently, revise their own work. In repetition tasks, learners have an opportunity to write a second draft in response to the same prompt (not revise the original draft) after seeing feedback on the first draft, following exposure to further input, or sometimes simply after the passage of time. For example, Adams (2003), in a study of written story reconstruction, found that learners who were allowed to discuss differences between their own production and their drafts reformulated by a native speaker wrote more target-like second versions of their stories compared to the second drafts of those without the same opportunity. Investigations of these two pedagogical techniques suggest that when learners have an opportunity to compare their work to that of others, or when they simply have the opportunity to reconsider the task after additional exposure to relevant input, their texts and the language in them change, in general for the better.

---

[1]Though see Wong (2001) for the effect of differences in input processing across modalities.

The affective aspects of the acts of speaking and writing are yet another avenue to consider in their relationship. Even if form-meaning connections are relatively robust, some learners are simply unwilling to try out IL forms in such a public and vulnerable context as conversation, or they may find the notion culturally dissonant. This reluctance is independent of whether they are actually capable of doing so. Some learners would prefer to try out language about which they do not feel confident in the safer, less public form of writing where they might get feedback from their teacher before going solo. They are also more likely to receive helpful feedback in this context. In writing, it is even possible for learners to request feedback on specific forms that concern them. In contrast, an error in spoken interaction might yield a funny look, a breakdown, or, if it is not crucial to communication, perhaps nothing at all. Learners might never be able to determine the accuracy of their hypotheses if they try them out only in conversation. Harklau (1994, 2002) notes that in her study of high school second language learners, interaction between them and their teacher was almost non-existent. She found that their spoken production was similarly minimal. To her surprise, most of their learning took place through interaction with written input. The bulk of their output was written as well. They got almost no feedback on their spoken production; in contrast, their teachers gave them considerably more feedback on their writing, generally in the form of explicit feedback on language form.

Hybrid Forms of Interaction

One way to cast further light on the interaction between the two modalities is to examine forms of language production that fall somewhere between writing and speaking. Two such forms are journaling and online chatting. Several authors have noted the effectiveness of journal writing in developing writing skills and, in some cases, language proficiency (Casanave, 1994; El-Koumy, 1998; Fazio, 2001; Peyton, 1990; Peyton & Staton, 1993; Weissberg, 2000a, 2000b). They argue that it is a safe place to try out new language, to experiment, but also, as with other types of writing, to receive useful feedback. It represents a hybrid genre that is written, yet two-way, personal, conversational in flavor, and generally with lower stakes than more formal academic writing. Weissberg, citing the private yet immediate nature of journaling, calls it a staging ground for syntactic acquisition. In his study, Weissberg compared the acquisition of syntactic features in the speech and writing of five second language learners of English. Although each of the learners displayed a unique pattern of acquisition in the two modalities, he found that writing (in dialogues) appeared generally to be "preferred for the emergence of new morphosyntactic forms" (2000a, p. 37). In addition, he found that learners' use of these forms was more accurate in writing than in speech, a finding consistent with some of the research on planning time in oral production.

Synchronous computer-mediated-communication (CMC) is yet another form that may shed light on speaking-writing connections. Research in CMC suggests that online chatting also shares characteristics of both writing and speaking (e.g., Payne, 2002; Pellettieri, 2000; Smith, 2003, 2004). Like journaling, CMC is written, two-way, low stakes, and conversational. The turn-taking time is much more forgiving than in an oral conversation but clearly much faster than in journaling. Smith (2004) reviews some of the demonstrated benefits of CMC over face-to-face interaction. These include increased participation among learners in terms of the quantity and complexity of the language produced in chat sessions. Warschauer and Kern (2000) maintain that the visual nature of the input in CMC increases learner's ability to focus on the formal aspects of language, which is often elusive in conversational interaction. Pellettieri (2000) also notes the impact of the visual representation on learners' ability to incorporate corrective feedback. Finally, CMC research also suggests that it brings out more diffident students who prefer not to speak in class and increases learners' willingness to take risks. Although not the focus of her study, Lam (2000) notes the role that online chatting played in the development of one learner's oral proficiency. Her study participant explicitly stated that he preferred to work things out in writing before using newly acquired features in spoken interaction.

In a study explicitly focused on the relationship between chatting and oral proficiency development, Payne (2002) examined the phenomenon in terms of working memory. He argues that chatting, because it offers a safe venue for trying out and strengthening new form-meaning connections, can assist in automization, thus freeing up working memory for acquisition of new forms. He explains that the processing advantages of online chatting may be several. First, the slower rate of the exchanges reduces processing demands. Demands on working memory are also reduced because interlocutor responses, instead of being quickly fading memory traces, are right there on the page, available for review. In other words, participants get more than one chance to process input and feedback on their output. In his own study, he found that those who engaged in online chatting showed greater gains on an oral proficiency test than those who did not. He concludes that there is a transfer of skills from writing to speaking.

Speaking into Writing

Research on the opposite direction of influence—that is, the impact of speaking on the development of L2 literacy—has been much more common. Such a relationship in general has perhaps never been in doubt. What follows explores a small area of this research, specifically investigations of the nature of transfer of knowledge gained in spoken interaction to written production and of the specific venues in which it has been shown to take place.

First, there is considerable evidence that talking about writing can improve the overall quality of writing (Ferris & Hedgcock, 2005; Hyland, 2003; Weissberg, 1994), at least in draft-to-draft changes. This assumption underlies much of what happens in both native speaker and L2 writing classrooms. However, there is less evidence of the impact of talking on movement toward more target-like language use in writing. We find some evidence for this influence primarily in three areas of research: investigations of the effect of teacher-student conferences, feedback in peer response groups, and writing center tutoring sessions.

In their study of teacher–L2 learner conferences, Pathey-Chavez and Ferris (1997) found that learners who contributed actively to the conversation in student-teacher writing conferences made more substantial revisions in their drafts, including changes at the sentence level. However, because the authors did not focus on issues of grammatical accuracy or word choice, it is difficult to draw any clear conclusions about their effects on language acquisition. Goldstein and Conrad (1990), in their study of writing conferences with L2 writers, obtained similar results: those students who participated in negotiation during conferences were more likely to make meaningful and successful revisions in their drafts. Again, these studies offer no specifics about draft-to-draft changes at the level of linguistic accuracy and complexity.

Although there is a considerable body of research on the effectiveness of peer feedback on revision, the primary focus is usually not on linguistic form (Ferris, 2003; Liu & Hansen, 2002). Indeed, advice to teachers on conducting peer response emphasizes content and rhetorical aspects of writing over grammatical form (Berg, 1999; Liu & Hansen, 2002). Much of peer response research also focuses on more macro-level issues—the overall difference in quality in the text and changes at the propositional level. This orientation, along with the emphasis in most of the common coding schemes for analyzing revision (e.g., Faigley & Witte, 1981), make it difficult to evaluate changes in grammatical or lexical accuracy or complexity. In addition, in many of these studies, the peer feedback is provided in writing, so the results cannot contribute to a discussion of the effect of speaking on writing. Such feedback does not allow the writer and responder to negotiate changes as oral responses do. Finally, in keeping with current pedagogical trends in peer response, in many of these studies, students were explicitly told not to focus on language issues, but to address content and rhetorical issues only.

Only one study of peer groups that used oral responses also separated out the effect of these discussions on changes at the linguistic level. Villamil and de Guerrero (1998) found that in spite of instructions to concentrate on content, peer responders and writers focused as much on grammatical issues as content and revised significantly at the sentence level. However, although this study did find that these comments generally led to positive changes in the drafts, the authors only noted change. They did not specify whether these changes resulted in increased grammatical accuracy or complexity.

The positive effects of collaboration are not limited to peer response groups in writing classes. In similar research on collaboration in other activities, Storch (1999) conducted a study of group work in performing form-focused activities (cloze exercise, text reconstruction, and a short composition). She found that learners who worked in pairs and discussed the activities had more accurate results than those who worked alone. Although in two of the exercises the participants were not writing, in the sense that they were not creating new text, this positive result is suggestive. By sharing their knowledge and engaging in dialogue, the learners were able to complete the activities more successfully than those who worked alone.

The opportunity to share and coconstruct knowledge has been discussed by researchers from a variety of other perspectives, most notably those working within socio-cultural theory. Numerous studies (Donato, 1994; Swain; 2000, Swain, Brooks, & Tocalli-Beller, 2002; Swain & Lapkin, 2002) have all found that collaborative dialogue during writing tasks can build knowledge that did not previously exist in the minds of any of the individual participants. Swain argues that collaborative metatalk—that is, conversation about language—may facilitate acquisition (see Weissberg, this volume). The role of talk is particularly important because, within the socio-cultural perspective, knowledge construction is mediated by language; articulation makes the new knowledge available for inspection and discussion. This, it is argued, is a precursor to the internalization of knowledge. This positive influence of collaborative dialogue is in addition to the other purported beneficial effects of output already noted, such as hypothesis testing, increased noticing, and fluency.

The positive impact of collaborative talk has been found in the interaction of peers, but it is perhaps even more evident in the interaction of learners with relative experts, such as writing center tutors. The writing center literature abounds with descriptions of sessions as "conversations," but there has been little exploration of the impact of the sessions on what writers do subsequently, and still less of their impact on the writers' language development. One study in this area (Williams, 2004) tried to provide some preliminary answers to the first question. Direct assessment of the writing center sessions is extraordinarily difficult to do because of the challenge of teasing out the impact of the interaction in the session from that of other potential factors. An additional difficulty is that although many ESL students come to the writing center for assistance with sentence-level questions, most writing center tutors are taught to focus on larger rhetorical issues (Gillespie & Lerner, 2004; Harris, 1986; McAndrew & Reigstad, 2002). This reduces the likelihood that the spoken interaction will influence IL development.

The focus of Williams (2004) was broader than the impact of speaking on grammatical accuracy in that it addressed all changes in the text, not just in language use. It traced aspects of a draft discussed in the session to changes in the subsequent draft. Of course, it is possible that many other factors also intervened between drafts: consideration of teacher feedback, help from friends, or simply time to reflect. Therefore, the results can only be suggestive. However, the drafts following writing center sessions do demonstrate that sentence-level changes in morpho-syntax and in lexical choice were the most prevalent type of revision. Most of the changes were discussed during the sessions. This was in spite of tutors' consistent efforts to give the sessions a broader, more rhetorical orientation. These draft-to-draft revisions may say nothing about permanent changes in the writers' ILs, of course. However, in the absence of this kind of evidence of more short-term improvements, it is unlikely that there will be any permanent change in IL. In these short-term changes, in which learners can try out new or more complex forms in the less pressured context of writing, and with the expert assistance of a tutor, perhaps we are seeing the forward edge of IL development.

One last area of research that may be relevant to the speaking-writing connection is verbal reporting of writing processes, such as think-aloud protocols and stimulated recalls. These research tools have been used to report on various learner processes (Gass & Mackey, 2000; Jourdenais, 2001). In particular, they have been used to indicate levels of awareness since it is impossible to report on anything unless one is aware of it. Much of this research is based on the assumption that these techniques are not reactive; that is, the act of reporting does not affect the cognitive processes about which the report is made (Bowles & Leow, 2005; Leow & Morgan-Short, 2004). Yet, it has been suggested that the verbal reports used to explore learners' thought processes may actually create learning opportunities for participants (Adams, 2003; Sachs & Polio, 2007; Swain & Lapkin, 2002).[2] While this presents a potential problem in terms of research methods, it nevertheless suggests some interesting possibilities. Adams (2003), in a study of story reconstruction, showed that writers who participated in stimulated recalls demonstrated more target-like versions of the story following the recalls than those who did not have this opportunity. This led Adams to conclude that the stimulated recalls increased noticing. Sachs & Polio (2007) conducted a study of reformulation that used concurrent think-aloud protocols. She found a clear association between the verbalization of the differences that participants noticed between their own first drafts and those reformulated by native speakers and the changes they later made in the revisions. If a difference between the two drafts was verbalized, then it was likely to be changed in the revision.

These are just some of the ways in which the relevant studies point to how the development of language proficiency may be related to the act of writing. It is likely that the growing body of research in all of these contexts will continue to provide evidence of the dynamic and complex nature of the bidirectional influence of speaking and writing.

REFERENCES

Adams, R. (2003). L2 output, reformulation and noticing: Implications for L2 development. *Language Teaching Research, 7,* 347–376.

Berg, C. (1999). The effects of trained peer response on ESL students' revision types and writing quality. *Journal of Second Language Writing, 8,* 215–241.

Bowles, M.A., & Leow, R. (2005). Reactivity and type of verbal report in SLA research methodology: Expanding the scope of investigation. *Studies in Second Language Acquisition, 27,* 415–438.

Carson, J. (1993). Reading for writing: Cognitive perspectives. In J. Carson & I. Leki (Eds.), *Reading in the composition classroom* (pp. 85–104). Boston: Heinle & Heinle.

Casanave, C. (1994). Language development in students' journals. *Journal of Second Language Writing, 3,* 179–201.

Cumming, A. (1989). Writing expertise and second language proficiency. *Language Learning, 39,* 81–141.

[2]The opposite may also be true: Reporting may drain cognitive resources, detracting from learner performance (Polio, 2002).

DeBot, K. (1996). The psycholinguistics of the output hypothesis. *Language Learning, 46,* 529–555.

DeKeyser, R. (2001). Automaticity and automization In P. Robinson (Ed.), *Cognition and second language instruction* (pp. 125–151). Cambridge, UK: Cambridge University Press.

———. (2003). Implicit and explicit learning. In C. Doughty & M. Long (Eds.), *The handbook of second language acquisition* (pp. 313–348). Oxford, UK: Blackwell.

———. (2007). Skill acquisition theory. In B. VanPatten & J. Williams (Eds.), *Theories in second language acquisition* (pp. 97–112). Mahwah, NJ: Lawrence Erlbaum.

De Larios, J., Marin, J., & Murphy, L. (2001). A temporal analysis of formulation processes in L1 and L2 writing. *Language Learning, 51,* 497–538.

Donato, R. (1994). Collective scaffolding in second language acquisition. In J. Lantolf & G. Appel (Eds.), *Vygotskian approaches to second language research* (pp. 33–56). Norwood, NJ: Ablex.

El-Koumy, A. (1998). *Effect of dialogue journal writing on EFL students' speaking skills.* (EDRS No. ED 424 772).

Ellis, N. (2007). The associate-cognitive creed. In B. VanPatten & J. Williams (Eds.), *Theories in second language acquisition* (pp. 77–95). Mahwah, NJ: Lawrence Erlbaum.

Ellis, R. (1993). The structural syllabus and second language acquisition. *TESOL Quarterly, 27,* 91–113.

Ellis, R., & Yuan, F. (2004). The effects of planning on fluency, complexity and accuracy in second language narrative writing. *Studies in Second Language Acquisition, 26,* 59–84.

Faigley, L., & Witte, S. (1981). Analyzing revision. *College Composition and Communication, 32,* 400–414.

Fazio, L. (2001). The effect of corrections and commentaries on the journal writing accuracy of minority- and majority-language students. *Journal of Second Language Writing, 10,* 235–249.

Ferris, D. (2003). *Response to student writing.* Mahwah, NJ: Lawrence Erlbaum.

Ferris, D., & Hedgcock, J. (2005). *Teaching ESL composition* (2nd Ed.) Mahwah, NJ: Lawrence Erlbaum.

Gass, S., & Mackey, A. (2000). *Stimulated recall methodology in second language research.* Mahwah, NJ: Lawrence Erlbaum.

Gillespie, P., & Lerner, N. (2004). *The Allyn and Bacon guide to peer tutoring* (2nd Ed.). Needham Heights, MA: Pearson.

Goldstein, L., & Conrad, S. (1990). Student input and negotiation of meaning in ESL writing conferences. *TESOL Quarterly, 24,* 443–460.

Grabe, W. (2003). Reading and writing relations: Second language perspectives on research and practice. In B. Kroll (Ed.), *Exploring the dynamics of second language writing* (pp. 242–262). Cambridge, UK: Cambridge University Press.

Harklau, L. (1994). ESL vs. mainstream classes: Contrasting L2 learning environments. *TESOL Quarterly, 28,* 241–272.

———. (2002). The role of writing in classroom second language acquisition. *Journal of Second Language Writing, 11,* 329–350.

Harris, M. (1986). *Writing one-on-one: The writing conference.* Urbana, IL: NCTE.

Hyland, K. (2003). Genre-based pedagogies: A social response to process. *Journal of Second Language Writing, 12,* 17–29.

———. (2004). *Second language writing.* Cambridge, UK: Cambridge University Press.

Izumi, S. (2002). Output, input enhancement, and the noticing hypothesis: An experimental study on ESL relativization. *Studies in Second Language Acquisition, 24,* 541–577.

Izumi, S., & Bigelow, M. (2000). Does output promote noticing and second language acquisition? *TESOL Quarterly, 34,* 239–278.

Jourdenais, R. (2001). Cognition, instruction and protocol analysis. In P. Robinson (Ed.), *Cognition and second language instruction* (pp. 354–375). Cambridge, UK: Cambridge University Press.

Krashen, S. (1981). *Second language acquisition and second language learning.* Oxford, UK: Pergamon.

———. (1982). *Principles and practice in second language acquisition.* Oxford, UK: Pergamon.

———. (1984). *Writing: Research, theory and applications.* Oxford, UK: Pergamon.

Lam, W. (2000). L2 literacy and the design of the self: A case study of a teenager writing on the Internet. *TESOL Quarterly, 34,* 457–482.

Leow, R., & Morgan-Short, K. (2004). To think aloud or not to think aloud: The issue of reactivity in SLA research methodology. *Studies in Second Language Acquisition, 26,* 35–57.

Liu, J., & Hansen, J. (2002). *Peer response in second language writing classrooms.* Ann Arbor: University of Michigan Press.

McAndrew, D., & Reigstad, T. (2002). *Tutoring writing: A practical guide for conferences.* Portsmouth, NH: Boynton/Cook.

Mehnert, U. (1998). The effects of different lengths of time for planning on second language performance. *Studies in Second Language Acquisition, 20,* 83–108.

Ortega, L. (1999). Planning and focus on form in L2 oral performance. *Studies in Second Language Acquisition, 21,* 109–145.

Pathey-Chavez, G., & Ferris, D. (1997). Writing conferences and the weaving of multi-voiced texts in college composition. *Research in the Teaching of English, 31,* 51–90.

Payne, J. (2002). Developing L2 oral proficiency through synchronous CMC: Output, working memory and interlanguage development. *CALICO Journal, 20,* 7–32.

Pellettieri, J. (2000). Negotiation in cyberspace. The role of chatting in the development of grammatical competence. In M. Warschauer & R. Kern (Eds.), *Network-based language teaching* (pp. 59–86). New York: Cambridge University Press.

Peyton, J. (1990). Dialogue journal writing and the acquisition of English grammatical morphology. In J. Peyton (Ed.), *Students and teachers writing together* (pp. 67–97). Alexandria, VA: TESOL.

Peyton, J., & Staton, J. (Eds.) (1993). *Dialogue journals in the multilingual classroom.* Norwood, NJ: Ablex.

Qi, D., & Lapkin, S. (2001). Exploring the role of noticing in a three-stage second language writing task. *Journal of Second Language Writing, 10,* 277–303.

Rott, S., Williams, J., & Cameron, R. (2002). The effect of multiple-choice L1 glosses and input-output cycles on lexical acquisition and retention. *Language Teaching Research, 6,* 183–222.

Sachs, R., & Polio, C. (2007). Learners' uses of two types of written feedback on an L2 writing revision task. *Studies in Second Language Acquisition, 29,* 67–100.

Sasaki, M., & Hirose, K. (1996). Explanatory variables for EFL students' expository writing. *Language Learning, 46,* 137–174.

Schoonen, R., van Gelderen, A., de Glopper, K., Hulstijn, J., Simis, A, Snellings, P., & Stevenson, M. (2003). First language and second language writing: The role of linguistic knowledge, speed of processing, and metacognitive knowledge. *Language Learning, 53,* 165–202.

Skehan, P., & Foster, P. (1997). Task type and task processing conditions as influences of foreign language performance. *Language Teaching Research, 1,* 185–211.

———. (2001). Cognition and tasks. In P. Robinson (Ed.), *Cognition and second language instruction,* (pp. 183–205). Cambridge, UK: Cambridge University Press.

Smith, B. (2003). Computer-mediated negotiated interaction: An expanded model. *Modern Language Journal, 87,* 38–57.

———. (2004) Computer-mediated negotiated interaction and lexical acquisition. *Studies in Second Language Acquisition, 26,* 365–398.

Storch, N. (1999). Are two heads better than one? Pairwork and grammatical accuracy. *System, 27,* 363–374.

Swain, M. (1995). Three functions of output in second language learning. In G. Cook & B. Seidlhofer (Eds.), *Principle and practice in applied linguistics* (pp. 125–144). Oxford, UK: Oxford University Press.

———. (1998). Focus on form through conscious reflection. In C. Doughty & J. Williams (Eds.), *Focus on form in classroom second language acquisition* (pp. 64–81). Cambridge, UK: Cambridge University Press.

———. (2000). The Output Hypothesis and beyond: Mediating acquisition through collaborative dialogue. In J. Lantolf, (Ed.). *Sociocultural theory and second language learning* (pp. 97–114). Oxford, UK: Oxford University Press.

Swain, M., Brooks, L., & Tocalli-Beller, A. (2002). Peer-peer dialogue as a means of second language learning. *Annual Review of Applied Linguistics, 22,* 171–185.

Swain, M., & Lapkin, S. (1995). Problems in output and the cognitive processes they generate: A step toward second language learning. *Applied Linguistics, 16,* 371–391.

———. (2002). Talking it through: Two French immersion students' response to reformulation. *International Journal of Educational Research, 3/4,* 285–304.

Tarone, E. (1982). Systematicity and attention in interlanguage. *Language Learning, 32,* 69–82.

Thornbury, S. (1997). Reformulation and reconstruction: Tasks that promote noticing. *ELT Journal, 51,* 326–335.

Vandergrift, L. (2006). Second language listening: Ability or language proficiency? *Modern Language Journal, 90,* 6–18.

VanPatten, B., Williams, J., & Rott, S. (2004). Form-meaning connections in second language acquisition. In B. VanPatten, J. Williams, S. Rott, & M. Overstreet (Eds.), *Form-meaning connections in second language acquisition* (pp. 1–26). Mahwah, NJ: Lawrence Erlbaum.

Villamil, O., & De Guerrero, M., (1998). Assessing the impact of peer revision on L2 writing. *Applied Linguistics, 19,* 491–514.

Warschauer, M., & Kern. R. (2000). Introduction: theory and practice of network-based language teaching. In M. Warschauer & R. Kern (Eds.), *Network-based language teaching* (pp. 1–19). Cambridge, UK: Cambridge University Press.

Weissberg, B. (1994). Speaking of writing: Some functions of talk in the ESL classroom. *Journal of Second Language Writing, 3,* 121–139.

———. (2000a). Developing relationships in the acquisition of English syntax: Writing versus speech. *Learning and Instruction, 10,* 37–53.

———. (2000b). On the interface of writing and speech: Acquiring syntax through journal writing. In G. Bräuer (Ed.), *Writing across languages* (pp. 71–88). Stamford, CT: Ablex.

Whalen, K., & Menard, N. (1995). L1 and L2 writers' strategic and linguistic knowledge: A model of multiple-level discourse processing. *Language Learning, 45,* 381–418.

White, R. (1987). Approaches to writing. In M. Long & J. Richards (Eds.), *Methodology in TESOL* (pp. 259–266). Rowley, MA: Newbury House.

Williams, J. (2004). Tutoring and revision: Second language writers in the writing center. *Journal of Second Language Writing, 13,* 173–201.

Williams, J., & Fernández, C. (2007). The role in interaction in input enhancement. In C. Gascoigne (Ed.), *Assessing the role of input enhancement in second language education* (pp. 107–127). Stillwater, OK: New Forums Press.

Wong, W. (2001). Modality and attention to form in the input. *Studies in Second Language Acquisition, 23,* 345–368.

Yuan, F., & Ellis, R. (2003). The effects of pre-task planning and on-line planning on fluency, complexity and accuracy in L2 monologic oral production. *Applied Linguistics, 24,* 1–27.

2

Critiquing the Vygotskian Approach to L2 Literacy

ROBERT WEISSBERG

Abstract

This chapter takes a critical look at the Vygotskian (socio-cultural) approach to second language literacy, specifically with respect to the development of L2 writing skills by adult learners. First, the basic tenets of socio-cultural theory are reviewed, as well as the claims that have been made in its behalf as an explanation for L2 learning and as an instructional model for L2 teaching. The difficulties in applying the socio-cultural model to writing instruction for adult L2 learners are then discussed. Finally, a *dialogue approach* to L2 writing instruction is proposed as a compromise between mainline socio-cultural theory and the realities of individual differences among adult L2 writers.

Over the past three decades, the applied linguistics community has gradually shifted its focus from linguistic and cognitive issues of individual language learners to a greater concern with learners' social contexts and the nature of their social interactions, a shift David Block has termed "the social turn" (2003). Symptomatic of this refocusing is the current interest among applied linguists, foreign language (FL), and second language (L2) teachers in socio-cultural theory (SCT), commonly associated with the work of the Russian theorists Vygotsky and Bakhtin, and in what it might suggest about the acquisition, development, and teaching of L2 skills (Lantolf, 2000; Johnson, 2004; Hall, Vitanova, & Marchenkova, 2005).

The shift toward a more socialized view of language learning has also been felt in the specific area of L2 literacy, as attested by the growing number of publications concerning the speaking-writing connection (Vann, 1981; Mangelsdorf, 1989; Blanton, 1992; de Guerrero & Villamil, 2000; Prior, 2001; Williams, 2002; Braxley, 2005; Weissberg, 2006a; and this volume). In the spirit of the social turn, this chapter looks critically at the claims of SCT as they have been applied in the field of L2 literacy and specifically to the speaking-writing connection that is the theme of this volume. After briefly reviewing what I believe are the relevant aspects of SCT to the teaching of L2 writers, I will offer an analysis of the appeal that the SCT approach holds for L2 writing teachers and researchers, and at the same time identify the pitfalls that I believe it entails. The claim I wish to establish is that SCT, appealing as it is, does not adequately address the instructional needs of many L2 writing students. I will further claim that a strong form of socio-cultural theory may actually obscure important differences in the acquisition of literacy skills among L2 learners and, in so doing, hinder their instruction. The chapter concludes by suggesting how SCT, critically re-examined, might be made more amenable to the classroom learning needs of a wider range of FL and L2 writers.

The Vygotskian Approach to Teaching and Learning

To establish the grounds for this critique, it is worth briefly reviewing the major tenets of socio-cultural theory as they pertain to teaching and learning language, and particularly to the L2 writing-speaking connection. First, SCT holds that for any learner, cognitive development takes place on two psychological "planes": one, the inter-psychological plane—that is, between and among people—and the other, the intra-psychological plane—that is, in the mind of the individual learner (Vygotsky, 1978). The order here is important; a central tenet of SCT is that the inter-psychological part of learning comes first. That is, social interaction precedes and is the necessary precursor to an individual's intellectual growth and development of higher-order cognitive functions. As Mitchell and Miles (1998) put it, "Learning is first social, then individual" (p. 145). If we accept this central premise of SCT, and if we wish to apply it as a general approach in our writing classrooms, we would then have to acknowledge that social tasks such as group brainstorming and peer revising do not merely facilitate the acquisition of L2 literacy; they are in fact essential to it.

Second, SCT holds that instructed learning takes place through assisted performance between the learner and an expert, a tutor or a more proficient peer (Donato, 1994; Ohta, 2001). Assisted performance takes place as tutor and learner work together in the zone of proximal development (ZPD), identified by the tutor as the psychological distance between what the learner can accomplish on her own and what she can accomplish with the tutor's assistance. The ZPD is created anew by the tutor for each learner and for each new learning problem.

Central to this enterprise is the mutual construction of "scaffolded" conversations between tutor and learner but guided by the tutor. Scaffolded dialogue is the verbal means by which the tutor helps the learner move through the ZPD. In L2 and FL contexts, this has been observed in the discourse that takes place between tutors and L2 writing students in university writing centers (Williams, 2002; Weissberg, 2006b) and between FL students working in pairs where one student is more expert than the other (Swain & Lapkin, 1998; Ohta, 2001). The end goal of assisted performance is the transformation of the learner's activity from "other-regulation" to "self-regulation," (Block, 2003, p. 101)—that is, to enable the learner to do tasks on her own that she was previously able to do only with the tutor's help.

If we accept this tenet of SCT, we must acknowledge the importance of providing students with opportunities to work one-on-one with more expert writers—in writing center tutorials, in conferences with instructors, and in pair and group work with more proficient peers. We would also have to recognize the responsibility placed on tutors and teachers to determine where each learner's ZPD lies for any given learning task and to acquire the skills needed to build scaffolded dialogues cooperatively with their students.

Third, SCT holds that the indispensable link between social interaction and individual learning is the psychological phenomenon known as inner speech—a silent, truncated version of oral language that learners internalize through their interactions with others and that goes underground, so to speak, to become the silent language of thought. Again, to quote Mitchell and Myles (1998), inner speech embodies "the use of language to regulate internal thought, without . . . external articulation" (p. 148). In learning literacy, inner speech is the bridge between conversation and composition. Again, if we take SCT seriously as an approach to teaching L2 writers, we would have to dedicate a sufficient amount of instructional time to activities and assignments that help students develop inner speech in their second language.

To summarize, what socio-cultural theory in its strong form implies for language teachers is that speaking and writing are developmentally linked—that the speaking-writing connection is psychologically valid and that teachers should exploit that link in their classroom practice. There is of course a good deal more to SCT than I have included in this brief overview (see especially the work of James Lantolf, 2000, for a thorough treatment of SCT as applied to second language acquisition, and Marysia Johnson, 2004, who applies SCT to teaching and testing, as well as to research), but these three premises are sufficient for our present purpose.

Speaking-Writing Connections in the Writing Classroom

How relevant are Vykgotsky's theories of learning and teaching in light of modern composition pedagogy? The significance of the former to the latter can be appreciated by viewing the teaching of writing through the lens of an analytical paradigm devised by Donald Rubin and Kenneth Kantor, pioneers in the area of speaking-writing connections (1984). (Another interesting analysis of speaking-writing connections in school settings is offered by Kevin Leander and Paul Prior, 2004.) In their article, Rubin and Kantor tip their socio-cultural hand early on when they state that "communication is situated in specific contexts; context cannot be avoided with describing processes of growth" (p. 48). This statement reflects the SCT emphasis on the historical and social setting of all learning (Schinke-Llano, 1995). Rubin and Kantor further reveal their SCT orientation as they trace the speaking-writing connection across three dimensions of communicative competence.

First they claim that because speaking and writing are inextricably linked, teachers should include classroom activities in both modalities to help their students develop coding abilities—that is, their ability to formulate ideas in writing (p. 56ff.). With enhanced coding skills, students are able to write with greater fluency, tighter organization, increased expressiveness, and a surer sense of voice. Rubin and Kantor recommend the use of narrative writing in particular, a rhetorical mode based on speech, to help students develop their expressive language and their ability to connect extended sequences of written text.

Increased facility in coding is only the most superficial dimension of communicative competence that learners tap by combining speaking and writing activities. Rubin and Kantor then discuss how, at a deeper level, building connections between speaking and writing helps student writers develop an increased sense of social awareness (p. 49ff.). This helps them develop a sense of writing for a specific audience and to develop a reader-based rhetorical style. Writers who are also experienced speakers are better able to imagine their eventual readers; they are able to sense what their readers already know, what they expect, and how their world view might affect their reaction to a piece of writing. In Rubin and Kantor's words, "[they] are able to tailor messages to their audience's perspective" (p. 51) "to make distinctions among types of audiences and anticipate the disposition of [their] listeners and readers" (1984, p. 56). Tapping their knowledge of oral communication, writers also learn to imagine the feedback an absent reader might give them (p. 43), and thus become more adept at constructing persuasive written arguments (Rubin & Kantor 1984). On the linguistic level, increased audience awareness helps writers to refine their lexical and syntactic choices and to provide their readers with helpful transitions and organization cues.

The idea that novice writers can develop a sense of audience through linked speaking and writing activities parallels Vygotsky's theory of the cognitive shift from the interpersonal plane of social discourse to the intra-personal plane of the learner's mind. In the context of composition, SCT helps us appreciate how the writer's memory of oral discourse is transformed into a conversation taking place wholly within the writer's mind, with an internalized and abstracted audience of readers.

At an even deeper cognitive level, Rubin and Kantor argue that by including both writing and speaking activities in their language classes teachers help students develop the ability to reconstruct their experiences in writing. That is, writing itself becomes a tool of thought for students. Accomplished writers, they say, learn not so much to think in order to write as to use their experiences as speakers and writers to learn to think:

> Speaking and writing are vehicles for sharing knowledge with others. But they are also instruments for helping us to make sense of things. . . . By searching for words to express ourselves, we discover what it is that we have to say. By linking those words in syntax, we discover relationships in the world (p. 62).

It's not just the case that learning to think helps us become better speakers and writers; just as important, by participating in speaking and listening activities, we become better thinkers. The notion that writing is a means of discovering what one wishes to write next echoes the SC idea that a writer's already-written text stimulates the production of inner speech, which in turn prompts the writer to produce still more text (Luria, 1969; Leont'yev,

1969; Bruffee, 1995). In applying this insight to the writing classroom, we help novice writers become more adept at inventing and discovering new ideas so that they can use the act of writing as a springboard for generating new ideas.

After exploring these three dimensions of communicative competence, Rubin and Kantor suggest that teachers exploit the speaking-writing connection by creating bridges—"synapses," they call them (1984, p. 71)—between the two modalities. They see the teacher's task as one of helping students bridge the gap from oracy to literacy by developing learning activities that use the former to leverage increased proficiency in the latter. In the two decades since Rubin and Kantor sketched this outline of the speaking-writing connection, we see composition teachers making regular and frequent use of a wide variety of synaptic activities in their classrooms, what we might term collectively a "talk-write" pedagogy (Zoellner, 1969)—the use of peer review groups, group composition activities, paired invention tasks, dialogue journal writing, writing conferences and tutorials, online chat rooms, and other practices that, to paraphrase Rubin and Kantor, help students release the power of speech and transfer it to their writing (1984, p. 71). Although the utility of some of these speech-based writing activities might be debated (see for example Liu and Hansen's 2002 summary of the controversy surrounding peer editing groups), few would argue that the teaching of writing, and L2 writing in particular, has not been generally enhanced by their incorporation into writing lessons and composition programs (Schinke-Llano, 1995).

The Appeal of SCT for L2 Writing Pedagogy

By exploiting speech-writing connections in their writing classes, teachers have, intentionally or not, adopted a socio-cultural approach toward their students' literacy development. For many teachers of L2 writers, the move toward a more socialized, interactive writing classroom is a natural progression from more traditional, teacher-centered styles of instruction (Gutierrez, 1994). What makes the socio-cultural approach appealing? The answer, I believe, lies in three rather seductive advantages that SCT offers to L2 writing practitioners.

First, SCT provides a unified theory of teaching and learning from which to view the acquisition of literacy and the teaching of writing—a theory, as Linda Schinke-Llano (1995) points out, that is "consistent, coherent and cohesive" (p. 21). The speaking-writing connection is the essence of this account—the unequivocal claim that novice writers depend, at least initially, on their speech base and ultimately on the development of their inner speech to "push" their literacy. Acceptance of this foundational claim leads teachers to implement social, speech-based activities in their L2 writing classes under the assumption that this will prompt the development of their L2 students' inner speech. As an added a bonus for theorists and researchers, SCT also suggests a wide range of empirical questions about the social nature of acquiring L2 literacy skills (see Marchenkova, 2005, and Grabois, 2004, for a discussion of the applicability of Vygotsky and Bakhtin's theories to research in L2 learning and teaching).

Second, SCT is compatible with a number of widely accepted beliefs about second language acquisition and with teaching practices based on those beliefs. For example, with its emphasis on assisted performance, SCT is congruent with current practices of error treatment that view a learner's interlanguage as a naturally developing outgrowth of the hypotheses she has formulated about L2 rules, and of her experiences testing them out in conversations with more proficient speakers. Granted, SC theorists would focus less on the learner's mental representation of the rules and more on the kinds of expert assistance she receives in moving from one level of rule approximation to the next; however, the general attitude on both sides toward learners' errors—their causes and their functions in the L2 learning process—is congruent. Other areas of overlap between socio-cultural theory and current L2 theory and pedagogy include the following:

- SCT coexists comfortably with the input hypothesis and the related notion of comprehensible input, in which instructional language is pitched by the teacher to a level just one step higher ("*i* + 1") than what the learner can easily comprehend or produce (Krashen, 1982). The latter bears obvious similarities to the socio-cultural notion of the ZPD, in which the tutor must identify the learner's current ability to master a task independently and then pitch subsequent instructional tasks at a slightly higher level. Again, the SC theorist would likely view the learner's processing of input more as a socially interactive phenomenon than as a strictly cognitive-linguistic one; nonetheless, the parallels between the two notions are difficult to ignore.
- An even better fit with SCT is the expanded version of the output hypothesis proposed by Merrill Swain (2000), where L2 acquisition is pushed forward by the learner's attempts to produce language, as well as to comprehend it. SC theorists would agree that although com-

prehensible input may be a necessary condition for second language acquisition, it is not sufficient; socially mediated output—conversational interaction—is critically important as well.

- In a similar vein, the interaction hypothesis (and its pedagogical realization in classroom tasks that require learners to negotiate meaning) is, as Linda Schinke-Llano (1995) and Jessica Williams (2002) have pointed out, closely allied with the SCT concept of scaffolding. All three concepts are concerned with promoting specific features of oral discourse between experts and novices that result in improved performance for the novice. (See Williams, 2002, and Weissberg, 2006b, for descriptions and analyses of the scaffolded dialogue at use in the writing center.)
- The recent interest in task-based instruction in L2 teaching would also win the approval of SC adherents, since tasks can promote group interaction and can make available multiple opportunities for scaffolding to occur between student and teacher and among students (Donato, 1994; Schinke-Llano, 1995). SCT proponents would ask us to recognize, however, that the task as set by the teacher and the actual activities in which students engage are not necessarily one and the same (Ohta, 2001, p. 232).

Last but not least, writing classrooms featuring a talk-write pedagogy informed by socio-cultural theory are attractive in that they support the growth of L2 students' proficiencies in both speech and writing. The two-for-one instructional dividend is particularly motivating for students whose learning styles favor social interaction over individual seat work. For them, the socio-cultural approach to L2 literacy pays off by providing a supportive classroom environment where learning to write is an enjoyable, collaborative social activity.

Thus, the socio-cultural approach to literacy learning provides convenient theoretical validation for many practices currently used in writing classes where L2 learners are enrolled. In light of this compatibility, it is important to examine critically the assumptions that SCT asks us to make about the nature of L2 writing and writers, especially adult writers who are already literate in their own languages. For as attractive as it appears at first glance, the socio-cultural approach to literacy learning glosses over important differences among L2 writers and promotes an overgeneralized, one-dimensional view of how L2 literacy is acquired. Consequently, it may lead us to make erroneous conclusions about how it should best be taught.

Three Caveats about SCT and L2 Writing

Three assumptions about L2 writing implicit in SCT seem to me to be particularly problematic. In one way or another they obscure what is actually happening in writing classrooms and what is being experienced by some L2 writers.

- *Assumption 1*: SCT asks us to assume that learning to write in an L2 is analogous, if not equivalent, to learning to write in an L1.
- *Assumption 2*: The SCT approach to L2 writing asks us to make unwarranted assumptions about the use of inner speech by L2 writers.
- *Assumption 3*: SCT assumes a model of second language acquisition in which a learner's L2 knowledge gained through speech transfers directly to the learner's writing.

Assumption 1: L1 and L2 Writing Are Developmentally Equivalent.

This assumption not only masks important differences between the two processes, but also obscures significant individual differences that distinguish some L2 writers from others (Leki, 1992; Reid, 1998). The problems here are both theoretical and practical. First, many applied linguists argue that the larger premise from which this assumption is derived (i.e., that second language acquisition is not qualitatively different from first language acquisition) is itself not true. Adult learners in fact do not learn additional languages in the same way as they learned their first. Not only do they no longer have unfettered access to universal grammar as they did when they were young children, as adults they have different, and various, cognitive approaches to language learning (see Bley-Vroman, 1989; Ellis, 1994; Lightbown & Spada, 1999; and Herschensohn, 2000, for discussions of this issue).

The assumption that L2 learners acquire literacy in an additional language in the same manner as they did in their first is likewise unwarranted. Yet by placing speech as the developmental precursor to writing, this is exactly the assumption that SCT asks us to make. At its base, the Vygotskian view of language learning is primarily a model of speech development; writing is dealt with as a secondary symbol system derived from speech (Johnson, 2004). This model undoubtedly holds for most, if not all, L1 learners, but not for all L2 learners (Sato, 1990). Adult L2 writers who are already literate in an L1, for example, are able to call on the invention strategies, rhetorical techniques, and even the turns of phrase, sentence structures, and lexical choices that serve them in their L1 writing (Weissberg, 2000). Whether or not these borrowed elements are always efficacious when applied by the writer in her L2 is not the issue; what is important is that these L1-referenced strategies place L1-literate L2 writers in a far different position from their L1 counterparts with respect to developing their writing skills.

Furthermore, because the SCT model of literacy acquisition is speech-based, it asks us to assume that speech is ipso facto the "modality of strength" for learners and, consequently, that including oral-based activities in the writing class will necessarily lead students to "bootstrap" themselves from their stronger modality (i.e., speech) to their weaker (writing) (Elbow, 2002). The practical classroom problems associated with this assumption are substantial. First, L2 learners differ with respect to their modality preference—that is, whether speech or writing is their primary acquisition driver (Sato, 1990; Pavlenko & Lantolf, 2000; Weissberg, 2000; Harklau, 2002). There is in fact no guarantee that a given L2 student's modality of strength is speech. For some adult learners, second language acquisition may be triggered more through literacy activities than through oral interaction. I think of Oscar, one of my former ESL writing students, whose spoken English was so much less developed than his written English that it would be highly unlikely for his speech to have had much bootstrapping impact on the growth of his L2 writing. Learners like Oscar may acquire written proficiency in an L2 with little or no gain in their spoken language (Weissberg, 2000).

In addition to the matter of modality preference, L2 learners also differ in their learning and social styles. As can be observed in any classroom where students are actively writing, some writers prefer to brainstorm, plan, compose, and revise on their own. For these writers, group work can be distracting, annoying, and even debilitating. I recall another adult L2 student of mine, Jesús, who was distracted by classroom talk to the point that he was virtually unable to complete tasks that involved group or pair work. Writing habits that students import from their L1 school experiences may also run headlong into the classroom methods used by their L2 writing teachers. Students, for example, who are accustomed to extended periods of silent seat work in their classes may have difficulty adapting to the intense socialization of the talk-write classroom.

Given the existence of learners like these, it seems misguided if not actually counter-productive to develop a pedagogy of L2 writing based on an inaccurate overgeneralization about how L2 literacy is acquired. Pavlenko and Lantolf (2000) have in fact created an alternative model of biliteracy based on learners like Oscar, learners whose "new voice" develops first in their writing. They claim that some adult immigrant writers begin to lose their old composing voices as they learn the second language, and that their new voice (in this case, an English one) often appears first in their writing. Writing is thus "a crucial stepping stone" for some adult immigrants in recovering their voices and their sense of self in their new culture (p. 168).

Because SCT invariably sees social interaction as the necessary trigger for cognition, it leaves us with a monolithic account of literacy acquisition, insensitive to differences in modality strength and cognitive style among L2 learners. We already know that what works well in our writing classes for some students works poorly or not at all for others, and part of that variation may well be explained by differences along these two parameters. In short, basing writing instruction around an SCT-influenced pedagogy can result in classrooms that do not serve all L2 writers well.

Assumption 2: Inner Speech Is a Psychological Reality for L2 Writers.

Recall that inner speech is the crucial link in the Vygotskian speech-to-writing argument. It is the means by which the learner transfers knowledge she has gained from the interpersonal plane of social interaction to the intrapersonal plane of cognition, and it is thus the conduit between social language and thought (Johnson, 2004, p. 161). The notion of inner speech as a tool for L2 writers is problematic, however, for despite a growing body of research in this area, inner speech is not, and by definition cannot, be directly observable. The evidence for inner speech as a universal phenomenon for L2 writers is at best indirect—students' self-reports, as in de Guerrero (1994); the use of "private speech" in the presence of an investigator, as in McCafferty (1992), or think-aloud protocols (equated by the author with private speech) revealing L1/L2 code switching, as in Woodall (2002). Unfortunately, the assertion that an L2 writer's think-aloud protocols are outward manifestations of her inner speech (see for example Woodall, 2002, and Prior, 2001) is unproven and probably untestable.

To further complicate matters, there is confusion in the published research between the terms "inner speech" and "private speech." Some authors use these labels interchangeably (see Grabois, 2004, for example), but in fact they are distinct constructs in socio-cultural theory. Inner speech is a wholly internalized, abbreviated form of language, while private speech, or speech-for-self, is uttered aloud by the learner but is not intended for interpersonal communication (see Ohta, 2001, for a thorough treatment of the distinction). L2 researchers investigating the uses of inner speech and private speech by L2 learners do not always recognize or articulate this distinction.

To compound the problem, research in the area of inner speech and private speech appears contradictory, as is evident in studies attempting to associate the use of inner speech with a learner's level of L2 proficiency. McCafferty (1992) reports that his more proficient subjects used less private speech, whereas de Guerrero's (1994) more proficient subjects reported using more extensive and more elaborated inner speech. Why there should be such a discrepancy is not clear. Logically, it would seem that inner speech would work best for L2 learners with a relatively advanced oral proficiency, yet a German acquaintance of mine, a highly proficient academic speaker and writer who publishes frequently in English, reports that she is unaware of any use of English inner speech in her writing process (Dagmar Haumman, personal communication). I have interviewed a number of my advanced ESL writing students who make a similar claim.

In sum, basing a pedagogy for L2 writers on the exploitation of inner speech is to some degree a case of wishful thinking. The results of Vygotsky-inspired L2 research are not yet conclusive or consistent enough to verify the existence of inner speech or private speech as universal phenomena for L2 writers, or to support the assertion that the latter is a reliable reflection of the former. Given the tentative nature of the research up to this point, it requires a substantial leap of faith to assume that inner speech functions for all L2 writers as the link between their social interaction and their writing, let alone to adopt a composition pedagogy that depends on it.

Assumption 3: A Learner's Knowledge Gained through Speech Transfers Directly to Writing.

Closely related to the problem of inner speech is another psycholinguistic issue: the absence in socio-cultural theory of a satisfactory mental model of exactly how linguistic knowledge is transferred from one production modality to the other (i.e., from speech to writing). This is especially problematic for L2 and FL practitioners, whose fields have traditionally been concerned with how best to represent linguistic knowledge—how it is acquired, stored, and accessed in the learner's mind (VanPatten, 2004). Clearly, SCT entails the assumption that modality transfer can and does take place; a central tenet of the theory is, after all, that knowledge gained in the social arena moves from the learner's interpersonal to her intrapersonal plane. As previously discussed, that transfer and internalization are accomplished through the medium of inner speech. However, there are serious problems with this explanation where L2 learners are concerned: the research evidence for the existence of L2 inner speech is indirect at best, and there is no evidence that it is by any means a universal phenomenon—that inner speech is available to all L2 learners. If, as Pavlenko and Lantolf (2000) claim, the goal of the SCT project in applied linguistics is not to replace traditional acquisition paradigms but to complement them (p. 156), some way needs to be found to model intermodality transfer. How exactly does linguistic material get from one modality to the other in the learner's mind? More generally, how can SCT be incorporated into existing models of L2 knowledge and acquisition?

In conventional approaches to second language acquisition, linguistic competence (i.e., the learner's "knowledge source" for the L2, or her "underlying mental representation" of acquired L2 knowledge [VanPatten, 2004, p. 29]) is a unitary construct that gives rise to both an individual's spoken and written output (Gass & Selinker, 2001, p. 238). This representation easily explains the transfer of a learner's L2 knowledge from speech to writing or vice versa: acquired L2 knowledge is integrated into the learner's competence and then may be manifested in either her spoken or written output. But SCT dispenses with the competence/performance dichotomy (Prior, 2001; Johnson 2004), shifting its focus from the formal problems of representing linguistic knowledge to viewing language as social communication, or in Bakhtin's formulation, to viewing language ability as a collection of "speech genres" available to the writer/speaker (Hall, Vitanova, & Marchenkov, 2005, pp. 2–3). In fact, SC theorists like Pavlenko and Lantolf (2000) explicitly question the traditional L2 acquisition model, preferring what they call a "participation metaphor" for language learning.

To resolve the speaking-writing transfer problem, one could accept the Bakhtinian assertion that "the appropriation of new voices" is what accounts for second language acquisition (Rodby, 1992; Johnson, 2004). Then we could assume that the learner's acquisition of L2 writing comes from unconscious memories of earlier encounters with L2 texts. Similarly, one could accept Block's (2003) multicompetence explanation, in which linguistic knowledge "bleeds" across a mental boundary from speech to writing. But neither of these options offers much beyond a rather poetic explanation for how L2 learners' speaking and writing modalities relate to each other dynamically. We are left then with a theory built on the rather shaky foundation of inner speech (see deGuerrero's 1994 diagram, p. 103), a tentative solution at best.

The problem here is that SCT is a *theory of learning with pedagogical implications*, not a fleshed-out view of second language acquisition or linguistic competence (Mitchell & Myles, 1998). In fact, there is a substantial gap between SCT and more traditional, cognitive/linguistic approaches to second language acquisition (see Gass, 1997, and Gass & Selinker, 2001, for example), a distinction that is dealt with at length by Block (2003). And given the explicitly social, non-linguistic orientation of much SC research (see Block's 2003 and Johnson's 2004 discussions), it is unlikely that a detailed explanation of the mental processes of L2 learners relevant to the speech-writing connection will be available any time soon. The upshot is that, unfortunately for teachers of L2 writers, SCT veils rather than illuminates the speech-writing connection.

The failure of socio-cultural theory to provide a convincing representation of linguistic knowledge is not merely a theoretical issue; it is a practical matter for teachers of L2 writers. Some L2 writers may be psychologically capable of accessing linguistic material from their L2 speech repertoire as they write, but others may not. Evidence I have presented elsewhere indicates that there are L2 writers for whom the boundary between L2 knowledge in speech and writing is not as porous as it is assumed by SCT. There are ESL learners whose spoken and written proficiencies develop quite independently of each other, and others for whom competence in the spoken language is so limited that it simply cannot be accessed during writing (Weissberg, 2000). This failure to adequately model linguistic knowledge and its transfer from one modality to another is not in itself an indictment of SCT; a theory ought not to be held accountable for ignoring questions it is not interested in to begin with. However, if teachers choose to adopt a socio-cultural account of L2 learning to inform their writing classrooms, they are obliged to acknowledge the psycholinguistic issues that impact their students' learning. If they do not, they are once again engaging in a leap of faith by assuming that their student writers are going to benefit from exploitation of the speaking-writing connection.

Socio-cultural theory thus remains an interesting and even appealing account of learning, but until it is incorporated into existing models of language acquisition and use, it remains inadequate to the task of explaining psychologically the speaking-writing connection, or more generally the acquisition of L2 literacy skills.

Dialogue and Speech

In light of these caveats, what positive contributions can socio-cultural theory make to classroom practice with L2 writers? Despite its monolithic view of the acquisition of literacy skills and its failure to provide a plausible mental model of the speaking-writing connection, I believe SCT holds significant pedagogical value, as long as it is not taken as a universal predictor of how all learners acquire L2 writing skills. To expand on this point, I conclude by posing, and attempting to answer, two questions that I believe speak directly to the essence of the problems raised in this chapter.

1. Is What Is Essentially an L1 Model of Literacy Development at all Suitable for L2 Writers?

The answer depends on the individual L2 writer, her modality preference for L2 acquisition, and her ability to transfer linguistic knowledge from one production modality to the other. Since a uniform developmental model cannot be assumed for all the L2 writers in a classroom, we must scrutinize our students individually to get at least a rough picture of how each one handles the writing-speaking interface. Which production modality is stronger? Does production in one modality appear to affect the other? We can determine this by being sensitive to the similarities and disjunctions between students' oral and written output of similar content over time. If we wish to do this systematically, we can sample and compare students' oral and written work early in the course and then monitor them periodically throughout the period of instruction.

Such a comparative analysis can help identify students for whom the oral-written interface is porous enough to allow for easy transfer of content, language, and invention strategies from speech to writing. It will also help us to identify students like Oscar, for whom the boundary is less porous and whose written English appears to develop independently from speech, or in the absence of any observable improvement in oral proficiency. It will also help identify students like Jesús, who do not function well in a highly interactive classroom. Remembering that instructional tasks based on social interaction may actually disadvantage such students, we should offer a variety of assignments and tasks in our writing classes, including some that de-emphasize or eliminate accompanying oral work. A certain amount of class time should be reserved for individual writing practice, unaccompanied by the hubbub of social talk. We must also be sure that non–orally oriented students have the choice of opting out of group and pair activities if they prefer to work on their own. There is something to be said for the splendid isolation of writing—for thinking over a writing assignment quietly and planning and writing it in solitude. For all writers, but especially for writers like Oscar and Jesús, there is a time for the talking to cease and the work of writing to begin.

2. What Role Can SCT and the Speaking-Writing Connection Play in the Education of L2 Writers?

To harness the power of speech in the writing classroom, socio-cultural theory suggests that we open up multiple opportunities for students to interact with each other, with their teachers and tutors, and with their own texts. However, experience with novice ESL writers like Oscar and Jesús, and with advanced ones like Dagmar, makes it difficult to argue for a strong version of socio-cultural theory in our work with L2 writers. In order to broaden the pedagogical application of SCT, we need to move away from a focus on talk per se. I would argue for a weaker version of the theory that envisions a classroom that supports dialogue in a variety of forms (Johnson, 2004; Marchenkova, 2005; Weissberg, 2006a; Wong, 2006). This modified application of SCT holds that, while dialogue is critical to the development of writing skills, not *all instructional dialogue need be external,* that we can appeal to the power of speech without always operationalizing it in the form of talk.

I define *dialogue* for this purpose as the conversations, both internal and external, that a writer has with a multitude of voices that inform her writing, not the least important of which is her own voice (Wong, 2006). The instructor's goal becomes not simply one of providing L2 student writers with opportunities for social talk but to inject the elements of dialogue into as many areas of their writing instruction as possible. In broadening our understanding of the speaking-writing connection, we can find non-oral but still dialogic equivalents to many of the interactive tasks prevalent in today's writing classrooms. Thus, the dialogue approach to L2 writing can include not only talk-write activities such as collaborative writing, peer revision groups, and conferencing, but also opportunities for students to develop their own internal dialogues about writing through journal writing (Peyton & Reed, 1990); by setting self-referencing writing assignments that ask students to incorporate and recast their earlier assignments into new texts; and by training writers to use self-questioning invention techniques known as "procedural facilitation (Bereiter & Scardamalia, 1982).

L2 writers can also communicate about their writing with their teachers and peers in written form rather than in face-to-face sessions. There are a number of ways for instructors to facilitate this, such as setting up online writing conferences (Bloch, 2002); by adopting dialogue-style written responses to students' work that allow students to respond with written comments of their own (Berzsenyi, 2001); and by allowing students to share their responses to each others' writing through writing rather than (or in addition to) peer group sessions. As Kate Braxley (2005) has noted, "not all students are able or willing" to engage in social interaction (p. 29). In acknowledging this fact, teachers should recognize that although not all L2 writers benefit from an overtly socialized classroom, all writers can benefit from developing dialogic strategies and techniques to facilitate writing in their new language. It seems to me this is the real advantage that socio-cultural theory offers the composition classroom.

To avoid creating unintended barriers to learning, teachers of L2 writers must carry on their own internal dialogue with Vygotskian learning theory. Since socio-cultural theory is itself a historical product of Marxist-influenced scholarship, it is entirely appropriate for writing instructors to engage in an on-going dialectic with SCT—pitting the obvious benefits of a socialized writing classroom on the one hand against the needs of their individual L2 students on the other. I am suggesting that the best way to make socio-cultural theory and the speaking-writing connection work for L2 writers is to resolve this tension by focusing not on speech but on dialogue.

REFERENCES

Bereiter, C., & Scardamalia, M. (1982). From conversation to composition: The role of instruction in a developmental process. In R. Glaser (Ed.), *Advances in instructional psychology, Vol. 2* (pp. 1–64). Hillsdale, NJ: Lawrence Erlbaum.

Berzsenyi, C. (2001). Comments to comments: Teachers and students in written dialog about critical revision. *Composition Studies, 29,* 71–92.

Blanton, L. (1992). Talking students into writing: Using oral fluency to develop literacy. *TESOL Journal, 1,* 23–26.

Bley-Vroman, R. (1989). What is the logical problem of foreign language learning? In S. Gass & J. Schachter (Eds.), *Linguistic perspectives of second language acquisition* (pp. 41–68). Cambridge, UK: University of Cambridge Press.

Bloch, J. (2002). Student/teacher interaction via email: The social context of Internet discourse. *Journal of Second Language Writing, 11,* 117–134.

Block, D. (2003). *The social turn in second language acquisition.* Washington, DC: Georgetown University Press.

Braxley, K. (2005). Mastering academic English: International graduate students' use of dialogue and speech genres to meet the writing demands of graduate school. In J. Hall, G. Vitanova, & L. Marchenkova (Eds.), *Dialogue with Bakhtin on second and foreign language learning* (pp. 11–32). Mahwah, NJ: Lawrence Erlbaum.

Bruffee, K. (1995). Peer tutoring and "the conversation of mankind." In C. Murphy & J. Law (Eds.), *Landmark essays on writing centers* (pp. 87–98). Davis, CA: Hermagoras Press.

de Guerrero, M. (1994). Form and functions of inner speech in adult second language learning. In J. Lantolf & G. Appel (Eds.), *Vygotskian approaches to second language research* (pp. 83–115). Norwood, NJ: Ablex.

de Guerrero, M., & Villamil, O. (2000). Activating the ZPD: Mutual scaffolding in peer revision. *Modern Language Journal, 84,* 51–68.

Donato, R. (1994). Collective scaffolding in second language learning. In J. Lantolf & G. Appel (Eds.), *Vygotskian approaches to second language research* (pp. 33–56). Norwood, NJ: Ablex.

Elbow, P. (2002). High stakes and low stakes in responding to student writing. In G. DeLuca, L. Fox, M. Johnson, & M. Kogen (Eds.), *Dialog on writing: Rethinking ESL, basic writing, and first-year composition.* Mahwah, NJ: Lawrence Erlbaum.

Ellis, R. (1994). *The study of second language acquisition.* Oxford, UK: Oxford University Press.

Gass, S. (1997). *Input, interaction and the second language learner.* Mahwah, NJ: Lawrence Erlbaum.

Gass, S., & Selinker, L. (2001). *Second language acquisition* (2nd Ed.). Mahwah, NJ: Lawrence Erlbaum.

Grabois, H. (2004). What does SCT research reveal about second language learning? In K. van Esch & O. St. John (Eds.), *New insights into foreign language learning and teaching* (pp. 35–49). Berlin: Peter Lang.

Gutierrez, K. (1994). How talk, context and script shape contexts for learning: A cross-case comparison of journal sharing. *Linguistics and Education, 5,* 335–365.

Hall, J., Vitanova, G., & Marchenkova, L. (Eds.). (2005). *Dialogue with Bakhtin on second and foreign language learning.* Mahwah, NJ: Lawrence Erlbaum.

Harklau, L. (2002). The role of writing in classroom second language acquisition. *Journal of Second Language Writing, 11,* 329–350.

Herschensohn, J. (2000). *The second time around: Minimalism and L2 acquisition.* Amsterdam: John Benjamins.

Johnson, M. (2004). *A philosophy of second language acquisition.* New Haven, CT: Yale University Press.

Krashen, S. (1982). *Principles and practice in second language acquisition.* Oxford, UK: Pergamon.

Lantolf, J. (Ed.) (2000). *Sociocultural theory and second language learning.* Oxford, UK: Oxford University Press.

Leander, K., & Prior, P. (2004). Speaking and writing: How talk and text interact in situated practices. In C. Bazerman & P. Prior (Eds.), *What writing does and how it does it* (pp. 201–237). Mahwah, NJ: Lawrence Erlbaum.

Leki, I. (1992). *Understanding ESL writers: A guide for teachers.* Portsmouth, NH: Boynton/Cook Heinemann.

Leont'yev, A. (1969). Inner speech and the processes of grammatical generations of utterances. *Soviet Psychology, 7,* 11–16.

Lightbown, P., & Spada, N. (1999). *How languages are learned.* Oxford, UK: Oxford University Press.

Liu, J., & Hansen, J. (2002). *Peer response in second language writing classrooms.* Ann Arbor: University of Michigan Press.

Luria, A. (1969). Speech development and the formation of mental processes. In M. Cole & I. Maltzman (Eds.), *A handbook of contemporary Soviet psychology* (pp. 121–162). New York: Basic Books.

McCafferty, S. (1992). The use of private speech by adult second language learners: A cross-cultural study. *Modern Language Journal, 76,* 179–189.

Mangelsdorf, K. (1989). Parallels between speaking and writing in second language acquisition. In D. Johnson & D. Roen (Eds.), *Richness in writing: Empowering ESL students* (pp. 134–145). New York: Longman.

Marchenkova, L. (2005). Language, culture, and self: The Bakhtin-Vygotsky encounter. In J. Hall, G. Vitanova, & L. Marchenkova (Eds.), *Dialogue with Bakhtin on second and foreign language learning* (pp. 171–188). Mahwah, NJ: Lawrence Erlbaum.

Mitchell, R., & Myles, F. (1998). *Second language learning theories.* London: Edward Arnold.

Ohta, A. (2001). *Second language acquisition processes in the classroom.* Mahwah, NJ: Lawrence Erlbaum.

Pavlenko, A., & Lantolf, J. (2000). Second language learning as participation and the (re)construction of selves. In J. Lantolf (Ed.), *Sociocultural theory and second language learning* (pp. 155–177). Oxford, UK: Oxford University Press.

Peyton, J., & Reed, L. (1990). *Dialog journal writing with non-native English speakers: A handbook for teachers.* Alexandria, VA: Teachers of English to Speakers of Other Languages.

Prior, P. (2001). Voices in text, mind, and society: Sociohistoric accounts of discourse acquisition and use. *Journal of Second Language Writing, 10,* 55–81.

Reid, J. (1998). "Eye" learners and "ear" learners: Identifying the needs of international students and U.S. resident writers. In P. Byrd & J. Reid (Eds.), *Grammar in the composition classroom: Essays on teaching ESL for college-bound students* (pp. 3–17). Boston: Heinle & Heinle.

Rodby, J. (1992). *Appropriating literacy: Writing and reading English as a second language.* Portsmouth, NH: Boynton/Cook.

Rubin, D., & Kantor, K. (1984). Talking and writing: Building communicative competence. In C. Thaiss & C. Suhor (Eds.), *Speaking and writing, K–12* (pp. 29–73). Urbana, IL: National Council of Teachers of English.

Sato, C. (1990). *The syntax of conversation in interlanguage development.* Tübingen, Germany: Gunter Narr Verlag.

Schinke-Llano, L. (1995). Reenvisioning the second language classroom: A Vygotskian approach. In F. Eckman, D. Highland, P. Lee, J. Milcham, & R. Weber (Eds.), *Second language acquisition theory and pedagogy* (pp. 21–28). Mahwah, NJ: Lawrence Erlbaum.

Swain, M. (2000). The output hypothesis and beyond: Mediating acquisition through collaborative dialog. In J. Lantolf (Ed.), *Sociocultural theory and second language learning* (pp. 97–114). Oxford, UK: University of Oxford Press.

Swain, M., & Lapkin, S. (1998). Interaction and second language learning: Two adolescent French immersion students working together. *Modern Language Journal, 82,* 320–337.

Vann, R. (1981). Bridging the gap between oral and written communication in EFL. In B. Kroll and R. Vann (Eds.), *Exploring speaking-writing relationships: Connections and contrasts* (pp. 154–177). Urbana, IL: National Council of Teachers of English.

VanPatten, B. (2004). Input and output in establishing form-meaning connections. In B. VanPatten, J. Williams, S. Rott, & M. Overstreet (Eds.), *Form-meaning connections in second language acquisition* (pp. 29–47). Mahwah, NJ: Lawrence Erlbaum.

Vygotsky, L. (1978). *Mind in society: The development of higher psychological processes* (M. Cole, V. John-Steiner, S. Scribner, & E. Souberman, Eds.). Cambridge, MA: Harvard University Press.

Weissberg, R. (2000). Developmental relationships in the acquisition of English syntax: Writing vs. speech. *Learning and Instruction, 10,* 37–53.

———. (2006a). *Connecting speaking & writing in L2 writing instruction.* Ann Arbor: University of Michigan Press.

———. (2006b). Scaffolded feedback: Conversations with advanced L2 writers. In K. Hyland & F. Hyland (Eds.), *Feedback in second language writing: Contexts and themes.* Cambridge, UK: Cambridge University Press.

Williams, J. (2002). Undergraduate second language writers in the writing center. *Journal of Basic Writing, 21,* 73–91.

Wong, S. (2006). *Dialogic approaches to TESOL: Where the ginkgo tree grows.* Mahwah, NJ: Lawrence Erlbaum.

Woodall, B. (2002). Language-switching: Using the L1 while writing in an L2. *Journal of Second Language Writing, 11,* 7–28.

Zoellner, R. (1969). Talk-write: A behavioral pedagogy for composition. *College English, 30,* 267–320.

3

Toward a Bakhtin-Inspired View of Oral and Written Discourse

LUDMILA A. MARCHENKOVA

Abstract

Bakhtin's theory of dialogue provides a conceptual basis for linking speaking and writing into a coherent whole. The aim of this chapter is to outline how the concern with the dialogic nature of speaking and writing manifests itself in Bakhtin's philosophy of language. It is argued that the dialogic principle extends into the mutual relation between speaking and writing. This relation is based further on the substantive goal that they help to accomplish: the formation of a person. The chapter closes with implications stemming from this approach for second language writing pedagogy.

The dialogic nature of speaking and writing is the foundation of their mutual connection. This idea was a constant concern for Mikhail Bakhtin (1895–1975), the literary theorist and philosopher of language whose insights have transformed our understanding of written and spoken discourses. Over the past three decades, studies of Bakhtin's work have had a widespread impact on scholarship in a number of academic disciplines. Recently scholars have begun to use his ideas in the debate on various aspects of second and foreign language and literacy learning (Hall, 1999, 2002; Hall, Vitanova, & Marchenkova, 2005; Johnson, 2004; Wong, 2006). The aim of this chapter is to outline how the concern with the dialogic nature of speaking and writing manifested itself in Bakhtin's philosophy of language. It will also be argued that the dialogic principle extends into the mutual relationship between speaking and writing. This relationship is further based on the substantive goal that speaking and writing help to accomplish: the formation of a person. Such an outline will offer a theory-based perspective on the connection between speaking and writing that draws on Bakhtin's understanding of these types of discourse. Bakhtin's view of oral and written discourses anticipates and lends support to attempts to recognize what Diane Belcher called "the synergistic interactions" between L2 speaking and writing when she proposed a colloquium for the 2006 TESOL Conference in Tampa, Florida. In addition, Bakhtin's theory of dialogue sets speaking and writing in a broader linguistic context that is important here because he views all language in dialogic terms and, as parts of this larger dialogic formation, spoken and written speech share in its overall dialogic nature.

Bakhtin rarely addresses oral and written discourses in separation from each other. His work is concentrated on literature, the novel in particular, and is thus focused on written language; spoken language is of interest to him mostly as the speech of literary characters. Accordingly, his theory contains concepts that can be equally applied to both speaking and writing. This fact is explicitly acknowledged by Bakhtin himself in many of his works (1981, 1984a, 1984b, 1986). Indeed, he repeatedly reminds the reader that his statements concern both types of discourse at once.

The Other's Word as an Other Language

Before addressing the dialogic nature of speaking and writing, it seems appropriate to touch on the question of transferring Bakhtin's ideas, articulated as they were primarily in literary theory, to the field of SLA. Bakhtin's ideas resonate with and contribute to current debates in L2 studies (Marchenkova, 2005). The possibility of applying his theory to discourses in a foreign and second language was both directly and indirectly acknowledged by Bakhtin himself. So far his statements on this topic have gone unnoticed in the Bakhtin studies literature. The most telling remark of this sort can be found in his essay "From notes made in 1970–71," written in the last years of Bakhtin's life. "I understand the other's word (utterance, speech work)," he writes, "to mean any word of any other person that is *spoken or written in his own (i.e., native) or in any other language* [italics added], that is, any word that is *not mine*" (Bakhtin, 1986, p. 143). This statement shows unequivocally that by "the other's word," Bakhtin refers both to native and foreign languages.

Bakhtin himself knew five languages in addition to his native Russian: German, English, French, Greek, and Latin (Alexandrova, 1999; Ivanov, 1999). Since he was equally fluent in Russian and German, it was easy for him to think of "the other's word" as spoken either in one's native or a foreign language. His major essay on philosophy of language, "Discourse in the Novel," may be understood as his account of "an individual's ideological becoming" or intellectual growth by assimilating the discourses of others. Speaking of authoritative discourse, Bakhtin again refers to a foreign language as the word of the other: "Often the authoritative word," he notes, "is in fact a word spoken by another in a foreign language" (1981, p. 343n).

Further, Bakhtin's frequent references to foreign cultures are relevant to what we now call intercultural communication. In the late 1960s–1970s, the time of the Cold War, he was particularly interested in "the relation between one's own society and other cultures that are foreign to it in space or time" (Holquist, 1986, p. xii). The gist of Bakhtin's attitude is summarized in this statement: "We must deal with the life and behavior of discourse in a contradictory and multi-languaged world" (Bakhtin, 1981, p. 275). And finally, Bakhtin believes that people who learn foreign languages change their very conception of language in the process. "For multilingual consciousness," he writes in his essay on heteroglossia, "language attains a new quality, becomes something quite different from what it is for a deaf, monolingual consciousness" (Bakhtin, 1996, V. 5, p. 157, my translation). By the metaphorical "deafness" of monolingual consciousness Bakhtin means a finalized, autonomous, and abstract view of language that is disconnected from the reality and context of use. Bakhtin's emphasis, especially in his literary theory, is on the heteroglossia within one language. However, the idea that the study of an additional language is an occasion for transformation of consciousness is highly relevant to the L2 learning context. True, Bakhtin's allusions to foreign languages are in most cases indirect. The historical context in which Bakhtin lived did not include the notion of a "second language" as it is understood in the discussions of SLA. Any language and culture, other than native, were foreign for him and others from his country. Still, this does not mean that Bakhtin and his contemporaries were oblivious to the question of second and foreign language as such. Bakhtin's close collaborator, Valentin Voloshinov, for example, explicitly discusses foreign language in his book *Marxism and the Philosophy of Language* (1929/1973, pp. 73–76). He believed that, while it had hitherto been ignored in linguistics, foreign language discourse has an enormous role to play in the development of language consciousness.

Dialogic Nature of Oral and Written Discourses

Turning now to the matter at hand, the following pertinent points need to be made. Bakhtin's theory of dialogue allows one to view speaking and writing as connected at a deep level. Bakhtin is predominantly interested in the communicative function of language and considers spoken and written communication as interactive or, in a broader sense, dialogic processes. They are connected, in other words, by their common dialogic nature. But there is an even deeper level of their mutual connectedness. According to Bakhtin, communication in general and oral and written discourses in particular ultimately involve the axiological and existential aspects of personhood. In other words, he views communication not as a value-neutral activity, but as having to do with people's most cherished values and with how they view themselves in the world. These aspects of discourse point to the broadest significance of the concept of dialogue: the latter embraces not only language narrowly understood, but also the fundamental issues of human existence. At the same time, the concept of dialogue, for Bakhtin, involves a whole series of other concepts. Each of these concepts shows, in turn, how basic dialogue is, in Bakhtin's view, to both oral and written discourses. In a number of essays Bakhtin makes statements that can be connected into an outline of his theory of dialogue as it pertains to the shared, dialogic nature of speaking and writing.

Internal Dialogism

Bakhtin examines dialogic relations in language in a variety of contexts and describes two types of dialogue. One is dialogue in the usual sense of the word: when two or more individuals are engaged in a verbal exchange. The other type is dialogue in the proper Bakhtinian sense: it reflects what he calls "the internal dialogism of the word, the dialogism that permeates its entire structure, all its semantic and expressive layers" (1981, p. 279). As he articulates this unique aspect of the concept, Bakhtin complains that it frequently escapes the attention of linguists and literary scholars. One could likewise note that this meaning of *dialogue* as a concept is still largely overlooked in applied linguistics and second language studies.

The dialogism of language manifests itself at the most basic level, in what Bakhtin calls *utterance.* "Language," Bakhtin argues, "is realized in the form of individual concrete utterances (oral and written) by participants in the various areas of human activity" (1986, p. 60). For him, any utterance used in communication with other people is internally dialogic because of its "dialogic orientations" (Bakhtin, 1981, p. 279; 1986, p. 92). In other words, an utterance is always directed toward another utterance or a rejoinder in dialogue. It intrinsically possesses an internal orientation toward an addressee in anticipation of a response; addressivity and responsiveness thus become its necessary conditions. "Each utterance refutes, affirms, supplements, and relies," Bakhtin believes, "on the others, presupposes them to be known, and somehow takes them into account" (1986, p. 91). This is true not only of oral utterances, but also of written ones, or texts. Some of Bakhtin's colleagues shared this conviction. Voloshinov (1973) spoke, for example, of the responsiveness of "a verbal performance in print." A text (such as a book) anticipates discussion or response in the form of "actual, real-life dialogue" or "printed reaction" in the form of book reviews or critical surveys. At the same time it responds to previous texts and thus engages "in ideological colloquy of large scale: it responds to something, objects to something, affirms something, anticipates possible responses and objections, seeks support, and so on" (p. 95).

Along with addressivity and responsiveness, there is another aspect of utterance in which Bakhtin discerns dialogic relations. This aspect can be understood as socio-historical, although Bakhtin never used this term himself. He describes this quality of utterance as:

> [The word] never gravitates toward a single consciousness or a single voice. The life of the word is contained in its transfer from one mouth to another, from one context to another context, from one social collective to another, from one generation to another generation. (1984a, p. 202)

An utterance, in other words, is not merely an individual unit, but also carries the historical contexts of its own current and prior uses. It is shaped by its past and anticipates its own future. By saying this, Bakhtin emphasizes that as speakers and writers we rely on a long-standing tradition of word use. The socio-historical aspect of internal dialogue is characterized by the presence of the others' words in one's utterance, by the words that have "already [been] spoken" (Bakhtin, 1981, pp. 279–280), the so-called "preceding links in the chain [of speech communication]" (Bakhtin, 1986a, p. 93). In Bakhtin's (1986a) own words, "our speech, that is, all our utterances [are] . . . filled with the words of our others" (p. 89).

Voice(s)

Utterance becomes possible only through the use of voice, which Bakhtin understood, once again, as both spoken and written modes of communication. The interaction of voices in an utterance can occur in a variety of ways, from peaceful collaboration to compromise to conflict: "Within the arena of almost every utterance an intense interaction and struggle between one's own and another's word is being waged, a process in which they oppose or dialogically interanimate each other" (Bakhtin, 1981, p. 354). The "intense interaction and struggle" makes possible the creation of one's own voice, that is, becoming the author of one's own discourse, a primary author, as it were, "a creator of the utterance whose position it expresses" (Bakhtin, 1984a, p. 184). This means that other voices are absorbed into our speech with the words and utterances of our others, either as anticipated responses of the listeners and readers or as already pronounced and filled with their own intentions and meanings through the channels of linguistic and cultural traditions. This is another way by which Bakhtin describes how through an utterance one's voice is linked to the social context of language. As Wertsch (1991) observes, Bakhtin "insisted that meaning can come into existence only when two or more voices come into contact: when the voice of a listener responds to a voice of a speaker" (p. 52). One could also say that every utterance has a secondary, implicit author, namely the addressee, whose anticipated response contributes to the utterance's semantic and syntactic characteristics. The presence of two such authors has been described by Bakhtin as "double-voicedness" (or "double-voicing").

It is worth noting that Bakhtin draws an interesting parallel between oral and written utterances. Both types of utterances, he thinks, can be used to produce either immediate action or delayed reaction. "Sooner or later what is heard and actively understood will find its response in the subsequent speech or behavior of the listener," Bakhtin remarks. "In most cases, genres of complex cultural communication are intended precisely for this kind of actively responsive understanding with delayed action" (1986, p. 69).

It is crucial to recognize that for Bakhtin voice is not merely an analytic concept, but a moral category. Wertsch (1991) remarks that Bakhtin saw in voice a manifestation of the speaker's or the writer's overall perspective, world view, conceptual horizon, intentions, and values (p. 51). Some linguistic anthropologists think of voice as a linguistically constructed persona (Duranti, 1997, p. 75). There is no clear distinction in the literature between the concepts of voice and identity. In Bakhtin's understanding, however, voice emphasizes primarily the moment of representation, a bridge between the author and the audience, something individual and unique for others to recognize and define as such. In other words, in voice the focus is on the author's self-expression for readers and listeners.

The concept of voice is also intimately associated, for Bakhtin (1986a), with the concept of authorship; he speaks, for example, of a search "for one's own (authorial) voice" (p. 91). Since the notion of the author connotes personhood and creativity, Bakhtin's voice has a personal, creative dimension. "With a creative attitude toward language," he insists, "there are no voiceless words that belong to no one" (Bakhtin, 1986, p. 124). Thus, voice in his understanding is both an individual and social phenomenon.

The concept of voice has proven to have a special appeal for authors working in L2 academic writing (Atkinson, 2001; Hirvela & Belcher, 2001; Hyland, 2002; Ivanic & Camps, 2001; Matsuda, 2001; Ramanathan & Atkinson, 1999; Ramanathan & Kaplan, 1996). It has generated significant discussion in various areas of L2 studies, and in recent years some authors have turned to Bakhtin for further insight on the question of identity (Cazden, 1993; Hall, 1995; Kramsch, 1993, 2000, 2003; Maguire & Graves, 2001; Pavlenko & Lantolf, 2000; Prior, 1998, 2001; Thesen, 1997; Toohey, 2000; Valdes, 2004; Vitanova, 2005).

Assimilation of the Other's Word

The word of one interlocutor can be authoritative, monologic, and admitting of no transformation by the other one. In this case Bakhtin refers to it as *authoritative discourse*. When one reproduces this discourse, one speaks in inverted commas, as it were; Bakhtin calls such speech "quoted." The same word, however, can become one's own, Bakhtin argues. He sees "an infinite gradation in the degree of foreignness (or assimilation) of words, their various distances from the speaker" (Bakhtin, 1986a, pp. 120-121). Where they have been assimilated by the interlocutor and become partially one's own, the words of the other are transformed into *internally persuasive discourse*. The relation between authoritative and internally persuasive discourses is a dynamic process:

> As a living socio-linguistic concrete thing . . . language, for the individual consciousness, lies on the borderline between oneself and the other. . . . It becomes "one's own" only when the speaker populates it with his own intention, his own accent, when he appropriates the word, adapting it to his own semantic and expressive intention. . . . One's own discourse is gradually and slowly wrought out of others' words that have been acknowledged and assimilated, and the boundaries between the two are at first scarcely perceptible. (Bakhtin, 1981, pp. 293–294, 345)

As Holquist (1981) notes, both authoritative and internally persuasive discourses are relevant to the general question about the growth of human consciousness. "Human coming-to-consciousness, in Bakhtin's view," he comments, "is a constant struggle between these two types of discourse: an attempt to assimilate more into one's own system, and the simultaneous freeing of one's own discourse from the authoritative word, or from previously used persuasive words that have ceased to mean" (pp. 424–425). Bakhtin sees one's own internally persuasive discourse in terms of "an intense interaction, a *struggle* with other internally persuasive discourses . . . within us for hegemony among various available verbal and ideological points of view, approaches, directions, and values" (1981, pp. 345–346).

An interesting and effective example of the interplay of authoritative and internally persuasive discourses is presented in Prior's (1998, 2001) study on mediated authorship. Prior views Bakhtin's categories as a framework for describing how language learning is linked to the formation of a person. He emphasizes the dialogic and dynamic nature of internally persuasive discourse through which "others' words, practices, and worlds are slowly and selectively reaccentuated and interwoven into the evolving formation of a particular personal consciousness" (Prior, 1998, pp. 216–218).

Ethical and Creative Word

Another significant facet of Bakhtin's view of language is that participation in oral and written communication is regarded as an ethical and creative act. Bakhtin understood expressing oneself in words as a moral struggle. Our entire discourse, according to Bakhtin, is saturated with ethical and aesthetic meanings. This is true of utterances within political, artistic, and even scientific contexts. Bakhtin (1990) insists that utterances come alive only insofar as they are "true or false, beautiful or ugly, sincere or deceitful, frank, cynical, authoritative" (p. 292). He is quite aware of the fact that such a view of language is at odds with the traditional linguistic approach, in which language is assumed to be value-neutral and to consist of abstract, schematic rules. By contrast, Bakhtin (1986) maintains that an utterance is not defined in merely formal terms, but possesses what he calls "contextual meaning" or, as he explains, "integrated meaning that relates to value to truth, beauty, and so forth and requires a *responsive* understanding, one that includes evaluation" (p. 125). Bakhtin also links the value-laden nature of discourse to its emotional charge (ibid., pp. 166–167).

One additional dimension of dialogue is that when one engages in it, Bakhtin believes, one inherently assumes responsibility for what one says to another person and for that person herself. It is not unusual for Bakhtin to speak of love as the main motivating force behind dialogue. The ethical and humanistic import of Bakhtin's theory has been noted by Holquist (1990): "Each time we talk, we literally enact values in our speech through the process of scripting our place and that of our listener in a culturally specific social scenario" (p. 63).

The creative aspect of language use can be traced back to Bakhtin's view of language as a creative medium and of utterance as always a potentially creative contribution to discourse. Bakhtin is primarily concerned with literary creativity, and his ideas about the creative nature of utterance lend support to regarding the learning of language in general as a creative process. Further, Bakhtin insists on a close connection among the cognitive, ethical, and creative aspects of language use. As a learner transcends the limits imposed on her by the authoritative discourse and gradually makes it her own internally persuasive one, her progress has an ethical and creative dimension. The ethical side consists of the transformation from a dependent position into one where she is in fuller command of her situation. The creative aspect consists of a similar transformation of the learner's activity from mere repetition of prior discourse into an independent revoicing of others' words and ultimately into authorship.

The Self and the Other

Finally, underlying the entire problem of dialogue in Bakhtin's thought is the relation between the self and the other. The concept of the "other" is highly relevant to SLA because the process of learning another language is based on the learner's interaction with another language, culture, and person(s). The relation between the self and the other is therefore a basic condition of the learner. Thus, the problem of the other is an indispensable part of any attempt to understand these processes. The existing theories do not provide a sufficient account of the other in language learning and cultural communication.

In Bakhtin's thought, by contrast, the concept of the other is richly elaborated and intimately linked to the rest of his theory of dialogue. Bakhtin especially stresses the significance of the other in linguistic consciousness and discourse. He also notes that traditional linguistic approaches are incapable of accommodating the concept of the other in their models of human interaction since the other's word is considered to be irrational from the standpoint of syntax (Bakhtin, 1986, p. 92). This mechanism of the relation between one's own and the other's word is described by Bakhtin in some detail: He views the work of this mechanism as assimilation of the other's word into one's own (Bakhtin, 1986, p. 168). He also emphasizes the significance of the other for identity formation (p. 143).

In Bakhtin's theory of dialogue, the other occupies a different position in comparison with the postmodernist view of it. In the latter, the other is marginalized, disenfranchised, non-Western, and disempowered. Bakhtin's notion of the other is much broader: the other is somebody who is not I, anyone other than me. In many cases Bakhtin describes the other as the authoritative side in discourse. These others are defined historically, culturally, and contextually. The other's word, for Bakhtin, may be that of parents, teachers, a religious authority, and a cultural-historical tradition (1981, p. 324). Further, Bakhtin views the self's relation to the other not merely in terms of resistance and rejection, but in terms of appropriating the other's authority by the self, a process through which the self shapes itself. This process does not end with the complete dissolution of the other; the other always remains part of the formula that defines the self.

In reading Bakhtin's statements about the relation between the self and the other, one must always bear in mind the Russian thinker's historical context. The self opposes the authoritative other in the same manner that Bakhtin resisted the ideological authority of the Soviet regime. He was himself a marginalized self, a person who was crippled physically, exiled by the government to a remote territory, and silenced by censorship. Bakhtin's ideological other was the oppressive political regime that rejected heteroglossia and polyphony. At the same time, Bakhtin manages not to view these relations between the self and the other as catastrophically antagonistic. Rather, he advocates a model in which they are necessary for each other and in which the marginalized self gradually appropriates the authority and power of its other.

The dynamic between the self and the other is reproduced, Bakhtin is convinced, not only in language, but also in the culture at large. There it may assume the shape of the interaction between the official, central, and written culture, on the one hand, and the folk, peripheral, and oral culture, on the other hand. Bakhtin develops this theme, not so much in his philosophy of language as in his philosophy of culture. In particular, he explores this interaction in his study of Francois Rabelais (1984b), in which restrictive medieval officialdom is set over and against the elemental energies of the "lower" popular culture.

The relations between the self and the other illustrate particularly well the shared dialogic nature of both oral and written discourses because these relations are equally indispensable, in Bakhtin's view, for both types of discourse. They are arguably the most fundamental level on which speaking and writing are connected with each other.

Bakhtin inherited the theme of a continuous dialogue between speaking and writing from the tradition of Russian literary criticism, where it was cast in terms of folk speech versus literary language and developed into the notions of heteroglossia and polyphony in literary texts, as well as into the intricate dynamics existing between "low" and "high" cultures. The concept of dialogue has not, to the best of my knowledge, been used in L2 studies to describe the relations between speaking and writing.

By the same token, even though they may not employ this concept to describe them, some authors address the need to examine the interactions between speaking and writing (de Guerrero & Villamil, 2000; Leander & Prior, 2004; Prior, 2001; Weissberg, 2006a, 2006b; Williams, 2004). These interactions can be seen through the prism of Bakhtin's theory of dialogue, which ultimately allows us to bring the four main groups of language skills together: speaking, listening, reading, and writing. All these skills are joined by their internal dialogic nature. "We are moving," wrote Horowitz and Samuels in 1987, "toward a redefinition of and integrated theory of speaking and writing, listening and reading" (p. 43). What they call "the mingling of oral and written language" is precisely in the center of Bakhtin's attention as both a literary and cultural theorist. His dialogic view of this "mingling" provides a new impetus for the redefinition that these authors hope for.

Pedagogical Implications

The discussion has focused on how Bakhtin can help us understand the parallelism between the linguistic phenomena of speaking and writing, a parallelism that rests on a shared dialogic nature. Whether a unit of expression so basic as an utterance to a theme so rarified as the relation between the self and the other, dialogic relations permeate both spoken and written discourses. Both types of discourse carry an axiological burden: they both possess irreducible ethical and creative dimensions. As such they form integral parts of a lived human experience. And finally, the inner dialogic nature of both speaking and writing serves as a basis for their mutual dialogic relation within the whole of language.

Such considerations lead to these questions:

- ❐ What are the implications of these insights for L2 writing teachers and researchers?
- ❐ What possibilities do they open?

One important implication is that teaching is not merely about transmitting skills but about transforming students as persons because the dynamics of this transformation are dialogic, both in the external and the internal sense. The external aspect of dialogic relations in the classroom has already been acknowledged and is being utilized in teaching methods such as group work, peer review, student-teacher conferences, and collaborative assignments. These methods are regarded, however, primarily as a means of improving the student's writing skills and meaning-making ability. They are seldom seen in the light of the formation of personhood, nor is the internal dialogism of language learning sufficiently recognized. The mechanism of the transformation of authoritative into internally persuasive discourse offered by Bakhtin illuminates the process by which students attain their own voices in speaking and writing. Such a process is not linguistic in the narrow sense of the word, but is also ethical and creative in nature. From the pedagogical point of view, the formation of personhood is an essential part of the process itself. Personal growth is, further, from the Bakhtinian perspective, not external to the acquisition of language skills, but the two are inextricably intertwined.

As she sums up the educational implications of Bakhtin's thought, Cazden remarks that "no forms of expression in natural languages are neutral referential codes. All bring with them—for all of us as speakers and writers—both pain and promise" (1993, p. 209). The difficulties that students experience as they overcome the external authority of texts and discourses in additional and disciplinary languages are not something accidental but belong to the nature of the process. It takes creative effort, motivation, responsibility, and agency for a learner to change from an anonymous voice to the author of one's own discourse. As learners develop their voices and sense of authorship, they empower themselves by assimilating the authoritative discourses and taking ownership of them. Adopting such a view suggests that a different set of criteria may be needed for evaluating writing, as well as providing correction and feedback. Plagiarism is a good example of a breakdown in this process: the student fails to assimilate the external authority of the existing text and to derive her own voice from it. By contrast, evaluative and reflective writing are examples of the proper deployment of this mechanism.

A dialogic approach points to the need for new ways of teaching direct and indirect speech, elaboration on quotations, summarizing, paraphrasing, reviewing texts, argumentation, critical-thinking and critical-writing skills, both as academic literacy practices and experiences guided by creative aspirations and ethical responsibilities. Another source of empowerment for our students is in the strengthened sense of value of their selves. Interpreting and evaluating texts in light of one's own experience and one's experience in light of the texts enhances our students' sense of value of their experiences and backgrounds (Blanton, 1998; Kramsch & Lam, 1999). As critical aspects of the formation of personhood, self-reflection, and self-expression can be facilitated by such genres as literacy narrative and learner (writer) autobiography that have already found recognition in our field and merit further attention (Canagarajah, 2004; Li, 1999, Pavlenko, 1998, 2001; Pavlenko & Lantolf, 2000).

It is encouraging to see researchers turning to the complexity and dynamics of personal identity of L2 learners both in a writing classroom and in broader multilingual contexts (Pavlenko & Blackledge, 2004). A growing awareness among researchers and practitioners of the issues associated with the learner's identity (Matsuda, Canagarajah, Harklau, Hyland, & Warschauer, 2003) underscores the value and importance of what Bakhtin calls "the initial mastery of speech" (1986, p. 143). The student's authorial voice can evolve only on the basis of the knowledge of syntax, grammar, vocabulary, and conventions of academic genres.

To adopt a Bakhtin-inspired type of pedagogy means bearing in mind that personhood takes shape in dialogue with other persons. Any class is, first and foremost, a group of persons whose self-identities manifest themselves only when there are other identities to whom their voices are addressed. They are engaged in a dialogue that, as Emerson says, "assumes that the healthy growth of any consciousness depends on its continual interaction with other voices, or worldviews" (1997, p. 36). The teacher is one of these persons and has the opportunity to change her worldview as a result of her interactions with students. The overall goal of this learning process, the transformation of personhood by means of communication with others, is the most substantive ground for the connection between speaking and writing.

REFERENCES

Alexandrova, R. I. (1999). Bakhtin, Mikhail Mikhailovich. In P. V. Alekseev (Ed.), *Filosofy Rossii XIX-XX stoletii* [Philosophers of Russia of XIX–XX centuries] (pp. 88–89). Moskva: Akademicheskii Proekt.

Atkinson, D. (2001). Reflections and refractions on the *JSLW* special issue on voice. *Journal of Second Language Writing, 10*(1–2), 107–124.

Bakhtin, M. M. (1981). *The dialogic imagination* (M. Holquist, Ed., C. Emerson & M. Holquist, Trans.). Austin: University of Texas Press.

———. (1984a). *Problems of Dostoevsky's poetics* (C. Emerson, Ed. & Trans.). Minneapolis: University of Minnesota Press.

———. (1984b). *Rabelais and his world* (H. Iswolsky, Trans.). Bloomington: Indiana University Press.

———. (1986). *Speech genres and other late essays* (C. Emerson & M. Holquist, Eds.; V. McGee, Trans.). Austin: University of Texas Press.

———. (1990). *Art and answerability: Early philosophical essays by M. M. Bakhtin* (M. Holquist & V. Liapunov, Eds.; V. Liapunov, Trans.). Austin: University of Texas Press.

———. (1996). *Sobranie sochinenii v semi tomakh*, t. 5 [Collected works in seven volumes, v. 5]. Moskva: Russkie Slovari.

Blanton L. L. (1998). Discourse, artifacts, and the Ozarks: Understanding academic literacy. In V. Zamel & R. Spack (Eds.), *Negotiating academic literacies: Teaching and learning across languages and cultures* (pp. 219–236). Mahwah, NJ: Lawrence Erlbaum.

Canagarajah, S. (2004). Multilingual writers and the struggle for voice in academic discourse. In A. Pavlenko & A Blackledge (Eds.), *Negotiation of identities in multilingual contexts* (pp. 266–289). Clevedon, UK: Multilingual Matters.

Cazden, C. (1993). Vygotsky, Hymes, and Bakhtin: From word to utterance and voice. In E.A. Forman, N. Minick, & C.A. Stone (Eds.), *Contexts for learning: Sociocultural dynamics in children's development* (pp. 197–212). New York: Oxford University Press.

de Guerrero, M. C., & Villamil, O. S. (2000). Activating the ZPD: Mutual scaffolding in L2 peer revision. *The Modern Language Journal. 84*(1), 51–68.

Duranti, A. (1997). *Linguistic anthropology*. Cambridge, UK: Cambridge University Press.

Emerson, C. (1997). *The first hundred years of Mikhail Bakhtin*. Princeton, NJ: Princeton University Press.

Hall, J. K. (1995). (Re)creating our worlds with words: A sociohistorical perspective of face-to-face interaction. *Applied Linguistics, 16*(2), 206–232.

———. (1999). A prosaics of interaction: The development of interactional competence in another language. In E. Hinkel (Ed.), *Culture in second language teaching and learning* (pp. 137–151). New York: Cambridge University Press.

———. (2002). *Teaching and researching: Language and culture*. Harlow, UK: Longman.

Hall, J. K., Vitanova, G., & Marchenkova, L. (Eds.). (2005). *Dialogue with Bakhtin on second and foreign language learning: New perspectives*. Mahwah, NJ: Lawrence Erlbaum.

Hirvela, A., & Belcher, D. (2001). Coming back to voice: The multiple voices and identities of mature multilingual writers. *Journal of Second Language Writing, 10*(1/2), 83–106.

Holquist, M. (1981). Glossary. In M. Holquist (Ed.), *The dialogic imagination: Four essays by M. M. Bakhtin* (pp. 423–434). Austin: University of Texas Press.

———. (1986). Introduction. In M. M. Bakhtin, *Speech genres and other late essays* (pp. ix-xxiii). Austin: University of Texas Press.

———. (1990). *Dialogism: Bakhtin and his world.* London: Routledge.

Horowitz, R., & Samuels, S. J. (Eds.). (1987). *Comprehending oral and written language.* San Diego, CA: Academic Press.

Hyland, K. (2002). Authority and invisibility: Authorial identity in academic writing. *Journal of Pragmatics, 34*(8), 1091–1112.

Ivanič, R., & Camps, D. (2001). I am how I sound: Voice as self-representation in L2 writing. *Journal of Second Language Writing, 10*(1–2), 3–33.

Ivanov, V. V. (1999, December). *Bakhtin's theory of language from the standpoint of modern linguistics.* Paper presented at the workshop, Bakhtin in Context(s), Indiana University, Bloomington.

Johnson, M. (2004). *A philosophy of second language acquisition.* New Haven, CT: Yale University Press.

Kramsch, C. (1993). *Context and culture in language teaching.* Oxford, UK: Oxford University Press.

———. (2000). Social discursive constructions of self in L2 learning. In Lantolf, J. P. (Ed.), *Sociocultural theory and second language learning* (pp. 133–153). Oxford, UK: Oxford University Press.

———. (2003). Identity, role and voice in cross-cultural (mis)communication. In J. House, G. Kasper, & S. Ross (Eds.), *Misunderstanding in social life* (pp. 129–153). London: Pearson Education.

Kramsch, C., & Lam, W. (1999). Textual identities: The importance of being non-native. In G. Braine (Ed.), *Non-native educators in English language teaching* (pp. 57–72). Mahwah, NJ: Lawrence Erlbaum.

Leander, K., & Prior, P. (2004). Speaking and writing: How talk and text interact in situated practices. In C. Bazerman & P. Prior (Eds.), W*hat writing does and how it does it* (pp. 201–237). Mahwah, NJ: Lawrence Erlbaum.

Li, X-M. (1999). Writing from the vantage point of the outsider/insider. In G. Braine (Ed.), *Non-native educators in English language teaching* (pp. 43–56). Mahwah, NJ: Lawrence Erlbaum.

Maguire, M. H., & Graves, B. (2001). Speaking personalities in primary school children's L2 writing. *TESOL Quarterly, 35*(4), 561–593.

Marchenkova, L. (2005). Language, culture, and self: The Bakhtin-Vygotsky encounter. In J. K. Hall, G. Vitanova, & L. Marchenkova (Eds.), *Dialogue with Bakhtin on second and foreign language learning: New perspectives* (pp. 171–188). Mahwah, NJ: Lawrence Erlbaum.

Matsuda, P. (2001). Voice in Japanese written discourse: Implications for second language writing. *Journal of Second Language Writing, 10*(1–2), 35–53.

Matsuda, P. K., Canagarajah, A. S., Harklau, L., Hyland, K., & Warschauer, M. (2003). Changing currents in second language writing research: A colloquium. *Journal of Second Language Writing, 12*(2), 151–179.

Pavlenko, A. (1998). Second language learning by adults: Testimonies of bilingual writers. *Issues in Applied Linguistics, 9*(1), 3–19.

———. (2001). 'In the world of the tradition I was unimagined': Negotiation of identities in cross-cultural autobiographies. *International Journal of Bilingualism* 5(3), 317–344.

Pavlenko, A., & Blackledge, A. (Eds.). (2004). *Negotiation of identities in multilingual contexts.* Clevedon, UK: Multilingual Matters.

Pavlenko, A., & Lantolf, J. P. (2000). Second language learning as participation and the (re)construction of selves. In Lantolf, J. P. (Ed.). *Sociocultural theory and second language learning* (pp. 155–177). Oxford, UK: Oxford University Press.

Prior, P. (1998). *Writing/disciplinarity: A sociohistoric account of literate activity in the academy.* Mahwah, NJ: Lawrence Erlbaum.

———. (2001). Voices in text, mind, and society: Sociohistoric accounts of discourse acquisition and use. *Journal of Second Language Writing, 10*(1–2), 55–81.

Ramanathan, V., & Atkinson, D. (1999). Individualism, academic writing, and ESL writers. *Journal of Second Language Writing, 8*(1), 45–75.

Ramanathan, V., & Kaplan, R. B. (1996). Audience and voice in current L1 composition texts: Some implications for ESL student writers. *Journal of Second Language Writing, 5*(1), 21–34.

Thesen, L. (1997). Voice, discourse, and transition: In search of new categories in EAP. *TESOL Quarterly, 31*(3), 487–513.

Toohey, K. (2000). *Learning English at school: Identity, social relations and classroom practice.* Clevedon, UK: Multilingual Matters.

Valdes, G. (2004). The teaching of academic language to minority second language learners. In A. F. Ball & S. W. Freedman (Eds.), *Bakhtinian perspectives on language, literacy, and learning* (pp. 65–98). Cambridge, UK: Cambridge University Press.

Vitanova, G. (2005). Authoring the self in a non-native language: A dialogic approach to agency and subjectivity. In J. K. Hall, G. Vitanova, & L. Marchenkova (Eds.), *Dialogue with Bakhtin on second and foreign language learning: New perspectives* (pp. 149–169). Mahwah, NJ: Lawrence Erlbaum.

Voloshinov, V. N. (1973). *Marxism and the philosophy of language* (L. Matejka & I. R. Titunik, Trans.). New York: Seminar Press.

Weissberg, R. (2006a). *Connecting speaking & writing in L2 writing instruction.* Ann Arbor: University of Michigan Press.

———. (2006b). Scaffolded feedback: Conversations with advanced L2 writers. In K. Hyland & F. Hyland (Eds.), *Feedback in second language writing: Contexts and themes.* Cambridge, UK: Cambridge University Press.

Wertsch, J. V. (1991). *Voices of the mind: A sociocultural approach to mediated action.* Cambridge, MA: Harvard University Press.

Williams, J. (2004). Tutoring and revision: Second language writers in the writing center. *Journal of Second Language Writing, 13*(3), 173–201.

Wong, S. (2006). *Dialogic approaches to TESOL: Where the gingko tree grows.* Mahwah, NJ: Lawrence Erlbaum.

4

Intertextual Connections between Spoken and Written Text: A Microanalysis of Doctoral Students' Textual Constructions

LISYA SELONI

Abstract

Despite the increasing literature on the academic literacy development of multilingual doctoral students, little is known about the intertextual links these students make during their construction of both written and spoken texts. In this chapter, I provide a perspective on speaking and writing connections by adopting the theoretical lens of intertextuality aimed at affirming the multiplicity and plurality of textual practices. I argue that by acting and reacting (Erickson & Shultz, 1977) to each other as speakers and writers in an intercultural space, adult multilingual students resist, challenge, and create hybrid forms of literacy practices, thus expanding the notion of text world construction (Kucer, 1985). Drawing from the scholarship on intercultural rhetoric and intertextuality as social construction, I present an intertextual analysis of six doctoral students' interactions within the context of what I call an "academic culture of collaboration." The study's results, which illustrate how multilingual doctoral students are empowered as academic writers while they create various intertextual links, challenge essentialist notions of writing and speaking practices.

With the advent of cultural globalization in the context of postmodern discourses in education, the notion of academic text has been redefined by many scholars in the fields of both L1 and L2 literacy studies (e.g.,

Bizzell, 1992, 2002; Flower, 2003; Hyland, 2000; Prior, 1998) As we move away from monolithic and static notions of discourses and cultures, there is now a greater awareness of how "text worlds" (Kucer, 1985) have been foregrounded as products of micro and macro social interactions. In this sociolinguistic and semiotic framework, texts are seen as social actions that are products of discursive practices (Bloome & Egan-Robertson, 1993; Gee, 1990; Kress, 1989, 2003; Street, 1985, 1993, 1995). In other words, texts are not merely located in readers and writers' minds; they are also embedded in social contexts existing and being constructed in relation to other texts (Bakhtin, 1981; Kress, 1989).

"Text world construction" (Kucer, 1985), in the context of the multiplicity and hybridity of cultures, does not merely involve linguistic production; it also involves socially and politically situated actions (Kress, 1993). Moreover, we are now realizing that discourse communities (Swales, 1990) that utilize certain agreed upon textual practices are hybrid and carry multiple sets of discourses and values. They may also include members from diverse linguistic, cultural, and rhetorical backgrounds, thus adding to their multiplicity and hybridity.

However, it is not necessarily the case that the experiences and perspectives of all these members are equally represented in discussions of such communities. One understudied example of this kind involves the academic experiences of multilingual doctoral students in Anglophone countries like the United States. Doctoral education is a crucial network space for constructing knowledge and displaying expertise because doctoral students are regularly engaged in the production of linguistically and intellectually sophisticated textual worlds utilizing various speaking and writing "rhetorical moves" (Swales, 1990). Students at the doctoral level are expected to be active participants in academic communities within their disciplinary fields by writing and speaking in certain ways. The academic world becomes more complex for students whose home language and culture are different than that of the mainstream within the university. Given the large number of foreign students in North American institutions,[1] it is worthwhile to investigate how multilingual and multiliterate nonnative–English speaking (NNES) students acquire, and socialize into, Western academic literacy practices and construct their own textual worlds on the way to becoming scholars in their chosen disciplinary realms.

[1]The number of international students enrolled in U.S. colleges and universities was recently reported as 564,766 according to the *Open Doors* 2006 annual report on international education published by the Institute of International Education (IIE). IIE reports that almost the half of this population came to the United States to pursue their graduate degree.

Many researchers in first and second language literacy education have begun to explore how novices acquire new sets of textual practices and socialize into their discourse communities (Belcher, 1994; Canagarajah, 2002; Casanave, 1995, 2002; Hirvela & Belcher 2001; Ivanĭc, 1998; Lea & Street, 1999; Prior 1995; Swales, 1990). These studies are valuable in the sense that they shed light on the types of literacy practices multilingual students need to apply or the kinds of social processes they tend to experience during their academic socialization period. On the other hand, given the highly interactive and collaborative nature of doctoral education in the United States (e.g., writing papers, working on group projects, making presentations inside and outside the classroom, engaging in academic conversations and discussions), little is known as to how doctoral students collectively co-construct knowledge about academic writing as they move through their doctoral experiences, though it seems safe to assume that such collaboration takes place among them. In addition, while a large body of research has focused on the writing practices of multilingual students in the process of enculturating into Anglophone academic discourse, little attention has been given to exploring the dialogic relations that presumably develop during the collective collaboration that occurs among doctoral students. It is in this collaboration that they encounter opportunities to establish intertextual connections between spoken and written texts while negotiating the demands and tasks that constitute doctoral education.

Drawing on this view of collaboration, this chapter argues that through dialogic exchanges (both oral and written), multilingual students at the doctoral level co-construct new textual worlds from the ones they encounter while reading for their courses, listening to professors' and classmates' comments in class, and interacting in face-to-face and online spaces. In other words, to borrow Casanave's important notion of "writing games," these students have to engage in certain academic practices where they "learn how to participate skillfully and flexibly in the academic writing games" (Casanave, 1995, p. 6) of doctoral education. While examining how graduate students learn to participate in their academic communities as novice members (Lave & Wegner, 1991), this chapter aims to illustrate the practices of an "academic culture of collaboration" in which a group of students from multiple cultural backgrounds creates and draws on various intertextual connections from both oral and written texts[2] while they make sense of the often unwritten

[2]Throughout this chapter, my use of the term *text* is influenced by Bloome et al. (2005), Kress (1995), and Street (1993), who describe text as written, oral, gestural, pictorial or electronic signs created among a group of people in social interaction.

rules and conventions of textual construction in academic writing within their disciplinary fields. Here "academic culture of collaboration" is defined as a set of social practices that include communicative and dialogic actions and interactions (Bakhtin, 1986) within an intercultural group of newcomers in a specific domain of academic discourse. Overall, as shown later, the practice of this academic culture of collaboration, which includes dynamic spoken and written interactions, reveals how doctoral students are willing to build "safe houses," which Pratt (1991) considers "social and intellectual spaces where groups can constitute themselves as horizontal, homogenous, sovereign communities with high degrees of trust, shared understandings, and temporary protection from legacies of oppression" (p. 40).

Textual Construction at the Graduate Level

Academic writing at the doctoral level moves beyond what Street (1995) calls the "autonomous model of literacy" (i.e., literacy as a set of generic and decontextualized skills) and appears instead as a situated practice that is more than merely learning about certain rhetorical moves. Multilingual students engaged in academic discourse at the graduate level constitute a unique population, as they need to "adapt smoothly to the linguistic and social milieu of their host environment and to the culture of their academic departments and institutions" (Braine, 2002, p. 60) while they shuttle between their home language and culture and the standard academic language and culture they are expected to use as doctoral students. The very nature of doctoral education is such that students—regardless of their first language and culture—have multiple joint experiences in classrooms or outside the classrooms while completing projects, writing papers, presenting at conferences, or informally conversing with one another. During these joint social interactions, students share and negotiate their emerging understandings of what is expected of them as doctoral-level students. Such joint interactions are especially crucial for multilingual students, who bring multiple cultures and languages that they juggle carefully while socializing into the academic discourse of their disciplinary fields. Both speaking and writing are at the heart of such activities. Therefore, it is essential for teachers who work with doctoral students and researchers to look into the speaking and writing worlds that such students engage in and create as they socialize into the academic discourse of their disciplinary fields.

Recently there has been an increasing interest in investigating the academic writing of multilingual graduate students. The research on their educational and disciplinary academic socialization has explored such issues as acquisition of genre (e.g., Belcher & Hirvela, 2005; Swales,1990; Tardy, 2006, Ventola & Mauranen, 1991), voice and identity in L2 writing (e.g., Hirvela & Belcher, 2001; Ivanič, 1998; Ivanič & Camps, 2001), and interactions with experts and mentors (e.g., Belcher, 1994; Casanave, 1995; Connor & Mayberry, 1996; Leki, 1995; Prior, 1998; Schneider & Fujishima, 1995). Several of these studies have emphasized the importance of interaction between peers and mentors, which is considered a significant aspect of academic socialization at the doctoral level.

Of particular relevance to this chapter is Casanave's (1995) study, in which she investigated the disciplinary socialization of doctoral students in a department of sociology. The results of her study illustrate how students and professors influence each other in a number of ways (e.g., students resisting certain writing tasks of the professors and professors changing their courses and writing tasks in response to students' resistance). She concluded that interactions among the doctoral students positively affected their academic socialization. Stressing the importance of "peopled environments" on the socialization period of doctoral students, Casanave asserts:

> It was the people with whom the students came into regular contact who shaped the socialization experiences from the first day. These people, whether professors, other members of the cohort or upper-year students, contributed in very real ways to the students' developing sense of what the field was like and of their own place in it. Students were pushed and pulled, confused and questioned, challenged and supported by those around them. It was in this peopled environment that they undertook their writing assignments. (p. 96)

Both in her 1995 study and in her later research, Casanave builds on the metaphor of "writing games," which she draws from feminist anthropologist Shelly Ortner's work. In her work, Ortner emphasizes that social life is composed of serious games that consist of "webs of relationship and interaction between multiple, shiftingly interrelated subject positions in which none are autonomous agents" (cited in Casanave, 2002, p. 17). Conceiving academic writing as a game-like structure, Casanave conceptualizes texts and writing as socially situated practice (see also Barton, Hamilton, and Ivanic, 2000). Yet, as this chapter will show, in order to play these "writing games," students may need to generate their own "academic culture of collaboration" where they draw on links between speaking and writing while "textualizing" (Bloome & Egan-Robertson, 1993) their experiences in academic writing. Next, the necessity of seeing doctoral students' textualizing from the framework of intertextuality, a central theoretical framework of this study, is explained.

The Intersection of People, Text, and Events: The Importance of Intertexuality in Doctoral Students' Worlds

Doctoral classrooms are comprised of diverse communities experiencing numerous and varied opportunities for academic text construction, and most construction involves combined writing and speaking activities. The nature of doctoral-level writing is such that it includes "peopled environments" (Casanave, 1995) that require ongoing social interaction among *people, texts, and literacy events*. Such experiences among multilingual doctoral students can be captured within the construct of an intersectionality[3] framework. In the context of doctoral education, it is important to consider the complexity and multilayered nature of people, texts and events as constructed and shaped by the intersection of various identity categories (i.e., intersectionalities) such as race, gender, class or other axes of social differentiation. Such identity categories could shape and are shaped by texts, contexts, and social events. Drawing on the work of Atkinson (2004), Connor (2004) identifies a need to explore the social interactions among "small cultures" (e.g., classrooms) within the paradigm of intercultural rhetoric. In the model I am proposing, the textual construction in an intercultural space such as today's doctoral classrooms (an example of such small cultures) contains several intertextual connections created among people, events, and texts that contribute to the creation of a space for an academic culture of collaboration. In such a sociolinguistically oriented perspective, the notion of intertextuality could be employed as a useful tool to understand the social interaction among doctoral students as well as investigate how they construct oral and written texts within an intercultural space.

In a nutshell, intertextuality means the juxtaposition of texts. My use of intertextuality in this analysis is built on social semiotics and discourse analytic understanding of intertextuality (e.g., Bloome & Egan-Robertson,

---

[3]*Intersectionality* is a methodological paradigm that is mainly used in the field of women's studies and sociology. Aiming to overcome various disciplinary boundaries, studies of intersectionality attempt to capture the complexity and multilayered nature of social life and start from the premise that one's gender, race, class, culture, or language are intertwined and always in flux. The subject of analysis in this conceptual framework includes "the multiple dimensions of social life and categories of analysis" (McCall, 2005, p. 1772). I intend to borrow this term to illustrate the relationship between people, events, and texts, as it rejects the separability of language, culture, race, gender, or social class and views them instead as changing and socially constructed categories.

1993; Ivanič, 2004). In this view, people in interaction constantly draw from various texts, constructing intertextual relationships by acting and reacting to each other (Bloome & Egan-Robertson, 1993). According to this social constructivist view of intertextuality, Bloome and Egan-Robertson argue that for an intertextual relationship to be socially significant, it should be proposed, recognized, and acknowledged. Drawing from various discussions of intercultural rhetoric (e.g., Connor, 2004; Flower, 2003; Scollon, 1995), New Literacy Studies (cf. Barton, Hamilton & Ivanič, 2000; Bloome & Egan-Robertson, 1993; Street, 1995) and intertexuality (e. g., Bloome & Egan-Robertson, 1993, 2004; Ivanič, 2004; Shurat-Faris & Bloome, 2004), the model proposed for an academic culture of collaboration includes the intersections of people, texts, and events and can be conceptualized as three circles that overlap, thus capturing the communicative processes and dynamic relationship among these three major components. While people in interaction use language, they make use of various semiotic tools in order to construct meaning and take social action (Bloome & Egan Robertson, 2004). Such a view of intertextuality could also contribute to our understanding of academic reading, writing, and speaking events in multilingual doctoral students' lives.

The notion of intertextuality is central to understanding the academic culture of collaboration and textual construction of the doctoral students in this study. Drawing from the intertextuality scholarship and social constructionist view of text, here texts are seen as socially constructed in various events. People in social interaction, as they "act and react" to each other, interpret, produce, and change texts according to their own immediate needs and expectations. In this framework, texts do not appear in isolation, as they always exist in the "sea of other texts" (Bazerman, 2004). The analysis of the intertextuality among the doctoral students in this study thus requires looking at texts in relation to other texts (e.g., oral, written, electronic). As Bazerman (2004) notes, "We can learn many things about texts by examining what is inscribed within the texts, but for a fuller understanding it is important to consider how texts move within and affect the social world of human action and human meaning" (p. 23). Similarly, in this study, exploring how doctoral students construct intertextual links with the academic culture of collaboration provides a broader perspective about how we can view textual construction in doctoral education, and it also offers a new set of thinking tools that help us better understand how peripheral participants in academic communities take up the literacy practices that are modeled for them.

In this study of the construction of an academic culture of collaboration, the students are seen connecting various resources in order to talk about their textual construction (e.g., writing a literature review) in academic writing, or as Bloome and Egan-Robertson (2004) argue, "textualizing" experiences. They frame such experiences as follows (Bloome and Egan-Robertson, 1993):

> A text is the product of textualizing. People textualize experience and the world in which they live, making those phenomena part of a language system (broadly defined). The result of textualizing experience can be a set of words, signs, representations, and so forth. But it might be other forms and products not usually associated with texts: architecture, rock formations, the stars in the sky, the wind, the ocean, emotion—these can all be texts, but their being texts depends on what people do. The stars in the sky are only a text if they have been made so, if they have been textualized. (p. 290)

With this in mind, the basic unit of analysis in this study is not the texts in isolation, but rather the people who are constantly "acting and reacting to each other" (Erickson & Schultz, 1977) in the course of textualizing. Within this framework, people are constituted as groups, and they are contexts for each other (Erickson & Schultz, 1977). As will be seen later, written and spoken texts within the social interactions of doctoral students are inter-wined, negotiated, and sometimes contested among the members of the support group.

The Study

The Contextual Background

The research in this chapter is part of a larger ethnographic study that explores the academic literacy socialization of multilingual doctoral students. This longitudinal study was conducted between September 2006 and June 2007 in the doctoral program within a college of education at a midwestern university. The data shared in this chapter were drawn from a microanalysis of the intertextuality of six doctoral students' spoken interaction within a student-driven doctoral support group. Inspired by an intensely self-reflective course in which a number of native and nonnative–English speaking teachers' issues emerged, a couple of students decided to continue the discussions about their needs and expectations as doctoral students with the hope of receiving some peer support for their courses, qualifying exams, and other academic practices common among doctoral programs. Facilitated by myself, the group, comprised of six multilingual first- and second-year doctoral students, met once a week. The students met in various places, such as classrooms and coffee houses, while conducting the support group meetings. The data shared in this chapter comes from a four-minute transcript of students' spoken interaction in one of the support group meetings.

Participants

The primary participants of this study were six multilingual doctoral students from a wide range of linguistic and cultural backgrounds: two students from Asia, two from Europe, one from the United States, and one from South America. All names used are pseudonyms.

Fang, who is from China, immigrated to Canada to pursue her master's degree. Upon completing it, she moved to the United States to pursue her doctoral degree in education. She had extensive experience in teaching and non-academic professions such as business. She was one of the most outspoken students in the group. This support group for her was "a strong emotional help," and, as she put it, she "gained knowledge, and more importantly, the power to face challenges in my academic study."

Another group member was Jewel. Born and educated in Cyprus, Jewel received her master's degree in the United Kingdom, and she came to the United States in 2006 to pursue her doctoral degree. Jewel also taught Greek in the same university, and she was one of the most active members of the group. She expressed her thoughts about the support group as follows: "I felt free to express my thoughts, ideas, feelings, and also to exchange suggestions."

Diana, another support group member, is from Albania. Diana immigrated to the United States in 1998, and in addition to her graduate schoolwork, she worked as an ESL teacher in a private school. She described her journey in graduate school as "establishing our new identity as graduate students while our family lives have their own demands." She added: "Exchanging ideas as doctoral students helped us to come out of a cocoon of isolation and learn to collaborate in the busy world of academic research." Diana was one of the group members the other students looked up to, and she provided constant mentorship in both academic and non-academic respects.

Also in the group was Carol, who was born and educated in Hong Kong and who moved to the United States in 2006 to pursue her doctoral degree. She hopes to find a job where she will teach Chinese pedagogy. She noted that she appreciated "the kind of multicultural environment that a student can emerge in such groups."

In addition, the support group had one male member, Mike, who was born and raised in Colombia and had immigrated to the United States in 2002 to pursue his graduate work. The existence of the support group in his life, he said, made the "burden of graduate studies less heavy."

There was also one domestic student in the group: Alexis, who lived and taught in Germany for a couple of years, was fluent in German, and who, at the time of the study, was in her second year of the doctoral program. She described her group experiences as follows: "This support group has awakened in me a sense of security as I become enculturated in the quickened pace and high-pressure world of doctoral studies." Alexis was especially active in the proofreading stage of the online manuscript.

It is useful to bear in mind that these students, who could be considered as "newcomers" to the academic community, had extensive experience in writing and speaking in various languages, including English. Therefore, they brought with them the sociolinguistic and cultural knowledge of various communities and discourses they belonged to. Although theoretically they were from different linguistic and culture backgrounds, one common denominator they shared was a sense of academic culture shock as they moved through their doctoral courses.

Data Collection and Analysis

The data collection took place between September 2006 and June 2007. In the larger study that this chapter is derived from, my research methods included a plethora of data gathering procedures, such as conducting ethnographic interviews, keeping a researcher diary, collecting student artifacts, audiorecording classroom discussions as well as our informal support group meetings, and videorecording some classroom discussions. The central methodology used was microanalysis of audio recorded and video recorded data; these data were complemented by in-depth interviews and classroom observations as well as tutoring sessions offered for some students' classroom papers. The microanalysis comes from interaction within a support group (which lasted about one academic quarter). During this experience, the researcher (Seloni) took the role of a participant observer and a mentor assisting the students in their search for answers to various academically related questions. The analysis of the data was ongoing and cyclical. The researcher went back and forth recursively while reading the transcriptions and looking for intertextual links the students made during their spoken interactions within the support group.

Results

The results section is composed of a narrative description of a support group transcription. The discussion of the construction of intertextual connections in the doctoral support group builds on Bloome & Egan-Robertson's (1993) five steps for analyzing intertextual links in classroom discourse. Bloome & Egan-Robertson suggest using five components to describe the social construction of intertextuality in their microanalysis of a fifteen-minute lesson of a first grade classroom: "(1) describing individual messages, (2) identifying the boundaries of interactional units, (3) locating the proposal, recognition, and acknowledgment of intertextuality, (4) describing the social consequences of intertextuality, (5) locating uses and references to written language" (p. 314). Following this procedure, to investigate the intertextual relationships in spoken text, the transcript of a four-minute segment of the discussion during one of these support group meetings was created. Next, a message-by-message analysis was conducted to describe the evolving events by indexing the texts and contexts referred to during the spoken interaction. The message units are determined on the basis of "contextualization cues"[4] (Gumperz, 1986), such as the stress and intonation of the speakers.

Narrative Description of the Transcription

The intertextuality that occurs in this transcript and the collaborative attempt to create a manuscript illustrate two important points: (1) Students textualize their academic writing experiences as graduate students by referring to various other texts; (2) students' construction of alternative literacy spaces—which include features of both oral and written interaction—reveals their attempts to search for empowerment and liberation in academic writing. Due to space limitations, relevant message units from the transcript will be quoted as opposed to providing the transcript itself. These message units reveal the intertextual connections the students established during the informal conversation in the support group. The students in this segment are in the midst of discussing their experiences with academic writing in graduate school.

[4]Contextualization cues, according to Gumperz (1986), are verbal, nonverbal or prosodic signs that speakers signal during the conversation: "Roughly speaking, a contextualization cue is any feature of linguistic form that contributes to the signaling of contextual presuppositions. Such cues may have a number of such linguistic realizations depending on the historically given linguistic repertoire of the participants" (p. 131).

The discussion starts with Diana's contribution about the strategies she uses to improve her academic writing: "Personally, I ask other people what experiences they had . . . . Classmates, professor, or if the professor is willing to read the paper, I ask him. I go to the writing center. Or my colleagues, they read it for me." Here she makes clear intertextual references to other texts (intertextuality) and contexts (intercontextuality) such as "writing centers" and "conversations with other people such as professors and classmates" while performing the conversational function of responding/informing. Following Diana's comments on obtaining assistance in academic writing, Carol provides an uptake (i.e., response) to her comments, beginning with the word *yeah*. However, it is not clear whether Carol acknowledges the intertextual link proposed by Diana; her response is ambiguous in its conversational function because it might not serve as an acknowledgement or recognition, but only as a transition to the new topic. Carol then proposes a new intertextual link: "And for me besides, the jargon, I mean big words. I would choose HIGH level vocabulary." (Capital letters are used to designate intonation <u>and</u> emphasis.) These are the words "which are good for theory building" in academic papers and, as she explains, "I try to use difficult words in one sentence at least two or three . . . . Because if you write, you know, just in SIMPLE language it doesn't look attractive at all to the professors."

Here, while apparently agreeing with Diana and taking her own turn in the conversation, Carol seems to believe that this approach would give her more legitimacy in her writing. Several lines later in the discussion, Diana requests more explanation of Carol's proposal by asking where she locates such vocabulary, and Carol offers specific examples drawn from the texts and contexts in which she finds disciplinary terminology intended to make her papers sound more academic, including scholarly work published by some of her professors ("For instance, I always look at . . . uhmm . . . the papers that Dr. X and Dr. Y write . . . .").

At this point in the interaction, we can see that the students are juxtaposing several texts in order to share their textual experiences with academic writing (i.e., Carol's search for "jargons"). Bloome et. al (2005) emphasize that in order for an intertextual link to be established, "a connection among events has to be reified by others; the participants have to acknowledge and recognize the connection, and the connection has to have some social consequence" (p. 44). In a similar vein, in this interaction and what comes after, the students are recognizing and acknowledging each other's textual references, which mostly derive from the classes they have taken together or the articles which they have all read.

The intertextual links established so far reflect a certain degree of social significance embedded in the desire to be a part of the relevant academic discourse community and to be recognized by its established members, such as professors. As the discussion proceeds, the intertextual link Carol made earlier was recognized and acknowledged, and it has social consequences. For instance, Fang picks up the intertextual link that Carol proposed, yet she indicates her discomfort about what Carol said about borrowing words from articles. Utilizing the conversational function of questioning, she asserts "that is the thing that I don't want to do," thus juxtaposing what Carol proposed against a new topic, what she calls "creative writing." Shortly thereafter, she claims her writerly identity and identifies herself as a "creative writer" who sometime finds writing in academic genre "like a torture." The simultaneous responses of other students, which come in later lines, illustrate that the intertextual link that Carol proposed has been socially established and collectively debated among the students.

Following Fang, Jewel also juxtaposes textual worlds in her speech: "BECAUSE we . . . every culture has its own WAY of writing. And well, in Greece when we write, we don't REPEAT what somebody else [said]." Here she establishes an intertextual link on two different levels: (1) at the level of intercultural rhetoric; (2) at the level of genre. She starts a new interactional unit[5] when she goes on to compare the rhetorical construction of American writing with that of Greek writing by saying that in Greek, people are "very very critical," and adds "but I understand that in America, people are more diplomatic, and the writing is more diplomatic." Notice that here Jewel is establishing a clear intertextual link between writing in Greek culture and Western academic culture.

On the other hand, her second attempt to construct intertextuality involves a reference to a specific academic genre. In this instance, she proposes an intertextual link that matches with the genre of literature review in academic writing. Although she does not explicitly indicate that she is juxtaposing the discussion with that specific academic genre, the example she provides ("Alexis says that and Mike says this, so probably both of THEM are RIGHT") seems to indicate a spoken version of a textual reference to the literature review genre, in which students are expected to build on others' research. Again, she juxtaposes this genre with that of Greek, when, as noted earlier, she says "in Greece, when we write we don't

[5]Bloome et al. (2005) point out that "interactional units can be viewed as the smallest units of social activity, that is by definition, an interactional unit involves both the actions and reactions of people toward each other" (p. 26).

REPEAT somebody else . . . . We say the same thing in our own way, but we are very, very CRITICAL." The rising intonation at the end of this statement signals her disagreement and astonishment relative to the rhetorical moves she is expected to make while writing a literature review as part of the world of academic writing. Moreover, the contextualization cues (i.e., overacting and mocking) in these remarks seem to indicate the verbosity and implicitness of academic writing she seems to experience.

The group discussion from this point centers on the intertextual proposal that Jewel put forth. From this point on, the students share more strongly their resistance to the genre of academic writing and discuss their sense of self-representation and culture in academic writing. For instance, consider Diana and Fang's interaction that follows shortly thereafter. Here, the spoken interaction revolves around the differences between academic writing and other sorts of writing, such as creative writing. Their interaction appears to be a response to the intertextual link that Jewel proposed about academic writing, that is, the genre of literature review. Diana states, "Academic setting dictates you what position you need to take." Many students' utterances overlap at this point. Although individual message units from other students are indecipherable, the cacophony of paralinguistic contextual cues signals their agreement with and support of this statement. Fang, for example, refers to "writing for the sake of publication only" and adds "I hope in my future I do not have to do those things." Diana immediately responds with "Yes, THANK YOU. THANK YOU . . . Go SISTER." Carol, however, then disrupts the general agreement on this point and illustrates a counter argument to what has been said about always citing others' voices when it comes to writing academically. Here she comments, "But this is the way academic game is being played, for the first time you have to put big names." This remark is followed by Fang and Jewel's rebuttals. Fang replies that "there should be a middle way. There SHOULD be." Jewel suggests that, in contrast to citing "big names" in the first part of the review and in concert with what Fang has just said, "Yes, in the second part, you have to say something but you are NOT . . . uhmm . . . straightforward." Here the students provide several uptakes as they react to Carol's views and talk about the "second part" of literature review, where the writer is expected to add his or her own opinion.

As the discussion proceeds, we see that the conversational segment in this part of the group interaction is a response to the intertextual links both Jewel and Carol provided previously. Diana and Jewel's comments challenge Carol's counterargument, where she asserted that one can also add his or her perspective in academic writing after quoting others, that is, by building on previous research. They emphasize that they believe that in this "second part," the writing "goes around and around . . . and who knows who said ORIGINALLY that word. It is not original" (Diana); one cannot be "straightforward" (Jewel). This illustrates that the intertextual link proposed earlier by Carol was acknowledged and recognized and has a social significance among the support group members.

On the other hand, a short while later Jewel again makes an intertextual reference to two texts they have read in their course work in order to support her point about not being "straightforward" in academic writing. The students' laughter and other contextualization cues that overlap with Jewel's comments show that they are also recognizing and acknowledging the set of intertextual links created by Jewel. For instance, Alexis offers the comment that "you have to validate your point because then you are allowed to make A POINT on your own until the day you become like Dr. X or somebody." Carol follows that remark with her observation that "I mean a BIG name, then you can have a chance to speak whatever you want."

As the discussion continues, Fang responds to the previous interactions as follows: "Even if you have some ideas, you have to read something." Alexis at this point takes the floor and provides an uptake to Fang's response as well as the previous spoken interaction that took place in the support group when he cites "the English slang" expression "hanging on someone's coat tail," which she sees as one of the moves expected of novice writers such as doctoral students, that is, being expected to quote published literature. In citing this expression, Alexis recognizes and acknowledges the intertextual links proposed so far and begins to describe the social significance of this intertextual link. This segment in the interaction also illustrates what Bloome and Egan-Roberson (1993) and Bloome et. al (2005) emphasize about the social significance of intertextual links. That is, the socially constructed intertextual links have been reified by the group members. In other words, throughout the support group discussion, the intertextual references made to both spoken and written texts have been acknowledged and recognized, illustrating the social significance of the intertextual links.

The intertextual links created by the students in this communicative interaction illustrate several important aspects of the speaking and writing connection, such as the inseparability of the micro- and macro-level linguistic processes that students are involved in while acquiring academic literacy, and the multidirectionality of spoken and written text within informally formed academic culture of collaborative discourses, such as the one described in this study. This narrative description of the students' support group interaction could also be seen as an example of a joint learning experience where students are voicing their concerns about the academic culture shock they have been experiencing as newcomers in the doctoral program. Through the academic culture of collaboration, they seem to build on each others' voices as well as the texts and contexts that exist outside their support group.

Moreover, as is evident in the narrative description of the transcript, these students seem to collaboratively construct the meaning of academic writing at the doctoral level. Although they are different individuals with different linguistic and cultural backgrounds, they are engaged in a "community conversation" (Flower, 2003) in which they are creating a shared understanding of what it means to construct an academic text. They are doing this by the intertextual links they created during their oral interactions. In so doing, the students are constantly working on an ongoing definition of academic literacy and collectively learning about the nuances of the doctoral community of practice by rigorously engaging in discussions about academic writing.

There are several social implications arising from these intertextual and intercontextual links in this social event. First of all, it looks as if writing in the academic context creates an authoritative distance between the writer and the text. Examples of this authoritative distance between the writer (multilingual doctoral students in this case) and the text (academic writing) can be seen throughout the students' spoken interaction about academic writing. For instance, Alexis' identification of quoting scholars (or "big names," as Carol calls them) via the English expression, "riding on someone's coat tail," or Fang's and Diana's comments on academic writing as writing "for the sake of publication only," suggest that students draw a line between academic writing and the self, and they try to establish a clear sense of authority in academic writing. Such discussions about the position of author and the authority in academic writing raise profound questions, such as Foucault's (1977/1984) well-known inquiry, "What is the author?" where he suggests that the author is an invention of modern times.

Moreover, the students' apparent resistance to academic writing is also an example of critical awareness of voice in academic writing (Ivanič & Camps, 2001). That is, the students are critiquing the "dictated" conventions of the disciplinary discourse community they are entering. Yet within this academic culture of collaboration, the students seem to freely voice their academic culture shock and co-construct the meaning of academic writing. For instance, while Diana and Fang are discussing what appears to them to be the monolithic features of academic writing and how they feel restricted by them, they comment that they wish to do more creative writing. Similarly, Jewel juxtaposes several texts from the classes that they all took together, and gives an example of the rhetorical moves they need to enact in order to build their theoretical framework in an academic paper ("It's like Street,

1986, and Bloome, 2000, and they agree"). Jewel's comments, which were articulated in an upbeat and a loud manner, prompted other responses that describe the academic writing games group members need to play in order to have a legitimate voice in academic discourse. The contextual cues signal not only their emerging genre awareness (i.e., their familiarity with the rhetorical moves they need to make in English academic writing), but also their collective resistance toward and problematizing of the dominant discourses they were encountering in their early years of doctoral education. Within this academic culture of collaboration (which mainly includes spoken interaction), these multilingual students are critically reflecting on their writing practices as doctoral students, negotiating the conflicting discourses, and attempting to resolve the academic conflicts they are experiencing. While so doing, they are making and drawing upon important connections between speaking and writing.

This narrative description of the students' support group interaction also suggests that the "writing games" students are playing at the doctoral level do not operate as a smooth and seamless experience. They do not simply learn the rules of the games and then become fully prepared to apply them; instead, they adapt or adjust the rules of these writing games through talking, negotiating, and sometimes resisting the conventions which constitute these academic writing games. In the course of doing so, they need (and in this case created) what Pratt (1991) has called a "safe house," that is, a collective space in which the complexities of their interaction could unfold in an environment of encouragement and positive reinforcement. In addition, the oral interactions of the students are evidence of the socially constructed nature of writing and illustrate "the importance of understanding how individual writers draw on resources from within and around themselves as they gradually learn to identify themselves as writers for particular communities or to recognize that they do not want to belong" (Casanave, 1995, p. 91).

In addition to the face-to-face interactions that these doctoral students engaged in, they collaboratively worked on a manuscript (in an online environment) about the benefits students derived from being a part of a support group during the beginning of their doctoral studies. (Due to space constraints, the analysis of this literacy practice will not be included in this chapter.) However, it is important to say a few words about this online interaction as, like the face-to-face dialogues in their support group, it reflects students' emerging agency, and their active attempts to problematize and appropriate the academic literacy practices that they are being exposed to in graduate school. Similar to what was seen earlier in the students' support group interaction, contesting the practices of academic discourse was also observed in these online spaces. Using a mixture of nonacademic and academic writing styles, the students negotiated the world of academic discourse in the online space as well. Some of the collaborative actions included providing help to each other with the lexical choices and rhetorical moves necessary to improve this text. The collaborative, multivoiced writing in this writing event operated as a hybrid genre where the students appropriated the literacy practices of graduate school to suit their own needs and expectations. In the online attempts to create a dialogic manuscript, students' interactions (e.g., providing online uptake to each other) show an understanding of the idea that students are ready to challenge and appropriate the textual practices around them. Moreover, by commenting on each others' texts and creating a dialogic text, they move away from the responsibility of single authorship as well as create a more equal power relationship among the group members.

Discussion and Conclusion

In this discussion of intertextuality, we have seen important manifestations of the ways in which multilingual graduate students can make meaning out of the writing games they are playing in their disciplinary fields. This study illustrates Bizzell's (1992, 2002) notion of hybrid academic discourses in which she points out that such alternative discourses challenge the dichotomy between students' vernacular discourses and school discourses, thus blurring the divide between academic and daily spoken interactions. Similarly, the doctoral students in this study challenged and problematized what they had been exposed to in their formal doctoral study experiences. At the same time, their interaction draws attention to the intertwined nature of speaking-writing relations. The collaborative nature of the students' academic culture of collaboration involved powerful meaning-making processes that enabled them to informally deconstruct and then reconstruct the academic literacy practices common at the doctoral level.

Writing in academia is an important means of knowledge construction. In the L2 literacy field, it is important to explore the day-to-day microsocial interactions that occur in order to shed light on how macro-level concerns in academic discourse play out in classrooms, as well as how and by whom knowledge and meaning are constructed. Working as a team rather than individuals within the communicative domain of an academic culture of collaboration (both in face-to-face and online interactions), the students in this study became active agents who gained the power to negotiate and question the textual practices that they were facing in the early years of their doctoral studies. Within this academic culture of collaboration, the students frequently provided uptakes, took up positions, and made intertextual links through indexing each other's oral narratives in interactions and indexing the scholarly articles they all read as a part of their doctoral education.

This analysis also illustrates that students' experiences are textualized within their narratives and interactions. These textualization practices reveal that text, especially at the doctoral level, is more than merely written or spoken in nature. The knowledge constructed about academic writing in the support group reveals the social significance of the actions and perceptions associated with academic writing. It was within the students' social and historical shared experiences both inside and outside of the classroom that they were able to appropriate the academic writing games that they were acquiring. Moreover, the students' textual construction included dialogues that adopted other voices and texts.

Researching intertextuality at the doctoral level within a microethnographic framework can open discussions and expand our views as to how texts are constructed and reconstructed through the written and oral interactions among people. This, in turn, can add to our understanding of the relationship between speaking and writing, and our understanding of intercultural rhetoric in L2 literacy. As opposed to mere textual analysis conducted in traditional contrastive rhetoric research, studies that focus on the social interaction (both spoken and written) in intercultural spaces, or—as Connor (2004) and Atkinson (2004) emphasize—studies that foreground a dynamic notion of culture and a context-sensitive analysis of discourse, could raise awareness of the interconnectedness among people, texts, and events found in the new domain of intercultural rhetoric, which posits that there is a dynamic and fluid connection among speaking, writing, and other nonlinguistic communication means such as gestural, electronic, or pictorial signs. Intertextuality, as conceptualized in intercultural rhetoric studies, could serve as a cornerstone in understanding the dynamic and evolving relationship between spoken and written text at the doctoral level. Looking at the intertextual links doctoral students establish in the course of acquiring academic literacy practices not only expands our views of academic textual worlds and intercultural rhetoric, it also increases awareness of the juxtaposed and interactive nature of texts and events (i.e., spoken, written, electronic, etc.).

In conclusion, the academic culture of collaboration (or intercultural academic collaboration) described through this analysis of intertextuality is comprised of a set of literacy practices in which students are not only swapping stories, but also engaging in a cross-cultural (or intercultural) meaning making activity. By building an academic culture of collaboration in their own informal communities of practice, they are talking about the writing games they are involved in. That is, they are acting in the doctoral world with the words they are constructing collaboratively. This collective construction of meaning making and resistance to authority within the academic culture of collaboration is an important step toward empowering multilingual students to appropriate academic literacy practices. As Canagarajah (2002) pointed out, "Students shouldn't be satisfied with just switching discourses as Bizzell argues, or fusing discourses as Zamel encouraged, but appropriating dominant discourses according to their interests and values to gain voice"(p. 40).

By looking at the intertextual links they constructed, in this study we can see students' struggles and their attempts to appropriate literacy practices. More specifically, such microanalyses suggest that multilingual students may be doing far more than merely acquiring the academic rhetorical conventions of their disciplinary fields; they may also be talking about negotiating, and attempting to adjust the academic literacy practices surrounding them. This is in line with Flower's (2003) claim that "intercultural rhetoric operates by definition and by choice in a space where *discourse practices* and *complex networks* of situated knowledge are known to differ. Moreover, it chooses to build the knowledge on the constructive potential and *reflective agency* of people" (p. 43, italics added). With this understanding of multilingual doctoral students' textual construction, we move the emphasis away from a view of people submissively accepting the academic rhetorical conventions they experience in their doctoral courses to a deeper understanding of how people use their agency to resist, challenge, and eventually creatively construct the rhetorics and texts around them (see also the growing emphasis on agency in L2 academic writing, such as Canagarajah, 2002; Casanave, 2002; Ivanič & Camps, 2001; Kubota & Lehner, 2004; Prior, 1995).

Kress (1997) wrote that "in a pluricultural or multicultural society the social histories of all individual members of that society will be histories of greater or lesser difference, producing social subjects who share significant social/cultural experiences, values, meanings and yet have significantly different experiences, values and meanings. In the production of any one text in any one social interaction there will be degrees of repetition (out of shared experience and knowledge) and degrees of difference" (p. 14). It was through this combination of shared understanding and difference in the academic culture of collaboration that the multilingual doctoral students in this study could negotiate the writing games that were expected of them. Lastly, the alternative literacy practices these students adopted, which include dynamic relations between written and spoken text and are influenced by the changing identity categories of people, could increase the possibility of empowering less authoritative, underrepresented student groups at all levels.

Acknowledgments

The study reported in this chapter was made possible by the doctoral students who participated in this research. Therefore, I am indebted to the students who let me hear their stories and showed their continuous support for this study. Also, I am grateful to Alan Hirvela and Diane Belcher for their helpful comments on the earlier drafts of this paper.

REFERENCES

Atkinson, D. (2004). Contrasting rhetorics/contrasting cultures: why contrastive rhetoric needs a better conceptualization of culture [Special issue on Contrastive Rhetoric]. *Journal of English for Academic Purposes, 3(3),* 271–289.

Bakhtin, M. (1981). Discourse in the novel. In M. Hoquist (Ed.). (C. Emerson & M. Holquist, Trans.), *The dialogic imagination* (pp. 259–422). Austin: University of Texas Press. (Original work published 1935)

———. (1986). The problem of speech genres. In C. Emerson & M. Holquist (Eds.). (V.W. McGee, Trans.), *Speech genres and other late essays* (pp. 60–102). Austin: University of Texas Press. (Original work published 1953)

Barton, D., Hamilton, M., & Ivanič, R. (Eds.). (2000). *Situated literacies. Reading and writing in context.* London: Routledge.

Bazerman, C. (2004). Intertextuality: How texts reply on other texts. In C. Bazerman & P. Prior Eds.), *What writing does and how it does it: An introduction to analyzing texts and textual practices* (pp. 83–96). Mahwah, NJ: Lawrence Erlbaum.

Belcher, D. (1994). The apprenticeship approach to advanced academic literacy: Graduate students and their mentors. *English for Specific Purposes, 13(1),* 23–34.

Belcher, D., & Hirvela, A. (2005). Writing the qualitative dissertation: What motivates and sustains commitment to a fuzzy genre? *Journal of English for Academic Purposes, 4(2),* 187–205.

Bizzell, P. (1992). *Academic discourse and critical consciousness.* Pittsburgh, PA: University of Pittsburgh Press.

———. (2002). The intellectual work of "mixed" forms of academic discourses. In C. Schroeder, H. Fox, P. Bizzell (Eds.), *ALT DIS: Alternative discourses and academy* (pp. 1–10). Portsmouth, NH: Heinemann.

Bloome, D., Carter, S. P., Christian, B.M, Otto, S. & Shuart-Faris, N. (2005). *Discourse analysis and the study of classroom language and literacy events—A microethnographic perspective.* Mahwah, NJ: Lawrence Erlbaum.

Bloome, D., & Egan-Robertson, A. (1993). The social construction of intertextuality in classroom reading and writing lessons. *Reading Research Quarterly, 28(4),* 305–333.

———. (2004).The social construction of intertextuality in classroom reading and writing lessons. In N. Shuart-Faris & D. Bloome (Eds.), *Use of intertextuality in classroom and educational research* (pp. 17–64). Greenwich, CT: Information Age Publishing.

Braine, G. (2002). Academic literacy and the nonnative speaker graduate student. *Journal of English for Academic Purposes, 1(1),* 59–68.

Canagarajah, S. (2002). Multilingual writers and the academic community: Towards a critical relationship. *Journal of English for Academic Purposes, 1(1),* 29–44.

Casanave, C. P. (1995). Locating interactions: Constructing contexts for composing in a graduate sociology program. In D. Belcher & G. Braine (Eds.), *Academic writing in a second language. Essays on research & pedagogy* (pp. 83–110). Norwood, NJ: Ablex.

———. (2002). *Writing games. Multicultural case studies of academic literacy practices in higher education.* Mahwah, NJ: Lawrence Erlbaum.

Connor, U. (2004). Intercultural rhetoric research: beyond texts. *Journal of English for Academic Purposes, 13(3),* 291–304.

Connor, U., & Mayberry, S. (1996). Learning discipline-specific academic writing. A case study of a Finnish graduate student in the United States. In E.Ventola & A. Mauranen (Eds.), *Academic writing: Intercultural and textual issues* (pp. 231–253). Philadelphia: John Benjamins.

Erickson, F., & Shultz, J. (1977). When is a context? *Newsletter of the Laboratory for Comparative Human Cognition, 1,* 5–12.

Flower, L. (2003). Talking across difference: Intercultural rhetoric and the search for situated knowledge. *College Composition and Communication, 55(1),* 1–31.

Foucault, M. (1977/1984). What is an author? In D. F. Bouchard (Ed.), *Language, counter-memory, practice: Selected essays and interviews* (pp. 113–138). Ithaca, NY: Cornell University Press. (Reprinted in *The Foucault reader,* pp. 101–120, Paul Rainbow, Ed., 1994, New York: Pantheon Books.)

Gee, J. P. (1990). *Social linguistics and literacies: Ideology in discourses.* London: Falmer Press.

Gumperz, J. J. (1986). *Discourse strategies.* New York: Cambridge University Press.

Hirvela, A., & Belcher, D. (2001). Coming back to voice. The multiple voices and identities of mature multilingual writers. *Journal of Second Language Writing, 10(1-2),* 83–106.

Hyland, K. (2000). *Disciplinary discourses: Social interactions in academic writing.* London: Longman.

Ivanič, R. (1998). *Writing and identity: The discursive construction of identity in academic writing.* Amsterdam: John Benjamins.

———. (2004). Intertextual practices in the construction of multimodal texts in inquiry-based learning. In N. Shuart-Ferris and D. Bloome (Eds.), *Use of intertextuality in classroom and educational research* (pp. 274–310). Greenwich, CT: Information Age Publishing.

Ivanič, R., & Camps, D. (2001). I am how I sound: Voice as self-representation in L2 writing. *Journal of Second Language Writing, 10(1-2),* 3–33.

Kress, G. (1989). *Linguistic processes in sociocultural practice.* Oxford: Oxford University Press.

———. (1993). Genre as social process. In B. Cope & M. Kalantzis (Eds.), *The powers of literacy: A genre approach to teaching writing* (pp. 22–37). London: The Falmer Press.

———. (1997). *Before writing: Rethinking the paths to literacy.* London: Routledge.

———. (2003). *Literacy in the new media age.* London: Routledge.

Kubota, R., & Lehner, A. (2004). Toward critical contrastive rhetoric. *Journal of Second Language Writing, 3(1),* 7–27.

Kucer, S. (1985). The making of meaning. Reading and writing as parallel processes. *Written Communication, 3(3),* 317–336.

Lave, J., & Wenger, E. (1991). *Situated learning: Legitimate peripheral participation.* New York: Cambridge University Press.

Lea, M. R., & Street, B. (1999). Writing as academic literacies: Understanding textual practices in higher education. In C.N. Candlin & K. Hayland (Eds.), *Writing texts, processes and practices* (pp. 62–81). Essex, UK: Longman.

Leki, I. (1995). Good writing: I know it when I see it. In D. Belcher & G.Braine (Eds.), *Academic writing in a second language: Essays on research & pedagogy* (pp. 26–43). Norwood, NJ: Ablex.

McCall, L. (2005). The complexity of intersectionality. *Journal of Women in Culture and Society, 3,* 1172–1800.

Ortner, S. B. (1966). *Making gender: The politics and erotics of culture.* Boston: Beacon Press.

Pratt, M. L. (1991). Arts of the contact zone. *Profession, 91(1),* 33–40.

Prior, P. A. (1995). Redefining the task: An ethnographic examination of writing and response in graduate seminars. In D. Belcher & G. Braine (Eds.), *Academic writing in a second language: Essays on research & pedagogy* (pp. 26–43). Norwood, NJ: Ablex.

———. (1998). *Writing/disciplinary: A sociohistoric account of literate activity in the academy.* Mahwah, NJ: Lawrence Erlbaum.

Schneider, M., & Fujishima, N. K. (1995). When practice doesn't make perfect: The case of an ESL graduate student. In D. Belcher & G. Braine (Eds.), *Academic writing in a second language: Essays on research & pedagogy* (pp. 3–22). Norwood, NJ: Ablex.

Scollon, R. (1995). Plagiarism and ideology: Identity in intercultural discourse. *Language in Society, 24*(1), 1–28.

Shuart-Faris, N., & Bloome, D. (Eds.). (2004). *Use of intertextuality in classroom and educational research.* Greenwich, CT: Information Age Publishing.

Street, B. (1985). *Literacy in theory and practice.* Cambridge, UK: Cambridge University Press.

———. (1993). *Cross-cultural approaches to literacy.* New York: Cambridge University Press.

———. (1995). *Social literacies: Critical approaches to literacy in development, ethnography and education.* London: Longman.

Swales, J. M. (1990). *Genre analysis: English in academic and research settings.* New York: Cambridge University Press.

Tardy, C. (2006). Researching first and second language genre learning: A comparative review and a look ahead. *Journal of Second Language Writing, 15*(1), 79–101.

Ventola, E., & Mauranen, A. (Eds.). (1991). *Academic writing: Intercultural and textual issues.* Philadelphia: John Benjamins.

5

Getting in Line: The Challenge (and Importance) of Speaking and Writing about Difficult Ideas

CHRISTINE PEARSON CASANAVE AND MIGUEL SOSA

Abstract

In this chapter, we discuss how important and rewarding it is to help students put difficult ideas into lines of words in speech and writing. We emphasize the value of personal contact in risk-free classrooms to achieve this goal. We first present an overview of some of our assumptions, followed by several vignettes exemplifying different kinds of difficulty. After describing four types of difficult ideas and topics, we then use examples from our own classes to discuss in further depth two kinds: one concerning cultural issues with EFL students and the other intellectual issues in a teacher education class. The combination of challenging topics, openness to new ideas, and a supportive environment where speech and writing mutually scaffold each encourages curiosity and communication.

"[U]nderstanding can emerge through an encounter with difficulty, and experiences of reading and writing will be enriched and enhanced if difficulty is addressed rather than ignored."

(Salvatori & Donahue, 2005, p. xxiv)

"If challenges are too low relative to one's skills one gets relaxed and then bored. If both challenges and skills are perceived to be low, one gets to feel apathetic."

(Csikszentmihalyi, 1997, p. 30)

"A 'resilient sense of efficacy,' Bandura (1994) argues, comes not from easy successes but from experience in surmounting obstacles with sustained effort (p. 72)."

(as cited in Belcher & Hirvela, 2005, p. 199)

In our teaching, we constantly seek ways to interest students in the topics we teach, to challenge them to do more than they think they can do, and to help them learn how to communicate important ideas to others in speech and writing. We cannot achieve any of these goals without asking them to engage with difficult ideas, which can then be turned into topics for speaking and writing. This idea applies as well to L1 students, to L1 and L2 students in teacher education, and to all of us as teachers. We also believe that speech and writing of many kinds can mutually scaffold our efforts at creating lines of words from complex multidimensional thoughts. In this respect, we are not making a directional argument about the benefits of speech on writing or writing on speech, although many examples in the literature do this (see, for example, Weissberg, 2006, as well as a number of chapters in this volume). Rather, our main focus is on the role of difficult ideas in the L2 language or teacher education class in challenging and motivating students, in connecting students and teachers, and in helping them and their teachers turn difficult multidimensional ideas into lines of words. Be prepared. We are not offering readers a piece of research, but an exploration of ideas. We both wonder and wander.

With educators and psychologists such as Neil Postman (1988), Howard Gardner (1999), Mihalyi Csikszentmihalyi (1997), Mariolina Salvatori and Patricia Donahue (2005), we begin with the assumption that challenge, complexity, and depth (so often absent in L2 classrooms) can promote motivation, critical thinking, engagement, and language development for both L1 and L2 speakers. With Nel Noddings (2006), we further assume that education at all levels, including in the L2 classroom, should fundamentally involve dialogue among students and teachers about important issues, in which many "why" questions are asked. We do not support, in other words, a separate skills approach to L2 education, even at lower proficiency levels. We also feel strongly that the best dialogue happens in person. But we also assume that "dialogue" includes not only talk between self and other (Weissberg, 2006), but also interactions that people have with texts and with graphic displays of ideas (cf. Bakhtin), as well as "inner speech" (in a Vygotskyan sense) and "private speech"—the silent and out loud discussions that older children and adults have with themselves as they are working out difficult ideas or processing difficult language (Lantolf & Thorne, 2006). All of these linguistic interactions constitute the mediations that connect and give expression to the worlds of experience and thought.

Lastly, we assume with Postman (1988) that language, spoken and written, must remain central to educational processes. As Lantolf and Thorne (2006) put it in their discussion of Vygotsky's conception of psychological tools or artifacts, the most "powerful and pervasive artifact of all [is] language" (p. 26). Even though multimedia literacy has become essential in all walks of our lives (Cope & Kalantzis, 2000; Kress, 2000, 2003), we are skeptical about some educators' (and some students') obsession with certain visual media, such as computer games (a highly gendered activity), in spite of arguments that they can promote the development of language and complex thought (e.g., Gee, 2004).

Gaming indeed can involve students and teachers in challenges and difficulty and even provide them with what Csikszentmihalyi (1975/2000, 1997) calls flow experiences, as Gee (2004) has documented, but this is not the kind of difficulty we are concerned with. We do agree with Kress (2000, p. 184) that written and spoken language cannot "be regarded as monomodal" and that we need "to rethink 'language' as a multimodal phenomenon." However, a primary concern of ours is how to help students and teachers transform difficult ideas into words for the purpose of person-to-person communication. We want to help students, and ourselves, communicate personally relevant, difficult ideas to others both within and outside our own cultures for the purpose of nurturing connections among people as well as stimulating intellectual growth. In other words, unlike Kress (2003) and others, we are not primarily concerned with preparing students for work in a multimedia world, but for personal communication on cultural and intellectual topics.

Our purpose in this essay is thus to convince readers, in particular novice language teachers, that this goal is a worthwhile one in our multimedia and commodified era, and that it is worth pursuing in our classrooms. Making lines of words in speech and writing about difficult ideas is challenging for everyone. However, mutual scaffolding of different kinds of talk and written text can assist all of us in creating these lines from complex multidimensional thoughts. Students and teachers are thus partners in the task of expressing difficult ideas.

To be honest, we must confess that we are especially concerned about engaging L2 students and their teachers in communication about difficult ideas because of trends we have seen in our EFL teaching experience in Japan, which is the context for our discussion in this chapter. We presume that many readers will find similar trends in their own teaching contexts, whether these are in second or foreign language settings. Certainly those teaching in North America will relate to our concerns, which, in a nutshell, are that (1) a testing craze has swept the educational world, and it is having depressing effects on what and how we teach and on students' motivation; (2) students we know seem to be doing little sustained conversing, reading, and writing in their classes, perhaps because their patience for deep and sustained thought is being reduced by a visual entertainment mode of teaching (and of living), and a cell-phone mode of communicating, characterized by fast-moving eye-candy bits and pieces; (3) this problem is exacerbated by ESL-EFL commercial text materials that seem to be increasingly vacuous as publishers (seeking global markets and hence fearful of offending?) seek to entertain with pictures, thus choosing not to challenge students with words and ideas; and (4) students' apparent apathy and boredom with school are escalating as EFL activities and materials become less challenging and less relevant to students' lives. Teachers, too, can become bored for the same reasons. People who are bored do not learn.

We may be wrong, but we feel that Japan is especially susceptible to these testing and media trends, both of which militate against sustained exploration of difficult topics in speech and writing (see, for example, McCrostie's 2006 condemnation of the TOEIC® bandwagon that is currently sweeping Japan). In conversations with and observations of teachers as well as from our readings, we learn that in many language classes, as well as in other kinds of classes, teachers tend to teach to the test, do a lesson and move on, teach to entertain with trivial if colorful materials, and teach for "coverage" (cf. Gardner, 1999). Pressures from within and outside the institution make it difficult to enact change (see McVeigh, 2002), with the result that we rarely immerse ourselves or our students over time in complex ideas, designed to be shared with others, particularly in the required English class.

In short, we have sensed that many students in Japan and elsewhere have little sense of purpose for studying—beyond passing a test or getting a diploma. These concerns are not new and have been expressed most passionately perhaps in the life work of Neil Postman (beginning with Postman and Weingartner, 1969) as well as in work by Gardner (1999), Csikszentmihalyi (1975/2000), McCourt (2005), and others, and, pertinent to our context, in Brian McVeigh's (2002) scathing if overstated indictment of Japanese higher education. These dilemmas affect both novice and experienced teachers and raise questions about how we prepare teachers in graduate language teacher education programs. We wish to add our small part to the discussion of these educational dilemmas. We want to be able to tell ourselves, future language teachers, and our students: Challenge yourself to explore difficult ideas; do not be afraid to try this; seek and nourish difficult ideas until you understand them. Use writing and speaking to foster your understanding: *The lines of words you create will both help you construct your interpretation of your world and will assist you in representing it to others.* (M. Rabinovitch, personal communication). This advice applies to all of us.

In the next part of the essay, we offer three vignettes to illustrate the challenge that all of us have in transforming difficult ideas into lines. One of the main problems is that difficult ideas, sensations, and felt experiences tend not to be linear, so that getting an idea into lines of words or concrete images challenges everyone. As Elliot Eisner (1997, p. 7) puts it, the "output" issue concerns "how we go about the magical task of reducing the multimedia world of our experience to a form of representation...." Next we discuss what we mean by "difficult ideas and topics" in the context of the L2 class and graduate language teacher education class. We then talk about ways we have used speech and writing in two very different classes in Japan to help students and ourselves find our way into and through two kinds of difficult topics, one cultural and the other intellectual. In our discussion, we emphasize that speech and writing interact to help students and teachers express difficult ideas.

Three Vignettes on the Transformation of Difficult Thoughts and Sensations into Lines of Words

Vignette 1

A scholar is walking along a deserted beach, thinking about an idea for a paper or a book. The idea is complex, challenging, and exciting. While walking and thinking, many ideas seem to come together with delicious clarity. On returning home, the scholar sits down immediately at the computer or at the kitchen table and attempts to put those "clear" ideas into writing. But nothing comes out, or nothing comes out right. Some words may appear on the screen or the writing pad, one word following another, but they do not capture the beauty and clarity and complexity of the sensations from the beach walk. She is stymied. "I need to talk to someone," she tells herself, "and then to go back to the beach to recapture the vision of what I was thinking and feeling, to talk to myself, with a note pad this time." Speech, writing, and sensation need to merge.

Vignette 2

A piano student is trying to learn a new piece. In his head he hears and feels what he wants his fingers to do as they move along a keyboard, one note or set of notes after another, following lines of music printed on a score. His challenge is to transform the score—a written text—and a felt sensation of sound, that may or may not be accompanied by images, into music that takes place in time, and to recreate what he hears and feels in his mind and body. Sing the notes, his piano teachers says. Then go away for a while and envision the sound and the bodily sensation of moving your fingers in ways that match what is in your head. For the pianist, as well as for the visual artist, the ability to translate into a tangible form a sensation or image or sound that is felt in the mind and body is never easy, but it is based on a personal (and quite strong) vision that keeps her or him focused. The vision is neither linear nor two dimensional. But the resulting product for the piano student is a series of convincing lines of sound that travel linearly in time.

Vignette 3

An intermediate or high-intermediate second language student (you, your students), bored by textbook exercises, longs to be challenged by something more interesting, which almost always means something more difficult and more interactive and almost always something outside the conventional school setting. Like the scholar and the piano student, the second language student experiences the world in complex ways, multidimensionally and multimodally, through body and mind. In the language class, we can draw on these experiences—what the student at some level already knows. To express the complexities of her lived experiences and embodied cultural knowledge and then to communicate with others both within and outside her own culture, she must merge experiences, emotions, images, beliefs, and sensations with language, squeezing out lines of words in speech and writing and letting the spoken and written words build on each other. But if she is doing this in her L2, she must hold to a belief that may make her fearful at first—she must believe that she does not have to wait until her language is error-free in order to transform her experiences and complex thoughts into lines of words. The lines do not need to be long. The grammar does not need to be perfect. They do need to connect with the student's mind, body, and experience. She also needs to be convinced that there is a receptive audience consisting of other people who are interested in what she has to say. In other words, she must be convinced that someone (in our example, a teacher and peers) is interested enough in her to listen well to her words and to help her put them into coherent lines that can be shared with others.

Types of Difficulty

There are many ways we can conceptualize difficulty in the L2 class or the teacher education class. The most common is linguistic difficulty (e.g., grammar, syntax). In this essay, we do not discuss this kind of difficulty; it is commonly discussed elsewhere. Instead we focus on ideas and topics that for one reason or another are difficult for students to speak and write about. We mention four kinds of difficult ideas below and discuss two of them in more depth.

1. Culturally Irrelevant Topics and Ideas

One type of difficult topic includes those topics that are completely foreign to students' culture, cultural knowledge, experience, background knowledge, and interest. Such topics may appear in textbooks that teachers are required to use. One book that Miguel was expected to use in Japan included one chapter about the history of aviation in the United States. Another chapter was about fashion in France during the reign of Louis XVI. In fact, such topics often lead these students to see the foreign language classroom as a boring place where topics are irrelevant and time is wasted. They know little or nothing about the topic, and if such information will not appear on a future examination, they see no reason to invest any effort in learning, speaking, or writing. In this chapter, we will not discuss this kind of difficult topic further because we believe that, in its many forms, it should be avoided.

2. Topics that Pose No Immediate Challenge

A second kind of difficult topic consists of those topics and ideas that have some relevance to students' lives and that may not be inherently difficult but are made difficult in a negative sense because there seems to be no way to engage with them. Answers are to be found in the textbook, or provided by the media or, in the worst cases, by the all-knowing teacher. These topics often include newspaper-style articles that textbook writers and teachers may use with the best of intentions, hoping to generate discussion. The problem arises when students have not been presented with the tools for analyzing the topic or idea from different perspectives. In such cases, students' lack of experience in generating alternative views of the same topic or problem only results in their inability to develop arguments. Students refrain from sharing any opinions simply because the answers seem too obvious: Read the conclusion at the end of the article and there is the answer. Then, fill in the blank. In other words, students are often asked to fish for the common and often obvious answer. The challenge of challenging the text is therefore lost, and there is no reason for speaking or writing. We will not discuss this type of difficult topic further except to say that apparently simple ideas and topics can be made more challenging and interesting by the way they are presented to students and by the activities that students are asked to engage in. Fixed-answer activities are not challenging; open and multianswer activities can be, particularly when the teacher is a co-learner with students.

3. Topics from Everyday Life Grounded in Tacit, Commonsense Assumptions

These are the topics and ideas that emerge from beliefs, assumptions, daily events and rituals, and interactions with others within students' own cultures and languages. One interesting thing about these topics is that they are always at hand, and one would think that students could easily consult their own knowledge of their own culture by talking to each other. Dictionaries are usually not necessary; examples abound. But such ideas and the topics we develop from them may pose a difficult challenge for ESL-EFL students and their teachers, according to our experiences and to what our students tell us. One reason may be that "common sense" is embodied, often tacit knowledge. Charlotte Linde (1993, p. 18) points out that common sense is "the system of assumptions and beliefs that are assumed to be shared by all competent members of the culture. Common-sense beliefs are so obvious and transparent to members of a given culture that they have difficulty perceiving them as assumptions." We should therefore not be surprised that students find it difficult to talk and write about ideas that fall under the umbrella of common sense.

First, students may see no reason to discuss such ideas, particularly in an EFL situation where classmates (if not the teacher) share commonsense assumptions. Why should they discuss or write about things that everyone knows? But once convinced to speak or write about such topics, what is difficult for them is to explicate tacit aspects of their own culture and then to organize what they want to say and how they want to say it. The ideas may be there, in the form of an embodied sense of cultural and personal knowledge, but the explanation and the commentary are difficult to piece together, to put into lines of words. In short, commonsense beliefs and everyday interactions and experiences are not inherently linear, but multidimensional and multisensorial as well as culturally embodied. All of us find it difficult to put such beliefs and experiences into lines of words. In the next section, Miguel relates a story about teaching this kind of difficulty in one of his university classes in Japan.

4. Intellectually Difficult Topics and Ideas

In perhaps the most common understanding of what a difficult topic or idea might be, we think of topics that are intellectually challenging: reading and interpreting a poem or other difficult reading; learning to speak and write about complex abstract subject matter; synthesizing ideas from multiple sources into a coherent linear representation in words; searching for verbal expression of difficult and complex personal emotions and thoughts (philosophies, ethics) (Salvatori & Donahue, 2005). For example, in our experiences, students at all levels, from high school to graduate school, and even teachers as well, may feel intimidated by difficult texts that they are asked to read and respond to critically and by abstract concepts that they are expected to talk and write about. Moreover, teachers themselves may not be experts at critical thinking (Noddings, 2006). Yet for both students and teachers, engaging with this kind of difficulty can be pleasurable, as Salvatori and Donahue (2005) have pointed out. Discussion can be animated and animating, writing of many kinds can be exploratory and experimental, and talk and text can feed into and off of one another. Paul Prior's (1998) research on the multiple influences on graduate students' writing and talk takes this broad view.

In the L2 class one goal is to devise intellectually challenging tasks that are not so far beyond students' L2 proficiency level or personal maturity that they are inaccessible. Students need to believe that a topic, even if difficult, is worth talking and writing about, and that they do not need to understand everything about it in order to get something from it. Similarly, in the graduate teacher education class, L1 and L2 students alike need to be encouraged to engage with material that can be challenging in any number of ways, again without fearing partial comprehension. Comprehension builds as abstract and partially comprehended ideas from readings are turned into lines of speech and writing through class discussions, response journals, email, and other readings and writings. In the next section, after Miguel's example, Chris will discuss the importance of asking graduate students to speak and write about difficult ideas not just occasionally, but throughout an entire term.

Examples from our Classes in Japan

Miguel's University English Class: "Learning to Talk and Write about Embodied Cultural Knowledge"

As teachers of English in Japan, we are aware that challenges in representing difficult ideas in a foreign language are often exacerbated by differences rooted in cultural and linguistic systems. We are also aware that embodied cultural knowledge may be difficult to talk and write about in both L1 and L2, except in stereotypical ways. (One reason that stereotypes persist is that they are so easy to talk and write about.) Hence, one type of difficult topic in the L2 class involves teachers and students working together to construct non-stereotypical explanations of cultural concepts.

Let me say a few words first about the difficulty of challenging stereotypes. David Matsumoto (2002) points out that many of the ideas and images about Japanese culture that people in Western countries as well as many Japanese have come to accept about themselves as standard are, in fact, myths. However, many of these ideas continue to be perpetuated by media, past and current literature about Japan, and in the discourse of prominent public figures. The belief persists, for example, both inside and outside Japan that Japan is uniquely homogeneous and unicultural and that the Japanese people are collectivist in orientation, sacrificing individual needs out of loyalty to group harmony. "These stereotypic images of the Japanese culture and people are no longer stereotypes," says Matsumoto; "they *are* the Japanese" (p. 16). Thus the "easy" topics—that is, the ones that students and teachers can talk and write about with little difficulty, are these widespread cultural stereotypes.

However, Matsumoto's research on cultural psychology has provided evidence that such ideas and images are not necessarily characteristic of the way people think and behave, particularly in the younger generations. He contends that the social changes that have taken place in Japan since the end of WW II, as well as changes in attitudes and behavior that have taken place as a result of economic growth, require that generations of young Japanese and non-Japanese alike re-examine their deeply held, often unarticulated assumptions about Japanese culture.

In our classrooms, we see these social changes as opportunities for us and our students to engage in exploring why people in their generation are developing a new way of thinking and what that thinking consists of. In the process, we hope that after exploring many difficult culturally based assumptions in writing, reading, and speaking, our students will be able to complicate and then explicate their views in ways that will not only help them forge connections with others, including their teachers, but that may also prevent (in some small way) the further spread of stereotypes.

In the example I give from one of my classes, I show how I have been trying to complicate students' thinking about deeply embedded cultural and linguistic concepts, ones prone to stereotyping. I teach reading and writing at a university that offers courses in Agricultural Science. Students attending my classes are in their second year, and on average, they have studied English for at least eight years, so they are not beginners. Interestingly, the majority of students attending my classes come from small communities throughout Japan. As a result of their upbringing, many of these students have varied assumptions about Japanese culture.

When I was asked to teach the reading and writing class, it was suggested that I select a book about American culture. Since I am not American and have spent about a quarter of my life in Japan, I thought it would be interesting to provide students with opportunities to review and explain concepts from their own cultural background knowledge. This is the kind of knowledge people usually take for granted and therefore feel little need to put into speech or writing. After some careful negotiation, the university agreed to my plan. The textbook I selected is a collection of essays written by Japanese students and edited by their teachers.

The book (*The Japanese Mind,* Davies & Ikeno, 2002) covers complex and difficult cultural topics such as *Chimmoku* (silence as part of communication), *Soto Uchi* (group culture: outsiders vs. insiders), *Honne to Tatemae* (expressing personally felt vs. other-oriented opinions), *Ie* (the patriarchal family system), *Bushido* (samurai-inspired way of life characterized by loyalty and honor), *Haragei* (implicit, non-verbal ways of communicating), and *Omiai* (selecting a marriage partner through mediated agreement). The book has sparked a number of controversial reviews, including the observation that many of the views are stereotypical, unexamined cultural concepts. This was a powerful reason to think that students would benefit if they had opportunities to explain their own culture, by drawing on examples from their daily life, and by questioning some of the stereotypical images and assumptions presented in the book under the umbrella of culture. One goal of the class is therefore to help students complicate (wrestle with, create a disturbance in) their tacit understanding of their own culture and then to help them put their understanding (and experience) and interpretation into lines of words.

In order to achieve this goal, I designed a course in which students read chapters in the book, draw on their knowledge of Japanese culture, and then provide tentative answers to questions that foreign residents of Japan or non-Japanese people may have about Japanese culture and language. Quite often, students do not expect that their teacher will ask them questions about their own language and how it represents their culture. Since I have struggled to understand many of these concepts in Japanese over the years, the course turns me into a student, while my students become teachers. This change of roles has given us the opportunity to construct ideas that require both parties to rely on the kind of mutual scaffolding that brings together four elements: (a) background knowledge on the topic; (b) reading about the topic; (c) speaking about the topic; and (d) writing about the topic. In my example of this class, this is the basic sequence we follow, although all elements work together in mutually supportive ways to help students construct lines of words that will express difficult ideas.

The mechanics of the class are as follows. Each week we address a different topic from the book. Very often, I begin the class by directing students' attention to a problem foreign people might have understanding some aspect of Japanese language and culture, or to a situation in which misunderstanding between a Japanese person and a non-Japanese might take place. We then discuss possible reasons as to why such misunderstandings happen. Sometimes I tell students stories about situations in which I have experienced intercultural misunderstanding, and ask them to think about why so many young Japanese often feel unable to provide explanations that go beyond perpetuating a stereotypical view. This initial talk prepares students for the reading and writing they will do next.

Students then read a chapter silently in class. They reread the chapter at home, draft a written response to one of the questions at the end of the chapter, and bring their writing to class. In class, students exchange drafts to read what another student has written and write a comment at the bottom of the sheet. Students can talk together during this activity. A student may work on a piece for three to six weeks, and during that time, he or she may ask several people, including me, to read it and give feedback. At the end of the semester students are required to submit their five best responses (out of twelve chapters), which are in turn read by other students the following year. I encourage this practice so that students have a real (if future) audience for their writing. In this way, class dynamics (exchanging assignments, having pair or small group discussions, working on drafts over several weeks) are intended to encourage students to share stories and viewpoints in speech and writing. In doing this, I hope that they will overcome any fear of writing they may have while also developing confidence in their ability to explain cultural concepts they often take for granted. At the end of the course, in addition to turning in their five revised pieces, students also take a short essay test on a concept from the book which they need to relate to current events. Students are urged to get written feedback from a peer during the last ten minutes of the test. A specific example of some class activities follows.

An Entry Point

After we have made an attempt to explain the topic for the week, we look at the *kanji* (Chinese-origin Japanese characters) that appear along with the English title or in the chapter,[1] and try to explain the concept in simple English. This is usually done in pairs. Students are asked to explain to each other—to the best of their ability—the topic, describe the *kanji* or paraphrase the concept.

At this point, I am acting as a moderator of sorts, telling the class the explanations provided by different groups of students. Often, according to what students have told me, translations in the book are inaccurate because they are too literal and do not convey current pragmatic usage (e.g., the kanji for judo is very poetic, but everyone today understands judo simply as a kind of wrestling). This pooled information creates an opportunity for everyone to see that there are infinite ways of using language and that producing an accurate explanation requires a certain amount of tinkering. We look at the characters and try to describe what their combination means beyond the linguistic level. At this point, we move from explaining the meaning of *kanji* as written language, and begin to analyze it as symbols that teach culture and cultural values. For example, in one chapter that discusses Japanese silence in communication, we analyze the *kanji* for "quiet." It depicts an adult human (大人) read as *otona*, combined with hiragana characters (しい) that suggest "-like." The combination of these characters results in the concept of "quiet." In other words, *otonashii*, 大人しい or adult-like, refers to a person who has attained the ability to control her or his thoughts and does not need to share them in public. Thus, one sign of adulthood might be considered the person's ability to be quiet in social situations in which people are expected to share a similar opinion. Of course, it is a myth that adults are silent

[1]The Davies and Ikeno book, although primarily in English, contains text in both English and Japanese. The Japanese appears in chapter titles, in phrases embedded in the English text, and in a glossary of terms in the back of the book.

and communicate silently, and even that Japanese classrooms are typically silent. Many teachers, both Japanese and non-Japanese, cannot get their students to stop chatting and get on with a lesson. The silence comes when teachers-as-authority-figures ask a student a question in front of classmates that has a right or wrong answer (see McVeigh's 2002 frustration in this regard).

In short, our entry point to the difficult topics in the book involves students in reading, speaking, and writing activities in which they begin by looking at the *kanji* for deeply embedded linguistic-cultural concepts that they tend not to question in their daily lives.

Going through a Chapter

After producing possible interpretations and translations for the *kanji*, we make a map to help us see how the chapter is organized. By outlining the chapter, and seeing the differences in how paragraphs are organized (in English the topic sentence tends to come at the beginning; in Japanese it often is the concluding sentence that carries the message), students gain practice at seeing how English text is organized. As students work in pairs to do this and to begin expressing the central cultural concept from the chapter, I go round the room and ask them to share with me their findings. As I listen to their discussions, I make trips to the board and write the most interesting ideas, in their words, so that the rest of the class can see what each group is talking about. Quite often, students' ideas generate new questions that I write on the board for everyone to see. This is a reminder that our task is to provide other people with tentative (not definite) explanations of cultural concepts they know well but may never have put explicitly into words before.

While students discuss the questions on the board, I continue to walk round the room, listening to their discussions. Most of the time, they speak in Japanese, but occasionally, there are some students who attempt to speak in English. Whenever possible, I try to create bilingual discussions—using both Japanese and English, so that we can maintain the flow of the conversation and feel what it is like to try to put ideas into lines of words—a challenge that exists in both L1 and L2. This is in no way an easy task. We are constantly required to negotiate meaning and construct sentences that will be satisfactory in both languages.

Once the topics and subtopics have been identified, I encourage students to write words that will help them remember the main idea behind each paragraph. Some students choose to write lists, while others write their "key" words either to the right or left side of the text in the book. We then proceed to read the entire chapter. Usually, this is done silently, with the occasional whisper of a student asking a peer about a word that may be new. With the help of the map, combined with the fact that the chapters are short, it is possible for students to finish reading a chapter within 20 minutes. Later, at home, students reread the chapter and draft their responses, which they bring to the next class and share with each other and with me.

Samples of Student Writing

My students are not used to revising their work. But one important idea I tell my students every week is that the process of writing takes time. Just as a chef never says, "I have produced the perfect recipe," or an artist or musician never claims to have attained perfection, I remind students that writing is a process and that we need to engage in what often feels like a struggle with difficult ideas and ways of expressing them. We talk together, and I give them written comments, as do their peers, and all of this written and spoken negotiation takes time. This process itself is inherently motivating. The long process pays off if students are willing to discover how fulfilling it can be. For example, when describing the concept of *Omiai* (selecting a marriage partner), one student took six weeks to express the following ideas on *Omiai* that partially counter the stereotype presented in the book:

> *Omiai* is a special way to meet a partner. To begin the process of *Omiai,* we exchange information by a mediator or a marriage agency. Then we decide to meet that person or not, from his profile and photo. Then, if both persons agree to go on to the next stage, the mediator introduces the couple to each other, probably the meeting along with their parents. Then, they have initial meeting that is called *Omiai.* We wear formal clothes and meet at formal places. During *Omiai,* the couple and their parents have a conversation. After the *Omiai* party, the couple sees each other periodically until they decide to get married or not.
>
> In the book *The Japanese Mind* it says that *Omiai* has many advantages. However, I think some of them are not true. It says that through *Omiai* we can learn about each other in detail. But I think to know each other well we use much time and many conversations. Therefore we cannot know well

> from some document or a short time formal conversation. Japanese formal words are not clear because we don't want to hurt other people's feelings. In initial meeting, we feel nervous and cannot talk like in usual. Besides, it says that Japanese people are busy and do not have time to look for a partner. The book says that *Omiai* helps busy people to find their husband or wife. Certainly some people may be like in this busy situation, however *Omiai* is not an activity like quickly shopping for a partner like the book gives an idea. (Mariko,[2] 2nd year student)

Another student expressed his ideas on the belief that Japanese people can communicate silently, again countering the simple idea presented in the book:

> In *The Japanese Mind*, the author defines that *Haragei* is a way of exchanging feelings and thoughts in an implicit way among the Japanese. I am afraid that we actually do not use it as this meaning. *Haragei* is the name of a technique for conveying our character without relying on gestures or words. In the original meaning, people used *Haragei* as the implicit way of signaling one's intentions. However, for people in my generation, *Haragei* has changed meaning to "relying on the force of one's personality to accomplish something" and we usually use *Haragei* in this sense. (Takehiro, 2nd year student)

In both cases, these students not only revised their English several times in response to comments from peers and me but managed to express complex ideas in ways that went beyond the stereotypes (of self and other) we were all familiar with. The description of these class activities demonstrates some ways that my students and I engage with difficult, culturally embedded ideas and begin to counter some of the common stereotypes about Japanese culture. Spoken and written language, both English and Japanese, work together to help students make sustained efforts to communicate with me and with each other about topics that are relevant to them. These sustained efforts would not be possible without the mutual scaffolding of risk-free speech and writing in two languages, or in a classroom that focuses only on isolated skills of speaking or writing. My students come to understand their own culture in more complex ways, and help me to understand it and the changes it is undergoing, as well.

---

[2]All names used in this chapter are pseudonyms.

Christine's Graduate Language Teacher Education Class

I regularly teach master's and doctoral students in language teacher education who are, or will be, teaching EFL students in Japan. I suppose I could keep their lives simple and help them learn recipes for teaching and research, but my goal instead is to engage them in complex research-related topics through discussion and writing.

Recently, in preparing to teach a doctoral course in qualitative inquiry at Temple University's Japan campus, I found myself recycling both concepts and even some readings from my own doctoral experience many years before. I had taken a year-long qualitative inquiry course early in my doctoral experience and found then that some of the readings and concepts were simply beyond me. Most of the other students were well into their coursework at the time and seemed to participate confidently in class discussions and to write without difficulty (of course, these were perceptions on the part of an intimidated newcomer to the field; in actuality, I think many others besides me were silent). I believe as well that some of those students belonged to study groups, which met regularly to discuss difficult readings and to put their evolving understandings into words. I did not have a study group. Moreover, we were not required to write reading response journals. As a result, much of what I read did not get processed regularly into speech and writing. The knowledge remained titillating but superficial, not embodied. I did end up five years later, however, writing a qualitative dissertation and after graduating conducted several qualitative research projects. The learning process has been long but rewarding.

For the course I was teaching at the time we drafted this essay, "Issues and Approaches in Qualitative Inquiry," I hoped to provide students (a comfortable cohort of working teachers, Japanese and non-Japanese, aged about 30 to 60) with a different experience from the one I had had. I also knew that the difficult ideas, concepts, and terminology would need to be recycled many times over the students' years in the doctoral program, so my goals for "embodiment" were modest. I opted not to use a textbook, which might have simplified concepts, approaches, and methods, but rather to put together a course reading packet. I knew that it would include readings that would challenge the students, all bright, but relative newcomers to complex issues in qualitative inquiry. Most had had just one introductory course. The readings also challenged (continue to challenge) me, and I had had some experience with qualitative inquiry before. They were packed with philosophical underpinnings of qualitative inquiry, obscure jargon (some in German), ambiguous and overlapping definitions, contested views, and in some cases writing styles that would not win any prizes in an essay contest. They covered topics such as the debates from some years ago on the "interpretive turn" in the social sciences, criteria for evaluating qualitative work, theoretical frameworks, and issues of writing and representation of self and others in research reports. These subtopics were both inherently difficult and interesting for me, and were ones I wished, along with the students, to learn more about. I thus represented myself as a co-learner who did not have all the answers and worked equally hard at trying to understand and represent in my own words the complex issues we were reading about.

The main difference between this class and some of the students' other graduate classes was that there were no lectures, no quizzes, no major final paper, and no tests, even though I had to give a grade at the end of the term. I assessed work through verbal feedback and a record of work completed. The main oral work of the class consisted of small group discussion of readings in which I participated as a circulating eavesdropper and occasional commenter and guide, and whole group sharing of issues brought up in the small groups. I provided reading guides for each set of readings, with space for students to make notes to use during their class discussions. There were also two short presentations per student on extra readings they had done.

The main written work consisted of three ungraded reading reaction papers due at regular intervals throughout the semester. For these papers, students chose several of the assigned readings to respond to and selected their own topic and title. I encouraged students to experiment in their writing in these reaction papers, which some did with gusto. They could rant and rave if they wished, write creatively, and mix conversational and formal styles. I responded in writing (by hand or electronically) and peers responded at least once. There was also a final short paper that asked students to respond to several readings of their own choice, in conjunction with their developing research interests and the themes of the course. We also used the white board as needed for notes and diagrams and email throughout the term. In other words, various kinds of spoken and written language at different levels of complexity and formality interacted and dovetailed throughout the semester to help students, and me, process and communicate difficult ideas. Speech and writing worked together as we assisted each other in transforming difficult, abstract ideas into lines of words that were beginning to feel embodied. These activities are not unusual, of course. I was simply trying to think about them in new ways.

In their reaction papers, written after many discussions on the difficult readings, some students expressed frustration, and others mentioned the changes they were undergoing. Oliver, a student from the United States, for example, like some of the other students, had little sympathy for the philosophical debates we encountered in the readings, but this did not stop him from dealing with the difficult questions:

> After reading this week's articles, my lack of philosophical reasoning skills quickly became apparent. My brain seems to prefer knowledge in small manageable chunks with a direct connection to practical experience, while I have difficulty grasping the larger abstract issues. Perhaps as a result, resolving existential issues like those raised in the Smith and Deemer (Smith & Deemer, 2000) article, have been a low priority for me. From my, albeit limited, experience, it seems like philosophical issues rarely get settled, and debate rages for generations (if not longer) with little consensus on the answers that are offered. I wonder if questions like *what is truth?* or *what is reality?* are any closer to being settled now than when they were debated by classical Greek philosophers thousands of years ago. And, to be honest, it seems the writers of what I've read have little interest in ending the discussion. I'm specifically thinking about overuse of unnecessary jargon, disagreement over trivial points, and failure to come together when viewpoints seem related... it seems that some relish the opportunity to pontificate from their pulpit. (Oliver, Reaction Paper 2)

In the next example, Lynne K. (an American of Japanese heritage who had lived in Japan for 30 years) responds creatively to several articles on writing and self-representation by writing a letter to sociologist Laurel Richardson for her third reaction paper:

> Dear Laurel (if I may),
> I don't know if it is appropriate to write fan letters to famous academics, but I have been inspired to do so. I cannot claim to be well-versed in your works, having read only a few articles these past few months, but I can say without a doubt that my whole outlook on what research and writing are has undergone a tremendous change, thanks to you. To tell you the truth, I had difficulty writing a paper and had a hunch that by writing this letter, somehow I would be able to articulate my thoughts. I would like to share with you how I have been shaped by writing and what I hope to accomplish with future writing projects. (Lynne K., Reaction Paper 3)

Another student who (like others) was trying to figure out where to situate his beliefs about knowledge and reality, said after the first month:

> Before doing the reading for our class, I suppose I might have described myself as a naïve realist (a term I thought I had invented until I noticed it on page 20 of Guba). Reading the assigned articles, as well as doing some additional reading on this question on the internet and participating in our class discussions, has helped me start to develop a more nuanced position. (Brett V, Reaction Paper 1)

Part of me wishes I could say that by the end of the term, we had all reached some closure on some of the difficult issues in qualitative inquiry. But closure would have shut off the discussion, which I knew needed to continue, perhaps indefinitely. I was happily struck by the (re)discovery that I continue to expand my own understanding of difficult ideas. So even though most of us felt frustrated that we had not been able to resolve any of the dilemmas that were brought up in the readings, many students expressed in their reaction papers, in email, and in person how they were changing and expanding intellectually as a result of the mutually supportive literacy practices we engaged in. Their eyes were being opened to new possibilities for themselves in research and writing. They, and I, used speech and writing to learn how better to express difficult, nonlinear ideas in more lines of words. The efforts brought us all closer together as a group. Connections were being forged between me and the students, and solidified among this student cohort, connections that I hope will continue in the coming years of students' doctoral study.

Final Thoughts

We continue to believe that transforming difficult ideas into spoken and written language is one of the most important activities we can do in a language class. It is language, after all, that connects one human being with another. We need more of these personal connections in our increasingly technological world. How all of us manage to do these transformations requires playing with thought and language, revising, replaying ideas in the presence of others, perhaps representing ideas graphically as well as linguistically, repeating many versions of the original idea until bits and pieces begin to find their way onto paper or screen, or into speech. In this way, we become deeply familiar with the original vision even as it transforms itself, and thus may become less fearful about it. Like the artist, writer, or piano student who must constantly work at matching a vision to a product without fear of criticism (Bayles & Orland, 1993), both the second language student and the graduate language education student can come to embrace the challenge of transforming a complex vision into lines of words. But in order to do this in the language class and the language teacher education class, teachers need to construct risk-free classroom environments in which topics connect to students' lives and interests and in which students and teachers support each other in the face of the inevitable frustration of no-fixed-answer classroom practices. Teachers also need to listen more, to transmit information and test less, to invest more in the interactive processes in the classroom, and perhaps worry less about the final product (e.g., a presentation, a final paper).

We are suggesting that teachers in both ESL-EFL classes and language teacher education classes conceptualize their spoken and written explorations of difficult ideas as social practices (Gee, 2006), and that teachers become co-learners with students in a joint project of engaging with difficulty. The distinction between teacher as knower and student as learner thus becomes blurred. It may make little sense, in other words, to focus on speaking and writing per se in classes where we hope to challenge students with difficult ideas, but to follow Gee's (2006) advice: "Because speech and writing so often go together and because both trade on contextual interactions for interpretation, it is often better to study *social practices* that include both writing and speech...." (p. 155, italics in original). In our classes, we tried to engage students in the practices of thinking about and expressing difficult ideas by means of different kinds of literacy activities (speaking, writing, reading) throughout a term. We could not identify any simple or linear relationship between speaking and writing in pursuit of this goal, even though in both of our classes, important works were pieces of writing. And there were no easy answers; because of this, there were always reasons to maintain efforts at communicating.

Equally important, we believe that teachers themselves can become models, for students, of complex thinkers who are engaged in the same kind of struggle. Teachers are thus viewed by students as fellow sojourners on journeys that are inherently interesting and challenging; students help us learn, as we help them do so. As Howard Gardner (1999, p. 134) noted, "Students take note when teachers are themselves continuing to learn, and when they appear to be excited by new discoveries." Together with students, teachers can thus experiment with what we see as an extraordinary human accomplishment, that of putting difficult multidimensional ideas into lines of words.

REFERENCES

Bayles, D., & Orland, T. (1993). *Art and fear: Observations on the perils and rewards of artmaking.* Santa Cruz, CA: The Image Continuum.

Belcher, D., & Hirvela, A. (2005). Writing the qualitative dissertation: What motivates and sustains commitment to a fuzzy genre? *Journal of English for Academic Purposes, 4(3),* 187–205.

Cope, B., & Kalantzis, M. (Eds.). (2000). *Multiliteracies: Literacy learning and the design of social futures.* London: Routledge.

Csikszentmihalyi, M. (1975/2000). *Beyond boredom and anxiety: Experiencing flow in work and play.* San Francisco: Jossey-Bass.

———. (1997). *Finding flow: The psychology of engagement with everyday life.* New York: Basic Books.

Davies, R. J., & Ikeno, O. (2002). *The Japanese mind: Understanding contemporary Japanese culture.* Boston: Tuttle Publishing.

Eisner, E. W. (1997). The promise and perils of alternative forms of data representation. *Educational Researcher, 26*(6), 4–10.

Gardner, H. (1999). *The disciplined mind: Beyond facts and standardized tests, the K–12 education that every child deserves.* New York: Penguin Books.

Gee, J. P. (2004). *Situated language and learning: A critique of traditional schooling.* London: Routledge.

———. (2006). Oral discourse in a world of literacy. *Research in the Teaching of English, 41*(2), 153–159.

Kress, G. (2000). Multimodality. In B. Cope & M. Kalantzis (Eds.), *Multiliteracies: Literacy learning and the design of social futures* (pp. 182–202). London: Routledge.

———. (2003). *Literacy in the new media age.* London: Routledge.

Lantolf, J. P., & Thorne, S. L. (2006). *Sociocultural theory and the genesis of second language development.* Oxford, UK: Oxford University Press.

Linde, C. (1993). *Life stories: The creation of coherence.* New York: Oxford University Press.

Matsumoto, D. (2002). *The New Japan: Debunking seven cultural stereotypes.* Yarmouth, ME: Intercultural Press.

McCourt, F. (2005). *Teacher man.* New York: Scribner.

McCrostie, J. (2006). Why are universities abandoning English teaching for TOEIC training? *On Cue, 14*(2), 30–32.

McVeigh, B. (2002). *The myth of Japanese higher education.* New York: M. E. Sharpe.

Noddings, N. (2006). *Critical lessons: What our schools should teach.* New York: Cambridge University Press.

Postman, N. (1988). *Conscientious objections: Stirring up trouble about language, technology, and education.* New York: Vintage Books.

Postman, N., & Weingartner, C. (1969). *Teaching as a subversive activity.* New York: Dell Publishing Co.

Prior, P. A. (1998). *Writing/disciplinarity: A sociohistoric account of literate activity in the academy.* Mahwah, NJ: Lawrence Erlbaum.

Salvatori, M. R., & Donahue, P. (2005). *The elements (and pleasures) of difficulty.* New York: Pearson Longman.

Weissberg, R. (2006). *Connecting speaking & writing in second language writing instruction.* Ann Arbor: University of Michigan Press.

6

An Investigation of Relationships between Spoken and Written Academic English: Lexical Bundles in the AWL and in MICASE

LUCY PICKERING AND PATRICIA BYRD

Abstract

The relationship between the language that students read in preparation for their classes and then hear in the classroom is complex. Not only does spoken academic language prioritize a different set of expressions than its written counterpart, even technical terms must be understood as they are represented by acoustic characteristics in the speech stream rather than as written forms. In this chapter, we use two corpora of academic English, the Michigan Corpus of Spoken Academic English (Simpson-Vlach, & Leicher 2006) and the Academic Word List (Coxhead, 2000) to examine some of these differences, specifically as they apply to four-word lexical bundles. In a comparison of the most frequently occurring bundles in each corpus, we propose that crucial differences in the structural and functional characteristics of bundles in each register suggest that one system of categorization is not sufficiently explanatory for both written and spoken academic discourse. A lack of recognition of the different discourse cues that prevail in a spoken versus written modality (i.e., intonation structure) can obscure crucial communicative differences between spoken and written realizations of the same (or similar) phrases and the variety of pedagogical purposes that they may perform. We address a number of important pedagogical implications that arise from our analysis and suggest that students will benefit from specific instruction on how to mediate between parallel written and spoken forms.

Connecting What Students Read to What They Hear in Class

In a reading assignment from a college or university textbook, students are likely to find the word *percent* used in sentences such as the following from the corpus created for the Academic Word List (AWL) (Coxhead, 2000)[1]:

> Rural dwellers comprised twenty percent of the population in 1954, dropping to sixteen percent in 1967. . . .

When students are in class listening to a university instructor, the same word is more likely to be heard in a statement like the following example from the Michigan Corpus of Academic Spoken English (MICASE):

> . . . however this compound uh binds to the extent of ninety-nine-point-eight percent, uh ninety-nine-point-five percent . . .

While the core meaning of *percent* remains essentially the same in both contexts, the use of the word in writing and speaking involves substantial differences that could be confusing for students as they attempt to connect their reading with what they hear in class.

The spoken data, for example, includes a number of disfluencies; in addition, *percent* is unstressed or deaccented by the speaker in these environments as it is assumed that the listener understands that this word rather than any other will be selected based on the context of the interaction (Brazil, 1997). In academic tasks in which students are working with their peers, the discourse context may become even more complex for the NNS listener. The following example from the MICASE corpus is replete with interactional discourse markers such as *like* or *you know what I mean* that make it increasingly difficult to follow the progression of the idea:

> Did you say that this, like from your research like, it was credited to Solomon? because like, when he wrote a lot of this stuff it was, after, like his, like he had turned away from God and come back, and it seems like... i don't know i just had this funny thought that, like, like if he had that kind of experience, like, if it was a man writing this it would be more likely to be about, like the actual, like

[1]We are grateful to Averil Coxhead for providing data from the AWL corpus in a format that was useable for our research and at the same time maintained the copyright security that she built into her corpus.

> less than metaphorical sense. you know like he was using all these metaphors to describe, like sexual relations but, it's probably less likely that, it was like, him thinking about this is God's union with Israel. you know what i mean?

Nattinger and DeCarrico (1992) highlight this contrast in the presentation of academic registers and note that

> texts for second language learners, especially writing and reading texts, usually provide more opportunity for learning the discourse markers necessary for the comprehension of written discourse. What is lacking is this same opportunity for learning spoken discourse markers. Undoubtedly, this gap occurs because our second language research has thus far not provided us with enough information concerning these structures. (p. 80)

To learn more about the connections between the academic language that students read in assigned texts to prepare for their classes and the spoken version of academic English that students hear from their instructors and peers in class, we investigated the most commonly used four-word lexical bundles that appear in AWL and in MICASE and their different realizations in speaking and writing.

Lexical bundles are defined by Cortes (2004) as a "sequence of three or more words that co-occur frequently in a particular register" (p. 397) and include sets such as *I don't know why* or *in the case of*. Biber and Conrad (1999) propose that the difference between lexical bundles and other lexical groupings such as "lexical phrases," "formulas," or "prefabricated units" is that these are complete structural units or fixed expressions, whereas lexical bundles tend not to be complete structural units. This structural difference also distinguishes the investigation of lexical bundles from previous studies of lexical phrases in the academic register (Flowerdew & Tauroza, 1995; Nattinger & DeCarrico, 1992; Shaw, 1994). Before moving to the analysis of the corpus data, we begin with a discussion of the motivations behind our selection of particular corpora and some of the challenges that working with these corpora bring to researchers.

Working with AWL and MICASE

Selection and Use of AWL and MICASE

For this project we wanted to use two corpora of academic English: one of written academic English and the other of spoken academic English. Research using corpus linguistic methods is hampered by the lack of public access to many of the corpora that are used in published research. Some corpora such as the *Longman Spoken and Written English* corpus (used in Biber, Johansson, Leech, Conrad, & Finegan, 1999) or the TOEFL® 2000 Spoken and Written Academic Language (T2K-SWAL) Corpus (used in Biber, Conrad, Reppen, Byrd, & Helt, 2002) are privately owned or controlled with access limited to a few scholars working on projects sanctioned by the owner of the corpus. Other corpora such as the Bank of English or the British National Corpus are available for researchers who can afford to pay subscription fees for access or for copies provided on CDs or for copies downloaded from the Internet. Still other corpora are developed by researchers for their own purposes with access restricted either because copyright permissions limit who can use the materials or copyright permission has not been sought and the developer quite reasonably does not want to take chances with legal results from sharing a corpus with somewhat shaky legal standing. Fortunately, some institutions and government agencies have moved ahead with the development of high-quality corpora that are freely and easily available for all scholars who can access the Internet. Among these is the MICASE, an excellent resource for research into academic English not just because it has been made freely available by the University of Michigan on the Internet, but because it provides transcripts of spoken academic English in addition to some sound files. The MICASE corpus comprises 190 hours (approximately 1.7 million words) of academic speech from 152 speech events at the University of Michigan (Simpson-Vlach & Leicher, 2006). A broad sample of the kinds of speech that occur in academic settings is represented including classroom events (small and large lectures, lab and discussion sections, student presentations) and non-classroom events (advising sessions, office hours, dissertation defenses, colloquia). We wanted to use MICASE because of its free public access for other researchers who might want to follow up on this current study; however, we ourselves worked both with the MICASE website and with transcripts and sound files on CD-ROM that had been purchased by our department for faculty and student research.[2]

Working with the AWL Corpus

Selection of a corpus of written academic English was more challenging because we wanted data that would be widely accessible to other researchers. Eventually, we were able to get data from the corpus created by Coxhead

[2]We thank Dr. Gayle Nelson, Chair of the Department of Applied Linguistics & ESL at Georgia State University, for her support of our research through purchase of the MICASE database and the WM Recorder software.

to develop the AWL. Although access to that corpus is highly restricted, we wanted to use that source because the AWL has become widely used both in teaching materials and in research. Copyright restrictions meant that we could not see the entire AWL corpus, but we were able to get lexical bundle data and concordance lines of adequate but limited length. Similar access to the AWL will be made available to other researchers through the publication of a study of collocations and lexical bundles in the AWL (Coxhead, Bunting, Byrd, & Moran, forthcoming).

Working with MICASE

Written transcripts corresponding to all 152 speech events comprising the corpus are freely available at an online interface, *http://micase.umdl.umich.edu/m/micase*; however, the written transcriptions and sound files are accessed independently. Seventy sound files representing a portion of the written transcripts are freely available online at *www.lsa.umich.edu/eli/micase.* A further 61 sound files may be purchased from the University of Michigan on CD-ROM, and approximately 21 speech events are unavailable as sound files. This distribution of sound files between CD-ROMs and streaming audio files (or unavailable data) makes research focused on the speech data a somewhat onerous and time-consuming process. Once a search has been undertaken within the written transcription files and the needed transcript(s) identified, the researcher must then search through both the CD-ROM lists and online streaming files list to find out if the accompanying sound file is obtainable (as it may be one of the unavailable sound files) and if so, from where.

Additional challenges became apparent when we subjected specific clips of the sound files to instrumental measurement using a Kay Pentax Model 4300b Computerized Speech Laboratory (CSL) in order to determine the acoustic correlates (specifically pitch or fundamental frequency traces) of targeted words or bundles. The MICASE sound files were recorded using a digital audiotape recorder (DAT) with external microphones; hence, the quality of each recording varies depending on the amount of external noise in the room (chairs scraping, students chatting, equipment being moved, and so on). In order to clip portions of the online streaming files, we used WM Recorder, a software that captured the streaming files and converted them into .wav files. Sound clips from the CD recordings were exported in .wav format using Apple Quicktime. Sound files were then analyzed by the CSL for pitch. Where possible depending on sound quality, all data was subjected to both types of auditory and instrumental analysis.

Four-Word Lexical Bundles in AWL and MICASE

Work by Douglas Biber and his colleagues (Biber, Conrad, & Cortes, 2004) provides a solid description of the frequency of lexical bundles in written and spoken registers. In their comparisons of how these bundles operate in academic prose and conversations, bundles are classified structurally and functionally. Consistent differences are found between registers, most notably a tendency in conversation toward interactional or stance-related bundles such as *I don't know whether, I'll tell you what, you might as well,* as opposed to an inclination toward referential expressions with high transactional value in academic prose *(in the form of, in the case of, the way in which),* suggesting that "bundles have important discourse functions that fit the context and purposes of the registers in which they are common" (p. 13).

Biber, Conrad, & Cortes (2004) focus exclusively on academic discourse and find a similar division of lexical bundles by spoken and written register despite the higher informational load carried by spoken teaching discourse as opposed to conversation. They describe teaching discourse as "an intermediate register" containing both expressions of "personal concerns and interactions" and statements demonstrating the prioritizing of "informational goals" (p. 374). Thus, in our analysis we anticipated similar findings regarding the structure and function of lexical bundles in the AWL and MICASE corpora.

Although frequency counts of transcribed speech are the established measure employed to demonstrate the differences between modalities, it is the case that spoken discourse is understood by listeners as a series of acoustic signals, and this creates the potential for overlooking an essential characteristic of spoken corpora if the acoustic realizations of these lexical groupings are ignored. By analyzing only the written transcripts of spoken data, we fail to consider a crucial aspect of the differences between the presentation of language in spoken and written academic registers that L2 learners will have to contend with. It is well established that features of intonation and stress form a natural link between linguistic and sociolinguistic aspects of the language as they are paramount in both communicating a speaker's perception of the relative importance of the information load carried by different elements of the utterance in discourse contexts and in expressing relationships between discourse participants (Brazil, 1997; Crystal, 1969; Gumperz, 1982; Halliday, 1967; Tench, 1996; Williams, 1986). In inner-circle varieties of English (i.e., North American, British, Canadian, Australian, and New Zealand English), it is commonly understood that important items are distinguished from surrounding discourse by increased prominence, or pitch excursions and contour shapes, or tones, such as the common pedagogical distinction made between the rising tone at the end of yes-no questions (Are you ➚LEAVing?) and the falling tone at the end of wh- questions (Where are you ➘GOing?)

A typical example of how prominence is realized in discourse is shown, in which the contrasts between *acidity* and *alkalinity*, *lower* and *higher*, and *acid* and *base* are emphasized by clearly perceptible pitch peaks indicated in CAPS.

> We use the pH meter to MEAsure the aCIdity or ALkalinity of COMpounds/ if the pH value is LOwer than SEven then it's an ACid/ if the value is LARger than SEven then it's a BASE/ (Levis & Pickering, 2004)

Conversely, information that the speaker assumes to be within the hearer's current understanding may be "deaccented" (Wennerstrom, 1997, 2001)—that is, deliberately uttered low in the speaker's pitch range:

> '...for the BIcycle in the U.S. versus the $_{\text{BIcycle}}$ in CHIna...'
> In this utterance, the word *bicycle* is first introduced with a high accent, but in the second intonational phrase it has a low accent because it is already assumed to be in the hearers' consciousness (2001: 38)

Such cases of prosodic saliency within a specific discourse context are described by Brazil (1997). In his model of discourse intonation, Brazil proposes that the way in which syllables are assigned or selected for prominence rests on the pragmatic intentions of the speaker. The paradigm consists of what possible choices could appear in each of the syntagmatic slots of the utterance based on both the constraints of the language system (the general paradigm) and on the non-linguistic situation or the situated context of the interaction (the existential paradigm). For example, given a potential tone unit such as "a parcel of books lay on the table" at least two possible prominence selections could be made:

a. A parcel of BOOKS lay on the Table
b. A PARcel of books lay on the TAble

In (a) the speaker presents a prominent choice of "BOOKS" as opposed to perhaps flowers or cups and makes a similar prominence choice regarding the location—that is, on the table as opposed to on the floor or on the chair. The choice of prominence on both syllables projects a situated context in which both these pieces of information are unrecoverable either from prior interaction or from constraints within the language system. Equally, by choosing not to make prominent certain other words in the unit, the speaker assumes that no choice needs to be made for listener comprehension. This assumption may be based on linguistic or non-linguistic factors. For example, a choice of "box" of books (another possibility in the paradigm) can be considered synonymous with the choice of "parcel," and books can be assumed to "lay" on a table as opposed to "stand up." In terms of linguistic factors, typical constraints on possible choices in the language system apply to the nonprominent function words such as *of* and *on,* which are predetermined by the language system or content words that have already been negotiated (e.g., A: Was the book there? B: There was a PARcel of books there).

Choices of prominence also frequently reflect one of the numerous examples of conventionalized intonational idioms or routinized lexical phrases that currently operate in the language and that speakers believe their hearer(s) will be familiar with (Ashby & Ashby, 1994). An example of how a speaker's use of stress reflects his or her understanding of idiomatic patterns is demonstrated using prosodic realizations of percent taken from the MICASE corpus:

a. FIFty NINE per CENT
b. Can we ABsolutely a HUNdred percent say this is how it HAppened.

In (a) the speaker selects "perCENT" for prominence that distinguishes it from other possible choices such as "eighty cases" or "eighty times." Figure 6.1 shows the pitch peak [or fundamental frequency (FO)] exercursion associated with this syllable. In contrast, in (b) *percent* appears as part of an idiomatic phrase that the speaker treats as understood and realizes as non-salient, as shown in Figure 6.2. Similar prosodic realizations of *percent* occurred with "a HUNdred percent CHANCE of SUCcess" and "a HUNdred percent guaranTEE."

Non-linguistic factors affecting choice of prominence are multifarious and range from immediate discourse context (e.g., an item being currently within view of the hearer) to assumed cultural or situational knowledge. Brazil (1997) notes for example that in certain expressions such as "SAKS 5th AVEnue" and "BOTtle of johnnie WALker" alternatives to the nonprominent "5th" and "johnnie" "scarcely come to mind," and that these examples "demonstrate how conversationalists may rely on shared understandings that either have a very wide or very circumscribed currency" (pp. 24–25).

Figure 6.1
FO reading of a prominent realization of *percent* from the MICASE corpus

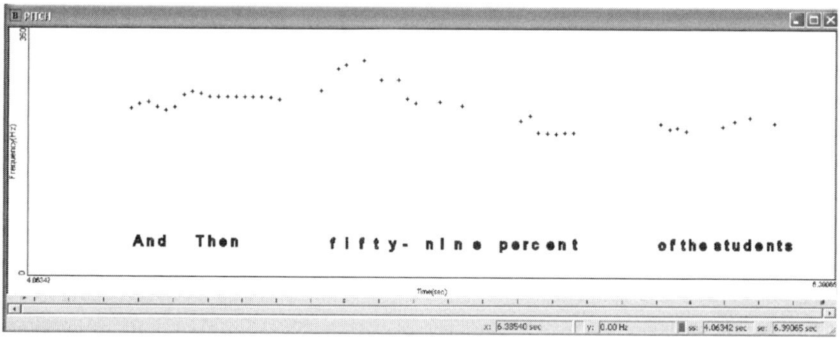

Figure 6.2
FO reading of a non-prominent realization of *percent* from the MICASE corpus

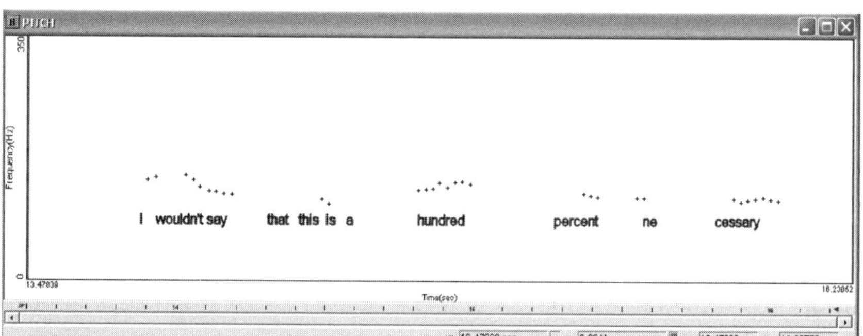

Additional examples of this kind of culturally assumed knowledge influencing choice of prominence include "SINgle white FEmale" and "LARGE metropolitan Area."

Within his discourse intonation model, Brazil also investigates the communicative function of tone or contour shape.[3] Using the principle of convergence, we can describe the social and informational significance of rising and

[3]We only discuss the parts of Brazil's comprehensive discourse intonation model that are directly relevant to the analysis we report here. We do not believe that this distorts the foundational tenets of the model in any way; however, we refer the reader to the complete account of the model as it is presented in Brazil (1997).

falling contour shapes as the result of the speaker's assumptions regarding the current knowledge state of the hearer and the speaker's desire to project shared, common ground. Tone choice indicates the common ground between speakers in the following way: Falling tones project a speaker's assumption that the information is a new assertion and unrecoverable from the prior context, whereas rising tones project the assumption that the information is part of a shared background and is recoverable for the hearer from the prior discourse or assumed common knowledge. The following example, taken from Pickering (2001), demonstrates how this might be used in a teaching context. The teacher in this chemistry laboratory lecture chooses to "remind" students of the results of a flame test that they conducted a few weeks earlier using rising tones to emphasize the shared knowledge:

> //you remember that potassium was ➚PURple// . . . and the third possibility is that there be no color at ➚ALL//

Speakers make certain tone choices depending on the context they wish to project. The teacher could equally have selected falling tone choices and projected a context in which he was "telling" them again.

> //you remember that potassium was ➘PURple//...and the third possibility is that there be no color at ➘ALL//

The *deictic* function of the rising tone (Nevalainen, 1992) has high pragmatic significance in that it can be used to overtly signal solidarity (Pickering, 1999) and to avoid the appearance of direct contradiction (Hewings, 1995).

While we can presume that these choices are interpreted effortlessly by native speaking participants based on their shared sociocultural and linguistic experience, it is reasonable to assume that for non-native listeners without this background many of these choices will present a challenge. This is particularly the case as traditional EFL/ESL instruction focuses primarily on individual items and far less on the "phraseological character" of natural language (Cheng, 2006). Moreover, both teaching and research rarely focus on the spoken realization of any of these expressions.

Biber (2006) acknowledges the contribution of "paralinguistic marking" under which he subsumes pitch as well as gesture, body language, and facial expressions. However, he does not investigate it further in this study of university language. Prosodic characteristics and the choice of prominence or non-prominence on specific items are prioritized in Lindemann and Mauranen (2001). They focus on the word *just* as it functions in a portion of the MICASE corpus. In their consideration of the phonetic shape of the word, including its prominence characteristics, the researchers found that when used as a "mitigator," *just* was generally realized as non-prominent, whereas when it operated as either an "emphasizer" or "particularizer," it was generally prominent, although there was some considerable overlap. Based on an informal study conducted by Lindemann and Mauranen (2001) to investigate the possibility of pragmatic misinterpretation by non-native listeners based on prominence patterns, they suggest that "in terms of teaching non-native speakers, this indicates a greater need to give attention to what might appear at first sight to be trivial matters (such as the phonetic form of *just*) in efforts to better prepare nonnative students for their socio-academic roles in USA universities" (p. 473).

Most recently, Warren (2006) specifically addresses prominence patterns in the Hong Kong Corpus of Spoken English, approximately half of which (one million words) has been prosodically transcribed. Also using Brazil's (1997) discourse intonation model, Warren traces lexical cohesive chains (Hoey, 1991) in job placement interviews (216 minutes of spoken data) and finds that prominence patterns are guided by what speakers perceive to be "situationally informative" (p. 311). In other words, prominence choices occur in response to local context and not as an intrinsic property of the word, a finding that supports Brazil's contention that prominence is speaker-selected and responsive to the immediate context of the interaction.

It seems clear then that non-native listeners will be at a considerable disadvantage when transferring information that they see on the page to comparable information that they hear. This obstacle may be even harder to overcome if, as Lindemann and Mauranen (2001) suggest, non-native listeners tend to focus on the lexical elements of the utterance and have difficulty integrating phonetic cues.

Procedure

Following Biber, Conrad, & Cortes (2004) and Cortes (2004), we limited our search to four-word lexical bundles and focused on the most frequently occurring lexical sequences of that length. The Wordlist tool from Wordsmith Tools 4.0 was used to develop lists of recurring four-word phrases: First, indexes were created with Wordlist for the complete MICASE and AWL corpora. These indexes were then used to search for four-word clusters[4] that were repeated

[4]The term *cluster* in Wordsmith Tools 4.0 corresponds to the *lexical bundle* used by Biber and his colleagues.

at least five times in the corpora. This approach provides data about lexical bundles that are characteristic of an entire corpus.[5] Various cut-off points have been used in the published literature on lexical bundles, based on the size of the corpora being analyzed. Generally, the larger a corpus, the more bundles that will be found, giving the researcher the ability to focus on highly frequent phrases at higher cut-off points. That is, there are no established standards for these cut-off points other than the general rule-of-thumb that the more frequent a phrase is, the more important it is for the corpus being studied. The usual practice is to norm the counts based on the appearance of clusters per million words. This norming makes it possible to compare the lexical bundles in corpora of different sizes like the AWL (3.8 million words) and the MICASE (1.7 million words). Because a cut-off of 10 per million words has been adopted in other published studies, we used that frequency for our basic standard and disregarded clusters that were repeated fewer times in the data.[6] Lexical bundles that involved proper nouns, such as *Victoria University of Wellington, the House of Lords,* or *the University of Michigan,* were left out of consideration, as were bundles that reflected special coding features of a corpus. Through this process of selection and elimination, we analyzed a total of 297 lexical bundles in AWL and 707 bundles in MICASE. This difference in numbers between the two registers accords with Biber, Conrad, & Cortes (2004) who found a much higher frequency of lexical bundles in classroom discourse as compared to written academic texts. Following previous work investigating lexical bundles in academic discourse, bundles in each corpus were classified by their structural and functional characteristics (Biber, 2006; Biber, Conrad, & Cortes, 2003; Biber, Conrad, & Cortes, 2004). In each case, because the number of cases of lexical bundles was so different between the two corpora, categories are shown as a percentage of the total.

Structural Characteristics

Studies of academic prose repeatedly report the prominence of long, complex noun phrases as the defining characteristic of such writing (e.g., Biber, 1988). Thus, the use of noun phrase fragments in the AWL as shown in Table 6.1 replicates previous studies as does the importance of prepositional phrase fragments since these are often post-nominal modifiers rather than

---

[5]Wordsmith Tools 4.0 can also create clusters from the Concord tool. These clusters focus on the behavior of particular words and phrases rather than on the linguistic characteristics of a corpus as a whole.

[6]Complete lists of clusters examined for the study are available from the authors.

Table 6.1
Structural Characteristics of Lexical Bundles in AWL and MICASE

	% Type 1 Verb Phrase Fragments	% Type 2 Dependent Clause Fragments	% Type 3 Noun Phrase & Prepositional Phrase Fragments
AWL	21	6	73
MICASE	54	20	26

free-standing adverbials. The contrast between the use of verb phrases in MICASE and in AWL accords with previous studies of these two types of academic communication: spoken academic communication involves both the verb-centric style of conversational English and the noun-centric style of academic writing in English. In addition to confirming the parallelism of these two corpora with other corpora and other reports of discourse analyses, this information reminds us strongly of the importance of selecting an appropriate corpus as the basis for discourse studies (see Baker, 2006, for a useful discussion of these issues).

Functional Characteristics

Overall results regarding the functional characteristics of lexical bundles are consistent with previous research into university language (Biber, 2006; Cortes, 2004). As shown in Table 6.2, in the AWL, referential bundles far outweigh any other functional type; in contrast, stance and interaction bundles, lexical groupings that express attitude or perform social functions in the discourse, account for a much larger proportion of lexical bundles in the MICASE corpus. In addition to the manifest difference in percentages in numbers of stance bundles, they were also qualitatively very different between the two modalities. Using the functional taxonomy developed in Biber, Conrad, & Cortes (2003, 2004) and Biber (2006), we find that in AWL, stance bundles appear as impersonal modality or attitudinal markers; typical examples are *is likely to be, it is possible to, should be able to, more likely to be, it may be that, would have to be.* By contrast, in MICASE the majority of these bundles appear as personal markers such as *I don't know what, oh I don't know, I think it was, you don't have to.* In this sense, the MICASE lexical bundles correspond more closely with lexical bundles found in conversation than in academic prose (Biber & Conrad, 1999). It is noteworthy that the functional category of text organizers comprises a similar percentage of the overall number of

Table 6.2

Functional Characteristics of Lexical Bundles in AWL and MICASE

	% Referential Bundles	% Stance & Interactional Bundles	% Text Organizers
AWL	72	17	11
MICASE	35	48	17

bundles found in AWL and MICASE. It is the case that university discourse has a high informational load regardless of modality and both teachers and textbook writers presumably strive to impose a clear organizational structure on that information using, in some part, text organizers.

In order to examine the issues of the different functions performed by lexical bundles and their prosodic realizations in spoken discourse, we present sample analyses of four of the most frequent lexical bundles to appear in MICASE (compared with use of each phrase in AWL): (a) *at the same time, (b) at the end of*; (c) *I don't know I*, and (d) *you know what I*. In Biber, Conrad, & Cortes (2004), both *at the same time* and *at the end of* are classified as referential expressions. However, Biber (2006) recategorizes *at the same time* as a text organizer, and in this study, we look at the text organizing function of *at the end of*. These variations in analysis are one of the problematic aspects presented to the researcher when attempting to implement a system of functional categories. While Biber, Conrad, & Cortes (2004) acknowledge the possible problem of categorizing multifunctional bundles by addressing issues such as dual function and categorization by "most common use," this lack of exactness that is inherent in meaning-based systems remains an ongoing problem for data analysis. In some cases, as shown by Lindemann and Mauranen (2001), prosodic shape can be a crucial cue, and we further demonstrate this in this sample analysis of the lexical bundle *at the same time*.

1. *At the same time* (97.65 uses per million words in MICASE, 60.53 uses per million words in AWL)

Within MICASE, this bundle is only rarely used to indicate "real time" sequential action, for example:

> i mean, we hafta, we need to heat up, the the mash but, not **at the same time** that we'll be cooling down, uh, [S2: yeah cuz everything's like step by step] the mash

In many cases it functions rather as a text organizer highlighting the temporal simultaneity between two referential expressions, for example,

> Gregor Mendel, who we talked about, was writing, in the, later nineteenth century. he was ar- his work was around **at the same time** as Charles Darwin.

Most important, however, for any consideration of the functional purposes of the bundle, it is used to underscore a contrast between two aspects of a single idea or person:

> a. i guess that's the thing that makes Buddhism particularly Zen Buddhism, so uh fascinating and **at the same time** so frustrating, for a lot of people;
>
> b. this is something very important a- about Marx to keep in your mind. he_ his take on capitalism is not simple. yes capitalism sucks. and that's what most people know about Marx. right? that that's what he said. **at the same time,** capitalism is great. and these two words are_ sort of, encapsulate these ideas.

This key organizational function is reflected in the typically highly prominent pitch structure with which the lexical bundle is realized when it functions as a text organizer and that is shown in Fig 6.3. The prosodic shape comprises a

Figure 6.3

FO Reading of a Prominent, Falling (Assertive) Contour in the Realization of *at the same time* from the MICASE Corpus

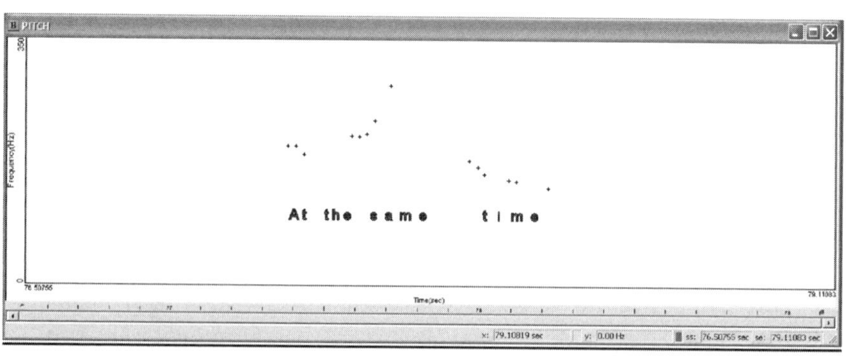

pitch prominent peak "at the SAME time" and a robust falling tone; a crucial signal to the listener that this is an important assertion.

2. *At the end of* (84.12 uses per million words in MICASE; 61.84 uses per million words in AWL)

At the end of is the sixth most frequent four-word lexical bundle in both the AWL and MICASE. Although categorized as a referential expression by Biber (2006), the phrase clearly fulfills a dual function in the MICASE corpus. In 60 percent of instances, it is used as a referential expression, for example:

> in the second century, **at the end of** the second century war had become a lot more complicated.

In the remaining 40 percent of cases, however, it is used as a discourse management marker and appears as part of classroom management talk—that is, as not indicating the organization of content but as indicating the organization of the class:

> a. you don't have the data and the outcome you can't write up your, discussion section, and so (i) should talk to (you) **at the end of** class.
>
> b. what i might wanna suggest is maybe **at the end of** the session i can show you a couple things. okay? mhm?
>
> c. alright we need a little calculator session **at the end of** of time today okay? cuz it is nice and easy to do it that way.

A useful distinction here is Coulthard and Montgomery's (1981) division of classroom content into main and subsidiary types. Main discourse comprises the informative content of the presentation, and the category of subsidiary content subsumes a variety of teaching discourse types concerned with class organization. Within spoken academic language, *at the end of* functions in both these capacities. The bundle demonstrates the difficulty of showing functional importance by use of frequency counts of a set phrase and suggests the need for a corresponding qualitative measure.

3. *I don't know I* (98.82 uses per million words in MICASE; 0 uses in AWL)

This lexical bundle frequently appears as a discourse device embedded in an utterance with other similar devices in strings such as *I don't know, I mean, I think it's* and is usually prosodically non-salient. This primary function as a "fluency device" (Nattinger & DeCarrico, 1992) is unique to the spoken modality, and its typical prosodic characteristics are a reflection of its importance for the speaker and corresponding unimportance in terms of semantic content for the hearer. This distinction, carried by both the lexical bundle and its prosodic realization, would seem to be key to an effective understanding of the discourse by a language learner. Thus, the verb *know* has become fixed in a phrase used by the instructor to hold the speaking space and to find time to think before speaking; that is, *know* is not any longer to be associated with epistemological stance but with a way of organizing spoken discourse in a manner that has become highly popular with large numbers of academics. In fact, we can demonstrate this difference using the Wordsmith Tools program to show that *know* appears 11,553 times (6795.88 per million) in the MICASE corpus, as opposed to 797 times (209.74 per million) in the AWL corpus. Thus, while we agree with Biber (2006) that a major purpose of university education is for teachers to help students learn to assess information and theory, we have found that the language of lexical bundles built around *know* might often need to be interpreted as text organizers or as teacher management bundles rather than as epistemic stance bundles.

4. *You know what I* (89.41 uses per million words in MICASE; 0 uses in AWL)

In contrast to *I don't know I*, this bundle appears most frequently in a prosodically salient pattern in which it collocates with *mean* or *I'm saying* to create the routinized expression *you know what I mean* or *you know what I'm saying*. This interactional device is considered to be an intonational idiom or "stereotype" (House, 1994) as it consistently appears with a final rising contour, for example, *you know what I* ➚ *MEAN*, *you know what I'm* ➚ *SAYing*, illustrated in Figure 6.4.

Particularly within classroom discourse, we recognize this kind of prosodic patterning as appearing on confirmation markers such as ➚ *Right* and ➚ *OK* (Nattinger & DeCarrico, 1992; Pica & Long, 1986). Such devices, however, frequently do not function as genuine confirmation markers. When used for confirmation, the speaker pauses and waits for verification from listeners, while in classroom uses of such language the teacher does not pause and wait for verification from the students, turning the phrase into a rhetorical question. This excerpt from the MICASE corpus demonstrates

Figure 6.4

FO Reading of a Prominent, Rising (Solidarity-Building) Contour in the Realization of *do you know what I mean* from the MICASE Corpus

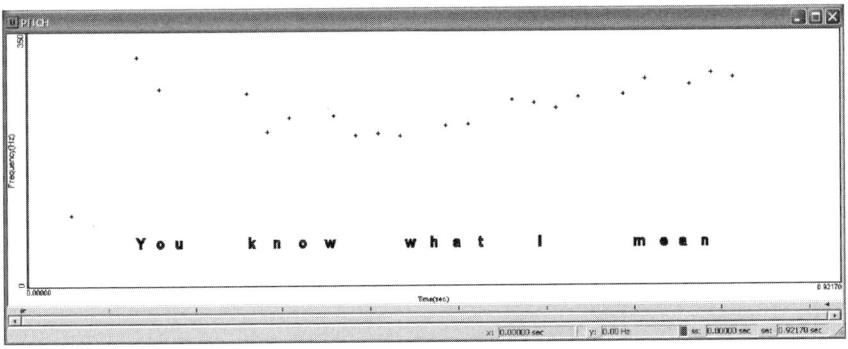

how these phrases might appear in this kind of succession in an academic lecture:

> with Durer he had a little, knife, **you know what i mean?** he had a little knife and he was managing it with his hand right? and and and when he did etchings he was managing it again with his hand and his fingers, he had control over this part of his arm. now this is heavy labor. so um, to carve stone especially stone of this size, we're not talking about a Venus of Willendorf size stone which is, uh you can hold in your hand, here we're talking about, a block of marble that's bigger than the artist. right?

Rather than being "confirmation markers," they appear to operate as "solidarity markers" used by the teacher to implicitly acknowledge a negotiation between speaker and hearer and to create a sense of mutual participation in the discourse (Pickering, 2001). This use is both a fairly straightforward yet important characteristic of spoken discourse that a focus on the spoken realization of the corpus allows us to isolate.

In addressing the functional appearances of *know* as opposed to its grammatical categorization, we suggest that categories that prioritize grammatical realization are not sufficient to detect the significant, functional differences between different prosodic realizations of lexical bundles and thus the variety of pedagogical purposes they may perform. In addition, we suggest that functional categorization that does not recognize the multitude of different purposes that may prevail in one modality versus another—that is, spoken vs. written discourse—and that may be communicated outside the lexico-grammatical system—that is, by intonational structure—will obscure crucial communicative differences between spoken and written realizations of the same (or similar) phrases. This interpretation is suggested in the significant numerical difference between the frequency of the appearance of *know* in each corpus discussed here. Such significant differences are unlikely to be satisfactorily interpreted by one all-inclusive system that encompasses both spoken and written discourse.

Pedagogical Implications

It is evident that there are both connections and dissonances between what students will read in their writing assignments and hear in their classroom lectures and peer study groups. In agreement with Schleppegrell, Achugar, and Orteiza (2004), we believe students will need help to construct "a coherent message and knowledge framework from texts" (p. 74), and that teachers should assume that textual realization (i.e. as spoken or as written text) will require different kinds of help. In fact, we may need to illuminate the singular nature of classroom discourse, a complex and demanding register which comprises the most lexical bundles of each functional category and is "at the same time informational, involved and produced with real-time production constraints" (Biber, 2006, p. 148).

The AWL wordlists provide teachers and materials writers with access to individual words and word families that are characteristic of written academic discourse across the many disciplinary areas that make up a modern university (Coxhead, 2000). As Coxhead explains, these words are seldom more than 8 percent of an academic text, with much of the rest of the vocabulary in the text coming from the 1,000 most frequent words in English. Additionally, the most frequent of the most frequent words are structural words such as *the* and *of* rather than lexical forms such as nouns, adjectives, adverbs, or verbs. The implication is that the academic words are presented in phrases that often take a pattern such as *the* .... *of the* ... or *the* ... *of* ..... Thus, learning to use the AWL words will mean learning to recognize, remember, access, and produce these longer strings. Teaching and learning vocabulary in phrases rather than just as individual words is a huge challenge because it goes against the traditional patterns of vocabulary instruction and demands information about how the words work in context. Another substantial challenge for teachers, materials writers, and curriculum designers is the yet unclear relationships and disconnections between the ways that academic words are used in writing compared to their use in academic speech. Publication of information about the phrases and collocations found in the AWL corpus of written English will certainly be of help (Coxhead et al., forthcoming), but additional information will be needed about the use of these same words in spoken academic discourse.

Although a number of researchers have suggested that recognition of "chunks" or "formulaic sequences" may enhance second language acquisition in the classroom (Jones & Haywood, 2002; Myles, Mitchell, & Hooper, 1999; Sinclair, 1991), the potential saliency of lexical bundles for second language development is a relatively new area of discussion. Warren (2006) in his discussion of intonation units suggests that we look beyond traditional lexico-grammatical units in order to assess the significance of prosodically based units and argues that the study of discourse intonation should become an established part of English language teaching. He further suggests that corpora such as those considered here might be examined in order to "serve as the basis for learning and teaching materials" (p. 321).

It seems clear that students will require help in "transferring" written forms to their spoken counterparts, both in dealing with specialized vocabulary (Murphy, 2004) and in recognizing idiomatic units that may be ubiquitous in academic spoken language in relaying specific functions. A more recent publication that might form a template for this is Cauldwell's (2003) *Streaming Speech,* which works entirely with natural, spontaneous discourse and highlights the pitch, pause, and intonationally idiomatic characteristics of conversational English for learners both for listening and speaking purposes. In the same way, materials developers who are targeting EAP listening comprehension might choose authentic lectures (from corpora such as the MICASE) in which the kinds of expressions we have looked at here are abundant rather than cleaned up, error-free spoken prose that will not allow learners to develop the kinds of listening skills that will make them most effective in the classroom. Finally, in addition to providing students with work on understanding authentic academic speech, materials and lessons need to help students learn to make the connections between what they read and what they hear in class.

REFERENCES

Ashby, P., & Ashby, M. (1995). Spelling aloud: a preliminary study of idiomatic intonation. In J. Windsor-Lewis (Ed.), *Studies in general and English phonetics* (pp. 145–154). London: Routledge.

Baker, P. (2006). *Using corpora in discourse analysis.* London: Continuum.

Biber, D. (1988). *Variation across speech and writing.* Cambridge, UK: Cambridge University Press.

———. (2006). *University language.* Amsterdam: John Benjamins.

Biber, D., & Conrad, S. (1999). Lexical bundles in conversation and academic prose. In H. Hasselgard & S. Oksefjell (Eds.), *Out of corpora: Studies in honour of Stig Johansson* (pp. 181–190). Amsterdam: Rodopi.

Biber, D., Conrad, S., & Cortes, V. (2003). Lexical bundles in speech and writing: An initial taxonomy. In A. Wilson, P. Rayson, & T. McEnery (Eds.), *Corpus linguistics by the lune: A festschrift for Geoffrey Leech* (pp. 71–92). Frankfurt: Peter Lang.

———. (2004). If you look at ...: Lexical bundles in university teaching and textbooks. *Applied Linguistics, 25*(3), 371–405.

Biber, D., Conrad, S., Reppen, R., Byrd, P., & Helt, M. (2002). Speaking and writing in the university: A multidimensional comparison. *TESOL Quarterly, 36*(1), 9–48.

Biber, D., Johansson, S., Leech, G., Conrad, S., & Finegan, E. (1999). *Longman grammar of spoken and written English.* Harlow, England: Pearson Education Limited.

Brazil, D. (1997). *The communicative value of intonation in English.* Cambridge, UK: Cambridge University Press.

Cauldwell, R. (2003). *Streaming speech.* Birmingham, UK: Speechinaction.

Cheng, W. (2006). Describing the extended meanings of lexical cohesion in a corpus of SARS spoken discourse. *International Journal of Corpus Linguistics, 11*(3), 189–208.

Cortes, V. (2004). Lexical bundles in published and student disciplinary writing: Examples from history and biology. *English for Specific Purposes, 23*(4), 397–423.

Coulthard, M., & Montgomery, M. (1981). *Studies in discourse analysis.* London: Thomas Litho Press.

Coxhead, A. (2000). A new academic word list. *TESOL Quarterly, 34*(2), 213–238.

Coxhead, A., Bunting, J., Byrd, P., & Moran, K. (forthcoming). *The Academic Word List: Collocations and recurrent phrases.* Ann Arbor: University of Michigan Press.

Crystal, D. (1969). *Prosodic systems and intonation in English.* Cambridge, UK: Cambridge University Press.

Flowerdew, J., & Tauroza, S. (1995). The effect of discourse markers on second language lecture comprehension. *Studies in Second Language Acquisition, 17*(4), 435–458.

Gumperz, J. (1982). *Discourse strategies.* Cambridge, UK: Cambridge University Press.

Halliday, M. (1967). *Intonation and grammar in British English.* The Hague: Mouton.

Hewings, M. (1995). Tone choice in the English intonation of non-native speakers. *International Review of Applied Linguistics, 3*(3), 251–265.

Hoey, M. (1991). *Patterns of lexis in text.* Oxford, UK: Oxford University Press.

House, J. (1994). Intonational stereotype: A reanalysis. In J. W. Lewis (Ed.), *Studies in general and English phonetics* (pp. 211–229). London: Routledge.

Jones, M., & Haywood, S. (2002). Facilitating the acquisition of formulaic sentences: An exploratory study in an EAP context. In R. Reppen, S. M. Fitzmaurice, & D. Biber (Eds.), *Using corpora to explore linguistic variation* (pp. 268–300). Philadelphia: John Benjamins.

Levis, J., & Pickering, L. (2004). Teaching intonation in discourse using speech visualization technology. *System, 32*(4), 505–524.

Lindemann, S., & Mauranen, A. (2001). "It's just real messy": The occurrence and function of just in a corpus of Academic speech. *English for Specific Purposes, 20*(Supplement 1), 459–475.

Murphy, J. (2004). Attending to word stress while learning new vocabulary. *English for Specific Purposes, 23*(1), 67–83.

Myles, F., Mitchell, R., & J. Hooper. (1999). Interrogative chunks in French L2. *Studies in Second Language Acquisition, 21*(1), 49–80.

Nattinger, J. R., & DeCarrico, J. S. (1992). *Lexical phrases and language teaching.* Oxford, UK: Oxford University Press.

Nevalainen, T. (1992). Intonation and discourse type. *Text, 12*(3), 397–427.

Pica, T., & Long, M. (1986). The classroom linguistic and conversational performance of experienced and inexperienced teachers. In R. Day (Ed.), *Talking to learn: Conversation in second language acquisition* (pp. 85–98). Rowley, MA: Newbury House.

Pickering, L. (1999). *An analysis of prosodic systems in the classroom discourse of native speaker and nonnative speaker teaching assistants.* Unpublished dissertation, University of Florida, Gainesville.

———. (2001). The role of tone choice in improving ITA communication in the classroom. *TESOL Quarterly, 35*(2), 233–255.

Schleppegrell, M. J., Achugar, M., & Orteiza, T. (2004). The grammar of history: Enhancing content-based instruction through a functional focus on language. *TESOL Quarterly, 38*(1), 67–93.

Shaw, P. (1994). Discourse competence in a framework for ITA training. In C. M. C. Myers (Ed.), *Discourse and performance of international teaching assistants* (pp. 27–51). Arlington, VA: TESOL.

Simpson-Vlach, R. S., & Leicher, S. (2006). *The MICASE handbook: A resource for users of the Michigan Corpus of Academic Spoken English.* Ann Arbor: University of Michigan Press.

Sinclair, J. (1991). *Corpus, concordance, collocation.* Oxford, UK: Oxford University Press.

Tench, P. (1996). *The intonation system of English.* London: Cassell.

Warren, M. (2006). Because of the role of er front office um in hotel: Lexical cohesion and discourse intonation. *International Journal of Corpus Linguistics, 11*(3), 305–323.

Wennerstrom, A. (1997). *Discourse intonation and second language acquisition: Three genre-based studies.* University of Washington, Seattle.

———. (2001). *The music of everyday speech.* Oxford, UK: Oxford University Press.

Williams, B. (1986). An acoustic study of some features of Welsh prosody. In C. Johns-Lewis (Ed.), *Intonation in discourse* (pp. 35–51). Kent, UK: Croom Helm Ltd.

Part 2

How Speaking Scaffolds Writing

7

Speaking of Absence: When the Connection Is Not There

An Essay on Loss in 2005 New Orleans and ESL Failure

LINDA LONON BLANTON

Abstract

Preferring an essay format as more expressive of emotion and exploration, I have situated my remarks on ESL speaking-writing in the context of the 2005 New Orleans flood. This may seem like an odd combination, but they—both my ESL research results and my disaster experience—share a burden of "absence" and "loss."

These days my brain works more in the realm of absence, in the realm of loss. Wasn't there a coffee shop on that corner, pre-Katrina? And, over there, how could that pile of lumber be a favorite New Orleans restaurant? A whole building could not be reduced to just enough wood for a picnic table. Not possible. And what about that linen suit of mine? Wasn't it in the bedroom closet? But I didn't see it in the pile of moldy clothes I dumped at the curb. Maybe, just maybe, I dropped it off at the cleaners a day or two before the storm. But where is the cleaners? Wasn't it over there?

Conceptualizing absence creates surreal sensations. Your eyes give a reading at odds with your mind's visual memory. You know it should be there, you know how it looked there, but it's not there. How do you mentally process the absence of a friend's house, a house you saw hundreds of times, when the only evidence that it was is the slab on which it sat? Did it actually exist? How could it suddenly not be there? How to reconcile what is from what should be? How to reconcile the absence of something familiar when you have no experience with other than its presence? What do you mean, it's not there?

Mold, rot, and destruction crowd my senses, disorient my brain. An odd time to search for connections to struggling English language students, but maybe there's something there. If their ESL program leads to the mainstream—to freshman English and into a full complement of college courses—we make certain assumptions about what should be there, do we not? For one, if the students are mainstreaming, then they are mainstreamable, right? They are literate. They wouldn't be in college if they weren't. Of course, they're ready for the instruction we provide, right? When we designed our ESL composition programs, we undoubtedly fretted over the mesh with mainstream English at the back end, but did we wonder if students would be ready at the front end? After all, if our first ESL course level is "be-gin-ning," what could possibly come before that?

Nothing is wrong with our ESL students that some good instruction won't fix, we may think. They need to read and write more. They need to read and write better. Of course, of course. But do we ask about a student's readiness for ESL writing, despite his best effort? Do we ask about the literacy underpinning that is necessary even to begin beginning composition work? What do you mean, it might not be there?

For a myriad of reasons, a student's readiness for ESL writing instruction isn't always there. What to do then? How to reconcile the absence of something expected, something assumed, when we have no experience with it other than its presence? How to conceptualize what is absent? Once conceptualized, how to proceed?

A speaker can be spoken to—ergo, she functions as a listener. She listens and speaks—or learns to speak—in response. A speaker who shows up in college can read—that is, she functions as a reader. If she's a reader, she can be instructed to function as a writer. These are assumed connections. They're assumed competences—even if existing as potentials to be realized, as dormant capabilities to be activated.

Historically, ESL educators decided that speaking went with listening. Reading with writing. Ham 'n eggs. Bread n' butter. That is how, years ago, instructors began to package ESL: listening-slash-speaking, reading-slash-writing. That is how programs were designed, how textbooks were written, how classroom lessons were framed.

But nowadays the students showing up on our doorsteps with disjointed prior schooling—the ones with lives disrupted by poverty, emigration, separation, resettlement—what about them? What goes with what? What we assume to be present in students' backgrounds—in their readiness to start even at point zero in our ESL programs—might just be absent. What do you mean, it might not be there?

In my own research with Generation 1.5 students (Blanton, 2005), I started out with certain assumptions, looking at what I thought would turn out to be poor composition instruction in both high school and college as the root of their current writing problems. Along the way, I happened to discover that my research subjects had almost identical childhood educational histories, although they were not of the same age, geographical origin, or length of U.S. residence. What they had in common, in addition to their disastrous U.S. school experience with ESL writing, was an abrupt and early halt to their childhood literacy development.

I realized that what was important was not so much the nature of students' more recent instruction but what had happened prior to this instruction. I needed to see that later segments of their schooling did not connect to earlier segments. To see how cruel were the timing and circumstance at the point in their lives when a bridge between earlier and later schooling needed to be constructed. And how disastrous was the absence of literacy experiences that could have provided the wherewithal for them to construct such a bridge.

I learned that at the end of their formal elementary schooling, these students stopped reading and writing altogether in their respective first languages. And they never subsequently began reading and writing—not really, not ever—in the new language either. In other words, once they had left behind schooling in the medium of the mother language—at about sixth grade—their literacy development never resumed, assuming theoretically that literacy development can "jump" languages. As I see it now, it was a given that these students, as young adults, would develop seemingly insurmountable writing problems in their second language. How could they not? After all, they never developed writing maturity in the first language before they stopped writing—really writing—altogether.

After the students' elementary school end of literacy instruction and immersion, followed by a long drought without meaningful reading and writing in any language (continuing to this day), enter traditional ESL composition instruction with its emphasis on error correction and grammatical-slash-rhetorical form. You can see where this is going. In the interest of brevity, let me say, perhaps unkindly, that the students' writing is now as flawed as it is primarily because of the post-immigration-to-the-USA instruction they received. Mind you, it wasn't wrong per se. Just wrong for them. And that is because the instruction was aimed not at literacy development but at preparing students for essay-centered composition courses, including—eventually, it was hoped—freshman English. Comparison/contrast, cause/effect, thesis/support—in other words, expository essay writing all the way.

Let's put it this way: these students' respective literacy foundations were not solid enough, not strong enough, to support the framework of rhetorical structures that their composition teachers would have them build. In the students' case, theirs were like the wobbly foundations of the floodwalls along the New Orleans drainage canals (what the media inaccurately called "levees"). The floodwall foundations, shallowly constructed by the U.S. Army Corps of Engineers in peaty and unstable soil (like bricks on jello), lacked the strength to hold their walls against pressure generated by storm water propelled backward from the lake. Both with the students' outcome in composition as with the canal walls, collapse was inevitable. (Now we know.)

Why did the students not profit from traditional composition instruction? Because for them it was premature. The students weren't yet literate enough to do what they were instructed to do. Why did the instruction prove so destructive? Because without a foundation of literacy to make it possible for them to perform as instructed, the students, as writers, defensively latched onto form, which, in their hands, manifested itself not even as the wretched and formulaic five-paragraph theme, but as a caricature of the wretched and formulaic five-paragraph theme.

In a nutshell, since the students hadn't yet acquired competence in written English, in its absence they substituted what they had learned, which were formulae. As a result, their writing was gibberish—a garble of mangled syntax shoehorned into First, blah, blah. Then, blah, blah. In conclusion, blah, blah. I'm not making fun. I'm sure their well-intentioned teachers didn't understand. With students like these over the years, I too often didn't understand. I didn't see what wasn't there. I didn't see the absence of literacy. I didn't understand until recently that successful composition instruction presumes a strong-enough foundation of literacy. Now I see that before students, any students, can write essays, language for them has to exist deeply and visually, has to have a written reality, has to be heard and seen.

The students I studied can speak English. Yes, indeed. It isn't perfect English. It isn't always grammatically correct English. But it's fluent English. They're at ease in speaking the language: they've made it their own. They have, for all intents and purposes, become American. So, oral fluency is not the issue.

Let me end by circling back and extrapolating from my research. First, during an early critical period when successful learners solidify literacy, my two subjects were instead separated from schooling in their mother language, and their literacy development as linked to their mother language stopped. Subsequent literacy development did not resume in English—due to the nature of their instruction, which, instead of promoting literacy, focused on error correction and the manipulation of form.

Generally speaking, literacy, at its foundational core, is representational of oral language. But for my two research subjects, oral and written language became "de-linked." As a result, for them literacy did not continue its development in the new language either. As I see it, the two did not have a continuing opportunity for literacy to be influenced and shaped by story experiences—as it always needs to be—or by activities spun off of stories, or by thinking-slash-writing in story narrative.

We all know that good writing—and especially good academic writing—is not just oral language written down. But at a critical time in literacy development, it is precisely that: oral language written down. When all goes well, later literacy takes on a life of its own, settling into a co-existence with oral language—related and intertwined, but not the same. For my research subjects, that never happened.

For them—and for students like them—the only chance in a literate world, let alone in our ESL programs, is re-linking oral and written language, particularly through story narrative. Such students need to write themselves back into the picture after an absence of long duration. Their thought, their expression, must have the chance to manifest itself in writing.

As it is now, these two students as writers are so disassociated from their own expression that it is not theirs. Their writing has little to do with them—with what they've experienced, with who they are in the world, what they think, what they've learned. I ask you to try writing without your brain, your heart, and your voice all connected to what your hand puts down. Your writing wouldn't make sense either.

What I'm talking about as a remedy is a very long shot since we don't know if literacy development, once interrupted in childhood, can resume in adulthood to the degree necessary for college work. But it is our only shot with students like these. Only then, I think, might we not need to ask about their readiness for writing instruction—what do you mean, it's not there. About New Orleans as it was, we will be asking for a very long time.

REFERENCE

Blanton, L. L. (2005). Student, interrupted: A tale of two would-be writers. *Journal of Second Language Writing, 14*(2), 105–121.

8

From Group Talk to Group Writing

LUXIN YANG

Abstract

This chapter argues that peer-peer dialogue, which appeared in this study in both an oral (group discussion) and a written mode (email exchanges) outside the classroom, facilitated the production of group papers in Commerce courses attended by two groups of Chinese-background ESL students over one semester of study. Data included group discussions, email exchanges, interviews, MSN chats, observations, questionnaires, and written documents (course-related materials and multiple drafts of the group papers). Data analysis showed a dialectic relationship between dialogue and writing in the production of group papers. Peer-peer dialogue allowed the students to clarify their understanding of subject matter concepts, generate ideas, and find proper writing forms in a natural context, thus contributing directly to their subsequent revisions. Such reconstruction generally occurred as the outcome of positive shared dialogue but was also the byproduct of criticism, rejection, and resistance to dialogue. Collectively, the reconstruction revealed in this study illustrates how peer-peer dialogue facilitates speaking-writing connections that lead to improved L2 writing.

There has been a growing interest in applying Vygotskian sociocultural theory to the field of SLA over the past twenty years (Zuengler & Miller, 2006). The socio-cultural theory of mind views learning as a mediated process, in which individuals actively construct their knowledge of the environment while engaging in goal-oriented activities. Learning takes place through a process of dialogic inquiry within a social group by pursuing authentic questions and constructing meaning through exploration (Wells, 1999, 2000). Vygotsky (1978) argued that learning takes place in the zone of proximal development (ZPD) of learners, which was defined as "the distance between the actual development level as determined by independent problem solving and the level of potential development as determined through problem solving under adult guidance or in collaboration with more capable peers" (p. 86). However, in recent years, a broader understanding of the scope of the ZPD has been put forward to include peer-peer interaction beyond expert/novice interaction (e.g., Lantolf, 2000a, 2000b; Swain, 2000; van Lier, 2000; Wells, 2002). Moreover, learning is never a benign activity. Internal tensions and contradictions contribute to the change and development of learning activity (Engeström & Miettinen, 1999).

A number of recent studies that drew on socio-cultural theory examined the dynamics of peer-peer interaction in second or foreign language (S/FL) classroom settings (e.g., DiCamilla & Antón, 1997; Donato, 1994; Huh, 2000; Kowal & Swain, 1994; Ohta, 2000, 2001; Storch, 2002, 2005; Swain & Lapkin, 1998, 2000; Takahashi, Austin, & Morimoto, 2000) and outside the classroom (Kobayashi, 2003; Tocalli-Beller, 2003). These studies demonstrate that students provide mutual assistance in their joint activity, shifting the expert role among peers during peer-peer interactions. Each member alternately builds on each other's comments and solves linguistic problems in oral and writing tasks. Of particular note, Kowal and Swain (1997), Ohta (2001), and Storch (2002) found that less proficient peers did provide assistance to more proficient peers in a collaborative pattern of interaction. These studies show that group tasks allow students to engage in collaborative dialogue in which they solve problems jointly by talking to each other in either their L1 or L2. Through this type of collaborative dialogue, learning occurs as students express their ideas by "saying" and then reflecting on what is said by others and themselves (Swain, 2000). Wells (2000) contends that it is frequently in the effort of saying that "speakers have the feeling of reaching a fuller or clearer understanding for themselves" (p. 74). In other words, collaborative dialogue, as a social cognitive tool, assists students' jointly constructed performance to outstrip their individual performance (Swain, 2000).

However, a number of researchers (e.g., Liang, 2004; Nyikos & Hashimoto, 1997; Parks & Raymond, 2004; Paulus, 1999; Storch, 2002; Swain, Brooks, & Tocalli-Beller, 2002; Tang & Tithecott, 1999) have identified certain adverse effects of collaborative work, such as greater reliance on teacher feedback, lack of confidence in one's abilities to offer useful feedback, and conflicts among students. Nelson and Murphy (1993) found that learners who interacted in a cooperative manner were more likely to use peer suggestions to revise their writing than those who interacted in a defensive manner. Similarly, Storch (2002) observed that collaborative and expert/novice patterns of dyadic interaction were more conducive to language learning than were patterns of dominant/dominant and dominant/passive dyad interaction.

Another likely phenomenon in group work is the use of L1 among L2 students for its convenience and speed in expressing ideas (Cook, 2001; Liang & Mohan, 2003). Researchers who take a Vygotskian theoretical perspective have argued that the L1 may act as a mediational tool, providing scaffolding support that learners need to acquire the L2 or to complete a task in the L2 (e.g., Antón & DiCamilla, 1998; Brooks & Donato, 1994; Huh, 2000; Swain & Lapkin, 1998, 2000), though the extent of using L1 in group work appears to be related to the L2 proficiency levels of students, the nature and familiarity of learning tasks, and time pressures of completing tasks (Brooks, Donato, & McGlone, 1997; Liang & Mohan, 2003; Swain & Lapkin, 1998, 2000). It is also possible that students might experience a dilemma in choosing between L1 use as a cognitive tool and L2 development as a learning goal (Liang & Mohan, 2003).

The L2 students in the reviewed studies engaged in group work for L2 production tasks in language-oriented courses. The findings of these studies reveal the possible language-related benefits that L2 students may gain through group work as well as the potential problems that may occur in L2 students' group work. However, while the use of L1 appears to facilitate L2 production or L2 task completion, students may encounter the dilemma noted by Liang and Mohan (2003) of using their L1 as a cognitive tool rather than practicing their L2 in group work. Notably, the student participants in these studies were at the level of lower or intermediate L2 proficiency. Little is known about how students with advanced L2 proficiency perform group work in mainstream university courses. The present case study examined the out-of-classroom writing of group-project assignments by two groups of Chinese ESL students enrolled in Business courses. As a part of a larger study (Yang, 2006), this chapter focuses on the role of peer-peer dialogue in writing group project assignments over one semester and what such dialogue reveals about the value of speaking-writing connections in a collaboratively oriented writing environment.

Method

Participants

The participants for this study consisted of two groups of Chinese ESL students, Yingxue's Group and Wenzhen's Group (all names are pseudonyms), from the Commerce program at two Canadian universities in southern Ontario. The two groups were formed voluntarily. I was led into the research sites by Yingxue and Wenzhen, whom I knew from their early participation in another project (see details in Cumming, 2006), beginning with their studies in an ESL academic preparation program and ending with their first-year studies at the university. At the time of the study, Yingxue and Wenzhen were each in their second year of the undergraduate Commerce program. Table 1 profiles the participating students' characteristics such as gender, age, years of learning English in the home country, education and work backgrounds in the home country, ESL courses taken, Test of English as a Foreign Language (TOEFL®)scores, start of studies at university in Canada, statuses (immigrant or international student), and future plans.

Yingxue worked with four other students—Fang, Liang, Jiang, and Guang—on the two group assignments (i.e., case presentation and term project) for the course called Information Systems Management. Later, Guang dropped the course because of his poor performance on the midterm exam. The members of Yingxue's group were all from Mainland China and native speakers of Mandarin. Yingxue was the only international student and had no work experience, whereas Fang, Liang, Jiang, and Guang all came to Canada as independent immigrants after having worked in China for from three to ten years. Yingxue was in her early 20s, Fang in her mid 20s, Liang in his late 20s, and Guang and Jiang were in their mid 30s. They had studied English as a foreign language in China for about six to twelve years, and three of them (Yingxue, Fang, and Jiang) had taken ESL courses in Canada for at least two semesters.

Wenzhen worked with three students—Ming, Qing, and Tong—on their marketing group project for the course called Foundations of Marketing. Wenzhen, Ming, and Tong were in their second year, whereas Qing was in her third year. Wenzhen was the only international student in this group; Ming and Qing held permanent residency in Canada, and Tong held Canadian citizenship at the time of the present study. Wenzhen, Ming, and Tong were all in their early 20s, while Qing was in her mid 20s. Wenzhen, Ming,

Table 1

Profile of Students

Students' pseudonyms	Yingxue	Fang	Liang	Jiang	Guang	Wenzhen	Ming	Qing	Tong
Gender	Female	Female	Male	Male	Male	Female	Female	Female	Male
Age	20	25	27	36	36	20	20	22	20
Years of EFL studies	6	6	12	7	10	8	10	10	9
Native language	Mandarin	Mandarin	Mandarin	Mandarin	Mandarin	Mandarin	Mandarin, Cantonese	Mandarin	Cantonese
Education/ work experience in home country	High school	College, computer programmer	B.Sc., engineer, insurance adjustor	B.A. (economics), businessman	B.A., Japanese translator	High school	One year university	Junior high school	Primary school
Arrival in Canada	Oct. 2000	May 2001	May 2002	Jun. 2001	Jun. 2000	Jan. 2001	Oct. 2001	Jun. 1998	Feb. 1996
Taking ESL courses	Yes	Yes	No	Yes	No	Yes	Yes	Yes	Yes
Start of studies at university in Canada	Jan. 2002	Sep. 2002	Sep. 2002	Jan. 2003	Sep. 2002	Sept. 2002	Sept. 2003	Sept. 2001	Sept. 2002
Status in Canada	International student	Immigrant	Immigrant	Immigrant	Immigrant	International student	Immigrant	Immigrant	Immigrant
Future plans	Accountant	Business	Insurance	Business	Companies in Japan	Business	Accountant	Business manager	Not clear

and Qing were from Mainland China and were native speakers of Mandarin. Ming was also a native speaker of Cantonese, as she grew up in a southern coastal city of China, where both Mandarin and Cantonese prevail. Tong was born in Hong Kong and immigrated to Canada with his parents upon completion of primary school. Tong could speak Cantonese and understand Mandarin spoken at a regular speed most of the time but could not write in Chinese because he had experienced so few opportunities to practice after he moved to Canada. All of them had studied English as a foreign language in China for about eight to ten years, and they all had taken ESL courses in Canada for at least one semester.

Data Collection

To investigate how the two groups of ESL students approached their group project assignments for the Commerce courses, a longitudinal case study approach was employed, one with a naturalistic, ethnographic orientation (Flowerdew, 2002; Johnson, 1992; Hammersley & Atkinson, 1995; Ramanathan & Atkinson, 1999). Each group was closely followed over one semester, and multiple sources of evidence were collected. Participants' accounts obtained through interviews, group discussions, email messages (including email exchanges between group members and my email inquiries to each group), and MSN (Messenger, an online concurrent chat program) discussions between certain student participants (Yingxue, Ming) and me were the major sources of data. Other sources of data, such as field notes from group meetings and classroom observations and related text-based artifacts (e.g., multiple drafts of assignments, course materials) were used to document the context.

Data Analysis

Interviews and group discussions were transcribed verbatim in the original language used (Chinese and English). Quotations presented in italics were originally spoken or written in Chinese, whereas those in regular typeface were originally spoken or written in English (and the latter are presented verbatim, without correction of grammatical infelicities). To follow the progression of the writing of the group assignments, I numbered the sequence of procedures for each group from the first week of the course. For each week, Mondays to Sundays were named as Days 1 to 7, respectively. The interviews, group discussions, email messages, and MSN chats were labelled as Week

X/ Day X in line with the schedule and sequence of each course, and I also identified them by the original calendar date (YY/MM/DD).

Adopting the qualitative research methods of analytic induction (Goetz & LeCompte, 1984) and constant comparison (Miles & Huberman, 1994), I read my data iteratively, searching for recurring themes or patterns in the activity of writing the group-project assignments and validating my interpretations "through constantly comparing one piece of data to another" (Strauss & Corbin, 1998, p.137). The participants also offered their feedback on the accuracy and plausibility of my interpretations over the course of this study. In this respect, the findings reported below were co-constructed through the interactions between the participants and me (Lincoln & Guba, 1985), though I have retained the advantageous position of being a researcher who eventually puts the results of the study into words.

Findings

Yingxue's Group

Yingxue's Group started to work on its term project paper soon after the topic was assigned: a debate over whether "Internet-based courses will replace the traditional classroom." To compose this paper, Yingxue's Group held three group discussions and conducted 24 email exchanges over a period of eight weeks. Excerpt 1 is Yingxue's summary of the first group discussion on the topic. (Jiang and Liang did not attend this discussion.)

Excerpt 1: Yingxue's summary of group discussion

We decided to <u>disagree</u> with the topic. Some aspects determined:

---

1. *Popularization*

   As not every corner of the world can have computers and access the Internet, people in the underdeveloped countries and areas will be deprived of the right of gaining education if "Internet-based courses will replace classrooms"
2. *Technology (technology is not perfect).* Internet courses *suite more* computer-based courses or essay-based, *but not the other courses such as mathematics oriented courses.* (e.g., statistics, which is really comprehensive to type the formula)

3. *Learning effect, self-discipline.*
   - *lack face-to-face communication. Questions cannot be solved immediately.* (take a long time to response)
   - *Eyesight will be hurt if working on computer for a long time.*
4. We come to school to learn not only knowledge but also group working, communication and so on
5. Teacher—learn from professor's personality

There are 5 TOPICS *on* ESSAY BODY. *Let's see if we can think of more topics. We can discuss further next time. I hope we can get our topics settled and* narrow down *our essay's* thesis. *Then we can start to do* RESEARCH.
(Yingxue, email 1, Week 4/Day 4, 10/02/03, 22:13:45)

Yingxue's email was written in mixed Chinese (English translation in italics) and English (in regular typeface). This summary then mediated the group's further interaction, as reflected in the exchanges between Liang and Yingxue. In his email (Excerpt 2), Liang pointed out that, according to the posted requirements, they should "discuss both sides of the topic, its advantages and disadvantages," rather than "distinguish right from wrong." He also suggested specifying their individual responsibilities earlier so that individual members could manage their workload efficiently. Yingxue had not read the requirements carefully when she had a discussion with Fang and Guang. Liang's email, as a mediating artifact, stimulated Yingxue to print out the posted requirements on the term paper and read them carefully. She then emailed her response to the whole group, reminding the group of the instructor's requirements and calling for another meeting (Excerpt 3). These three examples show how Yingxue's Group shared its ideas and negotiated an understanding of the assignment requirements through the written dialogue (email).

Excerpt 2: Liang's response to Yingxue's summary

Hi, Yingxue,
According to the requirement, I think we need to identify specific jobs and allocate them among the team members. The earlier the better, because we all can have sufficient time to collect information and coordinate ourselves toward the theme. Further, please carefully read the requirement posted on the web. I think our job is not to distinguish right from wrong, but discuss both sides of the topic, its advantages and disadvantages.
Liang (Liang, email 1, Week 4/Day 4, 10/02/03, 22:54:58)

Excerpt 3: Yingxue's reaction to Liang's response

Hi, guys
Sorry, guys. Liang just reminded me that we need to discuss the topic from both sides, advantages and disadvantages. I read the requirements by the professor again. It says as follows: "The term paper is structured as a debate, where both sides of a statement must be researched, documented and summarized. Maximum ten pages, double spaced, 12 point font, one inch margins, for the term paper (excluding references and attachments). The term paper is to be formatted using the term paper standard layout attached at the end of this document." So, we'd better arrange another meeting again. what do u [you] guys think about that. How about this Saturday? Or we don't meet, but u guys get ur [your] own opinions and type them to the documents I just sent.
hope get ur answers soon. tell me what do u prefer!
(Yingxue, email 2, Week 4/Day 4, 10/02/03, 23:13:55)

Prompted by Yingxue's call for another group meeting, Yingxue, Fang, Liang, and Jiang held a second group discussion on the term paper four weeks later. (Guang did not join them because he had dropped the course at that time.) Contradictions occurred in their discussion regarding the writing approach to be adopted and related rules of task division. Although they all intended to have an efficient approach to the topic without increasing their individual workload, the individual group members varied in their favored approach to the topic. For example, Liang explained that he preferred to approach the topic according to certain points, such as teacher and technology, and to divide the workload accordingly. A sub-group of two members was responsible for one or two points: finding out both pro (advantage) and con (disadvantage) evidence for each. In this way, the group members could work according to a clear objective and complete their individual work within a short period of time. However, as Excerpt 4 shows, Fang indicated that Liang's approach could actually double the workload because the instructor required them to use different references (at least one website, one journal article, and one book) for pro and con sides (turns 511 & 513). At the end of this excerpt, Jiang concluded that the dispute between Fang and Liang was in fact an issue of writing style (turn 517). Through this discussion, Yingxue's Group negotiated their writing approach to the topic and relevant macrostructure for the term paper.

Excerpt 4: The dispute between Fang and Liang

511 Fang: *I think you add more work on us. Why? You know, in general, the article is only about the con side or the pro side. Or-*

512 Liang: *Well, if you find one article, it will definitely have both pro and con sides. It is easy to find the article. If you can find the pro side, you can find the con side. I tell you, it is easy, because I have done the research.*

513 Fang: *But you know, our instructor's requirement is that the pro and con sides need to be from* different articles, different books. *According to his requirement, your method means more work for us, because your pro and con examples must be from different references. For example, regarding the* disadvantage *and* advantage *of* cost [for Internet-based courses], *I have to find two books.*

517 Jiang: *I think it's about the writing style. If we want to discuss the topic from the pro and con sides at the same time, we will divide our work according to Liang's suggestion. If we want to discuss the pro side first, then the con side, we divide our work in our* [Yingxue, Fang, Jiang] *way* [two sections: advantage and disadvantage].

(From Yingxue's Group's discussion 2, Week 8/Day 3, 10/29/03)

Note: Words in square brackets were inserted to clarify ambiguities.

Later, Jiang stated that he preferred to have two main sections—advantages and disadvantages—for the term paper because "*we haven't got sufficient information about the topic*" (turn 593, Yingxue's Group's discussion 2), which could allow them to divide the workload according to the points, as Liang had suggested. Yingxue also said, "*the advantage points* [evidence] *might not be in parallel with the disadvantage ones, so that's the style of this term paper*" (turn 605, Yingxue's Group's discussion 2). In short, Yingxue, Fang, and Jiang preferred to have two general sections—advantages and disadvantages—and then establish the relevant points under each section. After heated debate, they reached an agreement on the preliminary approach to the topic and to their task division. They decided to debate the topic in terms of both advantages and disadvantages regarding Internet-based courses. Liang was responsible for writing the advantages section, on which he had done some research; the others were responsible for writing the disadvantages section. Empowered by the ideas and direction produced through speaking, they were ready to move on to writing, thus illustrating a positive connection between speaking and writing.

Yingxue's Group then worked individually on the assigned task, sharing their drafts and offering comments via email. For example, Fang said, "I know it is not perfect, need advice!" (email, Week 8/Day 7). Jiang and Liang expressed their expectations for the emerging direction of their term paper: writing to "combine our respective parts to form a good paper" and "complete the project before we attend for lecture tomorrow" respectively, in their emails (Week 9/Day 2). Once they completed their individual tasks, Yingxue's Group held its third group discussion on the term paper, during which Yingxue, Fang, Jiang, and Liang commented on each other's drafts and discussed how to put their individual pieces of writing together. Excerpts 5 to 8 show how Yingxue helped Fang revise the paragraph on copyright after this discussion. Yingxue appeared to act as a more capable peer, providing scaffolding support to Fang. In Excerpt 5, Yingxue suggested that Fang read her comments embedded in Fang's initial draft, which were put into brackets and mainly written in Chinese (my English translation is in italics) (see Figure 1).

Figure 1

Yingxue's Comments on Fang's Copyright Paragraph, Week 9/Day 5

(1) Copyright is another big problem related to Internet-based courses that catches more and more attention around the world. (2) "According to the 1997 Global Piracy Report, four out of ten business software applications were pirated in 1997, with an annual dollar loss estimate of $11.4 billion. (3) Many software companies are reluctant to pursue the educational market due to concerns that several copies of purchased software may lead to millions of copies of illegal software, produced in the name of educating children"(Educator's Guide, 2002). (*I'm not sure if the above quotation is related to* INTERNET COURSES) (4) "Under current Copyright law, material written for websites, like all other forms of intellectual property, is copyrighted automatically."(Brooks, 279). (5) Therefore, the completed materials for online courses are intellectual property which have copyrights. (6) When professors post the materials found via Web, they have to be more careful about the copyright law. (7) This raises a problem between faculties and professors. (8) Regarding to textbook, copyright is an issue between the publishers and professors, which faculties are not involved in. (9) While the ownership of electronic materials is ambiguous since the faculties take charge in maintaining the course website so that they start seeking the possession of electronic materials. (*I think it's better to have a conclusion here. For example,* INTERNET COURSE *cannot replace traditional education. At least* COPYRIGHT LAW *does not have any new relevant regulations.*) (10) It changes the relationship between the faculties and professors. (*You must "be specific" in your writing, because NES readers expect you to have a clear explanation about the relationship between Cause and Effect. For example, your last sentence, what type of* relationship is "the relationship"? *You should explain it.*)

Note: The sentence numbers were inserted for ease of reading and comparison.

Excerpt 5: Yingxue's feedback to Fang's first draft of copyright paragraph

Hi, Fang
The following paragraph is extracted from Jiang's draft, which seems to have some of your previous writing. I have a few suggestions on your writing as an outsider. I've made some revisions. Please read it through carefully and see if I changed your ideas. If so, please do change them based on your original ideas!
(Yingxue, email 3, Week 9/Day 5, 03/11/07, 12:26:06)

After reading Yingxue's e-mail, Fang had a phone conversation with Yingxue about how to revise the paragraph on copyright:

Excerpt 6: Fang's reflection on her dialogue with Yingxue

Yingxue's idea *was that the professors cannot cite the materials freely when all the course materials need to be transferred into written texts. Actually I have thought about this when I wrote my first draft. In my first draft, I mentioned that* "when professors use some materials in their online courses, they should pay attention not to [be] against the copyright law." *If they don't teach* Internet courses, *they don't need to* pay attention to it. *Isn't that the same idea? Well, my writing didn't show the restriction of Internet courses. So we discussed and found other ways to say this issue. That is, the* professors *have restrictions when selecting course materials, because the materials have to be transferred into written texts. Then these materials will be regulated by* copyright law. (Fang, interview, 11/26/03)

Mediated by talking to Yingxue, Fang found an appropriate way to express her ideas about the restriction of copyright law on the posted course materials. Fang emailed Yingxue the revised draft (Figure 2) in the early morning of the following day. Compared to the draft in Figure 1, Fang rewrote the copyright paragraph as shown in Figure 2, in which only the quote (Sentence 9) from the original was retained. The content reflected what Fang and Yingxue discussed on the phone (Excerpt 6). Dialoguing with Yingxue, Fang was able to construct the copyright paragraph logically in line with the thesis of the whole group paper within a short period of time.

In the process of completing the group term paper, peer-peer dialogue helped Yingxue's Group better understand the instructor's requirements (e.g., Excerpts 1, 2, and 3) and discuss their approach to writing about the topic (e.g., Except 4). In an effort to construct a high-quality paper, peer-

Figure 2
Fang's Revised Copyright Paragraph, Week 9/Day 6

(1) Some copyright issue rise in Internet course, in term of using the other materials in Internet class, and the ownership of the course materials. (2) Preparing the materials of Internet class is a challenge for professors. (3) In traditional class, the professor can quote any materials they want, as long as they express it by oral. (4) In Internet class, all the material should be transferred into characters. (5) However, all the writing is regulated by copyright law, the professors should be careful of what they write. (6) They cannot quote anything freely in case of violating the law. (7) As a result, the content of the Internet class is limited. (8) The Internet class also raises the argument about the ownership of the course materials. (9) "Under current Copyright law, material written for websites, like all other forms of intellectual property, is copyrighted automatically."(Brooks, 279). (10) However, the owner of this property is not identified by law. (11) The ownership used to be the writer by default, recently the faculties start seeking the ownership of electronic materials. (12) They claim be the owner of the online material because they provide the hardware and software to set up and maintain the course website. (13) As the owner of the website, they should be the owner of the material on the website. (14) If the copyright issue could not be solved, it will hold back the development of the Internet class.

peer dialogue provided a valuable means for Yingxue's Group to seek and offer comments on individual drafts (e.g., Excerpts 5 and 6). Joint efforts helped them produce an A+ course paper (90 percent) and earned the course instructor's affirmative comments in the interview—"I think they did good research, and show good sources, and also they quote the sources. The content is good and how they organize is good..... They met all the requirements." In short, as the excerpts show, speaking to peers led directly to important changes in their individual writing and consequent overall improvement of the group's paper.

Wenzhen's Group

To complete the marketing project, Wenzhen's Group held three group discussions about writing the project proposal. After the third meeting, they sought feedback from their teaching assistant to make sure they were on the right track. They then held two group discussions to make decisions about how to proceed with the project writing. The purpose of their first group discussion was to decide what and where to market as their marketing project. Wenzhen and Ming each brought a few brochures on Shiseido products and a print copy of online information about Olay products to their first group discussion. After reviewing the materials on Shiseido and Olay products, Wenzhen, Ming, and Qing (Tong did not show up) reached a consensus that it would be best in terms of feasibility to select one product rather than one company for their marketing project. Compared to other, more available choices such as a computer, a cellular phone, alcoholic beverages, and an automobile, the three female students appeared to favor the skincare products because of their familiarity with and sound knowledge of them. The use of language regarding source information then caught their attention, especially when they discussed where to market skincare products, as Excerpt 7 shows.

Excerpt 7: Where to market?

182 Qing: *You need to do a* marketing program. *We need to select the market.*

183 Wenzhen: *Select the market?*

184 Qing: *In other words, where do you want to sell those products? Do we want to focus only on Canada?*

185 Wenzhen: *Not definitely.*

186 Qing: *I think we can turn to China or Asia if we don't want our instructor to verify all the information.*

187 Wenzhen: *But cosmetics products are worldwide products.*

188 Qing: *But we can't write a* marketing program *targeting the world market. That will be a super large project. We only need to write about 15 to 20 pages. If we have such a large project, definitely we cannot finish it on time.*

189 Wenzhen: *That's right.*

190 Ming: *But I think it is difficult to find* [English] *information about the Chinese market. The information is all in Chinese, which we would need to translate ourselves.*

191 Qing: *I think I would rather do translation myself. If we use the information from English references, for example, if we* copy or paste *some information, integrated with our own words, our instructor can easily find out we 'plagiarize' the references. If we use Chinese* *references, our instructor can't find out our references easily. And it is not difficult for us to translate the related information* [from Chinese into English].

......[discuss where to market *Shiseido* product, China or Canada]

234 Wenzhen: *I think translation is problematic. I mean, we'll have difficulty in writing if most of our information is in Chinese. If we have more information in English, we can feel the language when we read them, right? I don't mean that we copy the references in our writing, but it is easier for us to organize our ideas.*

235 Qing: *I understand what you mean.*

(From Wenzhen's Group's discussion 1, Week 6/Day 3, 02/11/04)

As this discussion proceeded, Qing ultimately discarded her choice of the target market (of China or Asia) and accepted the choice (of Canada) suggested by Wenzhen and Ming. Wenzhen's Group's agreement to rely on English sources for their marketing project reflected their intention of using English sources as a mediating guide to their writing, considering that they might not have enough appropriate vocabulary on their own to describe the product and market in their L2 (English). Based on their research, they later selected one of Shiseido's products, Total Revitalizing Cream, for the marketing project. Here, speaking shaped the direction of the writing that followed.

Excerpt 8 from the third group discussion shows how speaking helped Wenzhen's Group attend to the issue of marketing research, an essential part of the project, at the proposal writing stage. At the beginning of the discussion, Wenzhen, Ming, and Qing explained what they had already decided and acted on in their proposal writing because Tong missed the first two group discussions. Listening to their explanation, in Except 8, Tong posed questions (turns 56 and 62) intended to ensure that the draft proposal was based on research. Prompted by Tong's query, Wenzhen's Group then discussed how to do research (turns 64–75). For example, they could survey students (turn 65) and go to the shopping mall (e.g., Eaton's) or the cafeteria (e.g., Tim Horton's) for interviews (turns 70, 71, and 72). They could also draw on secondary source information (turn 73). As a result, Tong decided to add a section on research methods to the proposal at the end of this discussion. Tong used the group's ideas (bold print in Figure 3) in his description of research method and application, where Tong proposed the methods of data collection and data analysis for their marketing project.

Excerpt 8: Hypothesis or research?

56	**Tong:**	This is uh not a research, right?
57	**Wenzhen, Ming & Qing:**	No.
58	**Wenzhen:**	It's uh just-
59	**Ming:**	Things divided according to the uh last [meeting]
60	**Qing:**	We didn't call you, so
61	**Ming:**	We just write our outline-
62	**Tong:**	This is just hypothesis?
63	**Wenzhen:**	Yeah, we do our research later.
64	**Ming:**	We do interview or?
65	**Wenzhen:**	We have to make interviews, some interviews, give a survey to students,
66	**Ming:**	Well, this product is not for students, right?
67	**Tong:**	Yeah.
68	**Qing:**	We can do some just like
69	**Wenzhen:**	Not just for students, we can ask their opinions: what do you think of [this product]?
70	**Ming:**	Maybe we go to the Eaton
71	**Wenzhen:**	Yeah, we can do that, or go to café or Tim Horton. We can go to Eaton, we can go to different places.
72	**Ming:**	[they are] in different locations.
73	**Tong:**	Of course, secondary source is worth, they may have something on line.
74	**Ming:**	Yeah,
75	**Wenzhen:**	Yeah, but we have to use both primary and secondary sources.
76	**Ming:**	[it's] new product, we don't have much information about it
77	**Wenzhen:**	Yeah,
78	**Ming:**	I think this product is for the age 30 or 50 years old,
79	**Qing:**	So we need to do SWOT analysis.
80	**Ming:**	Yeah.

(From Wenzhen's Group's discussion 3, Week 8/Day 6, 03/06/04)

Figure 3 illustrates how Tong applied in writing the results of their spoken interaction.

Excerpt 9 further illustrates how speaking-writing connections were enacted as Wenzhen sought comments from her peers on her draft of the targeting and positioning section. In this excerpt, Wenzhen asked her group members to comment on her classification of the targeting consumers presented in the first paragraph of her initial draft (see Figure 4). This is followed in Excerpt 9 by the group members' responses to the writing she had produced.

Figure 3

Research Method and Application (by Tong), Week 8/Day 6

Due to the product's recent introduction, it is expected that there are little secondary date available for this project. Therefore, **the main focus of data gathering will be based upon on primary data**. Environmental scanning and **SWOT** assessment can be researched through secondary source on new environmental trends, factors such as the baby boomers (or population aging in general), Gender role (increased male usage of cosmetic products) among many others pose new opportunities and threats to the renewing cream. Psychographics and demographics can be researched through the use of **personal interviews, surveys,** or even Internet **questionnaire** such as VALS survey to determine what drives or influences customers to buy this cream. Finally, the marketing mix of Shiseido and other cosmetic companies can be found through the **packaging, interview with salesperson** and through the company itself.

After the essential data are collected, graphs such as perceptual maps, market share graphs, income distribution versus usage of the product and etc will be derived to compare with the group's hypothesis. From this step, we can conclude if the company's direction and the market demand are similar. Nonetheless, our group will provide a better marketing plan to this renewing cream if there are to be any discrepancies.

Figure 4

Targeting and Positioning (Excerpt) (1st draft by Wenzhen), Week 13/Day 3

The marketing objective of the Future Solution Total Revitalizing Cream is to reach women in Canada over 35 years old and **have** high income, especially those women who **immigranted** from Asian countries.

Note: The print in **bold** refers to where Wenzhen made her revisions later.

Excerpt 9: Commenting on Wenzhen's writing

53 **Wenzhen:** *I have some questions about* Asian women-

54 **Ming:** *In your* focus, *did you say-*

55 **Wenzhen:** *Now I am writing that my* target *is to* focus *on* women, *who have* high income *and are* Asian.

56 **Ming:** *So you are-*

57 **Wenzhen:** *Can I put these traits together?*

58 **Ming:** *In my draft* [of Market Segmentation], *one is* income, *one is* Asian women [Wenzhen is reading Ming's draft, noticing three subheads under Demographics—gender, age, and income distribution], *I think this classification is better.*

59 **Wenzhen:** *Do you think I can put these traits together or, I can't* cover *all the consumers-*

60 **Ming:** *According to this, uh, to* target *the professional women, their income, and Asian immigrants, but not all the Asian immigrant women have jobs here, like my mom* [housewife], *their* loyalty, *they have been using* Shiseido *for a long time. They will play an important role in making this new product successful in the market.*

61 **Wenzhen:** *This is multiple* marketing [segmentation]?

62 **Qing:** Yes, *multiple* marketing,

63 **Ming:** *Basically these three traits can cover* [the potential consumers], *they are related.*

64 **Wenzhen:** *I have a question: in your* [Ming] Segmentation, *you have mentioned the demographics, so could I select one or two traits in* marketing?

65 **Ming:** You can go this way: the market can be segmented according to age, and there are two targeting [groups], targeting is to combine them [Age + high income/ Age + Asian immigrants],

87 **Qing:** *How about you have three large sections? In the first paragraph, you talk about the age of targeting consumers in general. I mean, in your first* introduction *paragraph for* positioning, *you introduce the age of consumers. Then you further divide into two paragraphs: one paragraph about* Asian, *the other paragraph about* income.

88 **Wenzhen:** *Now I have two questions. For example, when I write* Positioning, *I divide the market into several pieces. Then when I write about* Targeting, *do I put them together or separate them? For example,*

one is about immigrants, *one is about* age above 30, *one is about* high income, *I write these three traits one by one?*

89 Qing: *separate them into three parts,* [thinking]

90 Wenzhen: *If I put them together, it will use* single segment concentration strategy to target the market. *Then I need to have several conditions-*

91 Ming: *Which strategy to use-*

92 Qing: *It will depend on whether you select one market or a couple of markets. Different market has different* market mix, *then you need to use* multiple segmentation strategy. *If you have* one market mix, *you will use* single segmentation strategy.

(From Wenzhen's Group's discussion 4, Week 13/Day 5, 04/09/04)

To generate answers to Wenzhen's questions, as Excerpt 9 shows, Wenzhen, Ming, and Qing shared their observations on marketing and their knowledge of marketing concepts through dialogue. Although they did not produce definitive answers to Wenzhen's questions, this discussion in Excerpt 9 indeed prompted revisions in Wenzhen's thinking and writing, as reflected in Figure 5, an excerpt from her revised draft. Figure 5 reveals substantial changes in writing that resulted from the dialogue that ensued in Excerpt 9 as the group members negotiated answers to the questions posed by Wenzhen. For example, based on this discussion, specifically mediated by Qing's ideas in turns 87 and 92, Wenzhen expanded her first paragraph by adding information regarding the special features of Shiseido's new product (bold print in Figure 5) to explain her rationale for targeting the "women over 35 years old with high income." Regarding the three traits to be emphasized (of high income, age, and being Asian women), Wenzhen stated in the last sentence of her first paragraph the decision to adopt the single-segment targeting approach: "We decided to use single-segment concentration strategy to target a particular group of people who are most likely to buy the product." In addition, she did some sentence level editing, such as correcting spelling errors and grammar mistakes (e.g., bold ***italics*** in Figure 5).

Excerpt 10 shows how Wenzhen's Group commented on Tong's draft about the SWOT (strength, weakness, opportunity, and threat) analysis that had been conducted. The excerpt shows how Tong's organization went beyond what Wenzhen, Ming, and Qing expected and how he demonstrated a mixed response in writing to the comments made in speaking. In his SWOT analysis, Tong had seven major sections, including Strength, Weakness, Baby Boomers, Direct Competition, Indirect Competition, Roles of Men and Women, and Desire for Convenience. Tong presented the Strengths

Figure 5

Positioning and Targeting (excerpt) (2nd draft by Wenzhen), Week 13/Day 3

The objective of our marketing plan to the Future Solution Total Revitalizing Cream is to reach women in Canada over 35 years old and ***with*** high income, especially those women who ***emigrated*** from Asian countries. **Shiseido has provided different lines of skin care products for women in various aging ranges during past several decades, such as the BENEFIANCE, designed to improve wrinkles, sagging, and roughness. PURENESS works well for young skin. SKIN CARE is good for combating early signs of aging to get a vibrant, beautiful complexion. Comparing with all the skin care products from Shiseido, Future Solution Total Revitalizing Cream has been expected to be a completely new product line in Shiseido due to its unique functions, extraordinary high price, luxurious social appeals, and its surprising efficiency. In order to expand the edge of the current customers and satisfy the needs of people who look for an extremely high quality product, we decide to use single-segment concentration strategy to target a particular group of people who are most likely to buy the product.**

and Weaknesses of the Shiseido Company and its product in the form of a paragraph. For the other five sections, Tong first gave a brief description about each section and then analyzed it from the perspective of Opportunity and/or Threat. Figure 6 provides an example from the section called "Baby Boomers," one in which Tong made only a minimal attempt to revise based on what had been said. It appeared that Wenzhen, Ming, and Qing preferred to organize the SWOT analysis into four parts (strengths, weakness, opportunities, and threats). Probably they realized that Tong might not fully understand their comments in Mandarin (which they used initially); they then switched to English from turn 196. However, Tong insisted on his approach to the SWOT analysis, indicating that it was better to spread four parts of the SWOT under environmental trends (turn 200). Obviously, Tong and his three peers had different opinions on the presentation of the SWOT analysis. To compromise, Tong later said he could put titles such as "consumers" and "market dynamics" in his SWOT analysis to make it clear.

Excerpt 10: Commenting on Tong's writing

192	**Wenzhen:**	*In our opinion, to write* SWOT, *we separate* SWOT, *that is, we have four sections*: S [strength], W [weakness], O [opportunity] and T [Threat].
193	**Qing:**	*He has many sub-sections, he has such a detailed classification.*
194	**Ming:**	*Let me have a look.*
195	**Qing:**	*You see he has* business role, opportunity, chain *in his later part,*
196	**Ming:**	You don't need to write every aspect,
197	**Qing:**	How about just separate into four parts and in each part you can uh for the opportunity you can include business role and separate it inside the opportunity.
198	**Tong:**	Oh, so we do the other way?
199	**Qing:**	That's better. Like that's SWOT, like four parts.
200	**Tong:**	It fits better this way that I explain SWOT under each trend [e.g., baby boomers].

(From Wenzhen's Group's discussion 4, Week 13/Day 5, 04/09/04)

Figure 6

Environmental Scan and SWOT Analysis (excerpt) (by Tong), Week 13/Day 3

Baby Boomers: Canada has one of the largest percentages of baby boomers in the world (at more than 33%). The baby boomers are the people "born between 1946 and 1966" and are now in their mid 30s to 50s. This sector is said to be more likely to "inherit" more wealth from aging parents. Both of these factors play a very important role to our product.

Opportunity: This is probably the best time to introduce a skin revitalizing product as the middle age population is the highest for many decades and will continue to be the case for at least 10 **yrs** to come.

Threat: Other cosmetic companies also see this golden opportunity and will also introduce their whole line of **anti aging** products to the market. Therefore, it is wise to test the market for a short period of time to check how sensitive customers are to this product and its price.

Note: The print in **bold** refers to where Tong revised later.

In spite of his resistance to his peers' suggestions regarding the organization of his SWOT analysis, Tong indeed took into account his peers' opinions in his revision by using a table format for a clearer presentation of his SWOT analysis. Tong put his four sections (Baby Boomers, Direct Competition, Indirect Competition, and Roles of Men and Women) into a table, adding three headings (i.e., Environmental Trend, Market Dynamics, and Company Issue). Figure 7 shows the changes that Tong made to the section on Baby Boomers. Tong spread the previous version of Baby Boomers (in Figure 6) under the three headings and also added one paragraph on strength, shown in bold print in Figure 7. He maintained his first two sections (Strength & Weakness) in the form of a paragraph, which he edited slightly, such as by making spelling corrections.

The groups got an A (80 percent) for the marketing project paper and positive comments from the teaching assistant. Wenzhen's Group was satisfied with the grade, as illustrated in Tong's words: "For the group assignment I think it is fair because the effort put in was quite high, so an A is good" (email interview, 04/06/09). They also agreed that the written comments on their project paper were consistent with what they had learned from the course and the weaknesses indicated were reasonable. Those weaknesses in their paper might have been avoided if they could have spent more time on reading through the paper carefully after putting all the individual drafts together:

> A good analysis & well-done job! (see my comments in the text!) Some sections that you may wish to pay more attention to are: (1) SWOT (a more effective organization?) (2) positioning map (elaboration on the information sources & competitors' position).

Discussion and Conclusion

The findings of this study point out the pedagogical value of peer-to-peer dialogue, in the form of group discussions (oral mode) and email exchanges (written mode), as a medium of learning and a cognitive tool in collaborative problem solving (e.g., Swain & Lapkin, 1998; Swain, 2000; Wells, 1999, 2000). They illustrate how speaking, as a mediating device, can connect to and shape writing that follows a process of negotiation and collaboration (e.g., Appel & Lantolf, 1994; DiCamilla & Antón, 1997; Donato, 1994; Huh, 2000; Kobayashi, 2003; Kowal & Swain, 1994; Swain & Lapkin, 1998, 2000). Speak-

Figure 7

SWOT Implications (excerpt) (by Tong), Week 16/Day 5

Environmental Trend	Market Dynamics	Company Issue
Baby Boomers (Age Demographics)	Canada has one of the largest baby boomers in the world (over 33%). The baby boomers are the people "born between 1946 and 1966" and are now in their mid 30s to 50s. This sector is said to be more likely to "inherit" more wealth from aging parents. Both of these factors play a very important role to our product.	Opportunity: This is probably the best time to introduce a skin revitalizing product as the middle age population is the highest for many decades and will continue to be the case for at least 10 ***years*** to come. Threat: Other cosmetic companies may see this golden opportunity and introduce their whole line of ***anti-aging*** products to the market, too. Therefore, it is wise to test the market for a short period of time and to check how sensitive customers are to this product and its price. **Shiseido's strength (factories in the U.S.) can provide supply in a short period of time. This means that even if our demand fluctuates (from small to very large), we can meet the demands in haste. Therefore, not a great deal of supply is needed at first to test the baby boomer's market (less risk).**

Note: The print in **bold** refers to what Tong added. **Bold *italics*** indicate the spelling changes Tong made.

ing to peers and hearing the speaking of peers allow students to clarify their understanding of instructors' requirements and subject matter concepts, generate ideas, and develop appropriate linguistic choices for presenting ideas in a natural context, leading to what they internalize and later use in individual writing. While sharing their own opinions, Yingxue's Group agreed on an understanding of the instructor's requirements (Excerpts 2 and 3) and the primary approach to the assigned topic (Excerpt 4); Wenzhen's Group narrowed down its target market and product choices (Excerpt 7) and developed the methods to be used in conducting the marketing research (Excerpt 8) at the stage of proposal writing. Dialoguing with Yingxue, Fang was able to organize the paragraph on copyright logically in accordance with the thesis of the group paper (Excerpts 5 and 6). Stimulated by discussion on research methods, Tong wrote the section on research method and application (see Figure 3) as a part of the proposal by integrating his peers' contributions with his own understanding of marketing research. By voicing her uncertainty about categorizing the potential consumers and hearing the comments of her peers (Excerpt 9), Wenzhen overcame her confusion and was able to make a substantial revision of her writing of the 'positioning and targeting' section for their marketing project paper (see Figure 5).

These examples illustrate the complementary relationship between speaking and writing in the production of writing, in contrast to the dichotomy of speaking and writing in traditional language study (Gere, 1987). These examples also show how writing is a social act. Even when students write on their own, there is still a continuing dialogue between them as individuals and the group or larger society (Gere, 1987), as reflected in how the students in the present study incorporated the outcome from peer-peer dialogue into their individual writing. As Bruffee (1984, p. 641) stated, "Writing is at once both two steps away from conversation and a return to conversation. We converse; we internalize conversation as a thought; and then by writing we re-immerse conversation in its external social medium." The results of this study provide support for this view of the connections between speaking and writing.

Furthermore, peer-peer dialogue (or group talk) in the present study collectively scaffolded each participant in maximizing his or her understanding of the subject concepts and locating linguistic capital for presenting content knowledge, "thus to augment the mediational resources that they can draw on" (Wells, 2002, p. 61) during the group tasks. In the process of developing the group project assignments, by speaking to each other, individual members of Yingxue's Group and Wenzhen's Group extended their knowledge and reasoning about the assigned academic tasks to higher levels of competence and consequently created a group zone of proximal development in and through which the whole group learned (Wegner, 2004), resulting in A or A+ grade for the course papers. Such co-construction not only occurred as the outcome of positive shared dialogue but also occurred as a consequence of criticism, rejection, and resistance to dialogue, such as in Fang's criticism of Liang's writing approach (Excerpt 4), Wenzhen and Ming's rejection of Qing's suggestions on the information sources (Excerpt 7), and Tong's resistance to his peers' suggestions about the organization of his writing (Excerpt 10). Questioning, commenting, or responding among group members through dialogue created an environment for joint understanding and for coordinating conflicting perspectives on a problem, which in turn enhanced individual intellectual performance, reflected in improved individual writing such as the revised drafts by Fang, Wenzhen, and Tong (Figures 2, 3, 5, and 7) and subsequent overall improvement of their group papers. Working together allowed Yingxue's Group and Wenzhen's Group to finish their research projects in good shape and on time. In brief, peer-peer dialogue facilitated their co-constructed performance, which outstripped their individual performance (Swain, 2000).

This study suggests the importance and educational value of group work in university mainstream courses for facilitating university students, especially ESL students, to better understand the course content and to present their content knowledge in appropriate language and form. In general, the ESL students who are accepted into university degree programs usually have met language requirements of universities, but they may have not fully reached native-like L2 proficiency. Group work can push ESL students naturally to interact with other ESL or native English-speaking students to extend their understanding of subject matter concepts and ease the process of presenting their content knowledge in L2 satisfactorily either in an oral mode (e.g., class presentations) or a written mode (e.g., course papers).

The study focused on two groups of ESL students with similar first language and cultural backgrounds in their study of one academic discipline. Future research needs to examine students from different cultural backgrounds and from various disciplines across different homogenous or mixed groups to verify for other university mainstream courses the connections between speaking and writing in constructing papers in L2 found in the present study. Moreover, the present study examined the co-construction of a research paper. Future research needs to examine the relationship between the production of other types of academic tasks (e.g., group presentations, lab reports) and speaking-writing connections through group interactions.

REFERENCES

Antón, M., & DiCamilla, F. J. (1998). Socio–cognitive functions of L1 collaborative interaction in the L2 classroom. *The Canadian Modern Language Review, 54,* 314–342.

Appel, G., & Lantolf, J. P. (1994). Speaking as mediation: A study of L1 and L2 recall tasks. *The Modern Language Journal, 78*(4), 437–452.

Brooks, F. B., & Donato, R. (1994). Vygotskyan approaches to understanding foreign language learner discourse during communicative tasks. *Hispania, 77*(2), 262–274.

Brooks, F. B., Donato, R. & McGlone, J. V. (1997). When are they going to say 'it' right? Understanding learner talk during pair–work activity. *Foreign Language Annals, 30,* 523–541.

Bruffee, K. A. (1984). Collaborative learning and the "conversation of mankind." *College English, 46*(7), 635–652.

Cook, V. (2001). Using the first language in the classroom. *The Canadian Modern Language Review, 57*(3), 402–423.

Cumming, A. (2006). *Goals for academic writing: ESL students and their instructors.* Amsterdam: John Benjamins.

Dicamilla, F. J., & Antón, M. (1997). Repetition in the collaborative discourse of L2 learners: A Vygotskian perspective. *The Canadian Modern Language Review, 53,* 609–633.

Donato, R. (1994). Collective scaffolding in second language learning. In J. P. Lantolf & G. Appel (Eds.), *Vygotskian approaches to second language research* (pp. 33–56). Norwood, NJ: Ablex.

Engeström, Y., & Miettinen, R. (1999). Introduction. In Y. Engeström, R. Miettinen, & R. Punamaki (Eds.), *Perspectives on activity theory* (pp. 1–16). Cambridge, UK: Cambridge University Press.

Flowerdew, J. (2002). Ethnographically inspired approaches to the study of academic discourse. In J. Flowerdew (Ed.), *Academic discourse* (pp. 235–252). Harlow, UK: Pearson.

Gere, A. R. (1987). *Writing groups: History, theory and implications.* Carbondale: Southern Illinois University Press.

Goetz, C., & LeCompte, M. (1984). *Ethnography and qualitative design in educational research.* Orlando, FL: Academic Press.

Hammersley, M, & Atkinson, P. (1995). *Ethnography: Principles in practice* (2nd ed.). London: Routledge.

Huh, M. (2000). A journey into L2 narrative with L1 collaborative dialogue. *Journal of the Applied Linguistics Association of Korea, 16*(2), 107–126.

Johnson, D. M. (1992). *Approaches to research in second language learning.* New York: Longman.

Kobayashi, M. (2003). The role of peer support in ESL students' accomplishment of oral academic tasks. *The Canadian Modern Language Review, 59*(3), 337–368.

Kowal, M., & Swain, M. (1994). Using collaborative language production tasks to promote students' language awareness. *Language Awareness, 3,* 73–93.

———. (1997). From semantic to syntactic processing: How can we promote it in the immersion classroom? In K. Johnson & M. Swain (Eds.), *Immersion education: Interactional perspectives* (pp. 284–309). Cambridge, UK: Cambridge University Press.

Lantolf, J. P. (2000a). Introducing sociocultural theory. In J. P. Lantolf (Ed.), *Sociocultural theory and second language learning* (pp. 1–26). Oxford, UK: Oxford University Press.

———. (2000b). Second language learning as a mediated process. *Language Teaching, 33,* 79–96.

Liang, X. (2004). Cooperative learning as a sociocultural practice. *The Canadian Modern Language Review, 60*(5), 637–668.

Liang, X., & Mohan, B. A. (2003). Dilemmas of cooperative learning and academic proficiency in two languages. *Journal of English for Academic Purposes, 2*(1), 35–51.

Lincoln, Y. S., & Guba, E. G. (1985). *Naturalistic inquiry.* Newbury Park, CA: Sage.

Miles, M., & Huberman, A. (1994). *Qualitative data analysis: An expanded sourcebook* (2nd edition). Thousand Oaks, CA: Sage.

Nelson, G. L., & Murphy, J. M. (1993). Peer response groups: Do L2 writers use peer comments in revising their drafts? *TESOL Quarterly, 27,* 135–141.

Nyikos, M., & Hashimoto, R. (1997). Constructivist theory applied to collaborative learning in teacher education: In search of ZPD. *The Modern Language Journal, 81*(4), 506–517.

Ohta, A. (2000). Rethinking interaction in SLA: Developmentally appropriate assistance in the zone of proximal development and the acquisition of L2 grammar. In J. P. Lantolf (Ed.), *Sociocultural theory and second language learning* (pp. 51–78). Oxford, UK: Oxford University Press.

———. (2001). Peer interactive tasks and assisted performance in classroom language learning. In A. S. Ohta (Ed.), *Second language acquisition processes in the classroom: Learning Japanese* (pp. 73–128). Mahwah, NJ: Lawrence Erlbaum.

Parks, S., & Raymond P. M. (2004). Strategy use by nonnative English–speaking students in an MBA Program: Not business as usual! *The Modern Language Journal, 88*(3), 374–389.

Paulus, T. M. (1999). The effect of peer and teacher feedback on student writing. *Journal of Second Language Writing, 8,* 265–289.

Ramanathan, V., & Atkinson, D. (1999). Ethnographic approaches and methods in L2 writing research: A critical guide and review. *Applied Linguistics, 20,* 44–70.

Storch, N. (2002). Patterns of interaction in ESL pair work. *Language Learning, 52,* 119–158.

———. (2005). Collaborative writing: Product, process, and students' reflections. *Journal of Second Language Writing, 14,* 153–173.

Strauss, A., & Corbin, J. (1998). *Basics of qualitative research: Techniques and procedures for developing grounded theory* (2nd ed.). Thousand Oaks, CA: Sage.

Swain, M. (2000). The output hypothesis and beyond: Mediating acquisition through collaborative dialogue. In J. P. Lantolf (Ed.), *Sociocultural theory and second language learning* (pp. 97–114). Oxford, UK: Oxford University Press.

Swain, M., Brooks, L., & Tocalli–Beller, A. (2002). Peer–peer dialogue as a means of second language learning. *Annual Review of Applied Linguistics, 22,* 171–185.

Swain, M., & Lapkin, S. (1998). Interaction and second language learning: Two adolescent French immersion students working together. *The Modern Language Journal, 82,* 320–337.

———. (2000). Task–based second language learning: The use of the first language. *Language Teaching Research, 4,* 251–274.

Takahashi, E., Austin, T., & Morimoto, Y. (2000). Social interaction and language development in an FLES classroom. In J. K. Hall & L. S. Verplaetse (Eds.), *Second and foreign language learning through classroom interaction* (pp. 139–159). Mahwah, NJ: Lawrence Erlbaum.

Tang, G. M., & Tithecott, J. (1999). Peer response in ESL writing. *TESL Canada Journal, 16,* 20–38.

Tocalli–Beller, A. (2003). Cognitive conflict, disagreement and repetition in collaborative groups: Affective and social dimensions from an insider's perspective. *The Canadian Modern Language Review, 60*(2), 143–171.

van Lier, L. (2000). From input to affordance: Social–interactive learning from an ecological perspective. In J. Lantolf (Ed.), *Sociocultural theory and second language learning* (pp. 245–259). Oxford, UK: Oxford University Press.

Vygotsky, L.S. (1978). *Mind in society: The development of higher psychological processes.* Cambridge, MA: Harvard University Press.

Wells, G. (1999). *Dialogic inquiry: Towards a sociocultural practice and theory of education.* Cambridge, UK: Cambridge University Press.

———. (2000). Dialogic inquiry in education: Building on the legacy of Vygotsky. In C. D. Lee & P. Smagorinsky (eds.), *Vygotskian perspectives on literacy research* (pp. 51–85). New York: Cambridge University Press.

———. (2002). The role of dialogue in activity theory. *Mind, Culture, and Activity, 9*(1), 43–66.

Yang, L. (2006). *Writing group–project assignments in commerce courses: Case studies of Chinese–Background ESL students at two Canadian universities.* Unpublished doctoral dissertation, University of Toronto.

Zuengler, J., & Miller, E. R. (2006). Cognitive and sociocultrual perspectives: Two parallel SLA worlds? *TESOL Quarterly, 40,* 35–58.

9

Scaffolding during the Writing Process: The Role of Informal Peer Interaction in Writing Workshops

FIONA HYLAND

Abstract

This chapter examines spoken interaction in writing workshops for ESL students in two classes on an English proficiency course, looking closely at the contextual features that help to give rise to the patterns of interaction between students and their peers. One important contextual feature is the way that the two participating teachers organized and managed their writing workshops. The chapter examines their procedures and interactions with the students and considers how these affected the student-student interactions during the workshops. It then focuses on the spoken interactions between the students in the two classes and examines the ways these interactions provided scaffolding for students' writing development during the writing process and what this suggests with respect to connections between speaking and writing.

Writing workshops are considered as important tools for writing improvement by teachers in both L1 and L2 contexts. The ideal writing workshop usually begins with some teacher-led input, which is then followed by students (working sometimes together and sometimes individually) "drafting, conferencing and sharing, revising, redrafting, editing, publishing and celebrating" (Peyton, Johns, Vincent, & Greenblatt, 1994, p. 470). Such workshops are often seen as potentially empowering environments for students since both the teacher and peers can be collaborators and facilitators in the writing process. Although writing is of course at the heart of any writing workshop, speaking plays a very crucial role since it is only through interaction and dialogue that sharing and consulting can take place. As such, these writing workshops are potentially fertile ground for the enactment of speaking-writing connections.

The Value of Interaction in the Writing Workshop

One benefit of writing workshops is that they offer the possibility of transformation of the classroom discourse from teacher transmission mode, in which the student writer is largely a passive recipient. Instead, they aim to foster "responsive/collaborative discourse," where the teacher encourages students to actively participate in an evolving and cooperative group conversation (Nystrand & Gamoran, 1991). This type of classroom dialogue, sometimes referred to as "dialogic instruction" (Wells, 1990), "instructional conversation" (Goldenberg, 1993), or "conversational dialogues" (Freedman & Sperling, 1985), encourages students to complete tasks they could not do on their own, thereby learning through dialogue and interaction with their teachers. Oral interaction with peers is seen as another essential aspect of writing workshops, providing practical and affective support and helping students to develop their confidence and autonomy as writers (De Guerrero & Villamil, 1994; Hyland, 2000b).

Such teacher-learner and learner-learner interaction while writing may help L2 writers develop both their cognitive and academic writing skills since it allows them to "propose, debate and critique ideas and language issues with the instructor, with each other and with the texts they write" (Weissberg, 2006a, p. 69). Through this dialogue, the students "learn to question assumptions, to extend and elaborate ideas, to start and finish topics, to reinstate and clarify ideas"—all of which are important aspects of academic writing, and thus "the writing classroom becomes the site for academic apprenticeship" (Weissberg, 2006a, p. 69-70) via interactions between speaking and writing.

However, some researchers have suggested that these views of the benefits of writing workshops and writing conferences in general may be somewhat idealistic and may gloss over their problematic aspects in L2 contexts. In terms of the teacher-student dialogue, Goldstein & Conrad (1990) point out that L2 learners may come from cultures that discourage informal interaction with authority figures such as teachers, and this can make it difficult for them to actively participate in conferences. Another factor that may have an impact on the quality and quantity of the dialogue in L2 conferences is the language level of students. Patthey-Chavez & Ferris (1997) suggest that less able students are more likely to follow suggestions from their teachers uncritically instead of actively negotiating during conferences.

The potential benefits of peer interactions in workshops may also be over idealized, as some research suggests that peer feedback generally has very little effect on students' writing (Mendonca & Johnson, 1994; Connor & Asenavage, 1994; Nelson & Carson, 1998; Sengupta, 1998; Tsui & Ng, 2000; Zhang, 1995). Comments from peers may not be widely used or trusted by students, as they may doubt whether their peers can give quality feedback (Hyland, 2000b; Leki, 1990; Lockhart & Ng, 1993; Mendoca & Johnson, 1994; Nelson & Murphy 1992, 1993). There are also concerns that students may give each other culturally inappropriate and overly critical feedback (Amores, 1997) or focus too much on surface errors. However, despite all these caveats, the various dialogues on writing that take place in writing workshops can be an important source of support for students and can provide them with scaffolding as they write. This scaffolding is at the heart of speaking-writing connections.

Scaffolding in Writing Workshops

The term *scaffolding* is generally used to describe the types of assistance and support offered to learners to help them move from assisted to independent performance (Wood, Brunner & Ross, 1976). Scaffolding is obviously an important aspect of dialogue in writing conferences and workshops and is usually considered as an essential part of the tutor-student discussion. It is, however, quite difficult to pinpoint what steps tutors can take to ensure they provide effective scaffolding in actual conferences. Weissberg (2006b) has attempted to do this by operationalizing scaffolding as a set of "observable discourse mechanisms." Using data from conferences, he illustrates how a tutor created verbal linkages to the L2 writer through lexical and phrasal repetition, questioning, phrase completion and extension, summary and paraphrase statements, and statements of personal affiliation. Such links were then used as a springboard to make instructional points. This could be viewed as scaffolding at the micro-level, focusing closely on specific aspects of student texts. However, teachers also provide support at a more macro-level, helping students to move through the writing process, and this can also be viewed as a form of scaffolding. In fact, this "nurturing" role may be most important for the writer's development. Wilcox (1997) looks at the attitudes of 12 middle school teachers and students concerning what makes a teacher good at conducting conferences. He identifies two roles for writing teachers in conferences, text-oriented instructor and student-oriented nurturer, and suggests that teachers see their most important role in writing conferences as that of "nurturer."

Scaffolding and Peers

Although the concept of scaffolding in the writing workshop context traditionally focuses on the dialogue between teacher and student, a scaffolding mechanism can also be observed in the dialogues between students. From a Vygotskian perspective, peer review can be seen as a formative developmental process that gives writers opportunities to interact with other students; this allows them to gain access to other perceptions and interpretations of their texts and to obtain support and guidance as they engage with the writing process. However, within the L2 context researchers have cautioned against idealizing all peer group interactions in this way—that is, as writers constructively helping each other and providing mutual scaffolding (Peyton, Johns, Vincent & Greenblatt, 1994). The reality is sometimes quite different, with the potential for misunderstandings and defensive and hostile behavior (Nelson & Murphy, 1993). Sometimes these misunderstandings and conflicts may be the result of cross-cultural issues, since ESL/EFL classes often include students from different cultural and educational backgrounds (Allaei & Connor, 1990). Students may have different expectations about aspects of group work, such as the roles of the members, the mechanics of the group, and politeness strategies, which can make it hard for them to function effectively as a group or to provide effective scaffolding to each other (Nelson & Murphy, 1992).

While much of the literature on the place of interaction in the writing workshop has focused on interactions on written drafts, there has also been some L1 research on the effects of pre-writing discussions between students. This research has suggested that students write better drafts after being given the opportunity to talk about the topic they are writing on (Kennedy, 1983; Sweigart, 1991). In the L2 context, Shi (1998) compared drafts written under three conditions—peer discussion, teacher-led discussion, and no discussion—but found no significant differences in the quality of writing produced. Nonetheless, she argued that pre-writing discussions were useful for scaffolding students' thinking and allowing students to explore their topics and generate a range of vocabulary items.

There is clearly a need to look more closely at the complexities of all the intricate and connected oral interactions taking place within writing workshops and the ways these interactions help to provide scaffolding and assist students' writing development. This chapter looks first at the different approaches, practices and procedures used by two teachers in their writing classes. It examines their management of their writing workshops and considers the extent to which the two teachers worked to foster the link between writing and speaking in their workshops. The paper then focuses on the spoken interactions between the students in the two classes and examines the ways these also provided scaffolding for the students' writing development.

Methodology and Participants

Research Setting

This was a naturalistic study, with data collected over a fourteen-week semester on a full-time Academic English course held at a university in New Zealand. The data are part of a larger longitudinal study that focused mainly on teacher written feedback, but also examined how such teacher written feedback interacted with other forms of feedback. As Goldstein and Conrad (1990, p. 459) point out, writing conferences are "dynamic events affected by context and participants"; therefore, research within a naturalistic setting was considered most appropriate.

Two classes were studied: one preparing students for undergraduate courses and one preparing them for post-graduate studies. The two teachers of these classes were experienced ESL/EFL teachers with an interest in teaching writing. Six ESL students (three from each class) were case study subjects. These students were selected as a representative sample of the different levels and nationalities on the course and ranged from low- to high-intermediate students. They included four female and two male students and were all from countries in the Asian region.

Data Collection

Data were gathered via pre- and post-course student questionnaires on student beliefs, attitudes, and practices regarding feedback; interviews with teachers and case study subjects; think-aloud protocols from the two teachers; and notes of observations of writing workshops. In addition, student writing, including drafts and revised versions of writing assignments, and related teacher and peer written feedback, was collected. In order to ensure confidentiality, teachers and students were given pseudonyms.

The writing workshops, held twice per week in both classes, were observed. As the researcher, I had taught a similar course in the previous semester and so brought some insider knowledge to the observer's role. The notes made during observations followed the guidelines discussed by Cohen and Manion (1994) with notes recording timing for events and interactions, participants and main activities. After sessions, more detailed notes were typed up, including diagrams of class layout and student positions. Member checking was carried out by passing the notes to the two teachers for their comments and observations. Then the notes were coded and the interactions were categorized. The categorizations were developed inductively from a close examination and coding and re-coding of the field notes.

Participants

Both classes were comparatively small. Class A had fifteen students from varied backgrounds, including Russia, Somalia, Vietnam, Korea, Indonesia, Japan, Taiwan, and Hong Kong. There were seven male and eight female students. The students were all of a fairly uniform degree of English language proficiency, ranging from low- to mid-intermediate level, but were diverse in terms of age and life experiences. They ranged from young school leavers to mature working adults, including diplomats. Although this class worked well together and co-operated when asked, the focus was on the individual, rather than the group, with few cohesive group links being observed and little social interaction among members outside the classroom.

All the sixteen students in Class B already had a first degree, though none had taken this in English. There were seven students from Thailand and six Chinese students, effectively splitting the class into two main groups, although there were also students from Poland, Japan and Korea. There were five male and eleven female students. The students' English language levels varied considerably, ranging from lower-intermediate to advanced level, and they were quite diverse in terms of life experiences. Some of them had just completed their first degrees, while others were mature adults. Unlike Class A, this class gave the appearance of being a cohesive and very close group, with many in-class jokes and banter among the members. Two out-of-class activities, a party and a trip to a restaurant, were organized and attended by all members of the class. However, students mainly worked with peers from the same language group during the writing workshops.

Two Teachers' Approaches to Writing and Managing Workshops

Joan and Class A: A Focus on Academic Writing and Individual Problem Solving

The students in Class A were taught by Joan. Joan had five years of ESL teaching experience and a diploma in Teaching English as a Second Language. This was the twelfth time she had taught the course, and having experimented with different approaches to teaching writing and reflected on the outcomes, she said in her interview that she now felt very comfortable with her writing program. She focused mainly on aspects of academic discourse and language issues, although she also taught students about the writing process. Her aim was: "to achieve a balance between time spent on overt teaching of ideas about writing such as how the process works, what academic writing is like, and common language problems; and time spent working with individual students in the workshops, looking at what their problems are and trying to solve them on a one to one basis." Joan felt that student-teacher discussion in writing workshops was an especially important aspect of her approach to teaching writing, since it allowed her to focus on individual problems and also allowed students to ask about previous written comments and take an active role in the discussion. Thus, she felt that she was in fact "getting feedback on the feedback," and this reassured her about its usefulness. She felt that the immediacy and directness of this interaction was what made it so useful in helping students to improve their writing:

> It's the oral interaction I guess I find most useful. . . . I guess it's more that I can gauge more how useful it is. . . . In the oral thing when we clarify something and they say, "Oh now I see!" Then I feel that . . . I'm getting the feedback on the feedback . . . because it's on the spot. . . . Because it's usable right then and there and they can clarify right then and there if they don't understand. . . . it's immediate, introducing an immediate problem you are dealing with right then and there.

Joan seemed unsure as to whether to encourage peer feedback on writing and was unconvinced of its general benefits:

> I haven't used it extensively and I think the thing with peer feedback is that the students do need training and quite a bit of help to make it useful and I don't always have the time. I guess I haven't felt that it's a sufficient priority to

> put the time into training them to do that. . . . The main benefit would be the opportunity for the students to see more of other peoples' writing . . . and to get more of a perception of how a reader reacts to what they are writing and I guess just a variety and another source of feedback, . . . it seems quite time consuming and I'm not sure whether it's justified by the length of time.

She did, however, believe that students were informally discussing their writing in her classes but was again unsure about the extent or focus of such interactions or their usefulness and was unwilling to make this discussion an integral part of the writing workshops: "I think it's happening a little bit informally. I guess I've mentioned this in class that they can talk to each other about their writing, so it's sort of informally encouraged, but I'm not sure that I'll do any formally." She also said, "I think I've noticed Jun and Seng Hee conferring a little bit, perhaps in Korean. And I think sometimes that can be useful for them to be able to confer in their own language."

So while she was happy to accept that peer discussions of writing were occurring in her class, she was unwilling to intervene or formalize this interaction, preferring to adopt a *laissez-faire* attitude to its emergence. Her own role as a resource person for discussions was always highlighted at the beginning of each workshop, and during workshops constant reminders such as, "Don't forget that I am here. Come and see me to discuss your writing" were given, but only once in her first workshop did she allude to the possibility of talking to other students. However, she did ask students to push their desks together and sit in self-selected groups of five or six students, which the observations suggest effectively created small "microcommunities" (Hirvela, 1999) for discussing writing and the writing process.

One formal interactive peer activity that forced students to talk about their writing was organized in Joan's class. This activity, called 3,2,1, could be considered a type of pre-writing discussion. It involved students explaining the main idea of their next assignment to a partner for three minutes, then getting the partner to repeat it back for one minute. Students then moved to new partners and told them their ideas in two minutes and finally in one minute with a third partner. This activity was noted to have an impact on the students, who appeared to both enjoy and benefit from it, as this extract from the observation data shows:

> Joan explains that she wants the students to explain the main idea of their second major assignment to a partner using the 3,2,1 technique. She tells the class that this will make their main ideas clearer. "Clear thinking is essential for writing a good essay." All the class explain their main idea to a partner for three minutes. Many of them find it difficult and struggle for words. Joan then tells them that

> their partner must repeat back their ideas in one minute. . . . Joan goes to the whiteboard and writes: listener = reader. She explains that the purpose is to see if the listener can understand. If they can't then maybe the main idea is not clear. The students all move on to a new partner and explain it to them for two minutes. This time they find it easier and start with fewer hesitations and appear much more confident. (Observation notes Class A)

Joan's *laissez faire* approach to peer discussion contrasted with her tight organization of her own writing conferences with the students. She gave very clear and very explicit instructions for these that put the onus firmly on the students in terms of initiating discussions and selecting the focus of those discussions. The students were told to be specific in their requests for help and to ask about particular problems with their writing. In the first workshop Joan explained their responsibilities to the students. She wanted to talk to all students at least once a week about their writing: "It's important that we talk." They could seek help from her or from other students, but it was up to them to initiate this interaction: "You tell me your problems. Come to me whenever you want help." Joan felt that it would be more helpful if the students identified their writing problems themselves and verbalized them to the teacher. In her interview she suggested this advice for new teachers of ESL about giving feedback in a conference: "Try to get students to identify their problems first... I think that's more effective feedback. If they perceive it as a problem, they are ready for an answer. It's a general learning principle that... if they've identified the problem, they've got more motivation to improve it."

She often reminded students: "Think of a specific problem. It will be more helpful." In the first workshop she gave the students some training in ways of asking specific questions:

> Joan circles "talk to Joan." She explains to the students that when they talk to her they need to be as specific as possible. She wants them to do some brainstorming now and think of some questions that are examples of specific questions. She says, "Can you look at this?" is not a specific question." The students laugh. Keith suggests grammar. Joan says that this is not specific enough. Seng Hee suggests, "Is this sentence correct? Joan suggests that this is better. Another student suggests, "Which tense should I use here?" Joan says, "This is good, very specific." (Extract from observation notes)

Thus for Joan the emphasis in the workshops was on the individual, with each student writing on his or her own, making his or her own diagnosis of writing problems and then working with the teacher to come up with solutions. The initiation and direction of most peer interactions that took place in the workshops was left to the students, but Joan's very clear modeling of the ways of identifying problems could have also served as a model for students when talking to each other about their writing.

Nadia and Class B: A Focus on Process Writing and Peer Interaction

Nadia, the teacher for Class B, had been teaching ESL students for thirteen years. One of her interests was creative writing, and she had written and published short stories herself. Nadia followed a process approach to teaching writing, strongly believing "writing is a process, not just a one-off thing," and she urged her students to "write, write, write" in order to improve their writing.

Oral interaction with students was seen as very important by Nadia, and in her interview she indicated that she saw her interactions in writing workshops as a crucial form of feedback because of the direct nature of the student-teacher interaction:

> I think an oral conference is probably the best thing you can do for students and that's why you have writing workshops where you can walk around and talk to the students . . . it's a one-to-one thing. You know you are actually doing it in front of them. You are showing them. Whereas in your writing, it's a kind of a third person thing where you are not actually physically present pointing it out. I think that's why the writing workshop situation is so important.

Like Joan, she viewed the writing conferences as a problem-solving opportunity involving the teacher, but unlike Joan, she saw her role as being to provide most of the direction:

> If I feel that there's somebody who has a problem which crops up all the time, then I tend to sit down with them and go through it with them. I sometimes talk to them about their writing—the things I've picked up and how they are dealing with that and where they can go to. . . . and where they can go to for work on the kind of grammar.

Peer written feedback and peer discussion were essential elements of Nadia's workshops because she was convinced that revising was the key to good writing and believed that students needed to receive as many sources and types of feedback as possible to help them with their revision. In her first workshop, she emphasized the collaborative nature of the workshop and the importance of peer interaction, telling students to use herself and the others in the class as resources, describing the workshops as "a really good time to use each other." She set up pre-discussion sessions before each writing task where the students in self-selected groups or pairs could brainstorm ideas together and discuss the essay topic before planning their own writings. The observation notes indicated that students took these very seriously:

> Zhang, Mei Ling, and Liang are discussing the question *Compare a free market economy with a planned economy in terms of economic growth.* They move on to a discussion about the political system in China, giving their personal feelings about it. Zhang feels that capitalism is wasteful and explains why he thinks that. All three start to blame the Soviet Union for China's economic problems. (Class B observation notes)

Nadia also used an adaptation of the 3,2,1 prewriting activity for prewriting discussion and, as in Joan's class, this was well received by students, as the observation notes show:

> The students are talking about their essay for four minutes to one student, then for three minutes to another and then for two minutes to another. All students are sitting and participating fully in this activity. The students who are listening bend forward to catch the other students' words. The speakers are animated. When it comes to the time to change partners, everyone does so very eagerly. There is a babble of noise and a cheerful atmosphere in the class. A lot of laughter can be heard as Nadia times them and tells them when their time is up. They appear reluctant to stop. Samorn says that the third time she spoke was the best. "I can think more about what I speak." (Class B observation notes)

Nadia also actively encouraged students to read and discuss each others' drafts during the workshops and formalized this by making them complete peer response sheets with set questions for each piece of writing:

> I get them to self evaluate their writing first of all and I get a peer to look at it and give them feedback on one aspect of it. They discuss it together. It's oral discussion in pairs, so they will discuss the written feedback they have done for each other. And then they hand in the peer feedback sheet, the self evaluation form, all the drafts for the essay that they've done so far, the brainstorming, all the notes. (Class B interview with teacher)

Most of Nadia's discussions with students began with Nadia doing circuits of the class, kneeling next to students or looking over their shoulders as they wrote. Unlike Joan, who insisted that students initiate and lead discussions with her, Nadia tended to intervene by providing direct comments on students' writing, and she usually initiated the interactions using openings like, "How's it going?" "Any problems?" "How are we doing here?" "How is your essay going?" She suggested in her interview that she preferred to give feedback in a global or holistic way, looking at the work as a whole rather than at individual problems. The classroom was arranged with all the desks pushed together, a bit like a refectory table with Nadia at the head. This meant that the class functioned more as a "macrocommunity" (Hirvela, 1999), and most peer interactions were between students and the persons sitting closest to them.

The descriptions of the two contexts show how very differently two individual teachers may treat writing workshops and promote the role of peer interaction within them. In Nadia's class, peer interaction was a crucial and formalized aspect of the workshops, but her own interactions with the students were very much less structured than Joan's. In Joan's class, the focus and conducting of peer interactions was mostly left up to the students, with very little encouragement or direction from the teacher, while expectations for the teacher/student interactions were very clearly laid out. The set up of the two classes with the creation of small microcommunities or groups in Joan's class and the sense of a more inclusive class-wide community in Nadia's class shows another contrast. With such a clear contrast, we might expect the nature and focus of peer interactions on writing in these two very different contexts to be quite different.

Patterns of Student-Student Interaction

The spoken interactions among the students in the two classes were examined to see how they provided scaffolding and support for students during the writing process (see Table 1). Because there was only one observer and students sometimes used their native languages for discussions, it was not possible to record all the interactions; it cannot be claimed that all the topics and discussions were covered in complete detail. However, as the classes were small, it was possible to make notes that covered nearly all the interactions.

Table 1
Student-Student Interactions on Writing

Focus of Interactions	Previous Feedback	Task Requirements	Writing Process	Written Draft	Total No. of Interactions
Class A	7 15%	12 25%	6 12%	23 48%	48 100%
Class B	13 23%	3 5%	0 0%	41 72%	57 100%

We have already seen that the two teachers had quite different stances and approaches to peer feedback, with Joan appearing to be quite unsure about its usefulness. Even though peers were mentioned once as a possible source of feedback to her class, little else was done to remind students of this or to reinforce the potential role of peer feedback or to encourage student/student interaction. On the other hand, we have noted that there was a very strong push from Nadia to make use of peers as readers, and this was reinforced a number of times throughout the workshops. It is not therefore surprising that a greater number of student-student interactions were observed in her workshops. What was interesting was the range of different types of interactions in both classes.

The students in Class B were more likely to discuss specific details of written drafts, often using the written feedback sheets as a guide or prompt, while the students in Class A tended to interact more fluidly and tended to focus more on ongoing aspects of the writing process, such as sorting out the task requirements or talking about the writing process itself. Joan's very clear instructions on how to use her as a resource person for problems relating to their written products may have encouraged her students to use her for those types of problems rather than their classmates. Nadia's students were sent clear messages to use everyone in the class as a reader and commentator on drafts. This was also reinforced by the (compulsory) written peer feedback sheet, which focused on specific aspects of the written drafts. Students were also more familiar with the process of writing. The stages in the process of writing were discussed at length by Nadia in her second workshop, and since all the students were post-graduates, they also had more direct experience with the whole writing process.

In addition to offering comments on each other's completed drafts, students in both classes consulted other students for practical assistance with both content and language at the immediate point of writing as they composed, as shown in these extracts from the observation notes:

> Kimiko asks about using the phrase *in my opinion* in an academic essay. Van tells her "That's OK." (Class A observation notes)

> Lin turns to Zhang and says, " I'm confused. Do I need to do like the long essay, say what I'm going to say and in the conclusion say what I've said? But this is short. I don't think it is necessary." Zhang says that he thinks it is. "Most essays you need to do this." (Class B observation notes)

> Samorn checks her sentence with Mei Ling. "So research shows that food colouring provoke an allergy"? Mei Ling says "induce." Samorn queries this. "Induce an allergy?" Mei Ling says, "yes." Lyn joins in. "What is the difference between provoke and induce? Do they mean the same thing?" (Class B observation notes)

One aspect focused on more in Class A than Class B was checking on task requirements. One student in Class A, Keith, had already completed one writing course and was often observed being a resource for his classmates, who believed he was more of an expert on what was required than they were and could therefore provide them with a role model:

> They continue to discuss the task requirements. Keith says that there are three kinds of writing on this course, journal writing, theme writing and assignments. The three others listen carefully and nod. He then discusses the topic he has chosen for his 600-word essay and his reasons for choosing it. (Class A observation notes)

> On Table C Maho is still talking as she looks at the tasks written on the whiteboard. She says it is very confusing. "What am I going to do first?" Keith comes over and tells her what needs to be done and explains that the plan, first draft and second draft all refer to the piece of work she is doing now. (Class A observation notes)

The observation notes also indicated that the students in both classes read each other's comments and feedback from the teacher with each other. Sometimes this seemed to be done specifically to share the teachers' comments:

> Chad . . . sits down reads the comments on Gina's writing and laughs. Then she reads Kris's comments. There is a lot of laughter and some discussion amongst all three about what the comments mean. (Class B observation notes)

> Joan gives out last week's test writing and the students read it silently. Kris shakes his head as he reads his comments and looks depressed. Table D then all look at Keith's comments together and laugh. (Class A observation notes)

The students also sought clarification of feedback they failed to understand from their classmates:

> Jeff and Chad are discussing a writing problem highlighted in Chad's feedback. Jeff says, "You can ask Joan. You need to ask Joan." (Class A observation notes)

> The students on table B are discussing their writing with each other. Van is talking about the teacher's comment "no promise to the reader" on his draft. He is canvassing different people on his table as to what it might mean. (Class A observation notes)

Students in Class A also discussed the process of writing itself. Perhaps because many of them were novices at academic writing and had not experienced process writing before, they turned to their classmates for confirmation that they were on the right track:

> Table D discuss what to do. Keith explains to the others. "You see, this is my first draft. Yesterday I checked my essay, now I will change some ideas and write my second draft." Abul nods. (Class A observation notes)

These examples provide some insight into the range of topics discussed and the various functions of the interactions and show how interaction in writing workshops involves much more than students simply commenting on each other's completed drafts.

Peer Support during the Writing Process

Spontaneous discussion and support are also an important part of the writing workshop. Dipardo & Freedman (1988) have argued for encouraging spontaneous peer talk during the writing process rather than using formalized peer feedback sheets to focus on drafts. Villamil and de Guerrero (1996) also point out the important role played by "affectivity" in peer interactions on writing. They suggest that this includes "camaraderie, empathy and concern for not hurting each other's feelings" (p. 65). As noted, the observations in the writing workshops suggested that such spontaneous and affective peer talk was both present and important in these two writing workshop contexts.

There were a large number of examples in the observation data of the students encouraging, supporting, and helping each other, without necessarily providing specific comments on writing. In Class A, 53 such episodes were noted, while there were 45 in Class B. Most instances were of the students turning to one another for impromptu support during the writing process. The importance of these informal interactions needs to be highlighted. De Guerrero and Villamil (1994, p. 492) suggest that such "about-task" and "off-task" discourse episodes may be serving a vital role for students both as "metatalk" and as affective support, as in the following examples from the observation notes:

> Keith turns to Jun and sighs and says "big problem." Jun asks him what the problem is. Keith says "Too much errors." Jun asks "Grammar?" and Keith replies "Yes grammar." They look at Keith's essay together. (Class A observation notes)
>
> Grace sits down and tells the other students on her table what Joan said were her problems, mainly to do with not having an academic tone. All four students discuss how to write in an academic way. Alex shakes his head. He says he finds this very difficult. (Class A observation notes)
>
> Sam is reading his feedback and turns to Lyn and sighs. He says, "Sometimes I want to get here in my writing." He extends his arm and points at his finger tips. "But I only get here." He points at his elbow. Lyn smiles sympathetically and nods. Sam sighs again and re-examines his paper. (Class B observation notes)
>
> Lyn looks at Zhang's essay, which looks almost complete. It is neat and ordered in paragraphs with no crossings out. She asks him how many words he has done. She says she finds it too difficult to give the two sides in a short essay. Zhang says he is sure she can do it. (Class B observation notes)

It was also interesting to see that these affective episodes were much more common in workshops where students had just received their drafts back with teacher feedback. More than 75 percent of all affective episodes were noted in workshops following feedback on drafts. It appears that students turned to their fellow students for reassurance most often when facing evaluations of their weaknesses in writing. On the other hand, when students were still working on initial drafts, they were more likely to discuss content or ask each other for practical assistance with language or organization.

Interaction outside the Classroom

Another important point about such informal oral peer interactions on writing is they are not necessarily limited to the classroom context. In both Classes A and B, students reported independently seeking the advice and guidance of others *outside* the classroom, where there were more opportunities for relaxed interaction. Two students, Liang and Keith, reported using their spouses (both more advanced L2 speakers), while others reported using flatmates or other ESL students. Both Liang and Keith suggested that because the relationship was a relaxed and friendly one, their spouses could provide affective support, feedback, and correction that could be supplemented by non-threatening but detailed oral discussion.

Liang gave each draft to her husband to look at, and he corrected the grammar and also gave her some suggestions about the comprehensibility of her writing. She indicated in her interview that she found the discussion this involved very useful:

> But I think the more important thing he can tell me which paragraph he don't understand what I mean, what I'm talking about. He always ask me "Why you say that? I don't understand what you speaking or why you use this sentence, can not understand the meaning." So when he asks the question I will think about what can I make it clear?

This quote shows that Liang did not see her role here as a passive one. She saw her husband's role as one where he alerted her to potential problems that she could then discuss with him and work on improving.

Nadia felt concerned about the very accurate language of Liang's writing and asked her on her draft of her first assignment: *Did you get some help with the editing?* After they discussed this, Liang was asked to submit all her future writing without consulting her husband. Liang wrote about this in her writing journal and indicated that she felt she was being denied access to an important source of feedback and interaction on her writing:

> I got the long essay yesterday. There were some mistakes and some sentences were not clear. I didn't ask my husband to revise the first draft, so there were lots of grammar mistakes. When I finish an essay, I usually give it to my husband. My husband corrects my mistakes and points out which sentence is not clear. I think it is good for me to learn how to write a correct essay. Sometimes I have

> good ideas, but I can not explain very well in English. My husband can give me advices to improve my writing. I always discuss some sentences with my husband and he teaches me grammar. In this way, I think I can improve my English ability. I like this kind of feedback. I can have more ideas about my essay during the discussion. (Journal entry)

Nadia responded to this with the following comment:

> *This is true—specially when you do university assignments next year. But now in terms of English learning, sometimes it's more important to try and learn from your own mistakes and self correct.*

Nadia felt that Liang was misusing peer feedback by enlisting her husband's help, rather than relying on her own resources. However, Liang believed that her discussion with her husband was scaffolding her development as a writer, viewing the interaction as a "collaborative endeavour" (Aljaafreh and Lantolf, 1994, p. 480). Liang considered her drafts as only a part of the writing process and not as final products, and she valued the collaborative face-to-face interaction with her husband as a learning opportunity, both in terms of language development, and also as a way of generating ideas. This is in line with the Vygotskyan concept that communicative collaboration with more skilled peers can lead to the development of the ability to solve problems independently (De Guerrero & Villamil, 1994).

On the other hand, Nadia saw the drafts as products with ownership issues and believed that Liang would develop more effectively as a writer if she functioned independently. Ownership here was a thorny issue, since the kind of discourse taking place between Liang and her husband may well have been the kind of peer collaboration Nadia was working hard to encourage in her classroom, and certainly in her interviews Liang indicated that she believed it was a collaborative discussion of her writing rather than a passive fixing up of her problems. Control and monitoring of this interaction by the teacher was, however, not possible since it took place outside the classroom, and this may be why Nadia felt uncomfortable with it. Nonetheless, the type of discourse that Liang was engaging in with her husband as an apprentice academic English writer was the type that would be invaluable to her later when she was writing independently for her Master's program. This highlights the difficulties teachers may feel when students take their exhortations to engage in active discussion and collaboration on their writing to a wider level.

Implications and Conclusions

This chapter has looked closely at two teachers and their management of workshops and has examined the student/student interactions within those workshops as a means of examining relationships between speaking and writing. The observations showed that these two teachers adopted different procedures in the way they handled their writing workshops. These differences could be related to the teachers' beliefs about the role of feedback and the process of writing for ESL students. There was an interesting contrast in the way the two teachers viewed and encouraged peer interaction in their workshops, with Nadia strongly encouraging peer feedback and Joan adopting a more *laissez-faire* approach and placing more emphasis on teacher/student interactions. In both classes, however, informal peer interactions on writing were observed frequently and were varied in their focus.

In order to help students to derive the maximum benefits of workshops, teachers need to consider their workshop management carefully and be clear about what they want to achieve. Although the workshops described were very different in their implementation, both had many positive aspects in terms of the interactions on writing taking place within them. Nadia's emphasis on students using each other as resources encouraged collaboration, while Joan's very focused approach to the teacher-student interactions in her workshops and the way she laid out the ground rules regarding roles and responsibilities in the interaction very clearly and consistently might also have provided an indirect model for student-student discussions on their writing. Her arrangement of the class into small groups or "microcommunities" of writers may also have facilitated student interaction by offering the students the security of working in a small community. It is interesting to note that peer discussion and verbal support evolved in both classes regardless of whether it was actively fostered or not, suggesting that students felt a need for such interaction.

Although it is beyond the scope of this chapter to try to directly link the various types of interactions with improvements or development in the students' writing, the chapter has sought to show the extent to which peer interaction is at the center of the writing workshop approach and to illustrate how spoken interaction during various stages of the writing process can help to scaffold and support writing. Oral interaction can be a starting point for students to develop and refine their ideas prior to writing, and the 3,2,1 activities observed in these workshops revealed the extent to which students both enjoyed and benefited from activities set up to encourage this type of discussion. Oral discussion can also be a way of confirming and elaborating their understanding of the writing task itself, as well as being of practical assistance. Such discussions can provide reassurance and serve as the kind of "academic apprenticeship" discussed by Weissberg (2006a). It can also be a catalyst to push students on with their writing and serve as a source of support when the writing task seems hard or the obstacles seem difficult to overcome. By discussing the challenges they face, students can articulate their problems, which is often the first step to solving them. Sharing problems also makes students aware that everyone experiences similar difficulties and thus makes these seem less oppressive. The potential of peers as critical readers has been established before in the literature on peer feedback, but we should not underestimate the importance of peer support or peer "nurturing" as a crucial aspect of the workshop environment and one that can help students to develop confidence and skills as writers.

We may also be overlooking the possible impact of interactions on writing that take place outside the classroom and their potential for student learning. This is a worthwhile area for research to further investigate and is a potential resource that writing teachers need to consider. Through investigations of students' self-selected outside sources of feedback, we could gauge the significance of this form of feedback, examining the extent to which these interactions occur, the types of interlocutors selected by students, and the ways that students use their own support networks on writing. It would be difficult to look closely at the actual dialogue of such interactions, but it is still an interesting area to research, since it is one where students have more control and autonomy over the selection of interlocutors and the focus of the feedback. Students, especially those preparing for an academic course, are not writing in a vacuum. They know there is a wide range of resources outside the classroom, including opportunities to discuss their writing and seek advice and support from friends and family. Teachers might also consider how they can help students to make the best possible use of these external interlocutors, so that the discussions that students engage in outside the classroom can be a collaborative learning opportunity rather than a fixing up of their problems.

The connection between speaking and writing in writing workshops is hard to unravel, since the interactions that take place in them involve a number of individuals with different motivations, and they encompass a wide range of topics and functions Although the workshops described in this chapter were very different in their implementation, both involved a rich variety of interactions. The chapter has tried to illustrate the complexity and range of such interactions and also to show how the students both valued and extended the role of dialogue on writing to provide each other with scaffolding on all aspects of the writing process, not just on their written products.

REFERENCES

Aljaafreh, A., & Lantolf, J. (1994). Negative feedback as regulation and second language learning in the zone of proximal development. *The Modern Language Journal, 78,* 465–483.

Allaei, S., & Connor, U. (1990). Exploring the dynamics of cross-cultural collaboration. *The Writing Instructor, 10,* 19–28.

Amores, M. J. (1997). A new perspective on peer editing. *Foreign Language Annals, 30,* 513–523.

Cohen, M., and Manion, L. (Eds.). (1994). *Research methods in education.* London: Croomhelm.

Connor, U., and Asenavage, K. (1994). Peer response groups in ESL writing classes: How much impact on revision? *Journal of Second Language Writing, 3,* 257–276.

De Guerrero, M. C. M., & Villamil, O. (1994). Social-cognitive dimensions of interaction in L2 peer revision. *The Modern Language Journal, 78,* 484–496.

Dipardo, A., & Freedman, S. W. (1988). Peer response groups in the writing classroom: Theoretical foundations and new directions. *Review of Educational Research, 58,* 119–149.

Freedman, S. W., & Sperling, M. (1985). Written language acquisition: The role of response and the writing conference. In S. W. Freedman (Ed.), *The acquisition of written knowledge: Response and revision* (pp. 106–130). Norwood, NJ: Ablex,

Goldenberg, C. (1993). Instructional conversations: promoting comprehension through discussion. *The Reading Teacher, 46,* 316–326.

Goldstein, L. M., & Conrad, S.M. (1990). Student input and negotiation of meaning in ESL writing conferences. *TESOL Quarterly, 24,* 443–460.

Hirvela, A. (1999). Collaborative writing instruction and communities of readers and writers. *TESOL Journal 8*(2), 7–12.

Hyland, F. (2000a). Teacher management of writing workshops: two case studies. *The Canadian Modern Language Review, 57,* 272–294. (Republished by arrangement with the *Asia Pacific Journal of Language in Education.*)

———. (2000b). ESL writers and Feedback: Giving more autonomy to students. *Journal of Language Teaching Research, 4,* 33–54.

Kennedy, G. E. (1983). *The nature and quality of compensatory oral expression and its effects on writing in students of college composition.* (ERIC Document No. 240 597)

Leki, I. (1990). Coaching from the margins: issues in written response. In B. Kroll (Ed.), *Second language writing: Research insights for the classroom* (pp. 57–68). Cambridge, UK: Cambridge University Press.

Lockhart C., & Ng, P. (1993). How useful is peer response? *Perspectives 5*(1), 17–29.

Mendonca, C.O., & Johnson, K. E. (1994). Peer review negotiations: Revision activities in ESL writing instruction. *TESOL Quarterly 28,* 745–768.

Nelson, G., & Carson, J. (1998). ESL students' perceptions of effectiveness in peer response groups. *Journal of Second Language Writing, 7,* 113–131.

Nelson, G., & Murphy, J. M. (1992). An L2 writing group: Task and social dimensions. *Journal of Second Language Writing, 1,* 171–193.

———. (1993). Peer response groups: Do L2 writers use peer comments in revising their drafts? *TESOL Quarterly, 27,* 135–141.

Nystrand, M., & Gamoran, A. (1991). Student engagement: When recitation becomes conversation. In H. C. Waxman and H. Walberg (Eds,) *Effective teaching: Current research* (pp. 257–276). Berkeley, CA: McCutchan.

Patthey-Chavez, G., & Ferris, D. (1997). Writing conferences and the weaving of multi-voiced texts in college composition. *Research in the Teaching of English, 31,* 51–90.

Peyton, K. P., Johns, C., Vincent, A., & Greenblatt, L. (1994). Implementing writing workshops with ESOL students: Visions and realities. *TESOL Quarterly, 28,* 469–487.

Sengupta, S. (1998). Peer evaluation: "I am not the teacher." *ELT Journal, 52*(1), 19–28.

Shi, L. (1998). Effects of prewriting discussions on adult ESL students' compositions. *Journal of Second Language Writing, 7,* 319–345.

Sweigart, W. (1991). Literacy as conversation: Classroom talk as text building. In J. Robinson (Ed.). *Conversations on the written word: Essays on language and literacy* (pp. 163–238). Portsmouth, NH: Boynton/Cook

Tsui, A., & Ng, M. (2000). Do secondary L2 writers benefit from peer comments? *Journal of Second Language Writing, 9,* 147–170.

Villamil, O. S., & de Guerrero, M. (1996). Peer revision in the L2 classroom: Social-cognitive activities, mediating strategies, and aspects of social behaviour. *Journal of Second Language Writing, 5,* 51–75.

Weissberg, R. (2006a). *Connecting speaking & writing in second language writing instruction.* Ann Arbor: University of Michigan Press.

———. (2006b). Conversations about writing: Building oral scaffolds with advanced L2 writers. In K. Hyland & F. Hyland (Eds.), *Feedback in Second Language Writing: Contexts and Issues* (pp. 246–265). New York: Cambridge University Press.

Wells, G. (1990). Talk about text: Where literacy is learned and taught. *Curriculum Inquiry, 20,* 369–405.

Wilcox, B. (1997). Two roles of a teacher during a writing conference. *Reading Teacher, 50,* 508–610.

Wood, D. J., Bruner, J. S., & Ross, G. (1976). The role of tutoring in problem-solving. *Journal of Child Psychology and Psychiatry, 17*(2), 89–100.

Zhang, S. (1995). Re-examining the affective advantages of peer feedback in the ESL writing class. *Journal of Second Language Writing, 4,* 209–222.

10

Multimodality and the Teaching of Advanced Academic Writing: A Genre Systems Perspective on Speaking-Writing Connections

CHRISTINE M. TARDY

Abstract

Genre-based pedagogies often advocate a "discovery" approach, which guides students through activities designed to raise awareness of specific features of key genres. The underlying assumption of such an approach is that writers begin to learn a genre (or, at least, certain features of the genre) through explicit analysis of and practice in that genre. Outside of the classroom, social and textual interactions within systems of genres also seem to play a crucial role in genre learning. This chapter describes how a systems-based view of genre—one that incorporates oral/aural, written, and even visual genres—can support the learning and teaching of advanced academic writing. The chapter outlines several principles of genre theory, bringing together the concepts of intertextuality, multimodality, and genre knowledge. Drawing on these principles, the chapter demonstrates how adopting a systems-oriented perspective may shift the focus of advanced genre-based writing instruction from isolated, written genres to intertextual genre activities that link spoken and written modalities. Finally, the chapter presents three pedagogical illustrations of a systems-based writing classroom.

Over the last few decades, genre-based pedagogies have become central to the teaching of English for Academic Purposes (EAP) and English for Specific

Purposes (ESP). Although various approaches to genre-based teaching have been described, the different orientations share a recognition of the important role that social context plays in writing. Many genre-based pedagogies advocate a "discovery" approach, which guides students through activities designed to raise awareness of specific features of key genres. A discovery approach makes intuitive sense for L2 writers, who often desire a concrete understanding of expectations for their writing (e.g., Angelova & Riazantseva, 1999; Blakeslee, 1997; Riazi, 1997). The underlying assumption of such an approach is that writers begin to learn a genre (or, at least, certain features of the genre) through explicit analysis of and practice in that genre.

Genre learning that occurs outside of classroom walls, research suggests, draws on some of these strategies as well. In "the real world," learners of a new genre often collect text samples, search out insights from expert users, and draw on guides, references, and templates to learn how to carry out the genre (Beaufort, 1999; Prior, 1998; Winsor, 1996, 2001); writers in non-classroom settings also learn through legitimate peripheral participation (Lave & Wenger, 1991), in which support from a more experienced guide gradually gives way to increasing participation and independence. In other words, situated genre learning is a social process, which draws on interactions with people and texts as a means of building the knowledge necessary for successful genre use. What emerges in studies of non-classroom genre learning, then, is a more complex picture of genre learning, in which writers build genre knowledge through interactions with multiple related genres, both oral and written. Indeed, genre theory has increasingly recognized the intertextual nature of genres as well, examining the ways in which texts intersect through genre chains, sets, or systems (see, for example, Bazerman, 1994; Devitt, 2004). These networks inevitably cross and mix modalities, including visual, oral/aural, and written "texts."

This chapter argues that a systems-based view of genre—one that incorporates oral/aural, written, and even visual genres—can add much to our understanding of the learning and teaching of single written genres in the writing classroom. An expanded pedagogical perspective that takes into account genre relations and both spoken and written interactions is particularly relevant to the teaching of advanced academic L2 writers, such as master's and doctoral students who are beginning the process of learning to participate in textually saturated disciplinary communities. The chapter begins by outlining several principles of genre theory, which connect notions of intertextuality, multimodality, and genre knowledge. Drawing on these principles, I consider how adopting a systems-oriented perspective may shift the focus of advanced genre-based writing instruction from isolated, written genres to intertextual genre activities that link spoken and written modalities. Finally, I describe such an expanded perspective by illustrating three pedagogical possibilities for writing instructors.

Intertextuality and Genre Knowledge

To use a genre is to participate in an intertextual system. Genre theory has emphasized the ways in which even the most mundane genres are linked to other texts, though the range of intertextuality may vary. The genre network surrounding a shopping list, for example, is more limited than that surrounding a federal tax form, but both texts are inseparably linked to other written and oral texts. Bakhtin (1986) outlines how this intertextual linking works on multiple levels, stressing the essentially social nature of text. He states that:

> Any concrete utterance is a link in the chain of speech communication of a particular sphere. The very boundaries of the utterance are determined by a change of speech subjects. Utterances are not indifferent to one another, and are not self-sufficient; they are aware of and mutually reflect one another. These mutual reflections determine their character. Each utterance is filled with echoes and reverberations of other utterances to which it is related by the communality of the sphere of speech communication. (p. 91)

In other words, genres can only be fully understood within the context of their use, which necessarily includes prior and subsequent texts.

As we participate in a particular sphere of communication—for example, a club, a neighborhood association, an academic discipline—we participate in a system of genres. The term *genre system* has been used to describe these "interrelated genres that interact with each other in specific settings" (Bazerman, 1994, p. 97). Because genre systems are used to carry out the work of a community, they both reflect and reinforce the community's ideologies and practices, providing us insights into a community. Yates and Orlikowski (2002) therefore argue that "understanding the interactions among genres and the communicative phenomena that emerge over time and space from genre interdependence gives us access to additional, larger insights" than the study of isolated genres can (p. 103). These insights, I would argue, are not just gained by genre theorists and researchers but also, crucially, by genre learners.

For novices, then, learning to participate in a new community includes learning the intertextual genre system. One needs to learn, for example, the generic resources available to respond to various exigencies. Consider the chain of genres involved in the typical blind peer review system: a submission letter and manuscript, an editor's request to peer readers, these readers' reviews, the editor's recommendations to the author, a revised manuscript with a response to the editor, and so on. Each stage in the process requires a response, and participants choose within a finite range of possible responses; a successful choice results in the continuation of communication, while an unexpected choice that lies outside of the generic possibilities may disrupt or even break down the genre chain.

Newcomers to a community must therefore learn the general paths and repertoires of communication that make up a community's genre system; that is, they must become familiar with how work gets carried out through genres. Graduate students and junior researchers, for instance, must become familiar with the genre system of blind peer review because knowledge of the system is essential to the submission process. In addition to this general intertextual knowledge, newcomers must learn to successfully produce specific genres within the system. In the early stages of community participation, a writer's focus is likely to be on the individual genres that hold primary importance for his or her own immediate goals. In the case of the peer review system, novice writers would tend toward greater investment in developing the manuscript itself than on their submission letter or written response to reviewers.

Knowledge of an individual genre is developed gradually, so a newcomer's understanding of it will likely be partial and rhetorically unsophisticated. Genre systems seem to play an important role in building this nascent knowledge. Through participation in a genre system, writers learn to understand how texts work—both individually and together—to carry out the particular goals of individuals and groups. They encounter some texts within the system that regulate practice explicitly, such as guidelines, handbooks, boilerplates, or evaluation criteria—texts that Giltrow (2002) refers to as "meta-genres." Participants also encounter genres that offer more implicit insight into the valued beliefs and practices of the community. They learn to borrow from the conventional discursive patterns that they encounter in the system, a process that Fairclough (1992) refers to as "interdiscursivity." As they experience the full range of texts that come to bear on central or key genres, writers also learn to "recontextualize" prior texts (Berkenkotter, 2001)—for example, incorporating notes, feedback, or proposals into a later text. Over time, genre expertise is built through the experience and practice that comes with community participation. Experts benefit from a "big picture" understanding of the genre system—they know who participates and what genres they use to participate. Experts have been through the system, playing various roles and participating in different stages of genre chains. In this way, expert knowledge of one genre incorporates an understanding of related genres.

Genre Systems and Multimodality

One would be hard pressed to identify a genre system that is monomodal, relying on, for example, only the written mode of communication. Rather, genres depend on interactions among participants, and those interactions take place through multiple modes (written, oral/aural, even visual and numerical), making genre systems both intertextual *and* multimodal. This phenomenon is easily illustrated though the example of a dissertation or thesis, a genre that much has been written about and one that has particular relevance to graduate L2 writers. The thesis is a rather unique genre in the sense that it is not something that writers can learn by carrying out the task repeatedly (as in a genre like the conference paper proposal, for example). Instead, writers generally face this task only one time in their life, although the task itself is carried out over a period of months or even years. Participation within an extended system of genres is a key to learning to write the thesis.

The thesis is of course part of a much larger genre system. Even before the thesis-writing task officially begins, a graduate student writes in many genres that lead up to (and feed into) the task, including perhaps course papers, lab reports, reading notes, conference papers, preliminary exam papers, or proposals. As the student embarks on the thesis itself, he or she may continue to produce some of these genres as well as new genres, such as data notes and memos, presentation papers and slides, progress reports, award applications, job applications, and perhaps journal articles. Each of these written texts is supported by numerous oral interactions, including seminars, lab discussions, oral presentations of papers and slides, advisor meetings, peer collaboration, formal and informal discussions, reading or writing groups, and oral defenses. Some graduate students keep blogs of their dissertation progress, while others create web pages that present their evolving ideas, incorporating visual genres as well. And then there are the genres that the student does not create but that nonetheless influence his or her understanding of the thesis as a genre: journal articles and books on the topic, conference and symposium papers within the field, protocol and formatting guidelines from the graduate school, formal and informal feedback from experts and peers, advice books or websites on dissertation writing, anecdotes or lore from others who have survived the process.

Although most of these genres bear little resemblance to a thesis in form, content, or rhetorical goals, together they help graduate writers build a richer understanding of the thesis. They feed into the writer's genre knowledge, creating a multilayered and increasingly sophisticated understanding of what the thesis aims to accomplish, what it might look like, what its disciplinary contribution might be, and how it might be composed, presented, and distributed to others.

Bazerman (2004) claims that "we create our texts out of the sea of former texts that surround us, the sea of language we live in" (p. 83); this sea of language is, crucially, both written and oral. Indeed, the influence of spoken language on written texts has been illustrated in numerous studies of academic writers. Prior's (1998) case studies of graduate student writers, for example, trace the ways in which graduate seminars, research group discussions, and advisor feedback influence the students' written texts both implicitly and explicitly. In her work with adult undergraduate writers, Ivanic (1998) is also able to locate both direct and indirect influences of spoken interactions on writers' texts, leading her to argue that "spoken and written language are inextricably intertwined in the acquisition of discourse" (p. 212). In a very different setting, Parks (2000) identifies oral collaboration as playing a key role in developing novice nurses' competence in writing patient care plans at work. Through "incidental collaboration" with experts at work, the newcomers learned to appropriate the linguistic, rhetorical, and informational features of the genre.

The earlier example of thesis writing also illustrates the importance of multimodality in shaping and building genre knowledge. Tables and charts, conversations, photographs, oral commentary, graphic models, and formal talks run throughout the thesis genre system; students encounter these multimodal texts as participants, creators, and observers, and the texts impact the writers in numerous ways. Most obviously, interlinked texts like these help writers build content knowledge of the topic. A statement made in an oral presentation or a question asked in the lab may be just as important (if not more) in building an understanding of the research problem as an article read in a journal. Linked multimodal texts also help writers build a complex knowledge of the thesis audience (both at the very local level and at a broader disciplinary level) and the goals of the document. It may be through participation at conferences, through discussions over lunch, or at seminars with guest speakers that graduate students gain "insider" knowledge of community goals, rhetorical strategies, and shared or competing ideologies. Oral interactions are often critical in building the procedural knowledge of how the thesis gets done, including perhaps the sequence of writing, procedures for collaboration and authorship, and the ways in which the material is presented to the larger research world. Through ancillary spoken genres, writers participate in patterns of disciplinary ways of communicating—the use of jargon, the strategies and forms of argumentation. Spoken texts—generic and non-generic—not only sustain and connect genre systems but also help newcomers build knowledge of the individual genres that constitute a network.

Multimodal Genre Systems and the Writing Classroom

While genre theory has moved into an intertextual view of genre, this systems-based lens has been adopted on a much more limited basis in discussions of genre learning, especially learning within the writing classroom. One exception can be found in the work of Russell (1997), who has emphasized the importance of genre systems in developing learners' situated understandings of genre as activity. Russell links genre systems to the activity systems that learners participate in—such as classrooms, workplaces, or disciplinary research. He argues that participation in a genre system provides students with access to discursive and material tools that can in turn expand their involvement in the larger activity systems of the discipline. Through this process, newcomers gradually become more "expert-like," as they gain familiarity with how things get done within the group. Building on Russell's claim, I would suggest that expanded participation in multimodal genre systems can also help learners develop a more sophisticated understanding of individual genres within the system. That is, as learners traverse interconnected genres through different modes, they gain insights that build their knowledge of key individual genres.

Although this genre system exposure and participation is vital in the learning process, Ivanic (1998) reminds us that "access to discourse is not random or arbitrary, but socially constrained" (p. 213). Several studies of international student L2 writers, for example, have suggested that these writers are often cut off from the social networks that support learning and success in graduate school (Dong, 1996, 1998; Shaw, 1991). In a study of five international students, Braxley (2005) found these students to see oral interactions—with friends, tutors, and instructors—as particularly important to writing development, yet the opportunities for these interactions were limited. In my own research with international graduate students, I noted a clear distinction in resource availability between those students who participated as members of research groups directed by a professor and non-thesis writing master's students who did not hold research assistant or teaching assistant positions (Tardy, 2004). Simply put, some students enjoy more access to the community—and thus more resources for genre learning—than others. This issue of resource availability is an important one that has received relatively little attention in pedagogical conversations. By broadening the perspective of advanced academic writing instruction to one of genre *systems*, instructors can find ways to provide "off-networked" students with at least some of the opportunities that aid in genre learning.

An Expanded Pedagogical Perspective: Multimodal Genre Systems

By and large, pedagogical discussions of genre-based learning have focused on the concept of "awareness-raising" through analysis of a specific genre, as described at the start of this chapter. A common feature in an advanced academic writing class, therefore, may be to ask students to collect samples of a research article in their field, analyze particular textual patterns (and deviations) among the samples, interview experts regarding the rhetorical basis of such patterns, and research some of the procedural conventions used to carry out the genre (see, for example, Hyland, 2004; Johns, 1997; Paltridge, 2001; Swales & Feak, 2000, 2004). Through this type of multidimensional genre analysis, learners can begin to demystify the largely invisible codes that structure writing practices and texts within specialized domains.

Activities like this have an important place in the classroom, as they allow students to filter out some of the rhetorical and linguistic complexities of genres. But what if classroom activities were to then proceed by moving beyond the individual genre, adopting the kind of systems-based perspective described? When genre-based pedagogy is refocused from a single genre perspective into a "systems-based" perspective, students gain opportunities to draw upon the intertextual and multimodal resources that are available to genre system participants.

A genre-system perspective into teaching academic writing draws on several basic principles of genre theory, as previously discussed. First, individual genres exist within a larger system of genres. Second, expert genre knowledge includes a sophisticated understanding of the system (or systems) to which that genre belongs. Third, genre systems are multimodal, including both oral/aural and written genres. As users traverse a genre system, they participate in multiple modes of communication, developing knowledge of individual genres through oral/aural texts, written texts, and even visual texts that make up the genre system.

The writing classroom is, of course, somewhat removed from the "situated learning" environments that are considered to be necessary for developing genre knowledge. Therefore, the goal of the teacher, in my view, should not be to replicate the "work" environment but instead to augment that environment. One strength of the classroom environment is that in altering the time and space of genres (e.g., devoting two weeks and multiple drafts to a text usually written under short time pressure), learners gain the opportunity to explore, analyze, and critique those genres to build a meta-awareness of individual genres *and* the systems that they exist within. A genre-systems framework lends itself extremely well to the graduate-level academic writing classroom, in which students are relatively new members of very specialized communities and must learn to communicate through the community's systems of oral and written genres. What might such a refocused genre-systems pedagogy look like within this context? I provide three illustrations of how a systems-based pedagogy may be adapted within the instructional setting of an advanced academic writing classroom.

Illustration #1: Panel Discussions

Most advanced academic writing classes can take on a systems-based perspective with relatively little readjustment. A unit focusing on writing article introductions, for example, could begin with a guest panel of experienced academic writers. The panel can be arranged to represent the various stages of the publishing process, so that one speaker describes his or her process in preparing and revising a manuscript for publication, another speaker describes his or her perspectives as a journal editor, and a third speaker describes his or her perspectives as an editorial member reviewing manuscripts. Alternatively, a panel could be formed to represent a range of disciplinary perspectives, each describing the publishing process from their disciplinary vantage point, perhaps sharing multiple drafts of a published article to illustrate the changes made to the introduction (or another section) in response to peer reviews or an editor's suggestions. Panelists may be asked to describe specifically the role of oral interactions (such as conversations with peers, advisors, or editors) in the writing process.

Guest speakers help to bring the writing process alive in a way that classroom discussions alone cannot. As students listen to experts talk about their writing, they gain insight into how writing is situated within the activity of research and therefore tied to the complex practices of knowledge making.

Inviting disciplinary expert writers into the writing classroom also creates a space for explicit discussion about writing among disciplinary members. These oral interactions can have a profound impact on students at the early stages of disciplinary participation.

Illustration #2: Genre System Portfolio

In the introductory chapter of their textbook, *English in Today's Research World*, Swales and Feak (2000) present the idea of genre networks through a task that asks students to map out a "genre planner," detailing the work to be completed—and the genres used to do so—over the course of the coming year. Through this task, students identify the oral and written genres of key importance to them, and they gain a sense of the sequential and intertextual relationships among these texts. Students can further develop this foundational understanding of genre system by assembling a "genre system portfolio." Building on the idea of literacy portfolios described by Johns (1997) and Hirvela (1997), a genre system portfolio allows students to collect artifacts from a target web of genres. Unlike the genre planner, the genre system portfolio includes not only those texts that the students must produce but also those that the student encounters—that is, those that the students' own texts recontextualize, respond to, or lead to.

A genre system portfolio may encompass a broad domain such as graduate research (see Figure 1), or it may detail the more immediate system surrounding a single genre of importance, such as a research article (see Figure 2). In either case, students should be encouraged to investigate both the written and oral genres that make up the system. Although it is far easier to obtain physical artifacts of written genres, evidence of oral genres should still be included; students could observe oral genres (such as conference presentations or seminar presentations) and write summaries of them, or they might create a multimedia portfolio that includes audio and video files as well as text files. Students should also be encouraged to collect not only the texts that respond to one another as part of a genre chain, but also the meta-genres that regulate the system and the expectations for individual genres, such as the evaluation criteria for a conference proposal or the graduate school's thesis formatting guidelines.

To collect relevant artifacts and to gain insight into their uses and contexts, students should work with one or more mentors. These mentors may be more experienced peers, content-area professors, and/or thesis advisors. The mentors can help students identify relevant genres, but even more importantly they serve as a resource for learning. Interviews with the mentor

Figure 1

Sample Contents for a Broad-Scale Genre System Portfolio: Graduate Research

	Primary Genres	Meta-Genres
Written genres	• Course papers • Lab reports • Response papers • Bibliographies • Preliminary exams • Research proposals • Conference proposals and papers • Conference handouts • Thesis/Dissertation • Book reviews • Journal articles • Newsletter articles • Professional listserv discussions • Fellowship and grant applications	• Course assignment sheets • Preliminary exam guidelines • Thesis timetables • Thesis formatting guidelines • Documentation style guidelines • Conference submission guidelines • Advice on research processes
Spoken genres	• Graduate seminar discussions • Research presentations • Preliminary oral exams • Oral thesis defense • Conference presentations	• Advice on thesis preparation • Information about specific journals, conferences, and professional organizations • Feedback or collaboration on writing and research

can be used to gather advice, anecdotes, or reflections of expert practices. Ideally, interviews serve the additional role of opening up communication between novices and experts; for students who have little interaction with professors (such as non-thesis writing master's students), these interviews may provide one of the few opportunities students have for social interaction with an expert in their field.

Finally, sequencing the contents of the portfolio is a crucial step in the assignment, as it is through this process that the students explicitly identify links and relationships among the genres. An additional portfolio requirement may be to prepare a cover letter that includes a discussion of these relationships, either in written form or visually through flowcharts, tables,

Figure 2

Sample Contents for a Focused Genre System Portfolio: Research Articles

	Chain of Genres	Meta-Genres
Written genres	• Sample articles • Submission cover letters • Editor-author correspondences • Sample manuscript reviews • Author bio-statements	• Journal guidelines for authors • Documentation style guidelines • Journal manuscript evaluation criteria
Spoken genres	• Guest talk or seminar related to published articles • Class discussions of published articles • Research group presentation of in-progress article	• Advice on manuscript preparation • Advice on the submission process • Information about specific journals • Feedback or collaboration on draft

or maps. Portfolios can be shared in small groups or as a whole class, so that students have the opportunity to see similarities and variations in intertextual systems across disciplinary communities or even specialized sub-fields.

Illustration #3: Genre System as Organizing Principle

A systems-based approach to teaching advanced academic writing can also be realized through an intertextual orientation to course design. In other words, the course syllabus may be organized around key genres within a system of focus (such as graduate school research). Assignments can be sequenced to purposefully move students through some of the key genres of academic research, highlighting the links between and among these texts. This approach is described by Hyland (2004), who presents genre networks as one possible organizing principle for a genre-based writing course, arguing that understanding the "event sequences" in which genres occur can help instructors order assignments and integrate written and spoken language in meaningful ways. Purposefully sequenced assignments can build students' textual resource pools, so that prior texts can be recontextualized in later assignments.

Beyond using genre systems as a means of sequencing major assignments, however, instructors may expand individual genre-centered assignments to help students "plug into" the multimodal genre system, thereby drawing on written, oral, and visual resources made available through the system. Consider, for example, the textual elements involved in the "event" of an academic conference paper—a task that is relevant and accessible to students at most stages of a graduate program. Conference papers are firmly embedded within a network of oral and written genres, some of which are illustrated in Figure 3. The right-hand column of the figure lists the written and oral meta-genres that provide writers with guidance in writing, revising, and presenting the conference paper. These texts may dictate content, format, and/or length; they may provide advice or describe the criteria by which the paper will be evaluated. In some fields, meta-genres also include written reviews of submitted papers or proposals, as these reviews will make explicit reference to strengths and weaknesses in the submitted paper or proposal. Another important resource within this genre system is samples of the target genre. Novices may turn to papers published in proceedings or their memories of oral presentations that they have heard. They may have access to conference papers given by peers or professors. These samples—whether explicitly analyzed or not—become an important part of a writer's understanding of the genre. Finally, the conference paper is linked to other

Figure 3

Oral and Written Texts Involved in Preparing an Academic Conference Paper

	Chain of Genres	Meta-Genres
Written genres	• Conference proposal • Sample conference papers • Presentation slides • Written paper for proceedings	• Conference website • Call for papers • Evaluation and submission criteria • Conference submission reviews
Spoken genres	• Seminar or meeting discussing the research • Oral presentation • Post-paper discussions	• Advice on conference submissions • Information about a specific conference • Feedback or collaboration on draft

texts in a chained sequence, or dialogue. It is written in response to but also concurrently with oral discussions of the topic, a proposal or abstract, a set of accompanying slides or handouts, an oral commentary which may differ somewhat from the written version, and perhaps formal or informal discussions following an oral presentation of the paper.

While the complexities of this genre network cannot possibly be replicated in the classroom, instructors can purposefully sequence activities that take students through parts of the network, helping students access at least some of the resources made available through participation in the genre system, as described.

1. *Research a particular conference forum.* At the start of the task, students research a conference in their field for which they will write a paper. This step might involve an exploration of the conference website, which should include a call for papers as well as any details specifying paper requirements and expectations. Students may also gather less formal information about the conference venue by speaking with peers and experts in their field. What reputation does the conference have? What is the typical manner of presentation? What kinds of topics are typically addressed and not addressed at this conference?
2. *Narrow research focus for the conference.* After an initial exploration of the forum, students can begin to narrow the focus for their conference papers. Individual conferences or peer groups can be used in this prewriting stage, giving students a chance to talk through their ideas before committing them to the page. For conferences that require a proposal or abstract, students can write this short text to focus in on their topic. Students who are submitting to conferences that require the submission of a full paper (typical in many scientific fields) may still find the task of writing a proposal or abstract to be useful in focusing down the content of the paper.
3. *Analyze and draft the target genre.* Before students begin to draft their papers, they should collect a small corpus of sample conference papers, which may be collected from experienced writers in the field or from conference proceedings for those in scientific and technical fields. These papers may come from the same conference they are "submitting" to or from a variety of conferences (giving an opportunity for comparative analysis). In this stage, students can look for conventional features as well as variations and acts of generic resistance or genre bending. Students should be encouraged, or even required, to discuss papers with a field expert to

gain an understanding of how the papers may be responded to by others. These sample papers and the discussions about them can provide important textual and discursive resources as students begin drafting their own conference paper.

4. *Share and revise conference paper or proposal.* Conferences, class discussions, teacher conferences, or discussions with advisors or mentors can provide valuable feedback on drafts. Such discussions can also give writers an opportunity to work out difficulties with the text and to consider alternative ways of expressing ideas.
5. *Prepare and present visual slides and oral commentary.* Creating a presentation requires students to use a new genre and new modes (visual and oral) to communicate the content of their paper. In some writing classrooms, it may be possible to have students give mini-presentations of their papers; in others, constraints of time or class disciplinary knowledge may make this option difficult. If pressed for time, students could be asked to present an overview of their research in a four-minute talk followed by two or three questions from peers. If students do not share a disciplinary background, they can be asked to re-focus their classroom talk for a lay audience. Doing so has the advantage of requiring students to concentrate on distilling the main argument or contribution of their work.
6. *Revise written conference paper.* Researchers often note that sharing work orally can be an important step toward improving written versions of research. A written text can then benefit not only from the feedback provided by peers but also from resulting revisions—that is, the very process of re-working and re-shaping the content of the work. Classroom settings often ask students to present their work orally only *after* a written text has been completed, but reversing the order of these tasks has certain advantages. Giving students revision time after an oral presentation can allow them to use what they learned from the presentation as they re-visit and revise their formal written paper.

These steps can be simplified or expanded, depending on the constraints and options within any given instructional setting. The assignment sequence may also be followed up by another task that could logically follow a conference paper, such as a research article or a thesis chapter.

A writing classroom is not the same as the world of disciplinary practice, and writers cannot build the kind of sophisticated genre knowledge of experts within the confines of the classroom setting. On the other hand, the classroom can provide valuable support that may not be otherwise available to learners. In fact, one benefit of the classroom is that it allows students to simplify the complexities of genre engagement, focusing only on textual forms or rhetorical contexts or even task procedures, rather than having to juggle all of these demands and expectations at once (Johns et al., in press). Classrooms can gradually build into these "stripped-down" tasks expanded views of genres, obliging students to consider the connections among various oral and written genres. Expanding the lens of genre-based pedagogy to the relevant systems of genres that students engage in (or hope to engage in) can likewise expand students' interaction with the oral and written texts that provide vital resources for learning, thus illustrating the valuable role that speaking-writing connections can play in an academic writing course.

REFERENCES

Angelova, M., & Riazantseva, A. (1999). "If you don't tell me, how can I know?" A case study of four international students learning to write the U.S. way. *Written Communication, 16,* 491–525.

Bakhtin, M. M. (1986). *Speech genres and other late essays* (V. W. McGee, Trans.; C. Emerson & M. Holquist, Eds.). Austin: University of Texas Press.

Bazerman, C. (1994). Systems of genres and the enactment of social intentions. In A. Freedman & P. Medway (Eds.), *Genre and the new rhetoric* (pp. 79–101). Bristol, PA: Taylor & Francis.

———. (2004). Intertextuality: How texts rely on other texts. In C. Bazerman & P. Prior (Eds.), *What writing does and how it does it: An introduction to analyzing texts and textual practices* (pp. 83–96). Mahwah, NJ: Lawrence Erlbaum.

Beaufort, A. (1999). *Writing in the real world: Making the transition from school to work.* New York: Teachers College Press.

Berkenkotter, C. (2001). Genre systems at work: DSM-IV and rhetorical recontextualization in psychotherapy paperwork. *Written Communication, 18,* 326–347.

Blakeslee, A. (1997). Activity, context, interaction, and authority: Learning to write scientific papers in situ. *Journal of Business and Technical Communication, 11,* 125–169.

Braxley, K. (2005). Mastering academic English: International graduate students' use of dialogue and speech genres to meet the writing demands of graduate school. In J. K. Hall, G. Vitanova, & L. Marchenkova (Eds.), *Dialogue with Bakhtin on second and foreign language learning: New perspectives* (pp. 11–32). Mahwah, NJ: Lawrence Erlbaum.

Devitt, A. J. (2004). *Writing genres.* Carbondale: Southern Illinois University Press.

Dong, Y. R. (1996). Learning how to use citations for knowledge transformation: Non-native doctoral students' dissertation writing in science. *Research in the Teaching of English, 30,* 428–457.

———. (1998). Non-native graduate students' thesis/dissertation writing in science: Self-reports by students and their advisors from two U.S. institutions. *English for Specific Purposes, 17,* 269–390.

Fairclough, N. (1992). *Discourse and social change.* Cambridge, UK: Polity Press.

Giltrow, J. (2002). Meta-genre. In R. Coe, L. Lingard, & T. Teslenko (Eds.), *The rhetoric and ideology of genre* (pp. 187–205). Creskill, NJ: Hampton Press.

Hirvela, A. (1997). "Disciplinary portfolios" and EAP writing instruction. *English for Specific Purposes, 16,* 83–100.

Hyland, K. (2004). *Genre and second language writing.* Ann Arbor: University of Michigan Press.

Ivanic, R. (1998). *Writing and identity: The discoursal construction of identity in academic writing.* Philadelphia: John Benjamins.

Johns, A. M. (1997). *Text, role, and context: Developing academic literacies.* Cambridge, UK: Cambridge University Press.

Johns, A. M., Bawarshi, A., Coe, R. M., Hyland, K., Paltridge, B., Reiff, M. J., & Tardy, C. M. (in press). Crossing the boundaries of genre studies: Commentaries by experts. *Journal of Second Language Writing.*

Lave, J., & Wenger, E. (1991). *Situated learning: Legitimate peripheral participation.* Cambridge, UK: Cambridge University Press.

Paltridge, B. (2001). *Genre and the language learning classroom.* Ann Arbor: University of Michigan Press.

Parks, S. (2000). Professional writing and the role of incidental collaboration: Evidence from a medical setting. *Journal of Second Language Writing, 9,* 101–122.

Prior, P. A. (1998). *Writing/disciplinarity: A sociohistoric account of literate activity in the academy.* Mahwah, NJ: Lawrence Erlbaum.

Riazi, A. (1997). Acquiring disciplinary literacy: A social-cognitive analysis of text production and learning among Iranian graduate students of education. *Journal of Second Language Writing, 6,* 105–137.

Russell, D. H. (1997). Rethinking genre in school and society: An activity theory analysis. *Written Communication, 14,* 504–554.

Shaw, P. (1991). Science research students' composing processes. *English for Specific Purposes, 10,* 189–206.

Swales, J. M., & Feak, C. B. (2000). *English in today's research world: A writing guide.* Ann Arbor: University of Michigan Press.

———. (2004). *Commentary for academic writing for graduate students, 2nd ed.* Ann Arbor: University of Michigan Press.

Tardy, C. M. (2004). *Exploring the interactions of writing instruction and disciplinary practice: Pathways of four multilingual writers.* Unpublished doctoral dissertation, Purdue University.

Winsor, D. A. (1996). *Writing like an engineer: A rhetorical education.* Mahwah, NJ: Lawrence Erlbaum.

———. (2001). Learning to do knowledge work in systems of distributed cognition. *Journal of Business and Technical Communication, 15*, 5–28.

Yates, J., & Orlikowski, W. (2002). Genre systems: Chronos and kairos in communicative interaction. In R. Coe, L. Lingard, & T. Teslenko (Eds.), *The rhetoric and ideology of genre* (pp. 103–121). Creskill, NJ: Hampton Press.

Part 3

How Writing Scaffolds Speaking

11

Writing to Speak: What Goes On across the Two-Way Street

DONALD L. RUBIN AND OKIM KANG

Abstract

Development in oral communication proficiency and in writing are mutually interdependent. Yet most theory and practice linking instruction in oral and written modalities treat speaking as the precursor, and writing performance as the outcome of particular value. To remedy that imbalance, it is useful to consider six ways in which written language serves as the foundation for oral performance: (1) Learning the print code advances metalinguistic awareness of speech. (2) Literacy advances metarhetorical awareness of speech strategies. (3) Talk is often the social consequence of writing. (4) Writing can script oral performances, as in speech writing. (5) Writing often guides face-to-face knowledge exchange, as in scientific poster presentations. (6) Writing often guides deliberative interaction, as in briefing documents used in collaborative decision making. Poster presentations and briefing documents can serve as paradigms for integrating instruction in oral and written communication.

More than 25 years ago Kantor and Rubin (1981; see also Rubin & Kantor, 1984) proposed a model of inter-related development in spoken and written discourse. They postulated that communication competence develops along three inter-related dimensions: coding, social awareness, and reconstruction of experience. Moreover, they claimed that along each of these dimensions, growth in speech affects growth in writing. Growth in writing, they likewise contended, reciprocally affects growth in speech. The arrows between development in speech and in writing are double-headed.

In depicting arrows pointing from speech to writing, Kantor and Rubin were simply rehearsing ground already well-trod at that time and further explicated in subsequent scholarship. A considerable body of developmental theory about emergent writing (e.g., Cook-Gumperz & Gumperz, 1981) as well as about life-span literacy learning in English (e.g. Rubin, 1987) and about languages other than English (Allen & Rubin, 1993) explicates the dependency of writing development on underlying oral skills. Scholars in L1 language development in particular seem to have reached consensus that literacy acquisition depends critically upon speech processing skills (e.g., Ravid & Tolchinsky, 2002; Thompkins & Binder, 2003; Verhoeven, 2002). In addition, a considerable body of pedagogical craft (e.g., Brice, 2004; Rubin & Dodd, 1987; see especially Weissberg, 2006, for L2 writing pedagogy) exploits that dependency of writing on speaking.

The arrow pointing from writing to speaking represents a territory not so well charted. Certainly scholars before (e.g., Gleason, 1961) Kantor & Rubin (1981) and after (e.g., Stotsky, 1987) acknowledge the possibility that speech and writing may be reciprocally dependent. J. Williams (this volume) does make important strides toward recognizing a "writing into speaking" process but asserts that at least in terms of second language acquisition, the impact of writing on speech must always be indirect, since oral competence ontologically precedes writing. But few scholars have pursued (descriptively) the ways in which writing supports oral development or oral processes. Neither, for that matter, did the Kantor & Rubin (1981) essay that serves as progenitor for this current exposition. The purpose of this chapter, then, is to redress that imbalance. Assuming that relationships between speech and writing constitute a two-way street, this chapter seeks to sketch out the kinds of trafficking that takes place from writing to speech. The latter part of this chapter discusses two common speech events that use writing as their foundation: the briefing in organizational communication and the poster presentation in scientific communication. Written documents are interwoven into the briefing in several ways, including the use of outlines or summaries as guides for the conduct of oral interaction. Similarly, at least one view of scientific posters is that they should serve to elicit face-to-face interaction among interested parties, but ought not really function as autonomous texts. This chapter concludes by suggesting that classes organized around a case/project curriculum are best equipped for helping students learn to navigate through the reciprocal relations between speech and writing.

Subordinating the Oral Code

It is not surprising that educational research and practice have emphasized the role of speech as a precursor to writing to the virtual exclusion of the complementary role—that is, speech as the teleology or consequential outcome of writing. Literacy theory usually treats writing as a more advanced code than speech. Speech is regarded as more primitive. Ontogenetically in L1 development and in most bilingual settings, speech does precede writing. And ontogenetically, acquiring the oral code seems to require less effort and less formal tutelage than acquiring the written code—though it is worth noting that both native speaking children and additional language learners divine a great deal more about literacy through ambient or out-of-school exposure than is sometimes appreciated (Harste, Woodward, & Burke, 1984).

In the context of foreign language instruction, calls for embracing communicative language teaching have for at least two decades encouraged a focus on oral communication as a self-consummatory goal, as opposed to merely in its instrumental role in scaffolding writing (Savignon, 1983). Yet mandates for communicative language teaching in English as a foreign language are still only slowly and imperfectly exerting impact on teaching and learning practices with respect to orality (Gatbonton & Segalowitz, 2005; Savignon & Wang, 2003). In most university foreign language curricula, language learning is often perceived as being at the service of the "real" work of literary study (Kern & Schultz, 2005). So it is writing and reading—and not talking and speaking—that are the real objects of direct, institutionally sanctioned instruction. Even when oral performance is invited in school settings, teachers may evaluate such talk according to the degree to which it conforms to literate conventions (Michaels, 1986).

Phylogenetically, speech is likewise regarded as more primitive than writing. While Ong (1982), for example, takes care to caution against associating negative value judgments with orality as opposed to literacy, it is clear that he and like-minded scholars regard the innovation of literacy—especially alphabetic literacy—as a crowning achievement of Western civilization (cf. Bizzell, 1988). According to much literacy theory, preliterate and oral cultures lack historical consciousness, lack psychological analysis, lack aesthetic critical sense, lack formal logical reasoning, and lack the attributes that contemporary Western industrialized societies prize most dearly. For related reasons, oral-based subcultures within a literate mainstream culture are likely to be perceived as menacing (Kinzer & Ruethling, 2004; Kochman, 1975).

Cognitively, speech is similarly often linked by literacy theory to less advanced, more primitive processes. In a foundational study on writing and thought, Emig (1977) argued that writing is a mode of learning uniquely suited for processing abstraction and for laying bare complex reasoning. Speech is often seen as the medium for transmitting or reproducing knowledge, whereas writing transforms knowledge (Olson, 1994, 2002; but for a less biased view from the same cognitive psychologist see Olson, 1995). In point of fact, this view is not correct, as literacy is often used solely for reproducing knowledge (Street, 1985), and oral discussion can indeed lead to significant transformations of knowledge, not all of which are evident from the surface syntax of informal speech (Berry, 1985).

Halliday (1987) presents a convincing counterdemonstration to this prevailing view of literacy theory, arguing in opposition to the view "of written language as richly endowed, while speech is a poor man's assemblage of shreds and patches" (p. 67). Halliday argues that speech is grammatically intricate, though lexically simple, and that speech is highly structured in just the ways necessary to accommodate to the needs of listeners. He concludes that writing and speaking are distinct semantic systems, different but co-equal modes of meaning. In other words, oral and written languages are on a structural-functional continuum, with different structures conventionally associated with different functions in context (Barton, 2004; Rubin, Goodrum & Hall, 1990; Rubin, Hafer & Arata, 2000).

The Role of Speech in Prevailing Writing Instruction

This Hallidayan (1987) perspective still exerts little influence on educational practices. Instead, the dominant view of orality as the precursor and handmaiden of literacy seems to guide most efforts at linking speaking and writing instruction. In the overwhelming preponderance of language arts activities or curricula, speech is subsumed into the process of composing written text, and writing is the goal toward which that process aims. Rubin and Dodd (1987; also Rubin, 1987) recognize three such ways in which speech activities are pressed into service to enhance writing.

First, speech activity can *accompany* various aspects of composing processes. Whole class pre-writing discussion has long been a mainstay for helping students discover subject matter about which to write. Discussion among peer response groups assists writers in gauging their audiences, in planning for revision, and in many other respects.

Speech activity can also serve as an *adjunct* to composing; that is, a portion of the composing might be conducted in talk rather than in writing.

In Zoellner's (1969) foundational talk-write methodology, for example, students draft their compositions in dialogue with a partner who serves as questioner/prompter and as scribe.

Finally, speech activities can serve a *calisthenic* function. As cognitive calisthenics, oral exercises may or may not lead up to a tangible written product. Instead, these activities develop the kinds of linguistic, social awareness, or epistemic skills that underlie writing of one kind or another. Rubin and Dodd (1987), by way of illustration, advocate a form of impromptu speech-making that helps students develop facility in "sculpting" meaningful and manageable topics from assigned prompts. Similar cognitive calisthenic linkages from speech to writing improvement characterize Cook's (2000) research on role-play activities with L1 elementary students and Brice's (2004) recommendations for story retelling, think-pair-share, and role playing to improve writing skills of learning disabled L1 speakers. In the context of L2 instruction, Weissberg (2006) demonstrates how dialogue-writing relationships are developed through such oral activities as small group problem-solving exercises and conferencing.

As valuable and productive as these activities may be for learning to write, they constitute an unbalanced stance toward the relation between speaking and writing. They represent mainly the arrow that points from speech to writing. Other kinds of communicative situations may utilize writing or written documents to mediate a speech event as ultimate outcome. One simple example of that kind of communication situation is the letter of introduction. Person A writes Person B about Person C for the ultimate purpose of facilitating an interview between B and C. It is the interview and not the letter that holds valence for the parties involved. To sensitize educators about the need for *fully* integrating speaking with writing, to think about a truly bidirectional arrow, it is helpful to briefly consider ways in which writing affects speech or speaking.

Influences of Writing on Speaking

Acquiring the Print Code Affects Metalinguistic Representation of Speech

Metalinguistic awareness—that is, awareness of language as an object—and acquisition of literacy are related. The development of script as a linguistic transcription system brings underlying linguistic structure into consciousness and renders it an object of study (Olson, 1994, 2002). When children can *visualize* language because they have cracked the print code, they consequently become more aware of the stream of speech as composed of segmentable units. Olson (2002) states that learning to read is to an important extent a matter of learning how to analyze one's speech in a new way, a way compatible with the properties of the writing system, and therefore the child has to learn to hear the sounds represented by letter in their own and others' speech. In this sense, good readers are more likely than novice readers to pronounce every phoneme aloud in certain words (and even to add some) (Ehri, 1985).

In studies comparing adult literates to nonliterates, major differences in general cognitive functioning are subtle at best. Where dramatic differences do emerge, however, is in literate adults' recognition of word and phonemic boundary units in speech and in their more complete realization of word pronunciations (Ferguson, 1981; Dellatolas, Willadino-Braga, Souza, Filho, Queiroz, & Deloche, 2003; Morais, Bertelson, Cary, & Alegria, 1986; Scribner & Cole, 1981). In contrast, illiterate adults rely heavily on semantic strategies rather than phonological strategies to perform lexical tasks (Reis & Castro-Caldas, 1997). In other words, acquisition of the ability to decode an alphabetic script changes the way in which individuals process oral languages in certain kinds of cognitive tasks (Tarone & Bigelow, 2005).

For nonalphabetic scripts, in which phonemes (or morphemes) can be mapped onto graphemes less reliably—and sometimes not at all—the impact of literacy on metalinguistic awareness is less well understood (Allen & Rubin, 1993).

Developing Written Discourse Affects Metarhetorical Awareness of Oral Structures

Although classical Greek rhetoricians like Plato and Aristotle were mainly concerned with the efficacy of oral discourse—they regarded writing simply as speech written down (Olson, 1994)—the claim has been made (e.g., Ong, 1982) that it was the advent of alphabetic literacy that enabled them to reflect on discourse as an object of inquiry. That is, the advent of writing enabled ancient civilizations to separate what is said from the manner of its saying, from the act of saying it, and from the sayer. And while there is little reliable proof of it, it seems that many "naïve" rhetoricians are sensitized to the structure of spoken discourse by extrapolating from writing. In speech class, the vocabulary of written structure describes units of speech; for example, "paragraph" refers to a unit of oral argument. In conversation, one person abjures, "Let me erase that and start over." For L1 language users, good readers are good listeners (Perfetti, 1987), probably because they know how to search for and detect rhetorical structures (since decoding is hardly an issue in L1 listening). Similarly, it is likely that good writers in their L1 are good speakers in their L1 (of at least certain kinds of discourse), probably because they are best able to deliberately manipulate rhetorical structure.

Talk Is Often the Social Consequence of Writing

While oral activities can often stimulate writing, the converse also holds true: people discuss their writing. Our written voices are quite literally linked to the oral voices (Dyson, 2000). Dyson (1990) observes,

> But talk's relationship with writing is not unidirectional. For writing in turn nurtures talk and thus the social relationships talk supports...[W]riting can channel talk in new ways, bringing about new kinds of human networks, networks woven through talk about text. (p. 100)

In classrooms that are permitted to function as learning communities, people treat writing as an object of conversation. They may talk about their writing processes, or they may talk about their texts as artifacts. For example, Swain and Lapkin's (1998) study showed that the dialogue between two learners in a French immersion class served as both a means of communication and as a cognitive tool as they attempted to solve the linguistic problem they faced while writing a short narrative.

Speaking as the social consequence of writing is consistent with Vygotskian theory and recent research on interaction in language learning, in that writing is seen to be firmly anchored to sociocultural contexts and local cultural practices (Dyson, 2000). Weissberg (2006) likewise reminds L2 writing specialists of Vygotskian perspectives on how social interaction is integrated with writing in an L2 learning community (see also Hall, Vitanova, & Marchenkova, 2005; Lantolf, 2000).

Writing Can Script Oral Performance

Speech writing, playwriting, and newscast writing are obvious examples of writing in the service of speech. The skilled speech writer or news writer seeks to produce a speech-like quality, a listenable message, though not necessarily to replicate the style of spontaneous talk (Einhorn, 1981; Quirk, 1982). In some cases, as in the speech never orated but only printed in the *Congressional Record*, the oral performance is just a pretext for a literacy event.

In other cases, as in a judge's oral instructions to a jury, the speech event is of real consequence, though the writing process (i.e., drafting judges' instructions to jurors) may take precious little cognizance of the needs of the judge as speaker or of the needs of jurors as listeners (Rubin, Hafer, & Arata, 2000).

Writing Can Guide Interaction

Because of its slower rate of production, the opportunity it provides for pausing and reflection and revision, and because writing permits attention to form and structure, writing is often a helpful tool for planning those kinds of talk that need to be planned. Instructors preparing for extemporaneous lectures write lecture notes. Political leaders planning to participate in live debates or news conferences or policy briefings write position papers as a way of clarifying issues in their own minds. Couples involved in interpersonal conflicts are urged to use journals to help analyze their feelings before engaging in talk. In these cases the written products will not script oral performances, but the processes of rendering thoughts in connected prose contribute to the speakers' ability to improvise cogent oral discourse.

One form of oral interaction that is sometimes treated in advanced language classes is the scientific poster presentation. In a typical poster session, presenters will have prepared materials to fit on a space of approximately 1.1 meters high by 1.75 meters wide. Since multiple posters are displayed simultaneously in an exhibition space, recommendations typically suggest that the posters be readable at some distance and contain headings and graphics that will capture the attention of casually roaming convention goers. In some cases, posters are left up for view over a day or more to enable extensive browsing, while in others, posters remain up for just a single concurrent session slot. In either event, some time is set aside for presenters to interact with interested colleagues.

What makes the poster presentation such an interesting genre is the relation between the poster "text" and the oral interaction that ensues. Some authorities regard the poster as an autonomous text, since it should convey a coherent message to viewers when it is on display in the absence of the presenter. Certainly any review of the various guidelines and tips for poster presentations that abound on the Internet or that professional organizations promulgate will reveal that the majority of the prescriptions pertain to graphical issues such as font size and use of charts and graphs.

Increasingly, however, authorities are noting that the value of a poster session must extend beyond the assemblage of static texts and graphics that comprise the posters themselves. For example, the American Society of Primatologists offers "Expanded Guidelines for Giving a Poster Presentation," intended for novice graduate students. It warns,

> You will be presenting your material in the midst of pandemonium as people elbow past each other toward friends or the hors-d'oeuvre[s] table, voices rise in vain efforts to be heard over the crowd, and someone spills wine on your new suit. . . .Think about the best way to present the material verbally to compliment [sic] what you have printed on your poster. (http://www.asp.org/education/howto_onPosters.html)

The oral skills needed to negotiate a poster presentation are actually quite complex. Presenters are wise to prepare a brief three-minute oral synopsis, and even a 30-second version of the same. They must be prepared to answer questions from both experts in the topic who are interested in methodological refinements as well as from generalists who are more interested in broader significance or applications. And presenters must know how to invite "lurkers" into the intangible boundaries of the presentation. Moreover, since potential audience members arrive on the scene at various points in time, the presenter must know how to juggle all of those functions more-or-less at once. A popular handbook for scientific presentations (Anholt, 2006) does devote several pages to the dynamic interplay between the text and the social interaction at poster sessions: "A well organized poster will make it easy for a newcomer to enter immediately in an ongoing explanation, after briefly viewing the title and a few of the summary headings above the figures" (p. 112).

Documents Guide Deliberative Interactions

The ultimate goal of scientific meetings in which posters are presented is to foster collaboration in scientific discovery. By the same token, collaborative decision-making is the norm in many private-sector as well as public-sector organizations. Even when a single individual is designated authority to make a decision, that person is likely to require the collaboration of other people in collecting and digesting information, in analyzing policy issues, and in identifying alternative plans of action. When these individuals come together to reach their decisions, they will engage in deliberative interaction. Examples of this sort of deliberative interaction include legislative hearings, "creative sessions" in advertising or public relations organizations, briefings between clients and their consultants in a variety of fields, and meetings of problem-solving teams in almost any profession, such as, accounting, engineering, architecture, marketing, and law. It is a common sort of interaction in complex organizations.

Because of the complexity of the information base and the policy issues that must be considered in such deliberative interactions, most often team members will prepare preliminary written documents. Those documents may become part of the record or archive of the organization, and once a decision is being implemented, technicians may from time to time consult those archives to ensure that they are working within the intended parameters. The documents may be indexed for ease of consultation, but they are usually cumbersome collections of raw data or precedents or regulations not useful for reader/talkers in action.

Instead of constantly consulting what may be a massive documentary record, for purposes of group discussion team members will produce some kind of briefing document—an executive summary, or at least an outline—that provides "talking points" to guide the interaction. The most effective of these briefing documents will take into account the needs of reader/talkers for an easily scannable page. Thus they make use of graphic devices, question/answer format, short and easily digestable units of organization, and the like.

The most effective of these briefing documents are also persuasive in subtle as well as in explicit ways. Explicit persuasive devices include listing priorities in order of importance and listing action options in order of desirability according to the drafter's criteria. More subtle persuasive devices include marshalling more and better authority for a desired outcome than for an opposing option, relying on the laws of primacy and recency to emphasize desired points (i.e., burying opposing positions in the middle of a list or document), and stating desired outcomes as assertions in the form of section headings.

Hawes (1976) explored the nature of briefing sessions as speech events and the role of written reports within those events. In his organizational case study, the document was used as a resource for a variety of interpersonal and political purposes (e.g., self-exculpation, rationalizing prior decisions, and the like). The talk surrounding the documents tended to focus on individuals' roles and motives rather than on the content of the document. The uses of the documents diverged radically from those texts' originally intended purposes. In his conclusions, Hawes is consistent with the view that organizational writing is often directed toward several audiences simultaneously and that effective preparation for organizational life must provide students with healthy doses of instruction in oral communication as well as written.

Poster Presentations and Briefings as Paradigms for Integrating Instruction in Speaking and Writing

Kantor and Rubin's (1981; Rubin & Kantor, 1984) bidirectional model of the relationship between oral and written language development may have been headed in the right direction(s), but it fails to fully capture the recurrent interplay between writing and speaking both in individuals' development as language users and in social and organizational uses of language. A more apt model might be a double helix with a writing strand and a speaking strand intertwined. At any particular stage one strand may be the focal outcome, drawing upon the other. But as a whole, the two strands are reciprocally supportive and leading in the same direction.

In social and organizational uses of language, the double helix well represents the progression of much collaborative discourse. The need to make some decisions may arise in the course of a meeting. An individual is assigned to research policy and action options. That individual talks to others to gain information. She may even commission others to write subsidiary portions of a report that will ultimately be submitted to the larger decision-making group. Writer/presenters at each level of preparation know that much of their "raw" report will go unread, will simply revert to archives. And at any rate the raw report is unsuited to guide deliberative interactions. The abstract briefing documents, therefore, "talking points," executive summaries, question and answer briefs, and the like. These briefing documents become artifacts that guide deliberative talk, used as resources of support by some individuals, as ethos building devices by others, as material to react against by still others. The group will eventually talk their way through to a final decision, and for reasons of documentary authoritativeness that decision will no doubt be recorded in writing.

In these ways writing and speaking loop back and forth between themselves (see also Kern & Shultz, 2005; Leander & Prior, 2004). To provide students with practice in this kind of integrated speaking and writing experience, curricula build upon case/project tasks. Such curricula are not uncommon in various kinds of technical writing courses in which students form teams to research, analyze, and propose solutions for some public construction project or management concern (e.g., Goldstein, 1980; Rafoth & Rubin, 1992).

Assignments need not require technical backgrounds, however. Students can be given freedom to find their own problems to address, and that process of deciding on the project's focus is itself an important learning device. Alternatively, the instructor may present students with case materials that define the problem for them and also provide most necessary research materials. Law school libraries often have excellent materials that may be used in this fashion, for example materials produced by the National Institute for Trial Advocacy or the American Trial Lawyers Association for use in mock trial demonstrations and competitions. When teacher-provided materials are used to circumscribe the project, naturally, the assignment becomes more of a simulation and consumes less time.

To be sure, the pedagogical recommendation that oral and written skills be taught in tandem is new to neither first nor second language instruction. Most existing writing-speaking pedagogies, however, do not even give lip service to the reciprocal nature of that relationship. Their ideas for speaking-writing pedagogies mainly treat speaking as a steppingstone to writing performance or proficiency (Rubin & Dodd, 1987; Weissberg, 2006). If language and literacy educators are serious about cultivating synergy between speaking and writing and about the primacy of social interaction, then they will redress that imbalance and bring practice into closer isomorphism with that theory. To do so, first and second language educators must recognize the myriad ways in which speaking serves as a teleological end or outcome of writing, and undertake teaching of institutionally and organizationally valued oral genres like briefing reports and poster presentations.

REFERENCES

Allen, J. E., & Rubin, D. L. (1993). Cross cultural factors affecting initial acquisition of literacy among children and adults. In S. Yussen and C. Adams (Eds.), *Reading across the life span* (pp. 3–32). New York: Springer-Verlagg.

Anholt, R. R. H. (2006). *Dazzle 'em with style: The art of oral scientific presentation* (2nd ed.). Burlington, MA: Elsevier Academic Press.

Barton, E. (2004). Linguistic discourse analysis: How the language in texts works. In C. Bazerman & P. Prior (Eds.), *What writing does and how it does it: An introduction to analyzing texts and textual practices* (pp. 57–82). Mahwah, NJ: Lawrence Erlbaum.

Berry, K. S. (1985). Talking to learn subject matter/Learning subject matter talk. *Language Arts, 62*, 34–42.

Bizzell, P. (1988). Arguing about literacy. *College English, 50*, 141–153.

Brice, R. (2004). Connecting oral and written language through applied writing strategies. *Intervention in School and Clinic, 40*(1), 38–47.

Cook, M. (2000). Writing and role play: A case for inclusion. *Reading, 34*(2), 74–78.

Cook-Gumperz, J., & Gumperz, J. J. (1981). From oral to written culture: The transition to literacy. In M. Farr Whiteman (Ed.), *Variation in writing: Functional and linguistic-cultural differences* (pp. 89–110). Hillsdale, NJ: Lawrence Erlbaum.

Dellatolas, G., Willadino-Braga, L., Souza, L., Filho, G., Queiroz, E., & Deloche, G. (2003). Cognitive consequences of early phases of literacy. *Journal of the International Neuropsychological Society, 9,* 771–782.

Dyson, A. H. (1990). Talking up a writing community: The role of talk in learning to write. In S. Hynds and D. Rubin (Eds.), *Perspectives on talking and learning* (pp. 99–114). Urbana, IL: National Council of Teachers of English.

———. (2000). Writing and the sea of voices: Oral language in, around, and about writing. In R. Indrisano, & J.R. Squire (Eds.), *Perspectives on writing* (pp. 45–65). Newark, DE: International Reading Association.

Ehri, L. (1985). Effects of printed language acquisition on speech. In D. Olson, N. Torrance, & A. Hildyard (Eds.), *Literacy, language and learning* (pp. 333–367). Cambridge, UK: Cambridge University Press.

Einhorn, L. J. (1981). The ghosts unmasked: A review of literature on speech-writing. *Communication Quarterly, 30,* 41–47.

Emig, J. (1977). Writing as a mode of learning. *College Composition and Communication, 28,* 122–128.

Ferguson, C. A. (1981). *Cognitive effects of literacy: Linguistic awareness in adult nonreaders.* Final Report NIE-G-80-0040. Stanford: Stanford University Department of Linguistics. (EDRS No. ED 222 857)

Gatbonton, E., & Segalowitz, N. (2005). Rethinking communicative language teaching: A focus on access to fluency. *The Canadian Modern Language Review, 61,* 325–353.

Gleason, H. A. (1961). *An introduction to descriptive linguistics.* New York: Holt Reinhart.

Goldstein, J. R. (1980). *Integrating interpersonal and small group oral communication skills into the technical writing course.* Paper presented at the International Technical Communication Conference, St. Louis Park, MN, May 1980. (EDRS No. ED 188 277)

Hall, J. K., & Verplaetse, L. S. (Eds.). (2000). *Second and foreign language learning through classroom interaction.* Mahwah, NJ: Lawrence Erlbaum.

Hall, J. K., & Vitanova, G., & Marchenkova, L. (Eds.) *Dialogue with Bakhtin on second and foreign language learning.* Mahwah, NJ: Lawrence Erlbaum.

Halliday, M. A. K. (1987). Spoken and written modes of meaning. In R. Horowitz and S. J. Samuels (Eds.), *Comprehending oral and written language* (pp. 55–82). San Diego: Academic Press.

Harste, J., Woodward, V., & Burke, C. (1984). *Language stories and literacy lessons.* Portsmouth, NH: Heinemann.

Hawes, L. C. (1976). How writing is used in talk: A study of communicative logic-in-use. *Quarterly Journal of Speech, 62,* 350–360.

Kantor, K. J., & Rubin, D. L. (1981). Between speaking and writing: Processes of differentiation. In B. Kroll & R. Vann (Eds.), *Exploring speaking-writing relationships: Comparison and contrasts* (pp. 55–81). Urbana, IL: National Council of Teacher of English.

Kern, R., & Schultz, J. M. (2005). Beyond orality: Investigating literacy and the literacy in second and foreign language instruction. *The Modern Language Journal, 89,* 381–392.

Kinzer, S., & Ruethling, G. (1 December, 2004). Hmong hunter charged with 6 murders is a shaman, friends and family say. *New York Times,* A10.

Kochman, T. (1975). Orality and literacy as factors of 'Black' and 'White' communicative behavior. *International Journal of the Sociology of Language. 3,* 95–118.

Lantolf, J. (Ed.) (2000). *Sociocultural theory and second language learning.* Cambridge, UK: Cambridge University Press.

Leander, K. & Prior, P. (2004). Speaking and writing: How talk and text interact in situated practices. In C. Bazerman & P. Prior (Eds.), *What writing does and how it does it* (pp. 201–237). Mahwah, NJ: Lawrence Erlbaum.

Michaels, S. (1986). Narrative presentations: An oral preparation for literacy with first graders. In J. Cook-Gumperz (Ed.), *The social construction of literacy* (pp. 94–116). Cambridge, UK: Cambridge University Press.

Morais, J., Bertelson, P., Cary, L., Alegria, J. (1986). Literacy training and speech segmentation. *Cognition, 24,* 45–64.

Olson, D. R. (1994). *The world on paper: The conceptual and cognitive implications of writing and reading.* New York: Cambridge University Press.

———. (1995). Conceptualizing the written word: An intellectual biography. *Written Communication, 12,* 277–297.

———. (2002). What writing does to the mind. In E. Amsel & J. P. Bymes (Eds.), *Language, literacy, and cognitive development: The development and consequences of symbolic communication* (pp. 153–166). Mahwah, NJ: Lawrence Erlbaum.

Ong, W. (1982). *Orality and literacy: The technologizing of the word.* London: Methuen.

Perfetti, C. A. (1987). Language, speech, and print: Some asymmetries in the acquisition of literacy. In R. Horowitz & S. J. Samuels (Eds.), *Comprehending oral and written language* (pp. 355–369). New York: Academic Press.

Quirk, R. (1982). *Style and communication in the English language.* London: Edward Arnold.

Rafoth, B. A., & Rubin, D. L. (1992). Speaking-writing curricula: New designs on an old idea. *Writing Program Administration, 15*(3), 17–29.

Ravid, D., & Tolchinsky, L. (2002). Developing linguistic literacy: A comprehensive model. *Journal of Child Language, 29,* 417–447.

Reis, A., & Castro-Caldas, A. (1997). Illiteracy: A cause for biased cognitive development. *Journal of the International Neuropsychological Society, 3,* 444–450.

Rubin, D. L. (1987). Divergence and convergence between oral and written communication. *Topics in Language Disorders, 7*(4), 1–18.

Rubin, D. L., & Dodd, W. M. (1987). *Talking into writing: Exercises for basic writers.* Urbana, IL: ERIC and National Council of Teachers of English.

Rubin, D. L., Goodrum, R., & Hall, B. (1990). Orality, oral-based culture and the academic writing of ESL learners. *Issues in Applied Linguistics, 1,* 56–76.

Rubin, D. L., Hafer, T., & Arata, K. (2000). Reading and listening to oral-based versus literate-based discourse. *Communication Education, 49,* 121–134.

Rubin, D. L., & Kantor, K. J. (1984). Talking and writing: Building communication competence. In C. Thaiss and C. Suhor (Eds.), *Speaking and writing* (pp. 29–74). Urbana, IL: National Council of Teachers of English.

Savignon, S. J. (1983). *Communicative competence: Theory and classroom practice.* Reading, MA: Addison-Wesley.

Savignon, S. J., & Wang, C. (2003). Communicative language teaching in EFL contexts: Learner attitude and perceptions. *International Review of Applied Linguistics, 41,* 223–251.

Scribner, S., & Cole, M. (1981). *The psychology of literacy.* Cambridge, MA: Harvard University Press.

Stotsky, S. (1987). A comparison of the two theories about development in written language: Implications for pedagogy and research. In R. Horowitz and S. J. Samuels (Eds.), *Comprehending oral and written language* (pp. 371–396). San Diego: Academic Press.

Street, B. (1985). *Literacy in theory and practice.* Cambridge, UK: Cambridge University Press.

Swain, M., & Lapkin, S. (1998). Interaction and second language learning: Two adolescent French immersion students working together. *The Modern Language Journal, 82,* 320–337.

Tarone, E. (2000). Still wrestling with "context" in interlanguage theory. *Annual Review of Applied Linguistics, 20,* 182–198.

Tarone, E., & Bigelow, M. (2005). Impact of literacy on oral language processing: Implications for second language acquisition research. *Annual Review of Applied Linguistics, 25,* 77–97.

Thompkins, A., & Binder, K. (2003). A comparison of factors affecting performance of functionally illiterate adults and children matched by reading level. *Reading Research Quarterly, 38* (2), 236–258.

Verhoeven, L. (2002). Sociocultural and cognitive constraints on literacy development. *Journal of Child Language, 29,* 282–288.

Weissberg, R. (2006). *Connecting speaking & writing in second language writing instruction.* Ann Arbor: University of Michigan Press.

Zoellner, R. (1969). Talk-write: A behavioral pedagogy for composition. *College English, 30,* 267–320.

12

Negotiating Online and In-Class Academic Conversations: Writing to Speak

GAYLE L. NELSON AND YANBIN LU

Abstract

This two-year qualitative case study investigated the academic socialization of a Chinese doctoral student, Yanbin Lu, one of the authors of this chapter, to a doctoral program in the United States. The findings suggest that the student's participation in the written conversation of online postings contributed to her participation during in-class academic conversations. Data consisted of transcripts of (1) key informant interviews over a two-year period, (2) oral journals, (3) stimulated recall interviews, (4) interviews with three faculty members, and (5) copies of Yanbin's online postings. Data were analyzed for recurring topics or themes. Two themes that recurred regularly in the data were Yanbin's negotiations with two unfamiliar pedagogical practices: posting online and speaking in class. Through the posting process of reading and responding to peers' postings, she experienced a shift in her perception of learning. The realization that she was learning from peers was significant and affected her perception of academic discussions/conversations and her behavior during class. These findings are important in that they provide support for the position that writing mediates speaking (writing → speaking).

As Williams (this volume) points out, the development of writing ability and oral proficiency is dynamic, complex, and bidirectional. The research that exists on the writing-speaking relationship is sparse (Weissberg, 1994, 2006), and what does exist is more likely to focus on the directionality of speaking impacting writing. One explanation for the primacy of this relationship (i.e., speaking → writing) is that oral language is seen as central to definitions of interlanguage competence (Williams, this volume). First language acquisition scholars have demonstrated that language development follows a natural progression from speaking to writing, and the work of SLA scholars has followed their lead. A second explanation stems from the socio-cultural work of the Russian psychologist Vygotsky, who conducted studies with children after the Russian Revolution. Based on approximately twenty years of cognitive research, Vygotsky claimed that higher cognitive functions, such as writing, emerge from social interaction internalized as "inner speech." In other words, emergent writing is inner speech—externalized (Weissberg, 2006). What made Vygotsky's contribution important was the essential place it gives to social interaction in the development of writing (Weissberg, 2006). Weissberg (this volume), however, argues that socio-cultural theory may not be compatible with L2 writing development or instruction. For instance, speech is not the primary modality for many second language learners; thus, the directionality of the relationship (i.e., speaking → writing) breaks down. Literacy activities (e.g., writing) may, in fact, activate SLA for some second language learners.

In this case study, we suggest that academic writing can mediate academic speaking, that the online postings that Yanbin wrote for her graduate courses contributed to her speaking in class discussions. When the study began over two years ago, Yanbin Lu was the "case" and Gayle Nelson was the researcher. However, after reading drafts of the manuscript as a validity measure to make sure her words, intent, and voice sounded authentic and true, and later after commenting on numerous drafts and writing a portion of the text, Yanbin became co-author. We will refer individually to the sections of the paper that we wrote.

Gayle's Account

This Study

When I began interviewing Yanbin Lu in the fall of 2004, I was interested in her academic socialization as a new doctoral student in the Department of Applied Linguistics and ESL at Georgia State University (GSU). More broadly, I was interested in how L2 graduate students participate in and negotiate membership in their new classroom communities. My work was informed by the work of Lave and Wenger (1991) and Wenger (1999). Lave and Wenger perceive learning as a socially situated process in which newcomers, by interacting with more experienced members, gradually become more competent in the ways of a new community of practice (CoP). New international graduate students may be socialized into many overlapping communities of practice: each discipline's community, the institutional community, and numerous classroom communities (Morita, 2004). Ideally, one way of being socialized into a particular academic community may resemble this—students observe that others (old-timers) have skills, strategies, and knowledge that they perceive as helpful in achieving their purposes. Newcomers perceive that if they are interested in acquiring these skills, strategies and knowledge, they might acquire them through participation.

Participation, according to Lave and Wenger (1991), leads to learning. Their theory of learning, legitimate peripheral participation (LPP), sees learning as gradual, purposeful, active, and social. According to this view, learning is not a product that can be measured by an exam or essay. It is an academic socialization process by which students "become increasingly competent in academic ways of knowing, speaking, and writing as they participate peripherally and legitimately in academic practices" (Morita, 2004, p. 576). The process of participating is also a process of becoming—of changing, of becoming a participant, of changing identities.

Methodology

This study used qualitative case study methodology of Yanbin Lu's socialization into the academic community of graduate school. Case study methodology is appropriate for investigating "contemporary phenomenon within its real-life context" . . . when the researchers deliberately want to cover contextual conditions (Yin, 1994, p. 13). I selected case study methodology for the potential of in-depth and detailed information and the understanding of one person's experiences over time. Initially, I was interested in Yanbin's socialization, but I also saw her "case" as possibly typical of other cases. Stake (2000) refers to this type of case study as instrumental, in that the case "facilitates our understanding of something else" (p. 437). The purpose of this study was to better understand the process by which second language graduate students participate and negotiate membership in U.S. academic communities. The data document Yanbin's experiences, thoughts, and feelings as she engages with both familiar and unfamiliar academic discourses over a two-year period.

Context

Yanbin started the doctoral program in the Department of Applied Linguistics and ESL at GSU in fall 2004. Yanbin took four courses her first semester: Second Language Acquisition (SLA), Research Design, Intercultural Communication (ICC), and Practicum. Courses included both MA and Ph.D. students. The method of instruction in both SLA and Research Design was primarily lecture, with the instructor asking students questions. Both ICC and Practicum involved class discussions. In fact, the ICC class was divided into half, with two groups of ten or eleven students that met for the semester. The whole class met once a week for 2.5 hours, one hour of which was dedicated to the smaller group discussions. I was the instructor for the ICC course. The seven students in the Practicum course discussed the ESL classes they were observing as well as current or former teaching experiences. In two of these courses (ICC and Practicum), students were required "to post" to a discussion group on course readings or experiences before each class. In the Research Design course, students posted occasionally. The requirement of "posting" is common in approximately half of the graduate courses in the department, and after two years in the program, Yanbin posted in 6 out of 12, or 50 percent, of her courses. Four of the twelve courses required postings once a week, with approximately one-screen-long messages as substantial responses to the readings or other classmates' messages. In one course (in Yanbin's fourth semester) the instructor asked for two postings a week with similar requirements, and in one course (in Yanbin's second semester) the instructor asked for five messages that could be short, but should be responses to different questions raised by the instructor or other classmates. In the first semester, as a newcomer who had just arrived from China, however, posting was a new practice for her.

Participant

Yanbin Lu, a female Chinese doctoral student in her mid-thirties, had recently begun her doctoral program when the study began and was in her third year of coursework when data collection ceased and data were analyzed. Yanbin had an MA degree in TEFL, had taught English at a Chinese university for ten years, and had never studied or taught outside China before her PhD work. When Yanbin began studying English in middle school, she first learned to read and write with her teachers following the grammar-translation method. For the first six years of studying English, she had no specific listening or speaking classes. She remembered memorizing new words, drilling sentence patterns, doing reading comprehension exercises, writing compositions, and translating from English to Chinese and Chinese to English. She called this approach "deaf and dumb English" and believes it is one of the reasons why she feels more comfortable writing than speaking English. When she entered college and studied as an English major undergraduate, she began to have separate classes dedicated to practicing the four skills—listening, speaking, reading, and writing.

Procedure

Because I was interested in Yanbin's perception of her social reality, the primary data collection procedure was the key informant interview. I conducted ten interview sessions with Yanbin during her first semester at GSU, four sessions during her fourth semester, and two sessions the summer following the fourth semester (interviews described below). As a measure of validity, ethnographic methodology calls for triangulation (Hammersley & Atkinson, 1995), the checking of inferences from one data source by comparing it to data from other data sources. In addition to interviews with Yanbin, other sources of data were interviews with three of Yanbin's professors (two interviews during her first semester and one during her fifth semester), my field notes, Yanbin's oral journal, Yanbin's course postings, videotapes of four intercultural communication classes, and stimulated recall interviews of those classes (described below). All of the interviews were audiotaped and transcribed; the interview analysis was based on the transcriptions.

After Yanbin had been in the United States three weeks, we began to meet weekly for approximately one hour to discuss her academic socialization. As the semester progressed, we met every other week. Initially I explained that the purpose of the study was to learn about her adjustment to a new academic community. Specifically, I was interested in what she noticed in her classes about instructors, about students, about student-instructor interactions, about assignments, about being a graduate student in the department, and about herself: behaviorally, cognitively, and affectively. In structuring the interviews, I followed Spradley's guidelines (1979), beginning with broad questions (i.e., grand tour) about Yanbin's experiences as a student in China and, over time, moving to more narrow questions about her current experiences. By the third interview, Yanbin began coming to the interviews with specific information that she wanted to tell me. My role was that of an interested listener (e.g., Can you tell me more? What about in your other classes?).

Yanbin also kept an oral journal on a small digital recorder that was easily transportable. She carried it with her so that she could record her thoughts as soon as possible (e.g., almost immediately after class). She spoke about aspects of life in Atlanta and GSU that surprised her (i.e., differences she was not expecting), practices that were different from what she was accustomed to, and so forth. To find out her thoughts during class, four of her ICC class sessions were videotaped to facilitate stimulated recall. Within one week of the videotaping, she observed the videotape with a research assistant (a doctoral student who had been trained in stimulated recall methodology) who stopped the videotape periodically to ask Yanbin what she was thinking and feeling. Following the guidelines set down by Gass and Mackey (2000), Yanbin was also invited to stop the videotape herself when she had something to say.

Data Analysis

Data have been examined multiple times throughout this study for recurring themes. I also checked my perception of the themes with Yanbin, and she informed me when I had misinterpreted a statement she had made. I also asked her about apparent contradictions in her interview data and she clarified any possible confusion, explaining the contradictions. Finally, she read drafts of this manuscript and made comments so that this final version represents her perceptions as well as my own. Two major themes that emerged from the data were Yanbin's negotiation of the practice of writing online course postings and the practice of speaking in class. From an LPP perspective, Yanbin was negotiating her competence in the classroom, and she perceived her challenges as learning to speak in class and learning to post online (see Lu and Nelson, 2008, for a description of her process of constructing a new identity through on-line postings). Of the two, speaking in class was a greater challenge.

Results and Discussion

Members of communities of practice work with others who share the same conditions and context, conditions that are central to the enterprise in which they are engaged. In this case study, the members are graduate students who collectively orchestrate their lives in order to become competent members of classroom and "graduate school" communities. Students negotiate the ebb and flow of graduate school by "acting as resources to each other, exchanging information, making sense of situations, sharing new tricks and new ideas . . ." (Lave & Wenger, 1991, p. 47). As a newcomer, Yanbin faced questions such as, Who am I in this new context? How am I supposed to "be" and "act" in this community? What do I need to learn (i.e., practice) in order to be both perceived as competent and to be competent?

Speaking in Class

During her first semester as a doctoral student, Yanbin observed that in many of her classes instructors encouraged students to speak and many students did, in fact, speak up in class. Yanbin was surprised by the frequency with which such discussions occurred. This practice (way of learning) of the new community is inconsistent with her former practices and also inconsistent with her identity and perception of appropriate student behavior.

During an early interview, she commented on the practice of students' asking questions and the discussion that results:

> *Y:* . . . and sometimes I think their [students'] questions are not directly related to what we are talking[about] now, so I, I would think, uh, it's kind of off-task, yeah, and for me, if I have common questions that's not related to the topic, I would not ask it in class. And sometimes in classes, we have discussion and . . . I think it's kind of a waste of time. (Interview, September 14, 2004).[1]

Midway through her first semester, while viewing a videotape of herself in her ICC classes, Yanbin again expressed this view. The interviewer asked her what she was thinking when another student raised her hand:

> *Y:* When she raised the question . . . I was thinking, if I were her, um, I would not ask this question because we are not on this topic. Yeah, I would just ask the question during the break or after class. (Stimulated Recall, October 6, 2004)

Yanbin's reluctance to speak during her first semester was noted by her instructors. As one instructor pointed out

> *I-1:* She has been and remains one of the, um, least talkative people in class, and the least likely to ask questions, but also, she clearly seems to be on top of the material. (Interview, October 20, 2004)

---

[1]The coding conventions are as follows: Y=Yanbin; the information in parentheses at the end of a quotation provides the type of data, such as, interview data, journal data or stimulated recall data, and the date on which the data were obtained (including year); I-1, I-2, and I-3 refer to Yanbin's instructors who were interviewed.

Often during her first semester, her preference was to sit quietly in class and listen to the instructor:

> *Y:* I'm more used to maybe, um, lecture-type. I think most Chinese students are like that, uh, they would, um, um sit there quietly and, uh, listen to the professor, maybe, and take notes. Yeah, and I feel more comfortable, like, in those classes. (Interview, October 12, 2004)

Even though Yanbin's identity as a Chinese student was strong and she had reservations about the effectiveness of class discussions, she wanted to be viewed as competent and she believed that being competent entailed speaking in class. As she expressed in an early interview, she wanted to speak:

> *Y:* I hope I can contribute something to the group discussion but I'm still getting used to it and I feel, um, um, obliged to say something in class. (Interview, September 14, 2004)

One night after ICC, she reflected on speaking in class in her oral journal:

> *Y:* . . . And uh, in the group discussion I didn't, couldn't contribute a lot, um or it's, um, sometimes . . . because I didn't have time to speak up. I lose the chance. . . . Sometimes I don't know what to say. (Journal, September 6, 2004)

By the time she "composed" what she wanted to say, the class discussion had often moved on to a different aspect of the topic.

During her initial weeks at GSU, Yanbin preferred not to speak in class and questioned the effectiveness of class discussions, particularly when students asked questions that were not directly related to the topic or issue under discussion. She was more comfortable in a lecture-style course. Yet she observed that in some classes, speaking was valued, and she wanted to be perceived as a competent graduate student, and competence involved speaking in class.

Situations for Speaking

The term *negotiation* conveys a "flavor of continuous interaction, of gradual achievement, and of give-and-take" (Lave & Wenger, 1999 p. 53). Yanbin's negotiation of the practice, speaking-in-class, was flavored in such a way. Data from her first semester indicate that Yanbin was more likely to speak in particular situations. For instance, she was likely to speak if she were asked a direct question by the instructor:

> *Y:* Dr. X asked me some questions, I answered but when they were having free discussion, I would just start listening. (Interview, November 2, 2004)

In two of her classes (Research Design, SLA), the instructors gave the students problems or exercises to do. Instructors would then call on students to provide the answers. In this controlled environment Yanbin also felt comfortable speaking.

Additionally, she spoke when interacting in pairs or small groups. For example, when ICC divided into small groups of three or four students, Yanbin felt at ease. She reflected in her journal:

> *Y:* I contributed something about this Confucius, Confucian ideas, but after we got back into the big circle, we have more than ten students and I find that I return back to the traditional Chinese student. (Journal, September 15, 2004)

Finally, it was easier for her to talk about topics with which she was familiar and had experience. In speaking about the Practicum, she revealed,

> *Y:* We would talk about teaching. I have that experience so I have, uh, something to contribute. (Interview, October 19, 2004)

The increase in Yanbin's speaking was corroborated by one of her instructors:

> *I-2:* She seemed to be very self-conscious and very reluctant to speak [at first], so I made a point of calling on her a lot . . . and the first few times I did that she was taken aback and a little startled, but then she got into the swing of things and now, . . . she seems to be more comfortable . . . and just the amount of speaking that she does in the class is, is much greater. (Interview, November 9, 2004)

During her first semester, when Yanbin spoke in class she preferred the more structured interaction of the instructor asking the question, student answering the question. As she wanted to be a competent member of the CoP, she found ways in which to participate in speaking practices that were comfortable for her. She felt relatively at ease when speaking in pairs or small groups about a topic with which she was knowledgeable or in which she had practical experience.

Writing as Postings

Whereas academic speaking was a new practice for Yanbin, the practice of academic writing was not. As a graduate student in China, she perceived herself as a relatively competent writer and she enjoyed writing. What was new to her in the context of GSU was writing-to-post. She had never heard of a "posting," was unfamiliar with the style or format, and did not know the purpose. Unlike speaking-in-class, postings were *required* and figured into the overall course grade in two of her courses from the outset of her first semester.[2] She had many questions. In her journal, she admitted,

> *Y:* I'm not very sure about the standards or criteria of such postings. I'm not familiar with the procedure of posting. (Journal, August 31, 2004)

Yanbin wanted to be viewed as competent and was concerned about being viewed as incompetent or unqualified by her peers as well as her professor. She wondered, "If I say something wrong or stupid, will the others laugh at me?" and believed mistakes would betray her incompetence (Lu & Nelson, 2008).

As with speaking, initially Yanbin's intended audience for the postings was her instructors. She was interested in other students' postings, but mainly as a model to understand the genre of posting. She was less interested in interacting with the content of the other students' postings or with the other students. She explained,

> *Y:* . . . after I read the students' postings, I will forget and when I'm writing my own posting, I will focus on the reading and the question, so I forget what my classmates have said. (Interview, September 7, 2004)

By the end of her first semester, however, a new set of relationships emerged. Lave and Wenger (1991) equate learning with increased participation. Yanbin increased her participation in the practice of posting. What did she learn?

[2]Yanbin notes that it is hard to quantify the amount of speaking one does in class, but it is easy to quantify the number of postings one posts online. If students do not post for a class, points would be deducted from their final grade, but if they do not speak up in one class, it would not affect their grade that obviously.

Was she being socialized into a new CoP? Was she learning the CoP's socially negotiated ways of learning?

Near the end of her first semester, and after posting three or four times a week, Yanbin explained how she learns from other students:

> *Y:* It's [the posting process] a good way to make me think about what I've read . . . and their [other students'] postings were from different perspectives and sometimes even solved my puzzles in the reading. (Interview, October 26, 2004)

Yanbin describes her emergent interactive identity in Lu and Nelson (2008). Her concerns about making language or content "errors" began to decrease after the fifth week of the semester. She began to interact with other group members, referring to them by name and asking them questions about their postings. By the eighth week she mentioned three members of her posting group in one paragraph and felt comfortable disagreeing with another student. This shift in Yanbin's online interaction with students and her communication style can be seen in her postings. One of her first postings in the ICC class demonstrates an academic impersonal quality:

> *Y:* In Kim's Structural Model, six dimensions of factors and their interdependent relationships are identified. The six dimensions of factors are 1) host communicative competence, . . . (Posting, September 6, 2004).[3]

A second posting from her teacher knowledge seminar taken during her fourth semester illustrates a more conversational style, easy interaction with other students, and the use of *I* (i.e., she is the agent):

> *Y:* Wow, Mi Jin, what a thorough synthesis! Both yours and Ben's summary helped recap the highlights of the class. I remembered what I learned in qualitative method class about ethnographic interview—usually we start with . . . . (Posting, January 23, 2006)

This shift in perception—that in addition to faculty, other students can contribute to one's learning—was an important realization for Yanbin. By participating in the postings, she started to understand the pedagogical

[3]The postings in ICC asked that students create an argument and thus demanded a certain type of prose. However, as the semester went on, Yanbin interacted more frequently with other students online.

underpinnings of both online discussion postings and in-class discussions in this new CoP. She was learning from other students.

By the fourth semester, she explicitly stated her perception of the purpose of classroom dialogue:

> *Y:* The function of class discussions is getting different perspectives of other classmates or getting a better understanding of the reading material. (Interview, February 7, 2006)

Although posting was a new genre for Yanbin, she learned the subtle and tacit rules for writing-to-post through participating in the practice of posting. She learned by reading and analyzing the postings of her peers and implementing what she learned in her own postings.

The Relation between Writing-to-Post and Speaking-in-Class

The relationship that unfolded between Yanbin's written postings and speaking in class was nuanced and complex. Can we say that the postings functioned as a rehearsal for discussing the readings in class? Can we say that after writing an idea or question or argument in the posting, she could then say those words out loud in class? The data do not seem to provide direct evidence for a linear relationship between posting and speaking, but we also cannot say that the writing *never* functioned as a rehearsal for speaking. There are, however, indirect ways in which the postings contributed to Yanbin's speaking in class.

Through online postings and interactions, students exchanged information, helped each other make sense of the readings, and, in fact, began a discussion of the readings. It may appear that the postings ought directly to contribute to students' speaking in class. For Yanbin, however, the class discussions frequently went in a direction that was unpredictable. Even though she may have had something to say, there was often not an opportunity in the class to say it:

> *Y:* Postings help me organize my thoughts but the discussion questions in class were not the same as the postings. (Interview, July 6, 2006)

As described in the previous section of this chapter, by participating in online postings, Yanbin began to learn from other students and modified her position on in-class discussions. Once she understood their pedagogical *raison d'être*, she was more inclined to want to speak in class. Her motivation to speak in class increased when she realized that students might learn from her.

The process of participating in the practice of posting also helped her understand the reading material and the overall topics. With this increased understanding came increased confidence:

> *Y:* Knowing that I understand a text better made me feel more confidence. I gradually got used to the environment. Especially later on. I knew I understood the reading and I felt more comfortable and I felt more comfortable speaking. (Interview, July 11, 2006)

Additionally, the posting process provided her with a sense of ownership of the course content. After working with the course material and writing about it and interacting with others online about the material, she began to own some ideas and also words. In describing this phenomenon, Yanbin gave examples of words from her assessment course that were strange to her until she used them in her writing:

> *Y:* *reliability, validity, practicality, authenticity*, . . . after I used them in my writing I could speak them and use them in discussions. After I digest a word, I'm able to use it. (Interview, July 25, 2006).

The most direct example of the posting-speaking relationship occurred during her fourth semester in the program. In a seminar on teacher knowledge, the students posted their ideas about particular topics. One week, Yanbin compared learning to teach with learning to swim. During the following class, the instructor praised her metaphor in front of the class and asked her to elaborate, giving her an opportunity to speak in class. Later Yanbin told me,

> *Y:* I said you have to practice a lot; you have to jump into the water and coordinate and practice, it's not enough to just learn theory. . . . (Interview, July 25, 2006)

At the beginning of her fifth semester as a doctoral student, Yanbin's speaking behavior in class was that of "an active participant." In the fall 2006, one of her instructors characterized her participation in this way:

> *I-3* . . . I can see that in small group discussions she is always engaged and talks to other group members. In large group discussion, she volunteers less often compared to some other students; however, she does volunteer to talk from time to time. She is not always quietly sitting there. Sometimes

> when a student talks, or has a question in a large group discussion setting, she would respond to another student's question or comment, so I would consider her an active participant in class. (Interview, September 12, 2006)

Yanbin talked in class, she responded to other students' questions or comments, and she volunteered in large group discussions. Was this change in her speaking behavior related to online postings or to overall academic socialization or to something else? This important question will be addressed through Yanbin's comments in the following section.

As pointed out earlier, this study is phenomenological. Its aim is to determine the essence of experience as perceived by the participant. In this study, the participant (and co-author) is Yanbin Lu.

Yanbin's Account

Two years ago when I first came to GSU, I became involved in this research project. The interviews and the oral journals are invaluable records of my academic life and my reflections and thoughts at that time, and the subsequent examination and analysis of these data turned out to be a self-improving and self-discovering process for myself.

As far as online postings and in-class discussions are concerned, I believe that the former contributed to the latter, maybe not directly, but they definitely contributed. How does writing online postings enhance in-class discussions? In retrospect, I think the writing task helps with speaking in the following three ways.

First, it helps me get better prepared for the class. If I'm not required to do online posting for a course, I tend to be content with superficial understanding of the reading materials. But, if I'm required to post answers to the study questions posed by the instructor, I have to read the articles or chapters very carefully and try to understand most, if not all, of the content. In addition, the writing up of postings helps me think over the readings and articulate my thoughts. Thus, I'm better prepared for the class, and in turn, the in-class discussion.

Second, it helped me see the value of peer discussion. I tended to think that discussion in class was not as effective as a lecture because I used to believe that the teacher was the best source of knowledge. This perception is probably due to my academic background in China, in which the class is traditionally dominated by the instructor lecturing. After I came to GSU, I found that in this community, an important classroom practice was discussion, including online discussion (posting). Through all these oral and written discussions (especially online posting), I have come to realize that my fellow classmates are also sources of knowledge, who have many brilliant ideas and points to enlighten me. Some of their postings helped me gain a better understanding of the reading materials; some of their viewpoints helped me gain another perspective that I had never thought of before. I can learn as much from them as from the professors.

Last, the posting process makes me see myself as a participating, competent member of the class. Class participation is required in almost all the classes I have taken at GSU. My oral participation in classes was minimal, especially in the first semester, and this posed a threat to me and my perception of myself as a competent class member. Online posting, on the other hand, removes the pressure of coming up with impromptu responses right then and there by extending the boundaries of traditional physical classrooms into cyberspace with no restrictions of time and space. I have as much time as I can afford to think over and reflect on others' comments, to formulate my own ideas, and to edit my writing before I post it. With online posting, I feel much more secure and confident, even though it is sometimes time-consuming. With online posting, I feel I'm also contributing to the class discussion, sometimes even with some good ideas for the class to share. With online posting, I feel more and more comfortable interacting with other class members and both the comfort and the interaction carry over to in-class discussions. At present, I no longer consider in-class discussion a big challenge for me. I have been acculturated into this discussion mode of class, have come to appreciate it, and have gotten used to speaking up whenever I feel like it.

In the fall 2006 semester, two visiting scholars came to our department from China, and in the first few weeks of classes, they expressed their worries to me, saying they could hardly follow what other class members were talking about, let alone take part in the discussions. I tried to console them with my own experience in the first semester and reassured them that as time went on they would get more and more accustomed to this approach of class discussion. I suddenly realized that I'm an old-timer in this community of practice now.

Gayle and Yanbin's Concluding Thoughts

Recently many scholars (e.g., Beauvois, 1998; Belcher, 1999) have written about the use of interactive online postings (frequently referred to as computer-mediated communication or CMC) and the possibilities it offers second (or third) language writers/speakers. Students are able to interact with each other without the constraints of time and space or the anxiety of face-to-face interaction. They have time to plan, think through and edit their postings, to be in control. In discussing the results of her work, Belcher (1999) notes,

> The most significant outcome of the new discursive environment . . . was that voices—not anonymous, but clearly, and to all appearances, confidently self-identified voices—which were never or seldom heard in class, were heard online. These online voices were . . . self-assured, confiding, and collegial. (p. 264)

Beauvois (1998) notes the conversation-like qualities of her students' CMC discussions: the fluidity of the communication, the use of language to negotiate meaning, topic initiation, and expressions of ideas and emotions, referring to the written interactions as "conversations in slow motion" (p. 198). The findings of this study are consistent with the work of other researchers who support CMC for offering a voice to a greater number of students and opportunities for students to interact with and learn from each other. What this study contributes to the literature on writing and speaking relationships is that the benefits of online interactive postings may extend to non-CMC activities, to other practices within the larger academic community, particularly to classroom discussions in which the goal of the instructor is for students to learn from each other. It also seems to have shown how writing-speaking relationships can be reinforced, and why it is useful to provide such reinforcement.

ACKNOWLEDGMENTS

Gayle Nelson: I would like to thank Diane Belcher for encouraging us to write this chapter and both Diane and Alan for providing supportive and thorough feedback; to Lauren Lukkarila for videotaping the classes, conducting the stimulated recall interviews, providing feedback on the manuscript and for insightful discussions on communities of practice; to Dara Suchke for transcribing the data quickly and accurately; and to the course instructors for their collegiality in participating in the interviews. I especially thank Yanbin Lu, who willingly agreed to work with me on this project in addition to all her coursework, teaching, and research assistantship responsibilities.

Yanbin Lu: I would like to thank Dr. Nelson for offering such a wonderful opportunity for me to participate in this research project, for inviting me to co-author this chapter, and for her continual encouragement and guidance in the course of my PhD study as well as this project. I am also grateful to Dr. Belcher for her constructive feedback and invaluable suggestions in the process of composing and revising this chapter.

REFERENCES

Beauvois, M. H. (1998). Conversations in slow motion: Computer-mediated communication in the foreign language classroom. *The Canadian Modern Language Review, 54,* 198–217.

Belcher, D. (1999). Authentic interaction in a virtual classroom: Leveling the playing field in a graduate seminar. *Computers and Composition, 16*(2), 253–267.

Gass, S., & Mackey, A. (2000). *Stimulated recall methodology in second language research.* Mahwah, NJ: Lawrence Erlbaum.

Hammersley, M., & Atkinson, P. (1995). *Ethnography: Principles in practice.* London: Routledge.

Lave, J., & Wenger, E. (1991). *Situated learning: Legitimate peripheral participation.* Cambridge, UK: Cambridge University Press.

Lea, M. R. (2005). Communities of practice in higher education. In D. Barton & K. Tusting (Eds.) *Beyond communities of practice: Language power, and social context.* (pp. 180–197). Cambridge, UK: Cambridge University Press.

Lu, Y., & Nelson, G. L. (2008). Negotiating on-line postings and publications: Identity construction through writing. In C. Casanave & Y. Li (Eds.). *Learning the literacy practices of graduate school: Insiders' reflections on academic enculturation* (pp. 150–165). Ann Arbor: University of Michigan Press.

Morita, N. (2004). Negotiating participation and identity in second language academic communities. *TESOL Quarterly, 38,* 573–603.

Spradley, J. P. (1979). *The ethnographic interview.* New York: Harcourt Brace Javanovich.

Stake, R. E. (2000). Case studies. In N. K. Denizon & Y. Lincoln (Eds.). *Handbook of qualitative research* (pp. 435–454), Thousand Oaks, CA: Sage.

Wenger, E. (1999). *Communities of practice: Learning, meaning, and identity.* Cambridge, UK: Cambridge University Press.

Weissberg, R. (1994). Speaking of writing: Some functions of talk in the ESL composition class. *Journal of Second Language Writing, 3,* 121–139.

———. (2006). *Connecting speaking & reading in second language instruction.* Ann Arbor: University of Michigan Press.

Yin, R. (1994). *Case study research: Design and methods* (2nd ed.). Beverly Hills, CA: Sage Publishing.

13

Does Writing Influence Learner Attention to Form?

REBECCA ADAMS AND LAUREN ROSS-FELDMAN

Abstract

While task-based language teaching has been widely promoted as a means of promoting language learning in classroom settings (e.g., R. Ellis, 2003), relatively little of this research has examined the role of task modality in promoting the interactional features that may lead to language learning. The current study compares the interactions of ESL learners (N = 44) as they complete tasks that require only spoken output with their interactions on tasks that require written as well as spoken language production. The results indicate that the inclusion of a writing component may promote more accurate language production, and that the opportunity to process content orally before engaging in writing can increase the likelihood of learners resolving language-related episodes.

While the importance of literacy in language acquisition and teaching has long been recognized, the primary focus of much research in many areas of second language research remains on spoken, rather than written, communication (Harklau, 2002). In studies of second language interaction and task-based language teaching in particular, little attention has been paid to the role of writing in creating opportunities for both language practice and language learning. The purpose of this study was to consider how the inclusion of writing in second language dyadic tasks can influence the way that learners create and make use of opportunities to learn second language form.

Language Production and Second Language Learning

Research on SLA has made it clear that target language production (i.e., speaking and writing) is a necessary component of language learning (e.g., Swain, 1995, 2005). Swain (1995) explains that "output pushes learners to process language more deeply (with more mental effort) than does input" (p. 126), suggesting that language production is not a result of the language learning process, but rather a part of the process. As Swain and Lapkin (2002) put it, production should be viewed "not only as a message to be conveyed, but as a tool in cognitive activity" (p. 285).

Swain (2005) points out that one of the ways that production promotes learning is through opportunities for students to notice form. Noticing can take place when learners, in the process of speaking or writing, perceive that they do not know how to express their intended meaning. A growing body of research supports a connection between noticing and learning (e.g., Adams, 2003; Mackey, 2006; Swain & Lapkin, 2002). One way that this takes place is through interaction. Second language interaction can focus attention on a particular form, allowing learners to notice when their output differs from the input they receive. During interaction, learners can also signal to the interlocutor that they do not have the requisite competence to express a proposition, allowing learners to recognize gaps and receive necessary input.

Swain also identifies hypothesis testing as a means of promoting learning through production. Swain and Lapkin (2002) studied output modifications that were the result of feedback and found evidence that students use output as a means of testing and refining hypotheses. They concluded that students used output opportunities as a way of gathering and internalizing metalinguistic information about the language. Similar to noticing, hypothesis testing is promoted in second language interaction. Learners use language production opportunities as a means of testing their interlanguage hypotheses. Through interaction with other speakers, they are able to determine (based on the comprehension of the interlocutor) whether their hypotheses need to be corrected or refined, and can receive the feedback to help them do so. Furthermore, negotiation and focus-on-form sequences embedded in meaningful interaction allow learners to break from the content of the discussion and turn their attention to the production of form in context.

Speaking vs. Writing

As Williams (this volume) explains, even as speaking and writing have been recognized as essential components of language learning, speaking has taken a leading role, with little research examining how writing itself contributes to second language acquisition, or how speaking and writing may interact. Of course, both speaking and writing provide opportunities for learners to produce output. However, in order for learners to notice the gap while speaking, they presumably need sufficient processing space available to hold both versions in memory and compare them. Recent research on the role of memory in learning from feedback (e.g., Mackey, Philp, Egi, Fujii, & Tatsumi, 2002), in forms-processing (see Doughty, 2001), and in lexical knowledge acquisition (e.g., Ellis & Sinclair, 1996) indicate that, with the ongoing processing demands of conversation, it is possible that learners are not always able to process oral feedback for learning. The demands of writing, on the other hand, are somewhat less immediate, possibly allowing learners some much-needed additional processing time. For example, Weissberg (2000) found that learners in his study were more likely to introduce new syntactic forms when writing than when speaking. As Williams (this volume) notes, research has indicated not only that learners introduce forms in their writing that they have not yet used in speaking, but also that using a form in the planned context of writing may lead to use in unplanned speaking contexts.

Also, when writing, learners may be able to separate the communication of meaning and form. Once ideas are recorded on paper, learners can orient themselves to the targetlikeness of their output. As Cumming (1989) points out, writing is a task that naturally encourages learners to attend to form and meaning. The product of a written task is an actual sample of written interlanguage, which learners can examine both during and after the writing process. Activities that incorporate writing, therefore, may be more likely to provide learners with opportunities to examine their own language production.

Written language production, then, may be especially helpful in promoting noticing. However, much of the research on writing and learner-learner interaction focuses on learners revising each others' texts (e.g., Lockhart & Ng, 1995; Villamil & de Guerrero, 1996); as Storch (2005) points out, "one of the drawbacks of peer reviews [...] is that the focus is often on the product of writing rather than the process of writing" (p. 154). In collaborative writing, as opposed to revision, learners work together to craft a single written product, and researchers can examine their writing process.

Collaborative writing samples are often shorter than writing produced by an individual working alone, but they are also characterized by higher linguistic accuracy, greater complexity, and higher scores on qualitative scales (Storch, 2005). Such collaboration has been empirically demonstrated to facilitate language learning (Adams, 2003; Lapkin, Swain, & Smith, 2002; Qi & Lapkin, 2001; Storch, 2001, 2002a, 2002b; Swain, Brooks, & Tocalli-Bender, 2002; Swain & Lapkin, 2002). Learners working together and adopting a collaborative stance have been shown to engage in "co-construction, extension of knowledge and provision of scaffolded assistance" (Storch, 2001, p. 46). Additionally, when learners engage in collaborative writing in a classroom setting, they know that their written product can be collected and examined by peers or teachers. It is possible that, for some learners, this increases the importance of producing targetlike language, which may in turn increase their orientation to form.

Influence of Task Modality on Focus-on-Form

A growing body of task-based language teaching research lends support to the particular effectiveness of written production in promoting attention to form. Several researchers have reported quite frequent occurrences of negotiation for meaning and other interactional modifications in tasks that require writing (e.g., Adams, 2003; Storch, 1998, 2001; Swain & Lapkin, 2002). While Foster (1998) suggests that, when speaking, learners may be unwilling to call attention to each others' errors unless a true communicative breakdown occurs, Storch (1998, 2001) reports that when writing cooperatively, learners may be willing to discuss form even when communication has not broken down.

Williams (1999) has suggested that tasks that incorporate writing may be perceived by learners as having a more language-oriented goal than tasks that require only speaking, perhaps because they are forced to confront language as an object as well as a tool for communication. This perception may make them more likely to focus more on form than they might if a writing component were not included. Williams' hypothesis seemed to hold true in a study by Ross-Feldman (in press). In her study, learners engaged in three interactive tasks. Two tasks were exclusively oral tasks; one combined speaking and writing. Not only did learners produce significantly more language-related episodes (LREs) on the combination task than on the speaking-only tasks, this was the only task that elicited attention to morphosyntax. The combination of writing and speaking in a single task seems to be especially effective in turning learners' attention to form.

The effectiveness of written production tasks in promoting attention to form is suggested by the following examples, drawn from Adams' (2003) study, which contrasted learner production in the speaking and writing sections of a picture story task. In the first two examples, the learners are engaged in an information gap task, seeking to understand a picture story for which each has half of the pictures. In Example 1, Learner 2 does not seem to understand what Learner 1 is saying, but does not indicate this:

Example 1. Speaking: No Negotiation Despite Miscomprehension

1. **Learner 1:** Hay es una maquina con un mano que que se levanta los pies de la mujer.
   [There is it is a machine with a hand that that lifts itself up the feet of the woman.]
2. **Learner 2:** (long pause) oh (long pause) huh

Following this turn, Learner 2 began to describe her picture, rather than seek to clarify what Learner 1 said. In Example 2, Learner 1 is clear in her desire to obtain information from Learner 2 about the grammaticality of her utterance. Yet Learner 2 ignores the attempt to focus on form, and the learners end up continuing to describe the pictures:

Example 2. Speaking: Negotiation Signal Ignored

1. **Learner 1:** Y la mujer continua estar durmiendo.
   [And the woman continues to be asleep]
2. **Learner 2:** Sí en la
   [Yes in the]
3. **Learner 1:** or continua dormiendo dormir?
   [or continues sleeping sleep?]
4. **Learner 2:** En en la pintura seis...
   [In in the picture six...]

When learners were writing the stories, however, they did not allow miscommunication to go unchecked. In Example 3, Learner 1 wants to use the Spanish word for *pillow (almohada)* but does not know it. Rather than ignoring her partner, as the learners in the previous examples do, Learner 2 works with her partner to come up with a way to describe the situation despite not knowing the lexical item herself:

Example 3. Speaking + Writing: Negotiation (Vocabulary)

1. **Learner 1:** Su cabeza está lejos de
[Her head is far from]
2. **Learner 2:** uh
3. **Learner 1:** Que es? (points to picture) OK?
[What is it?]
4. **Learner 2:** la uh pio de la cama
[at the uh 'pio' of the bed]
5. **Learner 1:** Los pies
[The feet]
6. **Learner 2:** Pie de la cama
[Foot of the bed]
7. **Learner 1:** Están on su, que es pillow?
[They are on his, what is pillow?]
8. **Learner 2:** No sé la palabra. No para rápido.
[I don't know the word. Not for fast]
9. **Learner 1:** Están en el primer parte de la cama
[They are on the first part of the bed]
10. **Learner 2:** Oh la cabeza de la cama.
[Oh, the head of the bed]
11. **Learner 1:** OK Oh en la cabeza de la cama
[OK, oh on the head of the bead]

This example was representative of how learners dealt with form during the writing section of the task. What is striking about these data is the change in these learners' willingness to engage in protracted discussions of form during writing, when they do not even seek to resolve miscommunication when just speaking. While the original purpose of that study was not to explore the influence of writing on speaking, but rather to examine the influence of a particular research methodology on learners' development, the data raised interesting questions about how the addition of a writing element to a speaking task can turn learners' attention to linguistic form. A later study (Adams, 2006) investigated the role that modality played in learner attention to form in a collaborative task. The results of that study indicated that learners engaged in more focus-on-form during the writing portion of the task than during the speaking-only portion, demonstrating that task modality may influence learner attention to form in interactive tasks, with collaborative writing tasks more successfully encouraging learners to focus on form than tasks that only require speaking.

Research Question

Prior research has shown that production through writing and through speaking can have different effects on learner tendency to focus on form during communication. While studies have indicated that learners focus on form more when writing than when speaking, little is known about how collaborative writing influences the way that learners attend to form. The purpose of this study was to examine whether the modality of production influences how learners engage in focus-on-form. The study investigated the following research question:

> *Do characteristics of focus-on-form differ between collaborative writing and speaking tasks?*

This study sought to determine whether the addition of a writing element influenced the way learners focused on form in interactive tasks with other learners. It was not the purpose of this study to contrast focus-on-form in tasks where learners only speak and in tasks where learners only write. While collaborative tasks may involve only speaking, collaborative tasks that involve only writing are rare and unnatural in a face-to-face setting. Rather, this study compared how learners focus on form in tasks where learners are only required to speak, and in tasks where learners are required to both speak and write.

Method

Participants

The participants in this study were 44 ESL learners in a community English learning program in a large urban center in the United States. The learners were all enrolled in high-intermediate classes (level four of a five-level series), based on their placement through in-house oral and written tests of reading, writing, oral communication, and grammar. All learners indicated that they had had very limited exposure to English before coming to the United States, despite having studied English in their countries. While most of the learners were working in the community, they often worked in jobs where their L1 was predominantly spoken, and where they had limited interactions with native speakers of English. Although these learners were learning in an ESL environment, they shared many similarities with learners in a foreign language environment who have restricted access to interaction with native speakers. For these learners in particular, it may be quite important they be able to benefit from classroom conversational opportunities. Table 1 summarizes important characteristics of these participants.

As can be seen from Table 1, the majority of the participants were speakers of Spanish, with relatively fewer speakers of the other languages. The mix of first languages included could not be controlled, as intact classes were used in this research. While this limitation should be considered in applying these results to other classes, the use of intact classes increases the pedagogical authenticity of the research.

Linguistic Targets

Because the purpose of the study was to examine learner focus-on-form during collaborative writing and speaking, tasks for the study drew learners' attention to specific structures. The tasks in this study were designed to

Table 1

Learner Characteristics

Characteristics	Treatment Group	
Age	Mean	32.3 years
	Range	20–51 years
Length of residence	Mean	3.69 years
	Range	1–15 years
Gender	Male	18
	Female	26
L1 Background		29 Spanish 4 Chinese 4 Amharic 3 Arabic 2 French 1 Vietnamese 1 Bengali

elicit the use of two target structures: locative prepositions and past tense morphology. Pilot testing of the treatment materials indicated that the tasks promoted the use of the target structures, but primary attention remained on communication.

Locative Prepositions

Locative prepositions are linguistically complex structures involving semantic, syntactic, and morphological competence. Semantically, locatives express a spatial relationship between two elements. This can be a particular point of difficulty, as these relationships are often encoded differently across languages. The locative prepositions targeted in this study were prepositional collocations (e.g., *next to, to the right of, across from*) involving learners' morphosyntactic knowledge. These locative collocations were chosen as linguistic targets for this study because their targetlike use involves both semantic and syntactic competence, both potential sites for focus-on-form.

Past Tense

In English, past tense is primarily encoded morphologically. Simple past tense is often taught early in second language curricula, and while past tense emerges rather early developmentally (e.g., Goldschneider & DeKeyser, 2001), even quite advanced learners may continue to make errors in past tense usage, including omitting past tense marking, and overgeneralizing regular past tense marking. Past tense was selected as a target for this study because the intermediate learners had received repeated instruction on it, but had not yet mastered its use.

Tasks

Two collaborative tasks were used in this study, one designed to elicit use of each of the target forms. Both tasks required learners to collaborate in order to arrive at solutions, so that both learners in each dyad had the opportunity to participate equally in the task completion.

Locatives Task

The locatives task required the learners to create the best possible seating plan for fictional characters using information, for example, about dinner party guests. Learners were given a picture of a table and chairs and a description of the participants for the event. They were asked first to come to a consensus about who should sit where and fill in a seating chart. After determining the seating plan, they were asked to complete a worksheet in which they described the position of each person at the table with reference to other people. Three different versions of this task were created; they were given to different dyads in this study at random. Different task versions were used to limit the possibility of particular task content influencing the outcomes.

Past Tense Task

For the past tense task, the learners were each given one half of a picture story (eight pictures total). For each picture, they were given a past date and time when it occurred. They were asked to orally reconstruct the story, and then to collaboratively write out the story. Because pictures can prompt present tense descriptions, the learners were orally instructed that the story occurred in the past, and their attention was specifically drawn to the date and time associated with each picture. Similar to the locatives task, three versions of this task were created and given to learners in the study at random.

Each task (locatives and past tense) included both an oral and a written component. They differed in terms of the order that the oral and written components needed to be completed. In the locative task, the learners shared all the information from the beginning of the task, and it was not possible for the learners to engage in the collaborative writing exercise describing where the participants were sitting before they had orally discussed the seating preferences and designed the seating chart. Twenty dyads completed this task. The design of the past tense task was less rigid. While each learner was given four pictures, they were not instructed to hide their pictures from their partners. Without this instruction, eleven dyads chose to conceal their pictures from their partner, only disclosing them after they had first reconstructed the story orally. These dyads then collaboratively wrote out the story, following the same order of speaking and writing as on the locatives task. The remaining nine dyads chose to reveal their set of pictures to their partner from the beginning of the task. These learners blended the collaborative discussion and the collaborative writing sections of the task. Thus, for just over half of the learners, the collaborative speaking and collaborative writing sections of the past tense task were carried out sequentially; for the remaining participants, these sections of the task were carried out simultaneously.

Procedure

The learners were divided into dyads by the researcher with input from the teacher to avoid pairing two very weak learners. Learners were audiorecorded as they completed both tasks with the same partner. Task order was randomized across dyads. The recordings were then transcribed by three independent researchers. Because of recording problems that precluded transcription, four task-based interactions (two each of dinner seating task and picture story task) were discarded at this stage. The transcriptions were then examined for evidence to determine whether the inclusion of collaborative writing in a dyadic task influenced the way that learners attended to form.

Coding

Because this study sought to determine whether task modality influenced the way learners engaged in focus-on-form, an internal cognitive process not directly visible to the researchers, learner discourse during the task-based interactions was coded for different phenomena that characterized both individual and collaborative focus-on-form.

The first stage of coding involved identifying language-related episodes (LREs) and instances of self-repair. LREs (and a similar construct, form-focused episodes) are segments of discourse where form becomes a central topic. For this study, LRE coding was based on Williams' (1999) definition, that LREs include "*all* interaction in which learners draw attention to form, that is, those that focus on form in the context of meaningful communication as well as those that are set apart from such communication and simply revolve around questions of form itself" (p. 595). This definition is similar to those used by other researchers, including Ellis, Basturkmen, & Loewen (2001) in describing attention to form when language learners are engaged in meaning-focused activities in groups or in full class settings. Prior research has connected LREs to subsequent learning in both native speaker-learner interactions (e.g., Loewen, 2005) and in learner-learner interactions (e.g., Adams, in press). LREs are normally considered collaborative focus-on-form; evidence of attention to form is usually coded as LREs only when more than one learner discusses the use of form. This understanding of LREs was adopted in the current study. Discussion of form by one learner, in which the interlocutor did not contribute, was included as self-repair. Collaborative discussion of form could occur in several ways, including episodes of discussions of form (see Example 4), as well as implicit or explicit feedback, and the use of metalinguistic information.

Example 4. Discussion of Form

Target: *Sat in a restaurant*

Learner 1: years ago, right? Years ago right? He was missing his wife who had died years ago. When, when, when a set, sit, set, set? Set in

Learner 2: Set

Learner 1: Set in the restaurant. Okay.

Learner 2: In the restaurant.

In this example, the learners are describing a picture story. Learner 1 attempts to describe a character entering a restaurant and sitting down. He is unsure of the correct form, and tries out two different alternatives, using question intonation to signal uncertainty. Learner 2 reinforces one of the forms, which Learner 1 then adopts. This sort of orientation to form may be beneficial for learning by allowing learners to make new form-meaning associations, or to reinforce existing associations. However, it should be remembered that in learner-learner interactions, as in this one, learners do not always arrive at a targetlike form (c.f., Adams, 2006). After the LREs were identified, their characteristics were coded to determine whether the inclusion of writing in the tasks influenced the characteristics of the focus-on-form. The coding schema used by Ellis, Basturkmen, & Loewen (2001) was adapted for this purpose. Figure 1 illustrates the coding schema used in this study.

LREs were categorized in four ways: target of focus, complexity of focus, directness of focus, and resolution. First, they were coded according to the target of the LRE, either Form or Meaning. If the LRE arose from a difficulty with formal linguistic aspects, such as morphology or pronunciation, the target of the LRE was coded as Form. If learners were primarily engaged in negotiation of meaning or discussing how to express an intended meaning, the target of the LRE was coded as Meaning. LREs were coded for target of the focus to see whether engaging in writing, rather than only speaking, pushed learners to attend to linguistic accuracy.

Second, each LRE was coded for complexity and categorized as either Simple or Complex. LREs that involved only a single attempt to solve a problem before it was resolved or dropped were coded as Simple; LREs that involved multiple attempts to solve a problem were considered Complex. In prior research (e.g., Ellis, Basturkmen, & Loewen, 2001), complex LREs

Figure 1
Coding

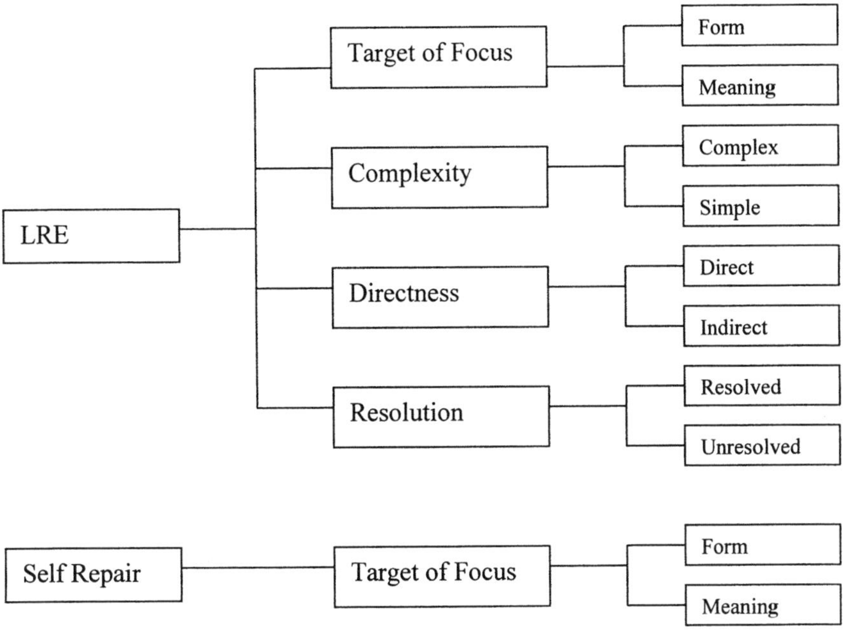

have been shown to be more likely to lead to uptake. The complexity of LREs was therefore examined to see whether engaging in writing allowed learners opportunities to have the longer discussions of form that are more likely to lead to linguistic restructuring.

Third, all LREs were coded for directness and categorized as either Direct or Indirect. Direct LREs were defined as those in which learners explicitly indicated that there was a problem, for example through the use of explicit feedback or metalinguistic information. Indirect LREs were those in which learners employed more implicit indications that problems had arisen—for example, implicit feedback or clarification requests. Engaging in more direct focus-on-form indicates that learners are overtly attending to form. Complex LREs, which involved more than one attempt, were coded as Direct if any direct attempts were included, because any explicit moves could influence how learners attended to form.

Finally, the resolution of the LRE was coded and categorized as either Resolved or Unresolved. LREs were coded as Resolved if the learner who had originally produced the utterance that prompted the LRE modified his output following direct or indirect attempts (either through correcting the original errors or by reformulating the utterance) or if the learners agreed on a solution in a discussion of form. LREs were coded as Unresolved if a learner simply repeated his original utterance or ignored feedback or attempts to discuss form and simply moved on with the task. Research on modified output (McDonough, 2005) and uptake (Loewen, 2005) indicates that resolving feedback and focus-on-form episodes promotes learning. It is important to point out here that a resolution was defined in terms of learners evidencing willingness to modify their output or coming to agreement. Resolving an LRE did not necessarily indicate that the learners produced a targetlike utterance. As noted, at times learners arrived at a non–target like resolution. However, as the difference between achieving a target-like resolution and a non–target like resolution is more likely related to learners' interlanguage knowledge than to the way they engage in focus-on-form, these were not distinguished for this study. Of interest here was how the structure of the task in terms of speaking and writing influenced learners' engagement in focus-on-form.

In addition to LREs, instances of self-repair were also identified to see if they occurred differently in writing or speaking. Self-repair was defined as any instance when a learner modified his own utterance in the same turn or in an adjacent turn without input from his interlocutor, as in Example 5:

Example 5. Self-Repair
Target: *Serving the soup*

Learner 1: Waitress is serving…is serving food at the man.

Learner 2: Uh-huh

Learner 1: I think she is serving the soup to him

In this example, even though Learner 2 speaks between the error and the repair, he does not seem to be involved in focusing on form here, so this was still considered self-repair. While LREs indicate collaborative focus-on-form, self-repair indicates individual attention to form, signaling learners' more autonomous efforts to monitor how they encoded meaning through linguistic form. Like LREs, instances of self-repair were further coded according to the target of the self-repair (Form or Meaning); the other categories of LRE coding did not apply to self-repair.

Analysis

After the data were coded, proportion scores were calculated for each dyad for each characteristic of the LREs and self-repair (e.g., the total number of direct LREs for each dyad was divided by their total number of LREs to determine the proportion of direct LREs). These data were submitted to two different types of analysis. First, in order to determine whether focus-on-form differed when learners were engaged in collaborative speaking and when they were engaged in collaborative writing, the characteristics of LREs and Self-Repair on the speaking and writing sections of the tasks were compared. To compare focus-on-form on the separate sections of this task, a non-parametric test, the Wilcoxian Signed Ranks test, was used. Non-parametric tests were selected because the limited number of dyads in the study precluded the assumption of a normal distribution of data. The second type of analysis carried out, Mann Whitney U, was used to compare the characteristics of focus-on-form of learners who completed the writing section of the past tense task sequentially with the speaking section to the focus-on-form characteristics of those who completed them simultaneously. This analysis and the results are described in detail below.

Results

Descriptive statistics for the characteristics of focus-on-form from the spoken and written sections of the locatives task are provided in Table 2.

Table 2

Characteristics of Focus-on-Form on the Locatives Task

Focus-on-Form Characteristics		Speaking			Speaking + Writing		
		N	Mean	Range	N	Mean	Range
LREs	Total	11		0–3	79		0–14
	Form	2	13%	0–2	31	43%	0–5
	Complex	2	13%	0–1	24	26%	0–8
	Direct	2	13%	0–2	31	30%	0–8
	Resolved	6	67%	0–1	60	78%	0–11
Self-Repair	Total	9		0–2	17		0–4
	Form	3	29%	0–1	10	52%	0–2

As can be seen in Table 2, there was clearly more focus-on-form when learners were engaged in writing on this task. These learners engaged in only eleven LREs while completing the speaking portion, but engaged in 79 LREs when engaged in writing. While not as dramatic a difference, learners also produced more self-repair in writing than in speaking. Additionally, when students were engaged in writing, a greater proportion of their LREs and self-repair were about form rather than meaning, and a greater proportion were complex, direct, and resolved. The clearest difference in the characteristics is found in the target of the LREs, where 30 percent more were about form when writing than when speaking. As explained, these data were submitted to Wilcoxian Signed Ranks tests for inferential analysis, as summarized in Table 3.

These analyses indicate that, during the collaborative writing portion of the task, learners were more likely to engage in LREs. None of the other measures reached significance at the .05 level. This may be related to the smaller numbers of participants included in the different analyses.

As explained, a similar analysis was carried out for the past tense task for the learners who engaged in the past tense task by discussing their pictures before revealing them to their partners and collaboratively writing the story. Descriptive statistics for this groups' orientation to form is provided in Table 4.

Again, the descriptive statistics indicate that the learners engaged in more LREs and produced more self-repair in the writing section of the task. Similar to the locatives task, when the learners were writing collaboratively, they engaged in more LREs targeted at resolving problems with linguistic form, produced more complex LREs, more direct LREs, and resolved more of their LREs. The resolution of LREs is particularly interesting here. Learners resolved the LREs at a higher rate in the past tense task over-

Table 3

Wilcoxian Signed Ranks for Locatives

		Z	ns/r	P
LREs	Total	–3.52	19	.00
	Form	–1.47	8	.14
	Complex	–1.36	8	.17
	Direct	–.94	8	.35
	Resolved	–.11	8	.92
Self-repair	Total	–1.64	19	.10
	Form	–.82	5	.41

Table 4

Characteristics of Focus-on-Form in the Past Tense Task

Focus-on-Form Characteristics		Speaking			Speaking + Writing		
		N	Mean	Range	N	Mean	Range
LREs	Total	30		0–8	66		0–15
	Form	7	19%	0–3	34	53%	0–11
	Complex	2	3%	0–2	6	12%	0–1
	Direct	7	22%	0–2	30	49%	0–11
	Resolved	22	73%	0–6	63	92%	0–24
Self-Repair	Total	25		0–6	32		0–5
	Form	18	67%	0–6	28	86%	0–4

all, and in the writing section of the task resolved all but three of the LREs.

Again, these data were submitted to a Wilcoxian Signed Ranks analysis to determine whether these differences were significant, as displayed in Table 5.

The Wilcoxian signed ranks tests did not reveal any significant differences between the focus-on-form in the speaking and writing sections of the test. However, three of the tests closely approached significance. These indicate that on the past tense task there was a strong trend for more LREs to be produced during the writing portion of the task, and for these LREs to be both focused on form and direct. Together, these findings provide emerging evidence that modality influenced focus-on-form in the past tense task. For the past tense task, there were no differences in self-repair (either amount or target of focus) between the spoken and written sections.

The previous analysis provided limited evidence that when these learners completed the writing portion of the task, the modality influenced the way they focused on form. Because both tasks were designed to allow learners to engage in the speaking-only section before the writing and speaking section, it is possible that shifts in how learners discussed form may be due either to the effects of adding the writing requirement or to the order of the sections of the task. Since the students discussed the content before they started writing, it could be argued that they attended to form differently in the writing section not because of the effects of modality, but because it was their second opportunity to process the content. However, as discussed, roughly half of the dyads integrated the speaking and writing sections of the past tense task, while the remaining learners first discussed the story and

Table 5
Wilcoxian Signed Ranks for Past Tense

		Z	ns/r	p
LREs	Total	–1.84	11	.06
	Form	–1.82	9	.06
	Complex	–1.16	9	.25
	Direct	–1.85	9	.06
	Resolved	–1.52	9	.13
Self-Repair	Total	–.96	11	.34
	Form	–.921	8	.36

then wrote it. Comparison of the characteristics of the focus-on-form of the dyads that engaged in the collaborative speaking and writing simultaneously to those that engaged in these sequentially allowed for separation of the effect of modality from the effect of task-order.[1] This comparison was carried out using a non-parametric test, the Mann Whitney U, which allows for analysis of the significance of the difference between the distributions of two independent samples.

Descriptive statistics for the characteristics of focus-on-form by students who engaged in speaking and then writing, and those who blended speaking and writing, are displayed in Table 6.

These descriptive statistics show mixed results for the effect of order on focus-on-form during writing. Overall, it does not seem that having engaged in processing the content for meaning during the speaking section allowed learners to focus more on form in the writing section, because learners who integrated the writing and speaking sections engaged in more LREs and produced more instances of self-repair than did the sequential group. Additionally, a greater percentage of their LREs were directed at form. The proportion of complex LREs and the proportion of direct LREs were similar to that of learners who engaged in writing after speaking. However, learners who engaged first in speaking and then in writing resolved a higher proportion of LREs. This could indicate that processing the content through speaking first helps learners to use opportunities to focus on form to greater

[1]This could have also been built into the design by designing tasks that required collaborative writing before engagement in collaborative speaking. However, such tasks would have been very unfamiliar to the learners in this study, and might have been perceived as inauthentic. Additionally, the current design allowed the learners autonomy to complete the task following their own strategies for task-management.

advantage. As explained, these data were submitted to a Mann Whitney U to determine whether or not these differences were statistically significant. The results of the analysis are presented in Table 7.

Overall, the order of engaging in speaking and writing did not influence the characteristics of focus-on-form. This indicates that the results of the prior analyses were more likely due to effects of producing output through writing than to having previously discussed the content in a collaborative speaking section of the task. There is only one exception to this: the resolution of LREs. The learners who first discussed the task before engaging in writing were significantly more likely to resolve LREs than learners who integrated the oral discussion and the collaborative writing. Thus, while only task modality influenced the amount of focus-on-form, the order in which students engaged in speaking and writing sections may have influenced the effectiveness of focus-on-form.

Table 6

Sequential vs. Simultaneous Engagement in Writing

Focus-on-Form Characteristics		Sequential			Simultaneous		
		N	Mean	Range	N	Mean	Range
LREs	Total	66		0–15	76		4–16
	Form	34	53%	0–11	56	77%	4–10
	Complex	6	12%	0–1	14	17%	0–6
	Direct	30	49%	0–11	36	40%	0–9
	Resolved	63	92%	0–24	46	61%	2–10
Self-Repair	Total	32		0–5	46		1–9
	Form	28	86%	0–4	42	93%	1–8

Table 7

Mann Whitney U for Past Tense

		Mean $Ranks_A$	Mean $Ranks_B$	U	p-value
LREs	Total	8.86	12.50	31.5	.17
	Form	8.15	12.06	26.5	.13
	Complex	9.10	11.00	36.0	.49
	Direct	9.95	10.06	44.5	.96
	Resolved	12.85	6.83	16.5	.02
Self-Repair	Total	8.45	13.00	27.0	.10
	Form	9.20	10.89	37.0	.55

Discussion

The purpose of this study was to determine whether the way that learners focused on form was influenced by engagement in writing during collaborative tasks. There were descriptive trends for learners' LREs to be targeted more on form, and for their LREs to be more complex, more direct, and resolved more often in writing than in speaking. However, the statistical analysis did not indicate that these differences were significant. On the analysis of the past tense task, the differences between the writing and speaking subtasks on the production of Form LREs and Direct LREs closely approached significance. These may indicate possible differences that were not uncovered due to the size of the data sample.

Additionally, the order in which learners engaged in speaking and writing was investigated through comparing the use of focus-on-form when learners engaged in speaking and writing sequentially and when they engaged in them simultaneously. This analysis showed that learners who engaged in the speaking section of the task before engaging in the writing section were significantly more likely to resolve their LREs. This finding is particularly striking in light of prior findings (Adams, 2006) that the order in which learners engaged in speaking and writing sections of a task (sequential or simultaneous) did not influence the amount of orientation to form, measured through the use of LREs and self-repair. Those findings seemed to indicate that prior engagement in speaking did not allow learners to turn their attention more to form in the subsequent writing. The current findings then point to the possibility that although order does not influence the amount of focus-on-form, it may influence the effectiveness of the focus-on-form that occurs. As mentioned, prior research (e.g., Loewen, 2005; McDonough, 2005) has found that learner responses to focus-on-form and feedback episodes strongly influence subsequent learning. Therefore, while task order may not influence opportunities to learn, it may influence how much use learners make of those opportunities.

Additionally, these findings indicated that engagement in writing did not influence learner use of self-repair. Just as the earlier study (Adams, 2006) indicated that engagement in writing did not influence the amount of self-repair, this study also showed that it did not influence the orientation of self-repair. Even if engaging in writing prompted students to attend more to form in their collaborative interactions, it clearly did not affect how they engaged in individual orientation to form through self-repair. Self-repair indicates that the learner is monitoring his or her own language production. The lack of influence on the characteristics of learner self-repair may be related to the nature of collaboration. One of the advantages of collaborative work is that it allows learners to bring the treatment of form from private, cognitive processing to shared, collaborative processing. As Villamil and de Guerrero (1996) point out, working together "offers [learners] an opportunity for bilateral, rather than unilateral, participation and learning; in other words, both peers may give and receive help, both peers may teach and learn" (p. 69). Changing modalities may impact LREs, which are a collaborative means of attending to form, more than self-repair because learner focus in dyadic tasks is oriented to the shared construction of meaning. This possibility is supported by the incidence of self-repair in these data; on both tasks there were more LREs than incidence of self-repair.

Limitations

When comparing these findings to those of other studies, it should be remembered that the amount of focus-on-form, the type of focus-on-form, and the characteristics of focus-on-form may have different effects on learning in classroom interactions that involve the teacher, and ones that involve only learners. Additionally, measuring learning that related to qualitatively different focus-on-form was beyond the scope of this study. Implications for subsequent learning should be drawn with caution.

Finally, as mentioned, it should not be assumed that learner use of LREs, or any differences in the characteristics of LREs, is automatically associated with greater learning. Because the learners completed these tasks with other learners, not every LRE resolution was in the direction of the target. While beyond the scope of this study, other research has indicated that learners can adopt their interlocutor's miscorrections and incorrect LRE resolutions (e.g., Adams, 2006). These findings may indicate that both modalities included in a task and the order they are engaged in the tasks influence the way that learners focus on form and the success of that focus in terms of resolution. However, increasing attention to accuracy or increasing resolutions of focus-on-form episodes does not necessarily mean that the resulting learner production is more accurate. In learner-learner interactions, the fact that learners have resolved a discussion of form does not necessarily imply that they have arrived at the correct form. And, as with focus-on-form in any context, learner resolution of an LRE does not necessarily indicate that they have internalized the form or restructured their interlanguage.

These data indicate that there may be differences in the way that learners focus on form when they are engaged in speaking and when they are engaged in writing. These findings may indicate that tasks that include a writing component can push students to focus more on accuracy during language production. They also demonstrate that providing learners with an opportunity to process content orally before engaging in writing can increase the likelihood of learners resolving language-related episodes. This has important implications for both second language researchers and teachers interested in how learners attend to form while communicating meaning. These results imply that the modalities included in the task design affect not only the amount of focus-on-form, but also the characteristics of focus-on-form. They also indicate that the order in which learners engage in speaking and writing can influence the success of focus-on-form. This has implications for our understanding of how prior processing of content impacts on subsequent processing of form. This serves as further evidence that engaging in language production through writing and through speaking offers learners different language learning opportunities.

REFERENCES

Adams, R. (2003). L2 output, reformulation, and noticing: Implications for IL development. *Language Teaching Research, 7,* 347–376.

———. (2006). L2 tasks and orientation to form: A role for modality? *ITL: International Journal of Applied Linguistics, 152,* 7–34.

———. (2007). Do second language learners benefit from interacting with each other? In A. Mackey (Ed.), *Conversational interaction in second language acquisition: A series of empirical studies* (pp. 29–51). Oxford, UK: Oxford University Press.

Cumming, A. (1989). Writing expertise and second language proficiency. *Language Learning, 39,* 81–141.

Doughty, C. (2001). Cognitive underpinnings of focus on form. In P. Robinson (Ed.), *Cognition and second language instruction* (pp. 206–257). Cambridge, UK: Cambridge University Press.

Ellis, N. C., & Sinclair, S. (1996). Working memory in the acquisition of vocabulary and syntax: Putting language in good order. *Quarterly Journal of Experimental Psychology, 49A,* 234–250.

Ellis, R. (2003). *Task-based language learning and teaching.* Oxford, UK: Oxford University Press.

Ellis, R., Basturkmen, H., & Loewen, S. (2001). Learner uptake in communicative ESL lessons. *Language Learning, 51,* 281–318.

Foster, P. (1998). A classroom perspective on the negotiation of meaning. *Applied Linguistics, 19,* 1–23.

Goldschneider, J. M., & DeKeyser, R. M. (2001). Explaining the "natural order of L2 morpheme acquisition" in English: A meta-analysis of multiple determinants. *Language Learning, 51,* 1–50.

Harklau, L. (2002). The role of writing in classroom second language acquisition. *Journal of Second Language Writing, 11,* 329–350.

Lapkin, S., Swain, M., & Smith, M. (2002). Reformulation and the learning of French pronominal verbs in a Canadian French immersion context. *The Modern Language Journal, 86,* 485–507.

Lockhart, C., & Ng, P. (1995). Analyzing talk in ESL peer response groups: Stances, functions, and content. *Language Learning, 45,* 605–655.

Loewen, S. (2005). Incidental focus on form and second language learning. *Studies in Second Language Acquisition, 27*(3), 361–386.

Mackey, A. (2006). Feedback, noticing and instructed second language learning. *Applied Linguistics, 27,* 405–430.

Mackey, A., Philp, J., Egi, T., Fujii, A., & Tatsumi, T. (2002). Individual differences in working memory, noticing of interactional feedback and L2 development. In P. Robinson (Ed.), *Individual differences and instructed language learning* (pp. 181–209). Philadelphia: John Benjamins.

McDonough, K. (2005). Identifying the impact of negative feedback and learners' responses on ESL question development. *Studies in Second Language Acquisition, 27*(1), 79–103.

Qi, D. S., & Lapkin, S. (2001). Exploring the role of noticing in a three-stage second language writing task. *Journal of Second Language Writing, 10,* 277–303.

Ross-Feldman, L. (2007). Interaction in the L2 classroom: Does gender influence learning opportunities. In A. Mackey (Ed.), *Conversational interaction and second language acquisition: A series of empirical studies* (pp. 63–77). Oxford, UK: Oxford University Press.

Storch, N. (1998). Comparing second language learners' attention to form across tasks. *Language Awareness, 7,* 176–191.

———. (2001). How collaborative is pair work? ESL tertiary students composing in pairs. *Language Teaching Research, 5,* 29–53.

———. (2002a). Patterns of interaction in ESL pair work. *Language Learning, 52,* 119–158.

———. (2002b). Relationships formed in dyadic interaction and opportunity for learning. *International Journal of Educational Research, 37,* 305–322.

———. (2005). Collaborative writing: Product, process, and students' reflections. *Journal of Second Language Writing, 14,* 153–173.

Swain, M. (1995). Three functions of output in second language learning. In G. Cook & B. Seidlhofer (Eds.), *Principle and practice in applied* lin-

guistics: Studies in honour of H.G. Widdowson (pp. 125–144). Oxford, UK: Oxford University Press.

———. (2005). The output hypothesis: Theory and research. In E. Hinkel (Ed.), *Handbook on research in second language teaching and learning* (pp. 471–484). Mahwah, NJ: Lawrence Erlbaum.

Swain, M., Brooks, L., & Tocalli-Bender, A. (2002). Peer-peer dialogue as a means of second language learning. *Annual Review of Applied Linguistics, 22,* 171–185.

Swain, M., & Lapkin, S. (2002). Talking it through: Two French immersion learners' response to reformulation. *International Journal of Educational Research, 37,* 285–304.

Villamil, O. S., & de Guerrero, M. C. M. (1996). Peer revision in the L2 Classroom: Social-cognitive activities, mediating strategies, and aspects of social behavior. *Journal of Second Language Writing, 5,* 51–75.

Weissberg, R. (2000). Developmental relationships in the acquisition of English syntax: Writing vs. speech. *Language and Instruction, 10,* 37–53.

Williams, J. (1999). Learner-generated attention to form. *Language Learning, 49,* 583–625.

Part 4

How Technology Bridges Speaking and Writing

14

Corpus Linguistics for Academic Literacies Mediated through Discussion Activities

LYNNE FLOWERDEW

Abstract

The use of corpora in language learning is well established, but three issues exist for enhancing the role of corpora in improving academic literacies. One issue concerns which corpus, or indeed other resources, should be consulted. Another consideration is how corpus work can be systematically integrated into the grammar and writing work of a course and not just used as an end in itself. A third aspect of using corpora in language work is that they tend to be used in a rather teacher-centered way with students mainly interacting with the computer. This chapter reports an attempt to use corpora in a more interactive way that encourages discussion-based peer response activities on a course where corpora have been integrated into the writing syllabus. I suggest that this type of corpus-based pedagogy provides an ideal bridge for linking the speaking-writing divide.

The use of corpora in language learning and teaching was first instigated by Johns, whose seminal work in this field is reported in Johns (1994), and Johns & King (2001). Various types of excellent corpus-based activities for general ELT and academic English, either in the form of pen-and-paper tasks derived from concordance output (indirect approach) or activities involving hands-on concordancing (direct approach), are described in Tribble & Jones

(1990), Thurstun & Candlin (1998a, 1998b), Milton (1998, 1999), Aston (1997) and Gavioli & Aston (2001). Recent years have seen an explosion in the exploitation of small, specialized corpora in various ESP areas (see Flowerdew, 2004, for an overview of such work). A recent volume by Gavioli (2005) and Lee & Swales's (2006) account of using specialized corpora with non–native speaking (NNS) doctoral students provide extremely insightful commentaries on the application of corpora in ESP teaching and learning. The increasingly mainstream role that corpora are now playing in enhancing ESP literacy is acknowledged in an overview article by Belcher (2006) on the current state of ESP.

However, this growth in the use of corpora has been accompanied by a more reflective, questioning attitude to the use of corpora, with more studies centered on evaluating various aspects of the whole corpora-learning process and product cycle. Cobb's (1997) study is noteworthy in this regard, in that it provides empirical evidence from a carefully designed series of vocabulary tests to show that there is a measurable gain in learning from hands-on concordancing. Other studies use student questionnaires and self-reporting to ascertain students' attitudes toward the usefulness of corpora (see Fan & Xu, 2002; Chambers & O'Sullivan, 2004; Gaskell & Cobb, 2004; Yoon & Hirvela, 2004; Chambers, 2005) and also teacher-initiated evaluations of student approaches to corpus investigation (Kennedy & Miceli, 2001, 2002). An article by Yoon & Hirvela (2004) provides a very useful critique of these evaluation-type studies.

There exist three issues, though, that hitherto have not received much attention in the literature. The first concerns which corpora or resources should be consulted, as pointed out in Chambers & O'Sullivan (2004):

> The concept of literacy now includes not only the knowledge and skills which are traditionally associated with that concept, but also the ability to select, evaluate and use the electronic tools and resources appropriate for the activity which is being undertaken. (p. 158)

In this respect, Davies (2004) reports on a program on student use of three main corpora for examining syntactic variation in Spanish, noting that sometimes students' intention was to use a corpus that was not the most appropriate for the research question they had formulated. This notion of making various corpora available to students (including the web), and sensitizing them as to which one is most appropriate for a particular search query, has not been explored much to date. This is an important aspect of corpus-based language work, which has been flagged for future development of the field by Bernardini (2002, 2004).

Another important consideration is how corpus work can be systematically integrated into the grammar and writing work of a course and not just used as an end in itself (Kennedy & Miceli, 2001). Both of these concerns seem to be embodied in the quotation from Chambers (2005):

> . . . there is little evidence to suggest that direct corpus consultation is coming to be seen as a complement or alternative to consultation of a dictionary, course book, or grammar by the majority of learners. There is thus a need for research to underpin the integration of corpora and concordancing in the language-learning environment. (p. 111)

A third aspect of using corpora in language work is that none of the current textbooks, although they contain very interesting ideas for exploiting corpora, explore the speaking-writing connection to any great extent, which is the focus of this volume.

Having students engage in talking about writing for making changes in drafts, whether it be through teacher-student conferencing or peer feedback and discussions, both of which can take place face-to-face or using electronic software, has been shown to benefit students' writing overall (Hyland, 2003). Peer feedback, discussed in depth in Ferris (2003) and Liu & Hansen (2002), has been classified in terms of three types, supporting, challenging, and editing (see Grabe & Kaplan, 1996). The first two involve commenting on ideas and structure of the text, while editing feedback relates to formal aspects of writing. However, as Williams (this volume) points out, most of the research has concentrated on revisions involving content or organizational aspects rather than grammatical or lexical features—that is, less emphasis has been given to the editing aspect.

This article sets out to show how, through a suite of peer response, discussion-based exercises, talking about certain language issues may help students not only improve their writing, but also foster 'an ability to select, evaluate and use the electronic tools and resources appropriate for the activity which is being undertaken' (Chambers & O'Sullivan, 2004, 158).

In the following section, I give an overview of the course, which progressed from speaking to writing through the integration of peer response activities to language points for follow-up consultation using various online resources.

Overview of the Course: The Speaking-Writing Connection

Following Leech (1997), cited in Bernardini (2004), I have adopted an approach that commences with teacher-directed "convergent" tasks, gradually moving toward "divergent" ones where students take on a more autonomous role in deciding on the language points for which to consult a corpus. In this discovery learning (DL) approach, the student is therefore very much considered as "the learner as traveler" (Bernardini, 2004).

In this 30-hour report writing course, students' first task is to decide on a suitable topic for their investigation. After finalizing their topic, each topic group is required to produce a one or two page outline of their project, organizing the information under suitable sub-headings (e.g., purpose and scope, justification, potential benefits). This outline is then passed to another project group for a Q & A session with the main aim of helping students with any clarification or elaboration points. Sometimes students also bring up language points, which are, of course, welcome, although they are not explicitly instructed to do this. Students also receive feedback on the content and organization from their class teacher, with any language errors underlined (although these outlines are mostly in point-form, certain language errors are still evident). I have found the underlining of language errors to be a very useful starting point in corpus consultation work. In this respect, Chambers brings up the nature of guidance to be provided by the language teacher, noting the usefulness of the marking of inappropriate language use. With this kind of "interim document" in hand, students can then access various online resources "in the context of interactive feedback" (Chambers, 2005, p. 171).

Once students have revised their initial outlines, I ask them to write the introductions to their project reports. These are then given to another group for peer review covering the content, organization, and language. As for vocabulary and grammar items, students are asked to underline these and correct them with their own version, using a tick against their suggestion for amendment if they are fairly certain they are right and to use a question mark against their revision if they are less sure. Sometimes students just underline a word or phrase, without making any revisions, saying that they have a feeling something is wrong about the language, but they don't know how to correct it. In this second stage, students are therefore given more responsibility for the error identification for follow-up corpus work.

It is hoped that the previously introduced corpus-awareness, confidence-building tasks will enable and motivate students sufficiently to use the resources on their own in the writing up of the final project report. In this latter stage, students thus follow up their own interests and queries as a result becoming more active and autonomous participants in the teaching-learning process (Bernardini, 2004). In a subsequent in-class discussion, students are encouraged to share their search questions and any problems and successes with other students.

The approach taken to error identification was very much indirect (see Ferris, 2002, for different levels of error identification) as the aim of these peer review tasks was to stimulate discussion among students and to get the learners to "use language to reflect on language use" (Swain, 1998, 68). Such peer response activities, which require students to use "collaborative metatalk," to use Swain's term, draw on Vygotskian socio-cultural theories of co-constructing knowledge through collaborative dialogue and negotiation, which is well documented in the literature. I also intentionally grouped weaker students with more proficient ones to foster productive dialogue through "assisted performance," thus drawing on another aspect of sociocultural theory (see Weissberg, this volume).

Williams (this volume) underscores the importance of such type of collaborative dialogue:

> The role of talk is particularly important because, within the sociocultural perspective, knowledge construction is mediated by language; articulation makes the new knowledge available for inspection and discussion. This, it is argued, is a precursor to the internalization of knowledge.

These peer response activities on language points not only require peer-to-peer interaction, but also "interaction" with online computer resources for students to validate their corrections, which generates further collaborative dialogue concerning interpretation of the corpus data. Thus, it can be said that knowledge construction is mediated by language and also language resources, as suggested earlier.

The Application of Corpora: From Speaking to Writing

In this section, I first outline the suite of online corpora and other electronic resources used such as various dictionaries and a thesaurus, all accessible under the same umbrella program, devised by my colleague Dr. John Milton. I then explain the various types of discussion activities that were set up to encourage students to articulate which online resource and search query they would use to correct the language errors and to voice aloud their interpretation of the corpus data.

Online Suite of Corpora and Other Resources

The literature on using corpora in the classroom tends to focus on either the use of individual small or large corpora. However, sometimes both are necessary, depending on the query (Flowerdew, 2006). The innovative Word Neighbors program (see Milton, 1998, 1999, for precursors of this tool) circumvents this problem by making available various sub-corpora for searching, in addition to the resources provided by the whole corpus of around 48 million words, as illustrated in Figure 1. Google® searches are also available in another window, if a particular item is not found in the whole corpus. One key feature of this program is that when a particular pattern is searched, the program automatically sorts and lists the word classes for each item in the pattern, thus bypassing the need for students to sort the items so that they can discern the different word classes (the left-hand column in Figure 2 provides an example of this feature).

Figure 1

Corpora Available under the Word Neighbors Tool

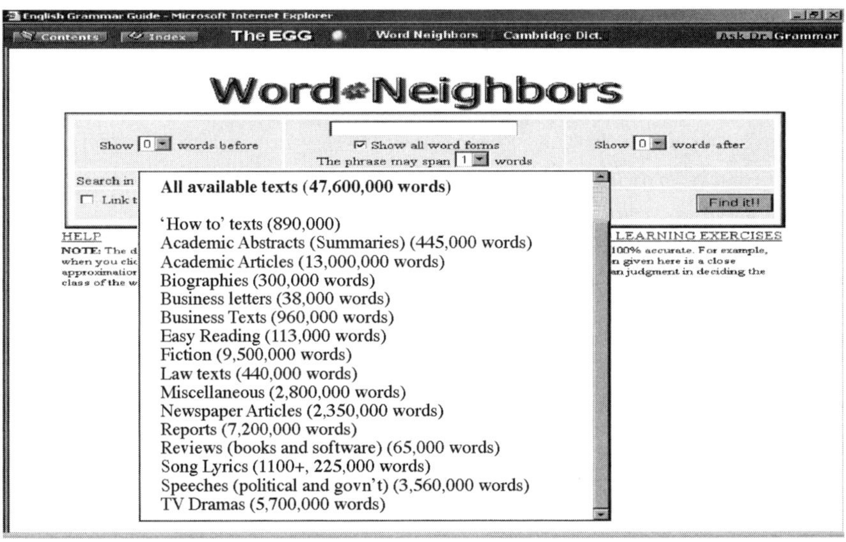

Figure 2

Results on Search for 'improvement' in the Reports Subcorpus

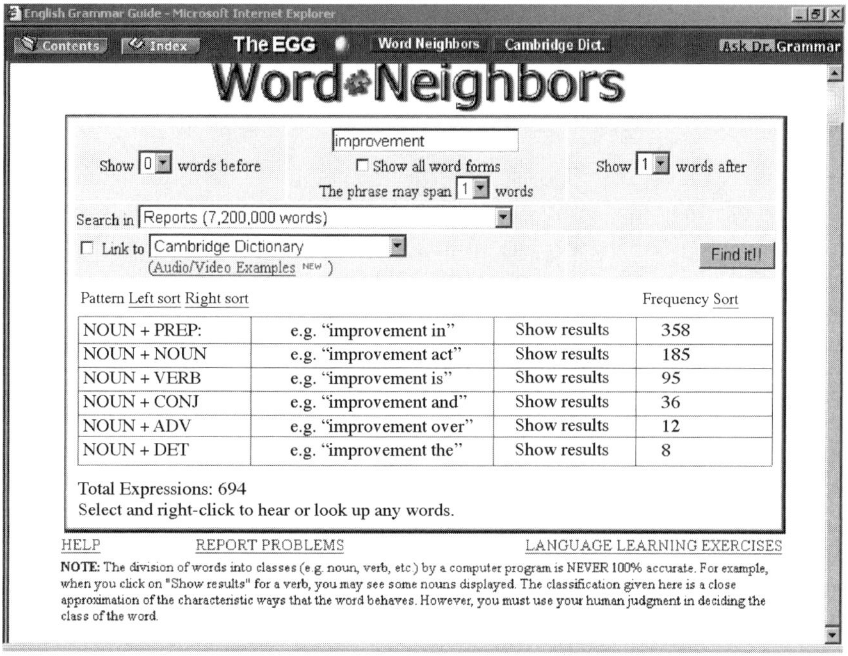

Figure 3

Other Online Resources Available under the Word Neighbors Tool

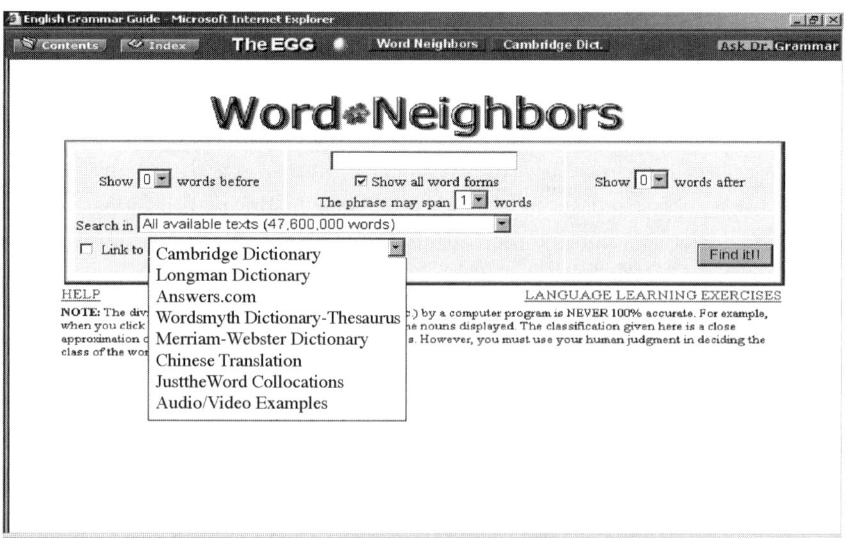

However, corpora are but one type of online resource in this age of newly emerging technologies. It should not be forgotten that corpora may not always be the most useful source to consult for a language query and that other resources such as dictionaries and thesauri may be more appropriate. Figure 3 shows other online resources available within Word Neighbors (an English Grammar Guide, EGG, specifically targeted at Hong Kong students' common errors, can also be accessed from this window).

With reference to these two main features of Word Neighbors, in the following section, I illustrate how these have been used to check various language points at the three stages of the writing process, mediated within a framework of discussion-based activities.

Discussion-Based Activities on Language Errors

As for the set-up of the discussion-based activities, these followed a similar format for each of the three stages. Students were divided into groups of three, resulting in about six groups in each class, and asked to address the following questions in their process of enquiry:

1. Which resource (corpus, dictionary, thesaurus) would be most appropriate?
2. If a corpus, would you use the whole corpus or sub-corpus or consult the web with Google®?
3. Which search word would you key in and what parameters would you set in Word Neighbors (i.e., the number of words to be shown before or after the search word)?

While students were involved in their discussions, I circulated among groups and noted down any interesting comments regarding search strategies, observations that surfaced for addressing in the round-up sessions at the end of the discussion activities.

Stage 1: Teacher-Identified Errors on Outlines

1. Choice of preposition: There will be a great improvement <u>on</u> students' attitude.

In the first part of the discussion, most students agreed that as *improvement* was a fairly common word, it would be very likely to occur in the seven million-word sub-corpus of reports (see Figure 1). They also had no trouble in deciding that the Show Words After button (located on the top right-hand side of the program, as shown in Figure 2) should be activated, as it was the preposition following *improvement* that was the item under consideration. Although some of the students felt quite sure that *in* was the correct preposition, a few said they felt confused, as they were sure they had seen *of* and *on* used after *improvement* before.

As Figure 2 illustrates, students can see at a glance that the NOUN + PREP category is the relevant one. A click on the Show Results button brings up the screen shown in Figure 4 for students to check their initial hypotheses against. Although the preposition *in* is the most frequently used one with *improvement,* as a few students surmised, *of* and *on* are also possible (and also quite a few other prepositions!). When See Contexts is shown, the examples given reveal that *improvement of* tends to be used with some type of skills or machines (e.g., *an improvement of the interface …*) and *improvement on* with reference to a previous or existing system. However, in this latter

Figure 4

Show Results for 'NOUN + PREP'

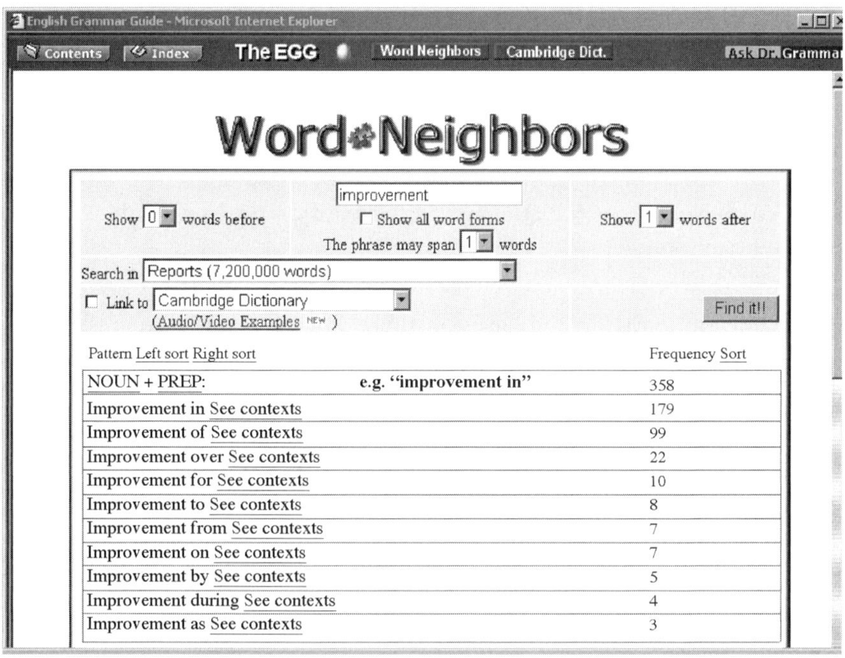

stage of the discussion activity, students had a little difficulty in interpreting the corpus data, as they had to be encouraged to examine the co-text of the phrase *improvement of...*, or *improvement on ...*, and read the concordance line for its *extended unit of meaning*.

After working through these stages, one student commented that "prepositions are so difficult for Hong Kong students and it is difficult to find the correct preposition in dictionaries so this is very useful." Interestingly, Yoon & Hirvela (2004) also noted from their students' overall evaluation of corpus use that the usage of prepositions was what was most emphasized in corpus searches and that students evaluated corpora to be very effective for acquiring the Verb + Prep construction.

2. Article Usage: <u>The</u> Victoria Harbour is becoming more and more narrow.

Regarding this article error, when I was circulating among the various discussion groups, I noticed that a common observation made by students was that it was very difficult to know whether to use articles with place names, as there didn't seem to be any rules. Also, students were undecided as to the choice of corpus in this case. Some students thought that the seven million-word corpus of reports, some of which related to Hong Kong issues, was huge, and therefore likely to contain this place name, although the corpus search disproved this. Students were then prompted either to choose another sub-corpus or do a Google® search. The majority of students suggested a Google® search (an ideal source for searching very infrequent words), which obviously gave examples of *Victoria Harbour*. However, in the follow-up reporting back session, it was found that these had been misinterpreted by a few students who extrapolated from an example such as the following that this place name was preceded by an article, not realizing it was functioning as a pre-modifier, partly on account of the fact that *cam* was an unfamiliar word to them:

> The Victoria Harbour cam captures some of the spectacular views of Victoria Harbour from various angles and at certain times of the day.

Surprisingly, only a couple of students suggested searching the two million-word newspaper corpus, made up of articles from English-based Hong Kong newspapers. This search proved fruitful, as it revealed several relevant examples.

Stage 2: Student-Identified Errors in Project Introductions

While allowing students a more autonomous role in error identification, I found that in their groups of three, students did not seem to find it easy to agree on the errors in the introduction sections of the project reports written by other groups, and, in the main, underlined certain words/phrases with a question mark, without noting a correct answer. Sometimes they made incorrect revisions, as noted, believing that the passive should be used instead of the active.

3. Active vs. Passive: This project <u>focuses on</u> the incidence of mosquitoes on campus →
This project <u>is focused on</u> ....

A search of each structure in the sub-corpus of reports revealed that both were possible, but there were only a handful of examples of the passive construction. Students were able to work out from a close reading of the concordance lines that in the passive it had the meaning of "to pay very close attention to something." When students saw the search results for *focus,* they were intrigued as to why there were so many examples in the present perfect, the second most frequent unit, as shown in Figure 5. An investigation of the wider context of this structure showed it to be used when previous research was introduced, to set up a critical evaluation of this work signaled by *However.* Bernardini (2000) advocates letting the students browse the corpus in a serendipitous fashion to follow up something that might just catch their eye. I have encouraged students to do this, as I believe it can lead to incidental learning of potentially useful structures and vocabulary and help students attain a more autonomous, divergent approach to learning. In other words, I encourage 'noticing' in the corpus output. As Swain (198, 66) remarks there are several levels of noticing, one of which is that: "Learners may simply notice a form in the target language due to the frequency or salience of the features themselves."

4. Collocation: We plan to <u>do</u> a survey on the usage of computers →
We plan to <u>carry out/conduct</u> a survey on ...

In the reporting back session after the group discussions, most students commented that *do* "did not sound quite right," and suggested either *carry out* or *conduct* as alternatives. They also considered the sub-corpus of reports

Figure 5
Search for 'focus' (All Word Forms)

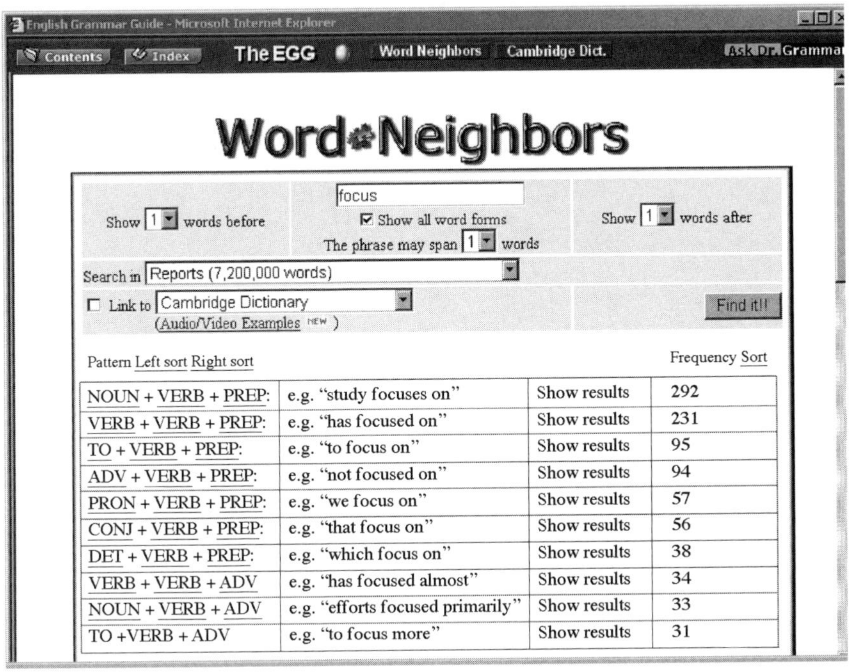

to be ideal for searching the noun *survey* and expected that it would show correct VERB + NOUN collocations. Somewhat to the students' surprise (and also mine, I must admit), there were useful verbs to collocate with the noun *survey* in this corpus, but these patterns were not easy to discern, because students were required to read through quite a number of concordance lines to identify appropriate VERB + NOUNS collocations for their context of writing, as evidenced by the results for the search shown in Figure 6.

This problematic example above then gave me the opportunity to remind students of another program, JustTheWord (available under other online resources shown in Figure 3). This program is an online collocations resource interfacing with the 100 million-word British National Corpus (BNC). The screenshot shows this to be a more appropriate online tool to use, with the cluster feature of particular use as the collocations are grouped semantically. In Figure 7, a glance at Cluster 1 confirmed students initial intuitions, but some were surprised to find that the verb *do* in Cluster 3 was acceptable. An examination of the concordance lines for this collocation revealed, though,

Figure 6
Search for a 'survey'

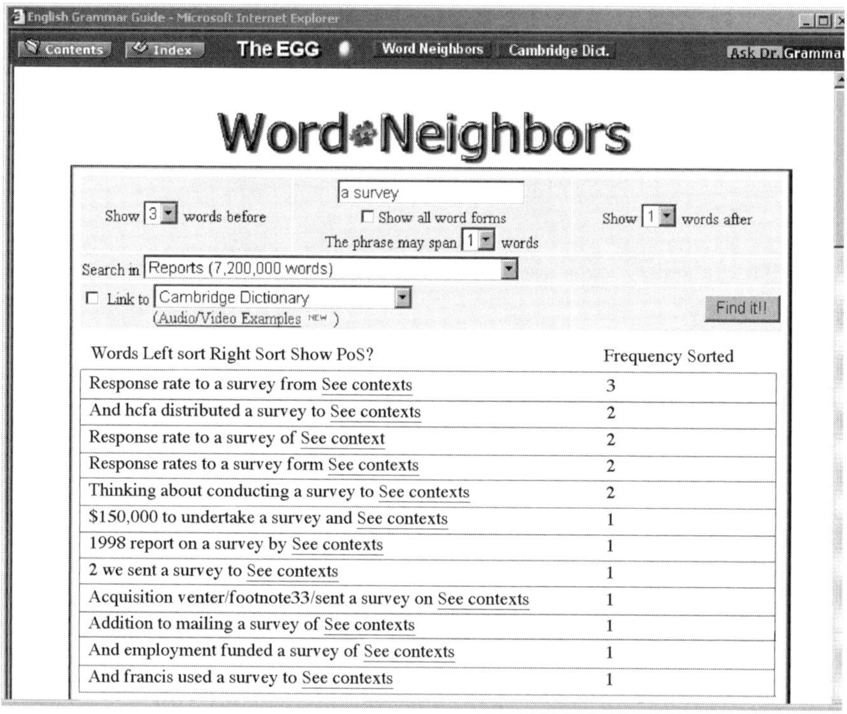

that it was mainly used in an informal setting in speaking, as in the following: *I mean, I haven't done a detailed survey on anything.*

One student then asked whether it was possible to say *implement a survey,* and if not, how one would use *implement.* A search on *implement* showed it to collocate frequently with *policy/plan/idea* thus providing useful collocations for students' project writing. Throughout these activities, I found that such kinds of unprompted questions from students were very motivating for them, as they seemed to appreciate the real-time processing aspect of the search.

5. **Word Choice: The mosquitoes around the university halls are irritating.**
   These <u>irritating</u> insects cause students to feel uncomfortable.

In their discussion groups, I noticed that a few students had brought up the repetition of *irritating* in the second sentence. However, in the reporting

Figure 7
Search for 'survey' in *JustTheWord* Collocations Program

V obj N*

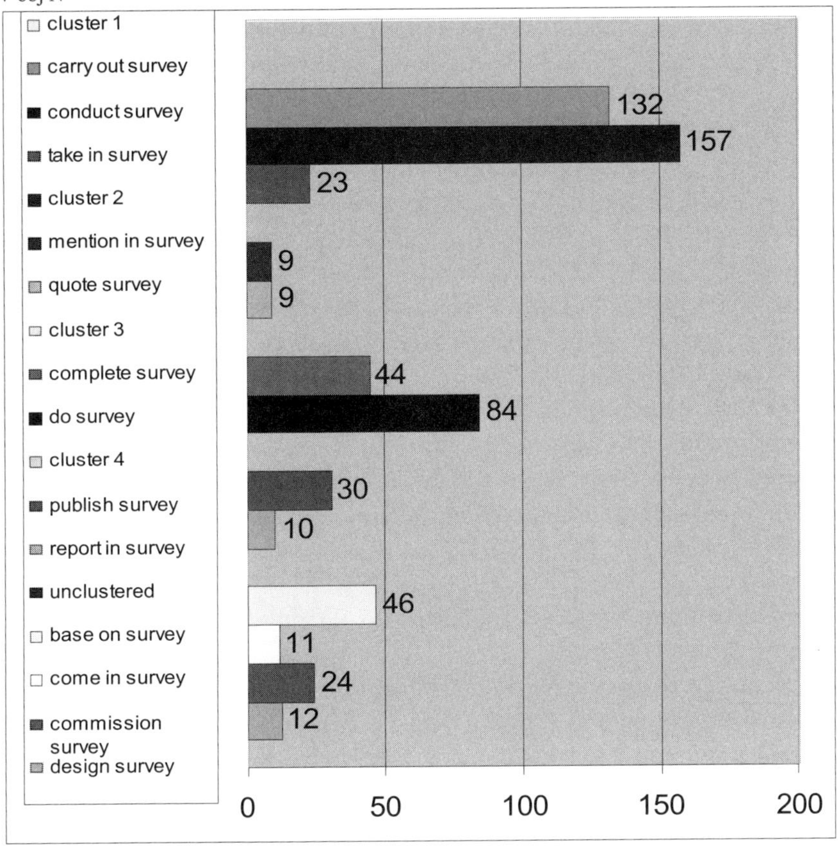

back session, students mentioned that they could not think of any replacement synonym, except for one student who suggested *vexing*. Students were aware that *vexing* was quite an uncommon word and, most, quite sensibly, suggested it would be best to do a Google search on the web for *vexing insects*. The fact that only four instances came up alerted students to the fact that this collocation, while possible, was extremely uncommon, leading to the conclusion that another adjective might be more appropriate. These results led students to totally reconsider their search strategy and consider other online resources. For this, they returned to the other online links accessible within Word Neighbors (see Figure 3), selecting the Wordsmyth-Dictionary Thesaurus to search for synonyms of *irritating*. *Annoying* was considered to be a suitable alternative. To double check the combination of *annoying insects* a Google® search was conducted, resulting in 24,600 hits.

Interestingly, a few students seemed to be mesmerized by a corpus of 48 million words, thinking that what to them seemed an enormous quantity of written text would doubtless contain examples of *annoying insects,* which it didn't. I feel that this trial-and-error approach, in the initial stages of corpus use, is a useful one for students, as it alerts them to the pitfalls of corpora and encourages them to evaluate whether the nature and size of a particular corpus is appropriate for a particular query.

The selected examples give an idea of how I approached the selection and searching of online corpora and other resources, mediated through discussion activities. I found it best to allocate about 15–20 minutes to such exercises every couple of weeks or so to deal with errors that were particularly problematic for learners at different stages of the project reports. Doing such tasks at regular intervals for short periods of time within a discussion-based framework meant that students did not feel overwhelmed by having to concentrate for too long analyzing and interpreting concordance lines, which they can find rather tedious if too much time is allocated to this kind of close reading.

Stage 3: Student-Generated Queries for Writing Up Final Report

It was hoped that after this regular in-class exposure, students would feel sufficiently motivated and confident to use all these online corpora and tools on an autonomous basis, without any intervention on my part, in the writing up of the final draft of their project report. Although I strongly encouraged students to make use of these sources, I did not insist on it, as I wanted students to take more responsibility for their own learning.

In follow-up informal class discussions to ascertain how students had used the resources, it was quite heartening to find that about a quarter of students had made the effort to use these resources outside class. Below I briefly describe the kind of language points students mentioned in their searches in the sub-corpus of reports.

In common with Yoon & Hirvela's students, my students also commented on the usefulness of corpora for checking prepositions, mentioning that they were unsure as to the preposition following the verb *aim.* Another salient verb for this project report is *recommend,* for which several students had checked whether it is possible to use the following structure: *We recommend to*

+VERB. One student had gone a step further by checking the grammatical structures for related words such as *propose* and *suggest,* observing from the concordance lines that *propose to* + VERB can be used. The same student then mentioned that he had tried to work out from scrutinizing the concordance lines if these three verbs differed in level of formality, but couldn't detect any noticeable differences and so gave up with this query. However, information on formal vs. informal language is provided in the *Longman Dictionary* with which the sub-corpus is linked (see Figure 3), in which *propose* is classified as [formal].

One particularly tricky query, both in terms of grammatical complexity and search strategy, concerned those change-of-state verbs such as *increase, decrease, develop,* which have three possible voices (active; passive; middle (or ergative). Celce-Murcia (2002, p. 147) gives a very insightful account of the problems these pose for students, noting that students misuse the passive in cases where the ergative should be used, such as, *Over the period of the study the learners' VOT values for ... were decreased.* One of my student queries was whether the passive or active (by which was meant the ergative) should be used in the following sentence: *With a very crowded schedule, students' level of motivation has decreased/was decreased.* Although the student had tried searching and found instances of each construction, he was not able to work out inductively the usage patterns from the truncated concordance lines. However, looking at this structure in a wider context (see Figure 8), Celce-Murcia's observation on voice choice could be confirmed: "With the verbs *increase* and *decrease* [the ergative] tends to be used when the inanimate subject is objectively or subjectively measurable (rather than an animate agent/dynamic instrument subject—both

Figure 8

Context Search for 'has decreased'

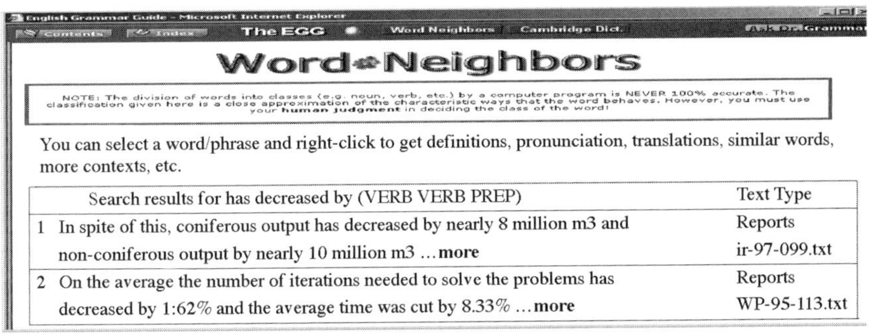

	Search results for has decreased by (VERB VERB PREP)	Text Type
1	In spite of this, coniferous output has decreased by nearly 8 million m3 and non-coniferous output by nearly 10 million m3 ...**more**	Reports ir-97-099.txt
2	On the average the number of iterations needed to solve the problems has decreased by 1:62% and the average time was cut by 8.33% ...**more**	Reports WP-95-113.txt

of which favor active voice—or a patient subject—for the passive voice" (p. 146).

In this chapter, I have attempted to show how using corpora and other online resources in a more interactive, student-centered way than is generally presented in books on exploiting corpora in pedagogy can provide valuable opportunities for enhancing written work through consciousness-raising speaking activities. Peer review tasks of written work can encourage collaborative dialogue among students in the identification of errors, and follow-up discussion-based activities can encourage students to articulate various stages of the corpus selection and search processes they undertake and their consequent interpretation of the concordance data.

However, this corpus-oriented strategy that exploits speaking to heighten students' awareness of grammar and lexis for improving their writing may not appeal to students with different cognitive styles. Field-dependent students who thrive in cooperative, interactive settings may benefit from this type of pedagogy. Field-independent learners who are known to prefer instruction emphasizing rules may not like the inductive approach to grammar inherent in the corpus-based approach, which this chapter has put forward as a bridge for linking speaking and writing. The speaking-writing connection in academic literacy development is well established, but the role that corpora can play in this partnership of modalities opens up many as yet relatively unexplored but tantalizing possibilities.

REFERENCES

Aston, G. (1997). Small and large corpora in language learning. In B. Lewandowska-Tomaszcayk & J. Melia (Eds.), *Practical applications in language corpora* (pp. 51–62). Lodz, Poland: Lodz University.

Belcher, D. (2006). English for specific purposes: Teaching to perceived needs and imagined futures in worlds of work, study, and everyday life. *TESOL Quarterly, 40*(1), 133–156.

Bernardini, S. (2000). Systematising serendipity: Proposals for concordancing large corpora with language learners. In L. Burnard & T. McEnery (Eds.), *Rethinking language pedagogy from a corpus perspective* (pp. 225–234). Frankfurt: Peter Lang.

———. (2002). Exploring new directions for discovery learning. In B. Kettemann & G. Marko (Eds.), *Teaching and learning by doing corpus analysis* (pp. 165–182). Amsterdam: Rodopi.

———. (2004). Corpora in the classroom: An overview and some reflections on future developments. In J. Sinclair (Ed.), *How to use corpora in language teaching* (pp. 15–36). Amsterdam: John Benjamins.

Celce-Murcia, M. (2002). On the use of selected grammatical features in academic writing. In M. Schleppegrell & C. Colombi (Eds.), *Developing advanced literacy in first and second languages* (pp. 143–157). Mahwah, NJ: Lawrence Erlbaum.

Chambers, A. (2005). Integrating corpus consultation in language studies. *Language Learning and Technology, 9*(2), 111–125.

Chambers, A., & O'Sullivan, I. (2004). Corpus consultation and advanced learners' writing skills in French. *ReCALL, 16*(1), 158–172.

Cobb, T. (1997). Is there any measurable learning from hands on concordancing? *System, 25*(3), 301–315.

Davies, M. (2004). Student use of large, annotated corpora to analyse syntactic variation. In G. Aston, Bernardini, S. & D. Stewart (Eds.), *Corpora and language learners* (pp. 257–269). Amsterdam: John Benjamins.

Fan, M., & Xu, X. (2002). An evaluation of an online bilingual corpus for the self-learning of legal English. *System, 30*(1), 47–63.

Ferris, D. (2002) *Treatment of error in second language student writing.* Ann Arbor: University of Michigan Press.

———. (2003) *Response to student writing.* Mahwah, NJ: Lawrence Erlbaum.

Flowerdew, L. (2004). The argument for using English specialized corpora to understand academic and professional language. In U. Connor & T. Upton (Eds.), *Discourse in the professions: Perspectives from corpus linguistics* (pp. 11–33). Amsterdam: John Benjamins.

———. (2005). Integrating traditional and critical approaches to syllabus design: the 'what,' the 'how' and the 'why?' *Journal of English for Academic Purposes, 4*(2), 135–147.

———. (2006). *Texts, tools, and contexts in corpus applications for writing.* Paper presented at 40th Annual TESOL Convention, Tampa, Florida.

Gaskell, D., & Cobb, T. (2004). Can learners use concordance feedback for writing errors? *System 32*(3), 301–319.

Gavioli, L. (2005). *Exploring corpora for ESP learning.* Amsterdam: John Benjamins.

Gavioli, L., & Aston, G. (2001). Enriching reality: language corpora in language pedagogy. *ELT Journal, 55*(3), 238–246.

Grabe, W., & Kaplan, R. (1996) *Theory and practice of writing.* London: Longman.

Hyland, K. (2003) *Second language writing.* Cambridge, UK: Cambridge University Press.

Johns, T. (1994). From printout to handout: Grammar and vocabulary teaching in the context of data-driven learning. In T. Odlin (Ed.), *Perspectives on pedagogical grammar* (pp. 293–313). Cambridge, UK: Cambridge University Press.

Johns, T., & King, P. (Eds.). (2001). *Classroom concordancing: English Language Research Journal, 4.* Birmingham, UK: University of Birmingham.

Kennedy, C., & Miceli, T. (2001). An evaluation of intermediate students' approaches to corpus investigation. *Language Learning and Technology, 5*(3), 77–90.

———. (2002). The CWIC project: Developing and using a corpus for intermediate Italian students. In B. Kettemann & G. Marko (Eds.), *Teaching and learning by doing corpus analysis* (pp. 183–192). Amsterdam: Rodopi.

Kettemann, B., & Marko, G. (Eds.). (2002). *Teaching and learning by doing corpus analysis.* Amsterdam: Rodopi.

Lee, D., & Swales, J. (2006). A corpus-based EAP course for NNS doctoral students: Moving from available specialized corpora to self-compiled corpora. *English for Specific Purposes, 25*(1), 56–75.

Leech, G. (1997) Teaching and language corpora: a convergence. In A. Wichmann et al. (Eds.), *Teaching and language corpora* (pp. 1–23). London: Longman.

Liu, J., & Hansen, J. (2002). *Peer response in second language writing classrooms.* Ann Arbor: University of Michigan Press.

Milton, J. (1998). Exploiting L1 and interlanguage corpora in the design of an electronic language learning and production environment. In S. Granger (Ed.), *Learner English on computer* (pp. 186–198). London: Longman.

———. (1999). Lexical thickets and electronic gateways: making text accessible by novice writers. In C. Candlin & K. Hyland (Eds.), *Writing: Texts, processes and practices* (pp. 221–243). London: Longman.

Swain, M. (1998). Focus on form through conscious reflection. In C. Doughty & J. Williams (Eds.), *Focus on form in classroom second language acquisition* (pp. 64–81). Cambridge, UK: Cambridge University Press.

Thurstun, J., & Candlin, C. (1998a). Concordancing and the teaching of the vocabulary of academic English. *English for Specific Purposes, 17*(3), 267–280.

———. (1998b). *Exploring academic English: A workbook for student essay writing.* Sydney: National Centre for English Language Teaching and Research.

Tribble, C., & Jones, G. (1990). *Concordances in the classroom.* Harlow, UK: Longman.

Yoon, H., & Hirvela, A. (2004). ESL student attitudes towards corpus use in L2 writing. *Journal of Second Language Writing, 13,* 257–283.

15

Blogging as a Bridge between Multiple Forms of Literacy: The Use of Blogs in an Academic Writing Class

JOEL BLOCH

Abstract

Blogging has emerged as one of the most important forms of computer-mediated communication for use in the L2 composition classroom. Like all forms of CMC, blogging contains elements of both oral and written forms of discourse; however, at the same time, research is beginning to show how blogging can be a unique form of discourse that offers students an opportunity to develop a sense of identify in their writing and to use their oral forms of discourse in one literacy context to develop writing skills in another literacy context. This chapter explores the possibilities that blogging offers as a form of discourse in helping students construct their own identity in their classroom assignments. The study examines the blogging and academic writing experiences of an East-African undergraduate as she attempts to develop her blogging skills and academic writing skills at the same time. The chapter shows how the student was able to exploit her ability to express herself in her blogs to cultivate her ability as an academic writer.

What makes forms of computer-mediated communication (CMC) relevant for a book on orality and literacy is that all such of forms of online discourse have long been seen from linguistic, rhetorical, and even legal perspectives as an amalgam of both oral and written forms of discourse, what Ong (1982) defined as a "secondary orality." Lunsford (2006) has further categorized this type of mixed discourse as a "secondary literacy," which she defines as "a literacy that is both highly inflected by oral forms, structures, and rhythms and highly aware of itself as writing, understood as variously organized and mediated systems of signification" (p. 170).

Recently there has been a great deal of interest in the use of CMC in the L2 composition classroom with respect to such applications as email, chat rooms, blogs, and listservs. The growing importance of CMC as a form of literacy has elevated the status of these types of secondary literacies, so that they are not only considered tools for aiding in the development of a student's print literacy skills but also as forms of literacy that need to be understood and perhaps learnt in the same way as are traditional forms of print literacies. Differences between these applications can be attributed to where they fall along an oral/written continuum. Different types of CMC incorporate these oral or vernacular forms of literacy to varying degrees; what they all have in common with vernacular forms of literacy is that they are often spontaneous forms of creation with the capacity to be easily and rapidly published.

Blogging has emerged as one of the most popular forms of CMC, as millions of blogs in a variety of different languages now populate the Internet. Blogs are a form of online journaling, similar in some ways to other kinds of web pages, but they can be frequently updated and, most important, can, through the use of what are called RSS (Really Simple Syndication) feeds, be easily aggregated so that readers can be notified whenever something new is published. Blood (2002) called blogs the first pure form of Internet discourse, and they have frequently been cited as an integral part of what is referred to as Web 2.0 (O'Reilley, 2005), a concept that portrays the Internet user as a producer of information as well as a consumer. As shown in the recent Pew/Internet survey, blogs are used for a variety of reasons, ranging from writing "to express yourself creatively" and "to document your personal experiences . . . with your friends" to writing "to share practical knowledge" or "to motivate other people to action" (Lenhart & Fox, 2006, p. iii).

We have discussed elsewhere how blogs can be used in these different ways in L2 composition classrooms (Bloch, 2007; Bloch & Crosby, 2006, 2008). This research has examined the use of blogs by Ethiopian Somali students, whose written forms of literacy had been, to use Blanton's (2005) term, "interrupted" by inconsistencies in access to school but who may also have developed strong forms of vernacular literacy during the time spent in an English language secondary school. These inconsistencies can place these students at risk in their ability to transition from high school to university, where a greater emphasis may be placed on learning and using academic forms of writing. On the other hand, these students may have stronger oral skills as a result of the time they have spent in English-speaking schools, which can be exploited in the development of their more formal, print-based literacies.

At the same time, Blanton finds that these students are not illiterate, but rather are literate to a different degree than students whose literacy development in both their first and second languages has been more consistent. In her discussion of an Ethiopian student, she argues that the student was "strangled" by the five-paragraph essay she had been forced to write (2005, p. 115). Blanton identifies a variety of aspects of school composing that can be problematic for these students, including the nature of the writing assignment, the role of oral language in the production of written discourse, the social relationships among the students, and the restrictive nature of classroom-based literacies.

These students have often been referred to by sociologists as belonging to Generation 1.5, a term used to distinguish them from the second generation born to immigrant parents as well as from adult immigrants (Rumbaut & Ima, 1988; Portes, 2001; Portes & Hao, 1998). Generation 1.5 students, by contrast, were born overseas and at some point in their school-age years emigrated to an Anglophone country like the United States, where they attend school and must learn to use English for academic and often other social purposes while also retaining at least some knowledge of the language and culture they were born into. Researchers have found that this group of students, given such a background, is far from monolithic and monolingual, with considerable variation across different ethnic and language groups as well as within them. The research has shown that these variations can result from their experiences as immigrants and their social, political, economic, and family backgrounds. Studies of their language learning experiences have shown that their language and culture experiences may similarly vary widely (Blanton, 2005; Harklau, Losey, & Siegal, 1999; Roberge, 2002).

In the great amount of research that has been conducted on the use of various forms of CMC in L2 composition classrooms, one emerging belief has been that the oral nature of these forms may be particularly important for students whose oral skills are stronger than their written skills, including Generation 1.5 students. Blogs, for example, are designed for the rapid publication of ideas, which may encourage a more spontaneous form of writing that resembles speech, particularly if the blogs are not corrected for grammatical errors (Bloch & Crosby, 2006).

Blogs are also believed to entail a different type of authorship than other forms of CMC, and this has added to their appeal among L2 composition teachers. What seems to make blogging different from other forms of CMC is that blogs often center on a writer or a small or large group of writers (Shirkey, 2003). By contrast, hypertexts, listservs, and Usenet groups, for the most part, are centered on issues that could be discussed by a wide variety of individuals. Unlike hypertexts, where authorship tends to be more decentralized (Bolter, 2001), the author or authors of a blog are often the central figures whose ideas or experiences other readers can interact with and comment on. While there are some blogs that are collectively authored, many of the most popular blogs are identified with a single author. Blogs often seem to be more print-like, perhaps because, despite the ease by which they are published, their function may be closer to that of an academic journal or a journalistic article and less conversational than electronic forms of discourse such as email or chat rooms. Nevertheless, they are rarely as formally written as traditional forms of essays or journalistic articles. Blogs are often rapidly updated and therefore retain some of the features of the more conventional forms of CMC.

The combination of these features makes blogging an interesting technology to use in the composition classroom, particularly with students whose oral forms of language may be better developed than their written forms. This chapter focuses on blogging, now one of the most popular forms of CMC, and looks at its use in the L2 composition classroom both as a facilitator for the generation of ideas and as what Blood (2002) calls a unique form of literacy. It discusses the blogging experiences of a Generation 1.5 student from Somalia and how she attempted to integrate her blog with her classroom assignments. I examine how blogging can be combined in an L2 composition classroom with more traditional forms of academic writing assignments in order to better understand the relationship between orality and literacy found in blogs and the ways in which this relationship can be utilized in academic composing.

A Pedagogical Context for Blogging

In the study discussed here, the context was an academic writing course for students who were just entering into the academy. The course focuses only on a single, highly controversial topic: how plagiarism should be defined and how it should be dealt with. The students read, wrote, discussed, and even took exams on the subject of plagiarism. Since the university was engaged at the time of the study discussed here in a highly publicized "crackdown" on plagiarism, an ongoing focus on this topic was seen as a way of engaging students in an authentic social context that could help them negotiate the complex demands of academic writing as well as to protect themselves against charges of academic misconduct. Although some of the students objected to focusing on a single topic through the entire course, it was felt that by focusing on just one topic, they could write from a developing sense of expertise on a complex subject.

Many of the students in this course come from Asia, but at the time of the study a few had emigrated from East Africa, particularly Somalia and Ethiopia. Large numbers of Somali refugees have, in recent years, escaped the ongoing turmoil in their country and settled in a few school districts surrounding the university where this research took place. The Somali literacy practices they brought with them are based in part on an older tradition used almost exclusively for reading the Qur'an and in part on a relatively new Somali literacy tradition that was begun in the earlier 1970s, after control of the government was seized by the military (Lewis, 1993). General Siyad, who was the military leader of the country at that time, argued that the literacy campaign was part of a larger plan to restructure the entire Somali society. He stated that

> This [literacy] will be the weapon to eradicate social balkanization and fragmentation into tribes and sects. It will bring about an absolute unity and there will be no room for any negative foreign cultural influences. (cited in Lewis, 1994, p. 150)

However, these goals were undermined by many years of civil war that disrupted every aspect of Somali society. Lewis argues that because of the continual political strife in the country, the goals of this literacy movement could not be achieved.

Therefore, for many from that region, the literacy development in their first language had been "interrupted," to use Blanton's (2005) term, by this strife. A key effect of such strife on these Generation 1.5 students' educational development is that often one form of literacy, usually a vernacular form, dominates over other forms. This problem is compounded by the lack of exposure to these other forms in their high school classes after they have immigrated to the United States.

The Somali students are not alone in this regard. Hillocks (2002) has found that students in American high schools often do not gain experience with a wide range of writing assignments. For these Generation 1.5 students, however, this lack of exposure can be especially problematic because of what Blanton (2005) calls a lack of a sense of textuality. Without a clear understanding of the dominant forms of academic literacy, the students who go on to college will later have difficulty with what Bartholomae (1985) calls "inventing the university," that is, learning what it means to write successfully in university courses.

The goal of using blogs in the academic writing course that served as the research base was to generate a dialogue among the students on the issues they were to write about in their academic papers and in their personal lives, although such dialogues often depend on the architecture of the blogging site and the nature of the prompts given to the students. Each student was expected to post at least 20 blogs on a class blog site that had been set up expressly for the course. The students were assigned two to three blogs a week on a variety of personal and classroom-based topics. They were graded on whether they completed the assignment and not on the quality of their writing. By freeing them from worrying about such issues as grammar and spelling, we hoped to take advantage of the power of oral expression in the development of the students' academic forms of literacy.

There were three formal writing assignments: a summary, an argumentative paper, and a synthesis paper. The goal of the summary paper was for students to begin to identify the key issues regarding the debate over plagiarism and learn how to paraphrase and report what they read. In the argumentative paper, they were asked their opinion about the use of the plagiarism-detection website *Turnitin.com*, which was discussed in one of the source texts they had read and was going to be employed by the university. The main goal here was to create a coherent argument that both refuted the ideas they disagreed with and used the ideas they agreed with to support their own claims. The third paper was a synthesis-response paper that discussed the key issues they had identified in the plagiarism debate. The goal was to have the students interweave their own ideas with the ideas that they had read in the assigned articles and with the ideas their classmates had discussed in their blogs. Each paper was expected to be about 500 words in length.

The incorporation of blogs into this pedagogical context was consistent with previous research, which has shown that Generation 1.5 students can use blogs to foster the development of their classroom writing ability and to gain richer experience with literacy events through the blogs themselves (Bloch, 2007; Bloch & Crosby, 2006, in press). In these studies, it was found that the students were often more comfortable using the more vernacular form of literacy common in blogging than they were with the more formal class assignments. The course discussed here generally consists of a combination of Generation 1.5 and international students, thus making it a suitable site to investigate the effects of blogging. The students were expected to write three papers plus two to three blogs per week. Each blog was at least 300 words in length. Although the academic papers counted for a greater proportion of the grade, they probably wrote more in their blogs.

The goal of the research described in this chapter is to deepen our understanding of the potential of blogging to help students better utilize their vernacular forms of literacy. This chapter explores the relationship between blogging and the essay writing experiences of a Somali student shuttling, as Canagarajah (2006) would say, between these various forms of literacy as she was entering the university. It was hoped that this study would enrich our understanding of the relationship between the more vernacular form of literacy found in blogs and the more academic forms of writing that were assigned in the classroom. The remainder of the chapter will discuss the blogging of one Somali student named Fidossa (a pseudonym) and her ability to shuttle between her blogs and her academic writing.

The Participant

Fidossa was born in Somalia and fled with her family to Kenya, from which she immigrated to the United States when she was in the tenth grade. At the time of the study, Fidossa was a first-year undergraduate who attended a branch campus of the university. She had been placed in the lowest-level course offered by the university's post-admission writing program for international students. Because there were no ESL courses at the branch campus, she had to commute about 50 miles a day to take this particular course. Fidossa reported that although she had little formal training, she could read and write in Somali and could read the Qur'an in Arabic; however, it was difficult to measure the degree of her literacy in either language. She also lacked a number of computer skills necessary for the course, such as how to send her files across the Internet and, most importantly for this discussion, how to blog.

Fidossa's Blogging and Essay Writing

Fidossa's Initial Blog

The primary goal of the first blogging assignment was to acquaint students with blogging and allow them to introduce themselves to their classmates and instructor, which we hoped would help build a sense of community in the classroom. None of the students reported having any experience blogging, but unlike her classmates, Fidossa had no experience with any form of online discourse. The students were asked to write as much as they could about themselves, and to do so as if they were speaking. Blogging could capture the oral nature of this writing while also allowing it to be posted permanently on the Internet so as to be available to be read at any time and at any speed. This archival aspect of blogging was one of its attractions as a pedagogical tool, since it was hoped that the students would access and make use of their previous blog postings as source texts during their essay writing experiences.

Sometimes, the students were asked to tell stories about their personal lives in their blogs, with the caveat that these blogs could be read by anyone outside the classroom. In this blog, Fidossa writes extensively about her experiences and her relationship with her family:

> my name is Fidossa. I am nineteen years old. I live with my parants and my young sibling. I am the oldest one that live with my parents currently. I have big brothers and sisters and they live back home. though I am the oldest one in my family, I have a lots of responsibilities that includes taking care my young sibling and being a role model for them because I am the first person for my family who is going college, I also help my young sibling to follow the foot steps I fellow, I also put alots of effort on my studies. eventhough, I am the first peroson to go college in my family in their eyes they seem like they are so proud of me, I like my family. to me family is every thing that encounter in my life. they are always there for you no matter how hard the circumstance is. I depend on my family in my believing system family is forever and friendship and others comes last to me.[1]

As we had found in our previous studies, students like Fidossa were able to produce a great deal of text. Her blog demonstrates her ability to express her hopes and goals for the future, as well as her feelings about her family to an audience with whom she was not well acquainted. A previous study of the blogging activities of an East African immigrant student provided some evidence of how the student participant may have incorporated interactive

[1]The blogs are uncorrected.

African forms of storytelling into her blog in order to interact with her classmates (Bloch & Crosby, in press). Some of the same strengths can be seen in the participant's storytelling here.

As would be expected from this storytelling tradition, Fidossa's language is primarily oral, which is consistent with what has been commonly claimed about CMC. Many of her sentences begin with *I,* and she gives a variety of examples that show different aspects of her life and her character. She describes how she takes care of her siblings and how she was the first in her family to go to college. Ivanĭc (1998) argues that how an individual represents herself in her writing is an intensely social process as the writer interacts with other people, and, as will be discussed later, with other texts. Fidossa's assumption that her audience would be interested in these details of her life may indicate her belief in the strength of her voice.

Since her more formal academic assignments required a great deal of what Halliday and Hasan (1976) call "coherence" and "cohesiveness," it is interesting to note these aspects of her writing in her blog. Coherence refers to the overall way in which a paper is organized and how its parts relate to each other, while cohesiveness refers to the relationship between sentences. The ability to make these kinds of connections between sentences was one of the key aspects of literacy that was discussed in the course. Because writers have more time to consider the relationships between sentences than do speakers, they are expected to more explicitly depict what those relationships are.

As Weissberg argues (2006), cohesiveness is an important component of oral dialogues, as it is in written discourse, as the speaker tries to convey a coherent message to the listener. This aspect of cohesiveness exists throughout Fidossa's blog. Her narrative weaves a number of themes around her story about her family. For example, she connects her college experience to the fact she was the first in her family to attend college, to her desire to be a role model to her siblings, and to her dependence on her family. Despite her thematic coherence, many of her sentences begin with *I,* with little use of the types of coordinating or subordinating connections found in more formal academic discourse. Fidossa could have created more hypotactic relationships by using markers like *even though* to establish the connection between her being the first person in her family to go to college and her parents' pride about her accomplishments.

Creating an Academic Voice

The main goal of the course was to help students develop an academic voice. Ivanĭc (2004) has discussed voice as a form of self-representation in a written form using a variety of different linguistic and sometimes visual features. The research of Gilbert and Mulkay (1984) and Latour (1988) on the deconstruction of academic writing shows that voice is present throughout an academic paper, although the nature of this voice may be expressed differently than in oral or less formal rhetorical contexts.

This course, which particularly focused on having students establish their voices in their written texts by interweaving their own ideas and opinions with those they had read from both their classmates and outside writers, required them to work with source texts in their writing in order to create a short academic paper dealing with some aspect of plagiarism. Academic papers using source texts are still the most highly valued means of expressing one's ideas in universities; thus, mastering their form is a key element for students entering into the academic community. It has been argued that through working with source texts—for example, by manipulating them, restructuring them, and by connecting them to other texts, the writer can reshape the information in new and different ways and thus better explore the connections between different ideas (Bazerman, 1988).

The famous dictum that "we stand on the shoulders of giants" metaphorically describes the relationship academic writers create between their own ideas and the ideas of others who have already published their work. A common problem that has been seen with Generation 1.5 students has been their inability to "weave" their ideas with the ideas from their source texts (Rose, 1989), similar to the problem of textuality that Blanton (2005) found.

The difficulty involved in acquiring an academic voice can be seen in the way some of these students veered from one extreme to another. Our previous experience with East African Generation 1.5 students indicated that many of them, particularly those who had been placed in the lowest-level composition course discussed in this chapter, had consistent problems with this aspect of textuality. Some of them worked so closely with the source texts that much of what they wrote bordered on plagiarism; others moved so far away from the texts, and so quickly, that they barely mentioned them at all. It was hoped that blogging would work as an alternative to these practices by giving the students a space to work with source texts in a social context.

In their first formal writing assignment, the students were asked to respond to a newspaper article about a high school girl who had been thrown out of an exclusive private school for plagiarizing (Heaton, 2003). Before the assignment was due, the students were asked to blog their opinions about the girl's act of plagiarism. Fidossa posted the following comments:

> It is obvious that, she committed plagiarism. she intentionally mentioned that a lots of people did extremely worse than what she did. I think the school authorities did the right thing for Haley. though, she was smart student, i still believe what she did was extremely wrong thing to do. As student your role is to do the best you can. the school was not mean to her it was the second time she did. the school do for her a favor by puting in probation the first time she commited plagarism...

As a heuristic for developing ideas that could be used later in her academic writing assignments (i.e., the essays), Fidossa's blog allows her to begin to explore a key issue in the discussion of plagiarism: whether "intentionality" should be a factor in judging the severity of the act. Britton (1980/1994) writes that shaping at the point of utterance involves exploring the data in order to perceive the patterns and cohesiveness of the data, unencumbered by the kinds of rigid plans and rules, which, as Blanton (2005) found, can "strangle" the writer. Britton (1980/1994) argues that through this shaping process, the writer becomes more aware of the emergent meaning of their written texts as well as the words and structures that accompany them, all of which the student writer can further shape when drafting and revising a paper.

The oral nature of blogging seemed to allow Fidossa a meaningful opportunity to explore the relationship between her own views and the various arguments about plagiarism issues discussed in the articles she had read about plagiarism. What was particularly interesting about her blog was how she moved from the source text to her response to what had happened. She begins her blog by briefly summarizing the story and then moves to her analysis of the text while attempting to weave her own opinions about whether the girl had in fact plagiarized and whether her punishment was fair. While she seems to be using some of the standard tropes often found in student papers—such as how students should do the best they can—that echo the voices of the authorities in the source text, she is, at the same time, extending the trope to include her own ideas regarding plagiarism and thus inserting her own voice into the discussion.

Fidossa's writing also shows some of the cohesiveness that academic forms of writing require. Cohesiveness gives the writer an opportunity to explore in more detail the relationships between sentences in a way that helps develop a specific claim. Fidossa seems to want to develop the argument that the student deserved her punishment. Unlike her first blog about her family, where she interwove a variety of issues, here she appears to be using a more structured type of organization, as each sentence focuses on reasons why the student deserved the punishment she received. She demonstrates her ability to use hypotactic relationships in the expression "though, she was smart student" as a way of conceding a point before going on to the next one. The use of hypotactic relationships has traditionally been seen as a means of distinguishing between written and oral forms of discourse (Halliday, 1985; Havelock, 1963). Although Fidossa does not always explicitly mark the relationships, she shows an awareness of how different ideas can be woven together.

The students were given a similar assignment in the next blog. They had read a second article about a college freshman who had plagiarized (Rose, 1989), and here they were asked to compare the acts of plagiarism in the two articles. This blog would be the basis for the next academic writing assignment, where they would be asked to write a more formal academic paper that used the two articles to explore the arguments about plagiarism these articles had raised. In her blog, Fidossa wrote:

> when we saw marita's plagirism due to her certain characterstics explained in detail such as english as asecond languge , personal expe- riences and cultural background ,when we say ,her english as second languge due to her languge barrier cannot let her to explained how to write her assigment .In another way her cultural back ground as stated by her father " donot talk unless you know " and her enviromental back ground grew upwith reservation inspeech ,but when we see Haley's it wasnot her first time to write her paper and she did exposed in differnt postion explained as above so I can say Marital shouldnot be punished as Haly's.

Fidossa expresses greater empathy toward Marita than toward Haley, a common response among the students in the course. Fidossa begins with another summary of the key issues regarding plagiarism, such as the differences in the language and cultural background of the student, and she begins to evaluate the significance of these issues and compare her alleged act of plagiarism with Haley's.

Her blog here reflects many of the goals that we had for the academic writing assignment she would later have to write. She gives a clear reason why the student may have plagiarized and cites the text to support her claim about how the cultural background of the student may have affected her plagiarism.

She then directly responds to the assignment's goal of comparing the two texts by arguing how the two cases of plagiarism were not the same. The presence of these elements of academic writing in this blog, as compared with her first blog about her personal life discussed above, may have resulted from differences in implementation caused by changes in the prompt, which was similar to the one used for her academic writing assignment. This blog lacks the more narrative quality of her more personal blogs. That she was responding to this prompt in different ways than she did the first one indicates that she had the ability to distinguish between different forms of writing. Still, an element of voice is present in her writing, such as in her assertion that Marital does not deserve the kind of punishment Haley received.

Shuttling between Blogging and Academic Writing

In this section I examine how Fidossa moved between her blogs and her classroom-based assignments, particularly in the context of the role of voice in her writing. In their next essay assignment, the students were asked to write an argumentative paper taking and developing a position on whether *Turnitin.com.*, a highly controversial website the university was using to help instructors check for plagiarism (Marsh, 2004), should be used to identify students who plagiarize. The students again began exploring the topic in their blogs. In the academic writing assignment, the students were then expected to cite both their own ideas from their blogs and ideas from their classmates' blogs either to critique opinions they disagreed with or to support claims they agreed with.

As Ivanǐc and Camps (2001) argue, voice involves an ability to discuss different issues and, perhaps more important, taking from different perspectives stances toward these issues. The purpose of this assignment was that the students could express their voices by examining the use of *Turnitin.com* from different perspectives and construct blogs about their own attitudes toward *Turnitin.com* and its potential adoption by the university. The students were first asked to visit the website (turnitin.com) and then blog about what was interesting to them and their reaction to what they found there. In Fidossa's first blog on this topic, she demonstrates both these aspects of voice. She begins by offering a short description of the website:

> Turnitin.com is a website based on catching plagarism owned by Turnitin.com, Inc. this is a business website that convince school everyone is a guilt untill proven a innonce.

She then continues by discussing her opinion about *Turnitin.com* and whether it is useful for teachers:

> The main idea of this webside is to profit from the schoo, by showing a report that this senctence was plagarized by this student. we don't know if the report is 100% accurate. I understand plagarims is pretty bad and who ever commited should learn their lesson, but I went this website to be free, and give us tips, suggestion and other useful tools that will prevent the spead of plagarism. all the website in th internet are free and its accessible to any student why not Turnitin.com is not accessible to the student. They is a point behind this and itis all about business. lots of teachers who used the Turnitin.com found it was incredible tools to use. they doubt they have for students was find easy way. they appreaciated the website. one teacher who have doubt for five student plagarized, when he went to the Turnitin.com found that four of the student committed plagarism. he view the website was the best tool ever to use. it make teachers job more easy. the website also indicate the exact where the material the student get from. I think it is also a good website if all the student and the professors have accessible and also if it was fre to use, when ever you want use.

In her blog, Fidossa is clearly able to establish her own stance toward both the importance of using *Turnitin.com* and its limitations and even weave some of the opinions she found on the website with her own. Here, for example, she summarizes the obviously positive testimonials she found on the site and then adds her own opinion: that it would be useful if both students and professors could access it and make use of it. However, there were certain limitations in Fidossa's ability to develop her argument. Her initial argument about the effectiveness of *Turnitin.com* is not entirely her own, but seems to have been assimilated from one of the articles that she had already read (Heaton, 2003). The article she had read about a student who was accused of plagiarism after her teacher had checked her paper using *Turnitin.com* briefly presented both sides of the debate by reviewing reasons why the program was effective and reasons why it should not be used. Interestingly, Fidossa begins to show aspects of her academic voice in the way she cites this text, as well as the testimonials given on the website, to support her argument. Her use of these texts reflects the kind of intertextuality we hoped she and the other students would achieve but also raises questions about attribution that, of course, were important in a course about plagiarism. Although she does not properly attribute these textual voices, Fidossa's ability to express her own ideas as well as incorporate voices from the texts she read illustrates, as Ivanĭc and Camps (2001) argue, how a variety of voices interact in academic writing.

An encouraging aspect in the development of Fidossa's academic voice is how she goes into much more depth about why she likes the article. Her next argument—that the site should be free—was more of her own since it had not been previously discussed in the classroom. She then develops this argument by offering a number of other reasons for why she likes the site. Unlike in her first blog, where her personal voice dominated, a stronger academic voice was beginning to emerge in this posting. Her ability to take a critical stand, both positively and negatively, is an important component of academic writing (e.g. Latour; 1988; Latour & Woolgar, 1986).

After writing the blog, the students were then asked to compose the first draft of their argumentative paper. The assignment was designed to help students synthesize their analysis of the website with their own opinions that they had previously blogged about. In this way, we hoped to integrate both a personal and academic voice into the development of an argument about how this plagiarism-detection program should be used. We see below how Fidossa attempted to construct this synthesis in her argumentative essay:

> Turnitin (Turnitin.com) is a website that prevents plagiarism; it is also world leading website that helps educators and student to check their assay. You have to be a member to check your work before you turn in to their professors.Turnitin. Com is like a business that convinces school everyone is guilt until they found innocence, so they can profit from the school. It is only accessible to the professors because they give the report to the professors not to the student.

Fidossa begins her argumentative paper by evaluating the significance of her topic *(world leading website)*, as she had been instructed to do in the class. Although she does not clearly establish her opinion about the use of *Turnitin.com*, she begins to position herself by laying out the issues she will later develop, particularly the question of giving students free access to the website and the role of *Turnitin.com* as a business. Both of these themes had already been developed in her blog; thus, it would appear that her ability to establish her voice in this paper was facilitated by the development of her voice in the blog.

Fidossa goes on in this section of her paper to further develop her argument. She injects her personal voice *(I understand . . .)* into the discussion as a way of first conceding that plagiarism is a problem but then going on to make her argument that using *Turnitin.com* is not the best way to deal with it:

> If the report is available to the professors why not to the student, and the question is how do we know how accurate this website is? Some one comes up with this idea to check plagiarism. I understand plagiarism is bad and who ever committed plagiarism learn their lesson. But I do not think this is the best way to determine if student plagiarized. Teachers can find out if student plagiarized their assays. I believer every teachers dedicated to their job. They have time to check if the assays belong to the student or if they steal from others website. I don't think teachers should support this website.

Fidossa was able to use the voice she had developed in her blog to position herself in regard to the topic of the paper. However, there were some limitations as well. For instance, it was hoped that she could better integrate the discussion in the article she had read with her own personal voice, something which she had previously blogged about. As noted earlier, one of the goals for this assignment was for the students to integrate source texts into their arguments. The students were required to integrate two sets of voices with their own: one set was from the article they had read (Heaton, 2003), and the other set came from their classmates' blogs. Fidossa had not, in her academic essay, met this goal as well as she had in her blog.

As with the student in Blanton's (2005) study, Fidossa may also have been somewhat "strangled" (p. 115), to use Blanton's term, at least to some extent, by the nature of the assignment. Throughout her drafting of this essay, she seemed to feel that there was a place in her paper where she could express her opinion and a place where she could not. The oral voice she used in her blog does not seem as strong in her essay, and, as a result, her academic voice dominates her evaluation, even though the assignment placed equal weight on using both voices. Her difficulty in drawing upon the various voices available to her could have resulted from an inability to understand what role these different voices should play in different writing environments. Her task representation of the assignment does not seem to include the recognition of the similarities between the modes of delivery that is a prerequisite for the transfer process to occur.

There are several possible reasons for this problem, perhaps beginning with how these various voices were conceptualized, or perhaps misconceptualized, in the blogging assignments. Blogs are forms of hypertexts and thus can be used to cite and to link to other source texts, an issue that is both complex and controversial (Howard, 2007). However, our implementation of the blogging pedagogy did not acknowledge or anticipate the possibility that multiple voices could exist within the blog itself. We encouraged students to focus primarily on their vernacular voice, and although we mentioned the possibility of hyperlinking, we did not require them to insert any links. As mentioned above, Fidossa cites a source in her blog but makes no reference to it, a practice that could be considered plagiarism (cf Howard, 2007). Perhaps, a different form of implementation of blogs in the course would have helped her integrate her different voices in different ways, a topic that could be of interest for future research.

Synthesizing Voices

In the final writing assignment, the students were asked to write a synthesis paper comparing different opinions, using the voices found in the texts they had read and in their classmates' blogs to both support their own claims and to critique the claims of those they disagreed with. This assignment was designed to highlight the important role that the students' own voices, as expressed in their blogs, could play in developing the intertextuality of the essay they were composing. In her first draft of this paper, Fidossa wrote about whether one of the students in the plagiarism story she had read should have been removed from school because she had been caught plagiarizing:

> However, Miss Lodge[2] felt that Halley committed plagiarism, but she do not want her daughter to be kicked out from the school. She stated that children need education not punishment. She felt that the punishment was too soon and too severe. Bonnie[3] agrees with Miss Lodge that the punishment was too harsh. According to bonnie if the student committed plagiarism they should get lower grade F. Or redo the assignment. Miss lode and bonnie [classmates} have the same idea when it come to plagiarism. They both agreed that Halley committed plagiarism, but they felt the punishment was too server.

[2]The mother of the student

[3]Fidossa's classmate

Fidossa was able to weave the voices from the article and the voice of her classmate (Bonnie) together, making it clear whose voice was whose, which was an important goal of the course. The students had been asked to cite texts in this way in order to understand how to distinguish between one's own voice and the voices of others. Here she cites her classmate Bonnie's claim that the student in the story should be expelled.

It was our belief that having the students use their classmates' blogs in these ways would help the students value each other's voices as well as enable them to gain a sense of textuality, which could in turn allow them to avoid accusations of plagiarism that might result from being accused of representing others' ideas as their own. Moreover, to have students understand how institutions, such as universities, understand plagiarism, citing sources in this way had a rhetorical dimension as well. The goal was for students to understand the rhetorical significance of using these other voices rather than relying only on their own, which might help them avoid leaving out the reference because of the mistaken notion that ideas expressed only in their own voices had power.

Fidossa seems to have assimilated that strategy: each sentence contains a subject, reporting verb, and a complement. She begins with the argument of the mother of the student about how her daughter was treated, and then explains her own arguments. However, despite the progress she seems to have made toward understanding the rhetorical dimension of citations, her instructor was still critical of how she developed her own ideas. He criticizes her for just "telling the story" and not developing her ideas. This lack of development of her own voice here is somewhat surprising since, as was discussed earlier, she had previously blogged extensively about the student's plagiarism.

Moreover, her writing often lacks grammatical precision and choice of appropriate vocabulary, as well as basics such as capitalization. Nevertheless, Fidossa seems to have "invented" a representation of academic writing that separates her concept of vernacular literacy from her print literacy. Although Fidossa was a particularly hard working student, her level of development is consistent with that of the other East African students we have studied (Bloch, 2007; Bloch & Crosby, in press). Fidossa can express her own opinion or she can summarize others' opinions; however, she still seems to have a problem with integrating the two different forms of literacy. She can produce essays that fulfill the requirements of the course, but she sometimes lacks development in her use of source texts as well as the degree of personal involvement she displayed in her blogs. Overall, however, blogging seemed to be a useful tool for helping students like Fidossa to integrate different writers' voices into an academic essay, although questions about the ability to shift between these different voices and transfer them from one text to another remain a topic for future research.

This chapter examined ways in which blogging can be implemented within an academic writing course pedagogy as a means of bridging the gap between a student's oral and written voices. The importance of using blogs to facilitate this process in our program arose from the enrollment of a new group of students, in this case immigrants or Generation 1.5 students from East Africa, whose oral literacy dominated their written literacy. Mina Shaughnessy (1977) wrote many years ago that new students coming into basic level writing courses make old premises problematic. The same argument can be made today.

However, what has changed since Shaughnessy's thoughts expressed in 1977 is the explosion of technologies that teachers can now incorporate into their classrooms. In this case, blogging seems to be able to mix both oral and written voices together in new approaches for creating relationships between readers and writers. However, it is clear that the blogs themselves do not determine the kind of writing produced. As Fidossa's blogging demonstrates, how blogs are implemented by the teachers and how they are appropriated by the students are critical factors impacting on the kinds of writing produced, something that is true of any technology.

Pedagogical Implications

As we have found in our previous research, Fidossa's use of blogging has revealed a great deal about how blogging, as well as CMC in general, can bridge the gap between the types of literacy students bring to the classroom and the types of literacy that academic writing classes demand. However, blogs were not simply used as a tool for helping Fidossa and her classmates develop their essays. Blogging itself can be seen as a unique form of technological literacy, one that is becoming increasingly popular around the world for both personal and academic purposes. Blogging also carries unique literacy demands. Fidossa had to master a number of computer skills, such as sending files across the Internet and posting her writing to blogs. At the same time, she was learning how to critically understand the nature of academic writing as well as the different ways that students respond to the institutionalized definitions and penalties involved in the discussion of plagiarism. In current writing pedagogy, becoming literate in an academic writing course often involves the ability to integrate a variety of literacies into an academic essay, with some forms of literacy valued more than others. The results of this study suggest that blogging is one of the forms of technological literacy that should be considered in second language writing pedagogy.

This kind of research also has implications for understanding the nature of blogging as a form of literacy. Blogging clearly differs from other forms of CMC in the greater focus it places on authorship. As a form of discourse, it lies along a continuum between the more oral forms of synchronous discourse and the more formal written discourse valued in the classroom. Where blogging lies on this continuum is not absolute; it depends on the nature of the writer and how she chooses to use the blogs. To the extent that it reflects more the orality of the blogger, it therefore can give greater value to the vernacular literacy of the student. Because of the greater permanence that blogs provide compared to some other forms of CMC, blogging can also provide an ongoing snapshot of the process by which the multiple voices of the author can be seen interacting throughout the course. Perhaps more important, the permanence of blogging gives the oral voice a sense of textuality that it may not have in class discussions or in other forms of classroom discourse. Blogs can be shared or used as texts by classmates or by students in other classes, which may add value to students' vernacular literacy that cannot be found in other writing contexts.

New technologies such as blogging, however, cannot simply be seen as aids in the teaching of composition. These new technologies are changing how all forms of writing are both written and published. Understanding their potential and their limitations across a variety of rhetorical contexts with a variety of users can help teachers decide whether blogging is an appropriate tool as well as a suitable form of discourse for use in the L2 composition classroom. This, in turn, can enhance our understanding of how links betweens speaking and writing can play out in the L2 composition classroom.

REFERENCES

Bartholomae, D. (1985). Inventing the university. In M. Rose (Ed.), *When a writer can't write: Studies in writer's block and composing-process problems* (pp. 134–165), New York: Guilford Press.

Bazerman, C. (1988). *Shaping written knowledge: The genre and activity of the experimental article in science.* Madison: University of Wisconsin Press.

Blanton, L.L. (2005). Student, interrupted: A tale of two would be writers. *Journal of Second Language Writing, 14,* 105–121.

Bloch, J. (2007). Abdullah's blogging: A generation 1.5 student enters the blogosphere. *Language Learning & Technology, 11,* 128–141. Retrieved July 31, 2007, from llt.msu.edu/vol11num2/bloch/default.html

Bloch, J., & Crosby, C. (2006). Creating a space for virtual democracy. *Essential Teacher, 3*(3), 38–41.

———. (2008). Blogging and academic writing development. In F. Zhang and B. Barber (Eds.), *Handbook on computer enhanced language acquisition and learning* (pp. 36–47). Hershey, PA: The Idea Group.

Blood, R. (2002). Introduction. In Editors of Perseus Publishing & R. Blood (Eds.), *We've got blog: How weblogs are changing our culture* (pp. ix–xiii). Cambridge, MA: Perseus Press.

Bolter, J. D. (2001). *Writing space: Computers, hypertext, and the remediation of print.* Mahwah, NJ: Lawrence Erlbaum.

Britton, J. (1980/1994). Shaping at the point of utterance. In R. Young & Y. Liu (Eds.) *Landmark essays on rhetorical invention in writing* (pp. 147–152). Davis, CA: Hermagoras Press.

Canagarajah, A. S. (2006). Toward a writing pedagogy of shuttling between languages: Learning from multilingual writers. *College English, 68,* 589–604.

Gilbert, N. J., & Mulkay, M. (1984). *Opening Pandora's box.* Cambridge, UK: Cambridge University Press.

Halliday, M.A.K. (1985). *Spoken and written language.* Oxford, UK: Oxford University Press.

Halliday, M.A.K., & Hasan, R. (1976). *Cohesion in English.* London: Longman.

Harklau, L, Losey K. M., & Siegal, M. (1999). Linguistically diverse students and college writing: What is equitable and appropriate? In L. Harklau, K. M. Losey, & M. Siegal (Eds.), *Generation 1.5 meets college composition: Issues in the teaching of writing to U.S.-educated learners of ESL* (pp. 1–16). Mahwah, NJ: Lawrence Erlbaum.

Havelock, E. A (1963). *Preface to Plato.* Cambridge, MA: Belknap Press.

Heaton, M. (2003, April 27). Are your kids cheating? *Cleveland Plain Dealer Sunday Magazine,* pp. 10–15.

Hillocks, G. (2002). *The testing trap: How state writing assessments control learning.* New York: Teachers' College Press.

Howard, R.M. (2007). Understanding "Internet plagiarism." *Computers and Composition 24,* 3–15.

Ivanič, R. (1998). *Writing and identity: The discoursal construction of identity in academic writing.* Amsterdam: John Benjamins.

———. (2004). Discourses of writing and learning to write. *Language and Education, 18,* 220–245.

Ivanič, R., & Camps, D. (2001). I am how I sound: Voice as self-representation in L2 writing. *Journal of Second Language Writing, 10,* 3–33.

Latour, B. (1988). *Science in action.* Cambridge, MA: Harvard University Press.

Latour, B., & Woolgar, S. (1986). *Laboratory life.* Princeton, NJ: Princeton University Press.

Lenhart, A., & Fox S. (2006). *Bloggers: A portrait of the internet's new storytellers.* Pew Internet & American Life Project. Retrieved November 13, 2007, from www.pewinternet.org/PPF/r/186/report_display.asp

Lewis, I. M. (1993). Literacy and cultural identify in the horn of Africa. In B.V. Street (Ed.), *Cross-cultural approaches to literacy* (pp.143–155). Cambridge, UK: Cambridge University Press.

Lunsford, A.A. (2006). Writing, technologies, and the fifth canon. *Computers and Composition, 23,* 289–177.

Marsh, B. (2004). Turnitin.com and the scriptural enterprise of plagiarism detection. *Computers and Composition, 21,* 427–438.

Ong, W. J. (1982). *Orality and literacy: The technologizing of the word.* London: Methuen.

O'Reilley, T. (2005). What is web 2.0: Design patterns and business models for the next generation of software. Retrieved December 3, 2005, from www.oreillynet.com/pub/a/oreilly/tim/news/2005/09/30/what-is-web-20.html?page=1

Portes, A. (2001). *Legacies: The story of the immigrant second generation.* Berkeley: University of California Press.

Portes, A., & Hao, L.X. (1998). E Pluribus Unum: Bilingualism and language loss in the second generation. *Sociology of Education, 71,* 269–294.

Roberge, M. (2002). California's generation 1.5 immigrants: What experiences, characteristics, and needs do they bring to our English classes? *The CATESOL Journal, 14*(1), 107–129.

Rose, M. (1989). *Lives on the boundary: A moving account of the struggles and achievements of America's educationally underprepared.* New York: Free Press.

Rumbaut, R. G., & Ima, K. (1988). *The adaptation of Southeast Asian refugee youth: A comparative study.* Final report to the Office of Resettlement. San Diego: San Diego State University. (ERIC Document Service Reproduction Service No. ED 299 372)

Shaughnessy, M. (1977). *Errors and expectations.* New York: Oxford University Press.

Shirkey, C. (2003). Power Laws, Weblogs, and Inequality. Retrieved September 27, 2005, from www.shirky.com/writings/powerlaw_weblog.html

Weissberg, R. (2006). *Connecting speaking & writing in second language writing instruction.* Ann Arbor: University of Michigan Press.

■ Afterword

"They've done it again," I thought to myself as I sat before the entire manuscript for this edited collection. And the phrase came to me as a sound image—not as a visual image, which didn't come until I started typing.

Once again, Diane Belcher and Alan Hirvela have put together a volume that usefully crosses over modalities of linguistic communication. The connection is undeniable even for me, a writing specialist who is always ready to refute—passionately, I might add—the early-20th-century views that speech should *always* be learned before writing; that speech *always* precedes writing; that speech *is* the language and writing is but an inaccurate, secondary representation of speech. But, as John Swales points out in his foreword to this volume, the connection between orality and literacy, or speech and writing, tends to be less obvious than the connection between reading and writing. Why?

One of the possible reasons is that language specialists working in Western intellectual traditions have been conditioned—by our disciplinary training—to think of them not as complementary but as competing areas of interest. In the dominant Western tradition, the history of antagonism goes back to ancient Greece, when Socrates chose not to acquire literacy because he considered it to be a hindrance to memory—an essential component of oratory. In ancient Western civilization, it was oratory that occupied a key position in education as well as social, political, economic, and religious affairs.

Literacy came to the fore as a highly privileged skill in the Judeo-Christian academic tradition, where it was used to preserve and disseminate (and sometimes withhold from the masses) the holy scripture and other important documents containing culturally valuable knowledge. The rise and fall of the Roman Empire and the spread of Latin as a *lingua franca* of legal and academic communication also led to the privileging of writing because of the conflated binary between Classic Latin/writing and vernaculars/speech. With the invention of literate technology such as the printing press and the development of dictionaries, writing became highly conventionalized, while spoken language was always in flux.

In the 18th and 19th centuries, the rise of nationalism and the desire for a national language in Europe, especially Germany, led to the development of philology—the study of national language, literature, and culture. While it united the study of speech and writing briefly, the situation began to change in the late 19th century with the rise of scientific linguistics with phonetics at its core. In their quest for respectability as a scientific discipline, linguists at the time drew a stark contrast between dead languages and living languages, conflating the distinction with that between writing and speech.

Thus began the audiolingual era, when descriptive linguists strenuously argued the primacy of speech. One of the key motivations was to correct the widening gap between the conventionalized spelling systems and the actual speech sounds they were supposed to represent, which precipitated spelling reform movements. Despite Saussure's distinction between *la langue* and *la parole*, it didn't occur to many language specialists back then that an alternative conception might be possible—that both speech and writing represented language and that each might be mediated by the other in the language acquisition and production processes. Disciplinarity blinds us as much as it enlightens us.

In the 1960s, second language writing finally became a subject of serious and sustained inquiry—initially in the context of U.S. higher education—for at least two reasons. First, the number of international ESL students had grown to the point that their literacy needs could no longer be ignored. Second, literature-oriented English specialists (i.e., prescriptive grammarians) were frustrated by linguists' insistence on the relevance of speech-focused linguistics to all areas of English teaching, and in order to deflect a series of attacks, some linguists felt they had to prove their worth by showing that they were not without interest in writing.

Fast forward to the present, and we see the study of spoken and written discourse well established in their own rights and in a wide variety of geographic and institutional contexts. The trend is to integrate the "four skills" that had traditionally been separated rather arbitrarily. Perhaps the time is ripe. It is no longer necessary to fight the ghosts of age-old disciplinary politics; it is no longer necessary to strenuously argue that we are interested only in speech or only in writing. It's OK to say that we are interested in addressing whatever issues that we find in our classrooms, using all available means.

The present volume brings together authors who represent a wide range of perspectives and agendas. They don't necessarily represent a unified theoretical perspective, or agree on how or to what extent orality and literacy interact with one another. Collectively, they have also presented many questions and gaps that need to be explored further. These qualities, of course, make for an excellent starting point of further discussion and inquiry into the relationship between speech and writing.

They've done it again, indeed.

Paul Kei Matsuda
Arizona State University

Contributors

Rebecca Adams is a lecturer in Linguistics and Applied Language Studies at Victoria University of Wellington, New Zealand. Her research focuses on the role of interactions among second language learners in promoting second language learning in classroom settings.

Diane Belcher, a professor of applied linguistics at Georgia State University, co-edits with Jun Liu the *Michigan Series on Teaching Multilingual Writers.* She and Alan Hirvela have guest-edited the *Journal of Second Language Writing* three times and collaborated on numerous other projects. Her research focuses mainly on advanced academic literacy.

Linda Lonon Blanton is Professor Emerita of English at the University of New Orleans, Louisiana. Newly retired, she spent her fall 2007 semester at Anatolia College, Thessaloniki, Greece, where she is assessing their K–12 English curriculum. She is a founding board member of the *Journal of Second Language Writing*. Her academic interests have taken her to Morocco, Tunisia, Senegal, Greece, Spain, and Portugal. And her academic writing includes a number of ESL textbooks yet in print. As for her home institution—the University of New Orleans—the English Department Intensive ESL Program, of which she was a co-founder, and the linguistics program, in which she taught, have both become victims of the 2005 flood.

Joel Bloch teaches ESL composition at Ohio State University. He has a PhD in rhetoric from Carnegie Mellon University and an MA in ESL and Education from the University of Michigan. His publications include articles on the use of technology, plagiarism, intercultural rhetoric, academic writing, and Chinese rhetoric.

Patricia Byrd, a professor in the Department of Applied Linguistics and ESL at Georgia State University, focuses her study and publication on issues in the use of English vocabulary and grammar in particular discourse settings. In addition to her research publications, she has edited with Cynthia Schuemann and Joy Reid EAP textbooks designed to prepare students for college study.

Christine Pearson Casanave resides part of the year in California and teaches at Temple University's Japan Campus in the Graduate College of Education in the fall. She spends most of her waking hours reviewing, editing, and writing manuscripts of various kinds.

Lynne Flowerdew teaches in the Language Centre, Hong Kong University of Science and Technology. Her main research interests include corpus linguistics, discourse analysis, genre analysis and EAP/ESP syllabus design. She has published numerous articles on various aspects of corpus linguistics. Her book, *Corpus-based Analyses of the Problem-Solution Pattern: A Phraseological Approach*, was published by John Benjamins in 2007.

Alan Hirvela is an associate professor of foreign/second language education and adolescent literacies at Ohio State University. His teaching includes courses on assessment, intercultural rhetoric, L2 reading research, methods of teaching English as a second/foreign language, and reading-writing connections. His research focuses, from a variety of perspectives, on the acquisition of L2 academic literacy. He is the author of *Connecting Reading & Writing in Second Language Writing Instruction* and co-editor (with Diane Belcher) of *Linking Literacies: Perspectives on L2 Reading-Writing Connections*, both published by the University of Michigan Press.

Fiona Hyland is currently a lecturer in the school of Culture, Language and Communication at the Institute of Education in the University of London. She previously taught and coordinated English language teacher education programs at the University of Hong Kong and has 28 years of experience teaching and researching in the areas of TESOL and teacher education. Her research interests include second language writing and feedback issues, learner autonomy and language assessment.

Okim Kang is an assistant professor of applied linguistics in the Department of English, Northern Arizona University. A native of South Korea, she has taught ESL and SLA in South Korea, New Zealand, and in the United States. She is also teaching classes in oral English and instructional communication for international teaching assistants. Her research focuses on oral proficiency assessment, L2 pronunciation, and World Englishes. She is a recipient of a Spaan Fellowship in language assessment from the University of Michigan and of the Louise McBee prize for educational leadership from University of Georgia. Kang was co-editor of the online *Journal of Language and Literacy Education* (2006).

Yanbin Lu is a doctoral student in the Department of Applied Linguistics and ESL at Georgia State University. Her research interests are teaching/learning and testing of ESL/EFL, especially computer-assisted teaching/learning and testing, and socio-cultural issues in second language acquisition.

Ludmila A. Marchenkova is a visiting assistant professor in the Department of Linguistics at Ohio University, where she teaches courses in applied linguistics, TESOL, and academic writing for international graduate students. She received her doctorate in second and foreign language education from Ohio State University. She has co-edited, with Joan Kelly Hall and Gergana Vitanova, *Dialogue with Bakhtin on second and foreign language learning: New perspectives* (Lawrence Erlbaum Associates, 2005).

Paul Kei Matsuda is associate professor of English at Arizona State University, where he works closely with doctoral students in rhetoric, composition, and applied linguistics as well as master's students in TESOL. He has founded and chairs the Symposium on Second Language Writing, and edits the Parlor Press Series on Second Language Writing.

Gayle L. Nelson, professor, Department of Applied Linguistics and ESL, Georgia State University, conducts research on second language writing, academic socialization, and cultural factors in second language acquisition. She has published in numerous journals including *Journal of Second Language Writing, Applied Linguistics, TESOL Quarterly,* and *Journal of Multilingual and Multicultural Development,* published numerous book chapters, and co-edited (with Pat Byrd) *Sustaining Professional Development.*

Lucy Pickering is assistant professor in the Department of Applied Linguistics and ESL at Georgia State University. Her research program focuses on analysis of prosodic systems including suprasegmental features such as stress and intonation in English and Papiamentu. She has a particular interest in exploring the pedagogical applications of speech analysis to ESL/EFL pedagogy and second language development.

Lauren Ross-Feldman is a recent graduate of Georgetown University with a PhD in Applied Linguistics. Her research interests are focused on interaction in SLA, task-based language teaching, and the influence of learner gender on language learning.

Donald L. Rubin is an emeritus professor of Speech Communication, Language & Literacy Education, and Linguistics at the University of Georgia. He is also an adjunct professor at Georgia State University and at Emory University. Rubin teaches mainly in areas of intercultural communication, second language learning, and research methods. His areas of particular research expertise include health communication message design, attitudinal responses to non-native speakers of English, and language assessment, especially oral communication. His research has been supported by funding from agencies such as the National Cancer Institute, American Legacy Foundation, U.S. Department of Education, and the Educational Testing Service. Rubin's research publications have appeared in such journals as *Health Communication, Research in the Teaching of English, Bilingualism and Bilingual Education,* and *Journal of Language and Social Psychology*. He was editor of the journal *Communication Education* (2003–2005, volumes 52–54).

Lisya Seloni is an assistant professor in the English Department at Indiana University of Pennsylvania. Her primary area of research revolves around the academic literacy and socialization practices of non-native English speaking graduate students in Anglophone universities, a topic she explored initially in her doctoral dissertation at Ohio State University.

Miguel Sosa has a dual career as a musician and an EFL teacher at several universities in the Tokyo area, including Tokyo University of Agriculture. In addition to playing several piano concerts a year, he is interested in how personal stories can connect students and teachers.

John M. Swales is professor emeritus of Linguistics at the University of Michigan, where he was also Director of the English Language Institute from 1985 to 2001. Previously, he had been Reader in ESP at Aston University in the UK, and before that Director of the English Language Servicing Unit at the University of Khartoum. Recent book-length publications include *Research Genres* (Cambridge University Press) and the second edition (with Chris Feak) of *Academic Writing for Graduate Students* (University of Michigan Press). Although officially retired, he remains active on a number of projects, including his memoirs (of sorts).

Christine M. Tardy is an assistant professor in the Department of Writing, Rhetoric, and Discourse at DePaul University in Chicago, where she teaches courses in writing, applied linguistics, and teacher education. Her research interests include genre theory and pedagogy, second language writing, global written communication, and ESL teacher education.

Robert Weissberg is retired from the Communication Studies Department at New Mexico State University, where he taught intensive ESL, academic writing, and courses in TESOL and applied linguistics. His primary area of research concerns developmental aspects of second language writing, particularly the interconnections between oral and written language for adult L2 learners.

Jessica Williams is a professor of Linguistics at the University of Illinois at Chicago, where she also directs the ESL and Less Commonly Taught Languages programs. She has published on a variety of topics, including second language writing, lexical acquisition, and the effect of focus on form. Her latest publications include an edited volume (with Bill VanPatten), *Theories in Second Language Acquisition* and the student text, *Academic Encounters: American Studies.*

Luxin Yang is currently associate professor of the National Research Center for Foreign Language Education and associate director of Language Education Testing Services at Beijing Foreign Studies University, China. She completed her Ph.D. in Second Language Education at the Ontario Institute for Studies in Education of the University of Toronto in January 2006. She is now actively involved in academic activities related to English as a foreign language education in China.

■ INDEX